Away for the WEEKEND™
N E W   E N G L A N D

by

Eleanor Berman

REVISED AND UPDATED

52 Great Getaways in the Six New England States for Every Season of the Year

Clarkson N. Potter, Inc./Publishers

Published by Clarkson N. Potter, Inc., 201 East 50th Street, New York, New York 10022 and distributed by Crown Publishers, Inc.

CLARKSON N. POTTER, POTTER, colophon, and AWAY FOR THE WEEKEND are trademarks of Clarkson N. Potter, Inc.

Manufactured in the United States of America

Library of Congress Cataloging-in-Publication Data

Berman, Eleanor
  Away for the weekend: New England.

  Includes index.
  1. New England—Description and travel—1981–
—Guide-books.   I. Title.
F2.3.B47   1988   917.4′0443   88-4085
ISBN 0-517-56950-7 (pbk.)

10 9 8 7 6 5 4 3

Revised Edition

Contents

Acknowledgments

My sincere thanks to the many state and local tourist offices that provided so much helpful information, particularly to the Vermont Travel Division for supplying the cover photo. And very special thanks to Terry Berman for her invaluable research assistance and to my editor, Shirley Wohl, for her help and encouragement.

Introduction

NEW ENGLAND has everything—craggy mountains and gentle rolling hills, placid lakes and the surging sea, quaint village greens and contemporary cities. Whether you want to ski or sail or lie on the beach, soak up culture or escape from civilization, spend a day in chic stores or explore virgin woods, you'll find what you are seeking in this rich and remarkable six-state area.

It's almost a problem. In a region so packed with attractions, how can you decide where to start? Should it be in the mountains of New Hampshire or Vermont, the beaches of Cape Cod or the rockbound shores of Maine, the "tall ships" at Mystic or the Maritime Museum at Bath?

Away for the Weekend invites you to sample them all, one at a time, as memorable weekend trips. In contrast to most guidebook writers, I have not separated the New England area by states or tried to list all the myriad attractions that each state has to offer. Instead, I have gone by the seasons, picking out some of the best places and special events to be found throughout the region at different times of the year.

There are a few things you should know from the start. The selections are admittedly personal, limited to locations and events I have visited and enjoyed. Though I have lived and traveled in New England for 20 years, and spent a whole year touring it to pick up what I had missed, with such bounty to choose from I have undoubtedly left out some places. Nor is every single sightseeing attraction, lodging, or restaurant in each location included. I've tried instead to give only the best—places I've either been to myself or had recommended to me by local sources or frequent visitors to these destinations.

Since New England country inns are one of the particular delights of the region, I've done my best to see and select special inns for each location covered, but keep in mind that this is a guide to destinations and events, not a guide to inns. The places listed here are those convenient for each specific weekend, and in some cases that will mean only motels or hotels. When a choice is available, I've given the inns, leaving the motel listings to local tourist guides or the Mobil and AAA publications.

Along with inns, bed-and-breakfast establishments have become increasingly popular with travelers. There is sometimes confusion as to what constitutes bed and breakfast. Small inns that serve breakfast only are listed here as inns. Lodgings that are rooms in a private home, with or without a private bath, are what is meant here by "B and Bs." These can be extremely pleasant places to stay both because they are economical and because they offer the chance to meet local residents and get some of the flavor of living in the area. Because it is impossible to mention every individual bed-and-breakfast lodging, I have included areawide registry headquarters in a list at the front of the book. Local registries, where available, are also given with the general information for each trip.

How to Use the Book

The format for the trips in *Away for the Weekend* assumes you have a normal two-day weekend to spend, arriving on Friday night and leaving late on Sunday. Fortunately, with the air service to cities such as Portland, Maine, and Burlington, Vermont, trips that once were impractical for weekend driving often can now be managed easily. Information regarding air transportation is included for each suggested trip, along with bus or train information for those who do not have cars or who prefer not to drive in the unpredictable winter months in New England. There is also a symbol indicating destinations that can be visited conveniently at least in part without a car.

For each trip, there is a suggested itinerary for a two-day stay, with added suggestions to accommodate varying tastes and time schedules. When there is enough to do to warrant a longer stay, a symbol at the start will tell you so. When you do have more than a weekend to spend, use the longer itineraries as a guide to plan a more interesting tour. If, for instance, you are touring the coast of Maine or the mountains of New Hampshire or Vermont, simply consult the maps and index for destinations that make for a convenient route.

Since the trips are arranged by seasons, you can read ahead about special events and reserve before it is too late. Even when seasons are not applicable to your schedule, you will find the lists of sights and accommodations useful.

Since special activities change with the seasons, you may find some destinations listed more than once. In the case of Boston, there is a separate chapter for families who want the sights best suited for the kids. An indication of the weekends most likely to appeal to families appears in the symbols at the start of each trip. You are, of course, the best judge of which trips your own children are likely to enjoy.

In many cases, the trips suggested are deliberately out of peak season. The seashore, for example, can be twice as nice in spring or fall, when both crowds and rates are at a minimum.

The symbols that indicate these various categories are:

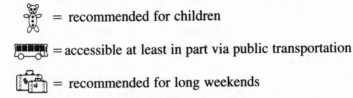

= recommended for children

= accessible at least in part via public transportation

= recommended for long weekends

As for prices, dollar signs indicate the range for lodging in a double room and dining as follows:

$ = under $50

$$ = $50 to $75

$$$ = $75 to $100

$$$$ = $100 to $125

$$$$$ = over $125

$ = most entrées under $10

$$ = entrées averaging $10 to $15

$$$ = most entrées over $15

$$$$ = expect to pay over $25 per person

$$$$$ = over $35 (usually means a prix fixe menu)

When prices bridge two categories, you will find two symbols. In seafood restaurants, a wide price range usually indicates the cost of lobster dinners, always the most expensive item on the menu.

For accommodations that include meals in their rates, three symbols are used:

CP = continental plan (breakfast only)

MAP = modified American plan (breakfast and dinner)

AP = American plan (all three meals)

All this information is as accurate as could be determined as of spring 1988, when the book went to press. In the months that elapse between the writing and the publication of any book, rates often change even before they can be put into print. For this reason, general price categories are used rather than specific rates. It is possible that even these general categories will change over time, with some of the places moving up into a more expensive range. Admissions fees to various attractions will probably go up as well, and hours sometimes change. So use the book as a general guide—an accurate one on the whole—but *always* check for current prices when you plan your trip. Telephone numbers are included for just this purpose.

If you find that any information here has become seriously inaccurate, or that a place has closed or gone downhill, I hope that you let me know in care of the publisher so that the entry can be corrected in the future. If you discover places I have missed, or have suggestions for future editions, I hope you'll let me know that as well.

The maps here are simplified to highlight exactly where the suggested destinations are located. They are not reliable guides as road maps, so be sure to have a detailed map in hand before you set out. One way to get an excellent free map of each state in New England is to write to the travel or tourism office of that state. These offices offer not only maps but detailed brochures on their state's attractions. Addresses are included at the end of this section.

In most cases, addresses for additional information are also given at the end of each itinerary. Do write away ahead of time, for the more you learn about your destination in advance, the more meaningful and enjoyable your visit will be.

One last warning: It almost goes without saying that for reservations in small country inns you must plan well ahead or risk disappointment. The same is true if you want to visit the shore at the height of the summer season or a ski resort during holiday periods. Most places offer refunds on deposits if you cancel with reasonable notice, so plan ahead—three or four months ahead is none too soon—and have your pick instead of having to settle for leftovers.

Writing this book has been a special pleasure. I began with the impression that I already knew a great deal about New England and its best places, but the more I traveled, the more I discovered that I had missed some special attractions, even in places I had visited before. And the more territory I covered, the more I appreciated what a remarkable area this really is. I gained a new understanding of my heritage as an American by visiting the historic sites where our nation was born, and a new awareness of nature's extraordinary generosity in the beauty that pervades this handful of fortunate states.

I hope *Away for the Weekend* will guide you to the same wonderful discoveries—as well as inspire you to find your own.

State Tourist Offices

Contact any of these state tourist offices for free maps and literature on attractions throughout the state, as well as for updated bed-and-breakfast registry listings:

Tourism Division
Connecticut Department of
Economic Development
210 Washington Street
Hartford, CT 06106
Toll free: (800) 243-1685
In Connecticut: (800)
842-7492

Maine Publicity Bureau
97 Winthrop Street
Hallowell, ME 04347
(207) 289-2423

Division of Tourism
State of Massachusetts
100 Cambridge Street
Boston, MA 02202
(617) 727-3201
Toll free: (800) 343-9072

Office of Vacation Travel
State of New Hampshire
PO Box 856
Concord, NH 03301
(603) 271-2666

Tourist Information
Department of Economic
Development
State of Rhode Island
7 Jackson Walkway
Providence, RI 02903
(401) 277-2601

Agency of Development and
Community Affairs
Vermont Travel Division
61 Elm Street
Montpelier, VT 05602
(802) 828-3236

or

Vermont State Chamber of
Commerce
PO Box 37
Montpelier, VT 05602
(802) 223-3443

Bed-and-Breakfast Registry Services

**COVERING ALL NEW
ENGLAND STATES**

Pineapple Hospitality
47 North Second Street
New Bedford, MA 02740
(617) 990-1696

Most state tourist offices also keep listings for their own state; write for the latest update.

CONNECTICUT

Nutmeg Bed and Breakfast
222 Girard Avenue
Hartford, CT 06105
(203) 236-6698

Bed and Breakfast Ltd.
PO Box 216
New Haven, CT 06513
(203) 469-3260

*Covered Bridge Bed and
Breakfast*
(Northwest Connecticut)
PO Box 447
Norfolk, CT 06058
(203) 542-5944

*Seacoast Landings Bed and
Breakfast Registry*
(coast communities, Old
Lyme and above)
133 Neptune Drive
Groton, CT 06340
(203) 442-1940

MAINE

*Bed and Breakfast Down
East Ltd.*
Macomber Mill Road
Box 547
Eastbrook, ME 04634
(207) 565-3517

Bed and Breakfast of Maine
32 Colonial Village
Falmouth, ME 04105
(207) 781-4528

MASSACHUSETTS

Berkshire Bed and Breakfast
(Western Massachusetts—
Berkshires, Sturbridge,
Springfield and Pioneer
Valley)
PO Box 211, Main Street
Williamsburg, MA 01096
(413) 268-7244

*Covered Bridge Bed and
Breakfast*
(some accommodations in
the Massachusetts
Berkshires)
PO Box 447
Norfolk, CT 06058
(203) 542-5944

Folkstone Bed and Breakfast
(Worcester, Sturbridge area)
PO Box 131, Station 1
Boylston, MA 01505
(508) 869-2687

Bed and Breakfast Cape Cod
Box 341
West Hyannisport, MA
02672
(508) 775-2772

House Guests Cape Cod
PO Box 1881
Orleans, MA 02653
(508) 896-7053

*Be Our Guest Bed and
Breakfast*
(Plymouth)
PO Box 1333
Plymouth, MA 02360
(508) 837-9867

*American Country Collection
of Bed and Breakfasts*
(Western Massachusetts)
984 Gloucester Place
Schenectady, NY 12309
(518) 370-4948

**For Boston–Cambridge
Area**

*New England Bed and
Breakfast, Inc.*
(also some Cape Cod,
Berkshires and lower Maine
listings)
1045 Centre Street
Newton, MA 02159
(617) 498-9819

*Bed and Breakfast
Cambridge and Greater
Boston*
Box 665
Cambridge, MA 02140
(617) 576-1492

Bed and Breakfast Associates
Bay Colony Ltd.
PO Box 166 Babson Park
Boston, MA 02157
(617) 449-5302

Bed and Breakfast
Brookline/Boston
Box 732
Brookline, MA 02146
(617) 277-2292

Greater Boston Hospitality
PO Box 1142
Brookline, MA 02146
(617) 277-5430

Host Homes of Boston
PO Box 117
Newton, MA 02168
(617) 244-1308

NEW HAMPSHIRE

New Hampshire Bed and
Breakfast
RFD 3, Box 53
Laconia, NH 03246
(603) 279-8348

RHODE ISLAND

Bed and Breakfast of Rhode
Island, Inc.
PO Box 3291
Newport, RI 02840
(401) 849-1298

Newport Bed and Breakfast
Castle Keep
44 Everett Street
Newport, RI 02840
(401) 846-0362

VERMONT

American Country Collection
of Bed and Breakfasts
984 Gloucester Place
Schenectady, NY 12309
(518) 370-4948

Vermont Bed and Breakfast
Reservation Service
PO Box 1
East Fairfield, VT 05448
(802) 827-3827

Hiking Information

Appalachian Mountain Club
5 Mount Joy Avenue
Boston, MA 02108
(617) 523-0636
Write for information on the
Appalachian Trail, White
Mountains, Monadnocks,
and other hiking throughout
New England

Green Mountain Club
PO Box 889
433 State Street
Montpelier, VT 05602
(802) 223-3463
Write for information on the
Long Trail and other hiking
in Vermont, including the
free publication "Day
Hiking in Vermont"

Churchill House Inn
RD 3
Brandon, VT 05733
(802) 247-3300
*Ask for the brochure "Hike
Inn to Inn: Country Inns
Along the Trail"*

Backcountry Publications
PO Box 175
Woodstock, VT 05091
(802) 457-1049
*Write for list and current
prices of "50 Hikes in
Maine," "50 Hikes in
Vermont," "50 Hikes in
New Hampshire's White
Mountains," and similar
publications, as well as for
books on bicycle touring*

SPRING

Overleaf: The rugged shoreline of Kennebunkport, Maine

Sights for All Seasons in Woodstock

When Laurance Rockefeller married Mary Billings French, the future of Woodstock, Vermont, was ensured.

Mary is the granddaughter of Frederick Billings, an early conservationist and native of Woodstock who went west long enough to make his fortune during the Gold Rush, then returned to establish a farm that was a model for dairy farmers and environmentalists throughout the state. Many of Vermont's green hills are the results of Billings's reforestation efforts.

Rockefeller, of course, was the guiding spirit behind Rockresorts, an organization that also has pioneered in conservation, developing model resorts that blend with and maximize the natural beauty of the environment.

Since the Rockefellers spend their summers at the Billings family home in Woodstock, it was almost inevitable that they would take an interest in the village, and the result is one of the most exquisite towns in Vermont, preserved in a manner befitting the Rockefeller tradition. Only one new home has been built around the village green in a century, and many of the original houses have been bought and meticulously restored by the Rockefellers, who lease them out to caring tenants.

The Rockefellers also own the Suicide Six Ski Resort, the Woodstock Country Club with its cross-country touring center, the Robert Trent Jones Golf Course, a slew of tennis courts and paddle tennis facilities, *and* the town's major inn—so you can be sure that all are kept in tip-top and tasteful condition.

If that's not enough activity for you, hiking, biking, and riding trails also abound around Woodstock, helping visitors make the most of this picturesque town with its meandering streams and covered bridges and mountain views. Indeed, there's something for everyone in Woodstock, even if it just means browsing through a selection of fine shops.

Though this is truly a town for all seasons, Woodstock is a particularly lovely and welcome destination in the soft green days of spring, that time of year between skiing season and summer when many Vermont areas offer little to do.

If you make your headquarters at Rockresorts' Woodstock Inn on the green, you'll find yourself in one of New England's more prestigious lodgings, built in 1969 to provide luxurious accommodations while blending with its Early American and rustic surroundings. It is Colonial in style and surrounded by landscaped gardens.

If there is any nip at all in the air, you'll likely be greeted with a welcoming fire in the huge fieldstone fireplace that dominates one wall of the lobby. The furnishings are country antique, the colors subdued, and the guest rooms adorned with handmade patchwork quilts. Even the menu in the dining room is more country than continental.

If the tab here is too steep in spite of the many weekend plans offered before the busy summer season, there are a few pleasant and more modest alternatives in town. The secluded Kedron Valley Inn, just a few miles away in the country, is unique, the kind of rustic inn you might expect to find out west, with excellent stables for riders.

Seeing Woodstock is easy, since everything is clustered within a couple of blocks of the green. The more than three dozen historic houses, all still privately owned, can be seen on a walk along Central and Elm streets, which intersect at the green. From Memorial Day on, you can visit one of the loveliest, the Dana House on Elm, an 1807 residence that was occupied by family descendents until 1944, when it became the home of the Woodstock Historical Society. There is a fine collection of period furnishings from 1800 to 1860, as well as many portraits, toys, costumes, and historical manuscripts on view. An adjoining barn holds a collection of antique farm, household, and artisans' tools and other artifacts of the past century.

Whether the building is open or not, be sure to walk around back for the view of the river and the picturesque Village Middle Bridge. When it was constructed in 1969 to replace the original, it became the first covered bridge built in the state since 1895.

There are two more covered bridges both east and west of town on Route 4. The 1877 Lincoln Bridge, four miles to the west, is the only known remaining wooden example of the Pratt truss, a style that found favor later in hundreds of steel bridges across the nation.

Besides the wooden bridges across its river, Woodstock boasts four authentic Paul Revere bells in its steeples. The 1808 Congregational Church on Elm Street houses the oldest. The others are in the Masonic Temple on Pleasant Street and in the Universalist Church on Church Street and the St. James Episcopal Church on Prospect, both on the side of the inn away from town.

Be forewarned that there are dozens of shops tempting you to detour as you take a stroll through Woodstock. Many of the stores listed in the local antiquer's guide are right in town. There are also plenty of stops for clothing, jewelry, gifts, crafts, and leather goods, and F. H. Gillingham & Sons, a general store owned by the same family since 1886, offers country housewares and Vermont specialty foods, including syrup and cheese.

For a change in sightseeing pace, tours are available from early May on at the Vermont Woodland Flora Exhibit, a collection of Vermont's native trees, wildflowers, and ferns in a naturalistic six-acre setting. Memorial Day usually marks the opening of the latest Rockefeller project: Billings Farm and Museum. This working dairy farm carries on the raising of prime Jersey cattle begun by Frederick Billings in 1871 and features a series of handsome restored barns housing exhibits on Vermont family farm life in the 1890s and some of the best-looking bossys to be seen outside the pages of a story book.

Once you've seen the sights and shopped the stores, what else you choose to do in Woodstock depends a lot on the weather and your inclinations. If sports are your choice, the golf course is usually back to playing condition by May, and all-weather tennis courts should be available even earlier. If it's too chilly for regular tennis, the paddle courts are waiting.

Woodstock Inn can furnish you with maps of the most scenic recommended routes for bikers, hikers, or joggers, and horses are available for hire nearby—a pleasant way to see the scenery even during Vermont's notorious spring "mud season."

There are also many scenic side trips to be made by car. One will take you to Quechee to see the gorge and waterfall and visit the riverside shop of glassblower Simon Pearce in a magnificently restored mill. Another road leads to Windsor, a longtime political center of the state with its own parade of historic houses, including the Windsor House, which serves as a state crafts center displaying the work of some 200 Vermont artisans. Still another route takes in the Crowley Cheese Factory and Weston, a thriving little shopping mecca that includes the Original Vermont Country Store and the Vermont Guild of Old-Time Crafts and Industries.

The most memorable and surprisingly moving side trip out of Woodstock is available from mid-May on, when the buildings are opened in Calvin Coolidge's birthplace, the Plymouth Notch Historic District in the tiny nearby hamlet of Plymouth.

At the attractive, small visitors' center built of Vermont slate, you will learn about Coolidge's life as well as about the modest frame house where Coolidge was raised—the home where his father, a notary public, administered the oath of office when Warren Harding's death cast Vice President Coolidge into the presidency in 1923. It stands as vivid evidence that ours is still a nation where a country boy can rise to greatness.

Within a distance no more than two city blocks, you can visit the one-room schoolhouse where Coolidge was taught, the simple farm homes of his family and friends, and the general store once operated by his father, as well as taste a sample of cheese in the 1890 cheese factory that is still run by the Coolidge family and visit the cemetery where six generations of the family are buried.

To see the exquisite tiny church built by the townspeople of Plymouth in 1842 and still in use, to feel the continuity of life in this dot of a town, and to stand on the front porch of a humble home rich in its mountain views is to understand some of the roots and reasons for our nation's strength.

You'll leave with a new appreciation of "Silent Cal" and empathize with his parting words when he left the White House: "We draw our presidents from the people. I came from them, I wish to be one of them again."

Woodstock Area Code: 802

DRIVING DIRECTIONS Woodstock is on Route 4, reached via I-91 to I-89. It is 148 miles from Boston, 260 miles from New York, and 166 miles from Hartford.

PUBLIC TRANSPORTATION Eastern Express and American Eagle air service to Lebanon, New Hampshire, 15 miles; Vermont Transit bus to Woodstock.

ACCOMMODATIONS *The Woodstock Inn and Resort,* 14 The Green, Woodstock, 457-1100, $$$–$$$$$, MAP available, many money-saving package plans available • *Kedron Valley Inn,* Route 106, PO Box 145, Woodstock, 457-1473, $$$$–$$$$$ MAP • *Village Inn of Woodstock,* 41 Pleasant Street, 457-2123, pleasant, modest in-town inn, $$$ CP • *Charleston House,* 21 Pleasant Street, 457-3843, stylishly furnished village home, $$$ CP • *Jackson House,* Route 4 West, Woodstock, 457-2065, elegant 1890s home, $$$–$$$$ CP • *Three Church Street*, at that address, comfortable bed and breakfast on the green, tennis and pool, $$$ CP.

BED AND BREAKFAST *Vermont Bed & Breakfast Reservation Service,* PO Box 1, East Fairfield, VT 05448, 827-3827.

DINING Woodstock Inn (see above), $$–$$$ • *The Prince and the Pauper,* 24 Elm Street, Woodstock, 457-1818, charming Colonial atmosphere, continental and nouvelle cuisine, prix fixe $$$ • *Barnard Inn,* Route 12, Barnard, 234-9961, excellent reputation, 1796 Colonial setting, $$$ • *Rumbleseat Rathskeller,* Woodstock East Shopping Center, 457-3609, informal fare in old stone farmhouse, $–$$. For a light lunch the Deli in town is hard to beat. Also see Quechee, page 69, and Hanover, page 206.

SIGHTSEEING *Dana House* (Woodstock Historical Society), 29 Elm Street, Woodstock, 457-1822. Hours: May to October, Monday to Saturday, 10 A.M. to 5 P.M. Adults, $2.00; children, $.50 ● *Billings Farm and Museum*, River Road, Woodstock, 457-2355. Hours: mid-May through October, daily 10 A.M. to 5 P.M. Adults, $4; children, $2.00 ● *Plymouth Notch Historic District*, Route 100A, Plymouth, 828-3226. Hours: daily mid-May to mid-October, 9:30 A.M. to 5:30 P.M. Adults $2; under 15 free.

INFORMATION   Woodstock Chamber of Commerce, 18 Central Street, Woodstock, VT 05091, 457-3555.

Getting Inspiration in Concord

By the rude bridge that arched the flood,
Their flag to April's breeze unfurled,
Here once the embattled farmers stood,
And fired the shot heard round the world
                          RALPH WALDO EMERSON

It was on April 19, 1775, that a brave band of farmers in Concord, Massachusetts, fired the fateful shot that meant the start of the American Revolution.

The spot and its significance, and the bravery of the minutemen who dared to fire against the mighty British crown, have been movingly marked and preserved to inspire us with patriotism even today—although it's hard to associate the present placid, prosperous little suburban town of Concord with such bloody goings-on.

It's easy, however, to see why the serenity of the town and the natural beauty of its countryside would have attracted a remarkable gathering of American literary giants in Concord in the nineteenth century. Emerson, who wrote *Nature* here, declared it a fit place for a poet, where a walk in the woods had "a breath of immortality in it." Hawthorne and Louisa May Alcott also lived and wrote here, as did Thoreau, whose Walden Pond is just outside town.

With such an extraordinary blend of history to its credit, Concord is a fascinating place to visit. You actually need three separate tours to appreciate all this small town has to offer in the way of military and literary lore and Early American architecture—and even then you haven't begun to enjoy the countryside.

Since its greatest fame rests on its pivotal role in the Revolution, it's well to start with a look at the Concord of 1775, a town of 1,600 people, mostly prosperous farmers, who were deeply involved in the movement to gain freedom from the oppression of Great Britain. As the place where Colonial supplies were being stored in anticipation of war, Concord became the target of a British confiscation mission. When General Gage's troops left Boston for Concord, Paul Revere helped spread the alarm with his famous ride.

Drive down Monument Street just beyond the center of town and you'll come to the North Bridge, a reconstruction of the simple wooden bridge where the fateful encounter began. The spot is marked by the famous minuteman statue—a young American farmer with musket and plow—created by Daniel Chester French, who was also famed for his Lincoln Memorial statue in Washington. The bridge is now part of Minuteman National Park, and the National Park Service has done its usual informative and tasteful job of bringing historical events to life. The site remains rural. You can cross the bridge and walk the path taken by the soldiers, following the action with plaques along the way as you head gradually uphill to the visitors' center for a panoramic view of the entire scene. In season there are guided tours as well.

Just before the bridge is the Bullet Hole House, where the British troops searched for supplies and fired a shot at the owner. The bullet hole may still be seen in the shed. The home is now a private residence, but visitors are welcome to inspect and touch the historic hole—and children are usually first in line to do so.

There are many other noteworthy remains of the April 19 events and of the early Revolutionary activities in Concord. You can see Colonel Barrett's farm, where the cache of arms was hidden—the target of the British army's mission to Concord. At Monument Square you can climb to the top of the Old Burying Ground where several Revolutionary families rest and see beyond it to the ridge running clear to Meriam's Corner, which the patriots marched along to follow the retreat of the British on the road below. The corner itself, known as Bloody Curve, was the site of another and far larger battle, the first real American attack of the Revolution.

Minuteman Park actually stretches all the way from Concord to Lexington, along Route 2A, the road the British followed on their way from an early-morning skirmish on Lexington Green and again on the way back to Boston following the Concord battle, when further fighting took place all along the route. The Battle Road visitors' center, on Route 2A just outside Lexington, has its own exhibit room and a movie and orientation program. If you want to follow the entire sequence of events of April 19, you'll have to include not only the park but also the town of Lexington, another pleasant Colonial site with its share of historic buildings.

But if you have just a weekend, you may prefer to stick to Concord, where you can take a welcome lunch break at the Colonial Inn, a 1716 landmark right on the green in the center of town and another storage site for Colonial arms. As you munch your Colonial chicken pie or Boston scrod, you'll actually be starting your literary tour of Concord. Thoreau's family lived in the old part of the inn when it was still a private home; after the inn began taking in lodgers, it became known as Thoreau House.

You should also take note of another important literary spot, the home of Reverend William Emerson, Ralph Waldo's grandfather. The house, known as the Old Manse, was so close to the North Bridge that the Reverend Emerson actually watched the Battle of Concord from an upstairs window. Descendants of the Emerson family lived here for 169 years, except for a period from 1842 to 1845 when Nathaniel Hawthorne and his bride, Sophia Peabody, rented the house. It was here that Hawthorne wrote *Mosses from an Old Manse.*

Hawthorne moved away to Salem but returned to Concord in 1852 to the home known as the Wayside, where he remained for the rest of his life. There's an orientation program and a half-hour tour here to tell you about the Wayside's interesting inhabitants.

The Alcott family also stayed at the Wayside while their home was being completed, but it was the Orchard House, where they lived for 20 years, that became the setting for *Little Women.* The tour here includes many of Louisa's mementos, including the costumes used by the Alcott girls when they gave their famous plays. Outside is the School of Philosophy, where great thinkers of the day studied and spoke; the school was founded by Bronson Alcott and Ralph Waldo Emerson, the two leaders of the American Transcendentalist movement.

Emerson's own home, where he moved with his wife, Lidian, in 1835 and remained until his death in 1882, is known simply as Emerson House. The guides will show you a collection of many of his books, personal effects, and furniture.

Thoreau, the only one of the resident writers who was a native son, loved the town and once wrote, "I have never got over my surprise that I should have been born into the most estimable place in all the world. . . ."

The Thoreau Lyceum, headquarters of the Thoreau Society, is an institution devoted to the preservation of Thoreau's ideals. It contains much of his memorabilia and features a replica of his famous Walden cabin on the grounds. There are changing exhibits here, as well as a research library and a book and gift shop. Thoreau's wilderness outpost, Walden Pond, is now part of a state recreational reserve, enjoyed by boaters, swimmers, and fishermen. Take a walk down the nature trail to the lovely pond and the stones that mark the site of the original cabin, and you can see why the spot was enough to inspire Thoreau.

Both Thoreau and Bronson Alcott were sent to the Old Jail in town when they refused to pay the poll tax as a protest against government-supported slavery. The incident was the inspiration for Thoreau's famous essay "On Civil Disobedience."

You'll learn still more about Concord's extraordinary group of writers at the lovely 1873 Concord Library, which houses their manuscripts as well as a statue of Emerson and busts of the others done by Daniel Chester French. Emerson's study and the furnishings of Thoreau's Walden House are on display at the Concord Museum, which offers a tour of period rooms and galleries dating from 1680 to 1890, with pieces from the homes of Concord families and such patriotic memorabilia as Paul Revere's lantern and artifacts from the Battle of North Bridge.

All of Concord's writers are buried on Authors' Ridge in Sleepy Hollow Cemetery, just outside the town on Route 62.

If all these sights become overwhelming, take a shopping break downtown. Concord these days is basically an upscale suburban town, and most of the shops on Main and Walden are geared more for local residents than for tourists. You'll find conservative clothing, as well as a variety of galleries and gift shops. If you want a souvenir of your visit, a good bet is the Tri-Con Gift Shop housed in historic Wright Tavern, British headquarters on that fateful April 19 long ago. If you stop for ice cream at the Vermont Creamery, you'll find cheeses and other specialty products grown and made in the Green Mountain State.

On Sunday, you might want to take part of the morning for the architectural walking tour provided in a $1 brochure published by the Concord Chamber of Commerce and available from the information booth on Heywood Street and at several locations in town. It will lead you down Monument, Liberty, and Main streets and Lowell and Lexington roads, along brick sidewalks abutting the green and gravel paths just out of the town center, past lovely and historic homes and white-spired Colonial churches dating from the early 1700s to the mid-1850s.

One, the 1750 home of Jonathan Ball, now houses the Concord Art Association, which holds regular exhibitions. Another only-in-Concord attraction is the Grapevine Cottage, former home of Ephraim Wales Bull, who planted the wild grapes that eventually developed into the ubiquitous Concord grape. A plaque marks his accomplishment, and a grape arbor still thrives by the side of the house.

Finally, you can have your pick of places to get back to nature and explore some of the scenery that inspired Concord's literati. There's Walden Pond preserve, as well as the Great Meadows National Wildlife Refuge, with headquarters in nearby Sudbury. Or if you'd rather glide along in a canoe, as Emerson and Thoreau once did, head for South Bridge Boathouse in Concord and paddle your way along Concord's three rivers: the Concord, Sudbury, and Assabet.

If young children are along, you may want to take the 10-mile drive to the headquarters of the Massachusetts Audubon Society at Drumlin Farm in Lincoln, a 220-acre preserve with lots of friendly barnyard animals as well as walking and hiking trails and a picnic area. There's an excellent nature-oriented gift shop here.

It's fun to make this trip around Patriot's Day, April 19, when both Concord and Lexington have early-morning reenactments and other festivities to mark the date. The festivities, which change from year to year, are sometimes scheduled on a weekend rather than on the actual day, so it's best to check each Chamber of Commerce for the current year's schedule.

Concord is probably at its most beautiful in mid-May, when its fine Colonial homes are set off by the pinks, purples, and whites of the flowering trees. But whenever you make the trip, you're almost sure to find the town a treasure trove of history as well as a chance to emulate Thoreau and get back, at least a bit, to nature.

Concord Area Code: 508

DRIVING DIRECTIONS   Concord is on Route 2, reached from I-495 or Route 128. Route 2A, the Battle Road, leads from Lexington to Concord. It is 20 miles west of Boston, 248 miles from New York, and 138 miles from Hartford.

PUBLIC TRANSPORTATION   For many residents, Concord is a commuter outpost for Boston, so there is frequent train service from North Station. Buses from Williamstown also travel east on Route 2. Many of the sights are within walking distance of the Colonial Inn and the center of town.

ACCOMMODATIONS   *Longfellow's Wayside Inn,* off Route 20, South Sudbury, MA, 443-8846, a real charmer, worth the ten-mile drive, a 1702 Colonial beautifully restored by the Ford Foundation and operated by a nonprofit trust; just ten rooms, so reserve well ahead, $$ ● *Hawthorne Inn,* Route 2A, 369-5610, a lovely 1870 home, but with just five rooms, so again, reserve early, $$$ CP ● *Colonial Inn,* Monument Square, 369-9200, prize location on the green, with rooms in the old inn or new motel wing, $$–$$$$ ● *Howard Johnson,* 740 Elm Street (Route 2), 369-6100—if there's no room at an inn, this is at least a nicely kept motel choice, $$$.

BED AND BREAKFAST   *Bed and Breakfast in Minuteman Country,* 8 Linmoor Terrace, Lexington, MA 02173, 861-7063.

DINING   *Longfellow's Wayside Inn* (see above), popular, so reserve early, $$–$$$ • *Colonial Inn* (see above), $–$$ • *Chez Claude,* Route 2A, Acton, 263-3325, popular French restaurant, $$–$$$ • *The Rusty Scupper,* Nagog Square (off Route 2A), Acton, 263-8327, seafood, salad bar, $$–$$$ • *A Different Drummer,* 86 Thoreau Street in the restored railroad station complex in Concord, is good for lunch or a light meal, 369-8700, as is *Walden Station,* 24 Walden Street, 371-2233, a restored firehouse; both are $–$$.

SIGHTSEEING *Minuteman National Historical Park,* North Bridge Visitors' Center, Liberty Street (PO Box 160), 369-6993. Hours: daily 8:30 A.M. to 5 P.M. Free • *The Old Manse,* Monument Street at the Old North Bridge, 369-3909. Hours: June to October, Thursday to Monday 10 A.M. to 4:30 P.M., Sundays from 1 P.M. Adults, $2.50; children 11 to 16, $1; children under 11, $.75. • *The Wayside,* Lexington Road (Route 2A), 369-6975. Hours: April to October, Thursday to Monday 9 A.M. to 5:30 P.M. Adults, $.75; children, free • *Orchard House,* 399 Lexington Road (2A), 369-4118. Hours: April to mid-September, Monday to Saturday 10 A.M. to 4:30 P.M., Sundays and mid-September through October from 1 P.M. • *Emerson House,* 28 Cambridge Turnpike at Lexington Road (2A), 369-2236. Hours: Monday to Saturday 10 A.M. to 4:30 P.M.; Sunday from 2 P.M. Adults, $2.50; children 6 to 17, $1 • *Thoreau Lyceum,* 156 Belknap Street, 369-5912. Hours: Monday to Saturday 10 A.M. to 5 P.M., Sunday from 2 P.M. Adults, $2; children 8 to 18, $1 • *Concord Museum,* 200 Lexington Road, 369-9609, guided tours. Hours: Monday to Saturday 10 A.M. to 4 P.M., Sunday from 1 P.M. Adults, $2; children under 15, $1 • *Concord Free Public Library,* 129 Main Street, 369-2309. Hours: Monday to Friday 9 A.M. to 9 P.M., Saturday 9 A.M. to 5 P.M., Sunday 2 P.M. to 5 P.M. Closed weekends July and August. Free • *Walden Pond State Reservation,* 915 Walden Street, 369-3254. Hours: open daily until dark. $3 vehicle fee, May to mid-October. • *Drumlin Farm Education Center,* South Great Road (Route 117), Lincoln, 259-9807. Hours: Tuesday to Sunday 9 A.M. to 5 P.M. Adults, $4; children 3 to 16, $3 • *Great Meadows National Wildlife Refuge,* Weir Hill Road (off Route 68), Sudbury, 443-4661. Hours: daily mid-April to mid-October, sunrise to sunset. Free. Education center open 9 A.M. to 4 P.M.

INFORMATION Concord Chamber of Commerce, ½ Main Street, Concord, MA 01742, 369-3120.

Herbs and History in Connecticut

Adelma Grenier Simmons is a performer. Audiences are rapt when she talks about the herbs she grows at Caprilands, her 50-acre farm in Coventry, Connecticut. And when she tells you that sage and other herbs preserve a person's youth, you're likely to become a believer, seeing the energy and charm of the grandmotherly Mrs. Simmons.

Visitors to Caprilands not only learn about herbs and their uses and tour the 30 gardens on the property; they are also treated to one of Mrs. Simmons's legendary five-course luncheons, served in her eighteenth-century farmhouse and flavored with her home-grown seasonings. It's a very special day, and one that leaves you in easy driving range of Norwich, where you can discover some Colonial history as well as a thoroughly modern inn and health spa.

A visit to Caprilands begins at 11 A.M. with one of Mrs. Simmons's colorful introductions to herbs, delivered in a Colonial barn whose rafters are festooned with bunches of drying lavender and other fragrant plants. Her herbal lore, the result of half a lifetime of study, is both factual and fanciful. In the spring, she concentrates on teaching you how to plan and plant your own garden, with a lecture spiced with humor and legends.

She may tell you, for example, that silver rosemary improves the mind and memory, so it's a good idea to plant it "in case you have need of that. Rosemary is also good for making tea," Mrs. Simmons adds, "and if that doesn't work, you can wash your dog's hair with it."

Following the lecture comes a tour of the gardens, where touches of the Simmons wit and whimsy abound. There's a heart-shaped garden, a garden planted only with silvery plants, and a Shakespeare garden filled with the bard's quotations on herbs. In all there are 300 kinds of herbs to be found.

After the tour comes lunch, seated at long tables crammed into the three main-floor rooms of the farmhouse. Mrs. Simmons circulates from room to room visiting with her guests, but she won't give away her recipes or tell what herbs you're tasting until the meal is over. "Then it's too late," she chuckles. After lunch, Mrs. Simmons can usually be found autographing some of her more than two dozen recipe books. Guests are free to wander once again through the gardens or to browse in the heavenly scented gift shop, which features, among other things, Caprilands herbs that have been dried and packaged. There is also a most attractive greenhouse gallery with herb plants, seeds, and hanging baskets for sale.

It's about half an hour's drive from Coventry to Norwich and the recently remodeled Norwich Inn. At this posh, pastel California-style inn and spa you'll be able to work off your luncheon calories in one of the most stylish gym complexes to be found in this part of the country, then be massaged and pampered to your heart's delight, with all the facilities of a luxury resort.

The present town of Norwich may not look too promising at first glance, but there is a surprising slice of history to be found here. Norwich was one of the 12 largest cities in the colonies in 1776, and one Christopher Leffingwell was a major reason. The industrious Mr. Leffingwell established not only the first paper mill in Connecticut but a stocking factory, pottery works, chocolate and fulling mills, a clothier's shop, and a dye house. He was a chief supplier for the Continental Army and a leading citizen of the colonies.

His home, now open to the public and the chief sightseeing attraction in Norwich, was also an inn that entertained many dignitaries; today it is one of the outstanding remaining Colonial dwellings in the state.

The two-story structure was expanded over the years, so it is actually two homes brought together with an addition at the rear, with sections dating from 1675 to 1765. The interior has been authentically restored and beautifully furnished by the Society of Founders of Norwich. Among its highlights is the George Washington Parlor, named in honor of a visit paid here by the general in 1776. The room is furnished with the kinds of rare pieces usually found only in museums or private collections.

The Great South Parlor, the most formal room in the house, also contains prize eighteenth-century pieces, including a Massachusetts block-front chest-on-chest, a cherry desk, and Chippendale chairs around a Queen Anne tea table set with valuable Oriental china. The floorboards in the parlor are the originals, measuring a good 24 inches across.

The Society of Founders has also issued a set of four walking tour pamphlets, available for purchase, to guide you to many other outstanding houses from the town's long and eventful past. The Norwich town tour, through the earliest areas settled, includes many houses dating from the 1700s. One, the Simon Huntington Jr. Tavern, goes back to 1690.

Other tours take you through three centuries of architectural styles, with particularly fine homes to be found in the Chelsea Parade and the Little Plain and Broadway sections of town. Each of the noteworthy houses is illustrated in the guide, and clear maps are provided to find them.

If you sleep late on Sunday, you can fill the afternoon in Norwich alone, but you'll also be near some of the best attractions on the Connecticut shore. New London's Coast Guard Academy and Groton's Submarine Memorial are just a 10-minute drive away, and 20 minutes will bring you to Mystic Seaport.

Golfers may prefer to forget it all and stay close to home to take advantage of the course right next door to the inn, and on warm days there is a delightful outdoor terrace next to the pool with expansive views of the greens.

If you plan a herbs-and-history weekend, remember that reservations are a necessity at Caprilands, and the earlier the better, since Mrs. Simmons is becoming something of a local legend. She tells her guests that caraway is believed to bring those who eat it back to the place where they tasted it. Whether she laces her luncheon dishes with this herb or not, guests here do tend to return again and bring their friends—and the 50 seats in the house fill up in a hurry.

Connecticut Area Code: 203

DRIVING DIRECTIONS   Caprilands is on Silver Street, first left after the intersection of Route 31. The best direct route to Caprilands is I-84 west from Hartford, an extension of the Mass Pike (I-90) from the east. Take the Rockville-Coventry exit (Route 31) south, turn left on Route 44, and take the second right to Silver Street. Coventry is about 70 miles from Boston, 140 miles from New York, and 30 miles southeast of Hartford. Norwich is on Connecticut Route 32 south of Coventry.

ACCOMMODATIONS AND DINING   *Norwich Inn,* 607 West Thames Street (Route 32), Norwich, 886-2401, $$$. The other possibility is to stay in Hartford and add city sights to your weekend agenda. See page 209 for Hartford information.

SIGHTSEEING   *Caprilands Herb Farm,* Silver Street, Coventry, CT 06238, 742-7244. Hours: daily 9 A.M. to 5 P.M. Visits to gardens and gift shops, free; lecture and luncheon, $15 (check in case of recent price change). Reservations essential ● *Leffingwell Inn,* 348 Washington Street, Norwich, 889-9440. Hours: Tuesday to Saturday 10 A.M. to 12 noon and 2 P.M. to 4 P.M., Sunday 2 P.M. to 4 P.M.; winter hours, by appointment. Adults, $3; children, $1.

INFORMATION   Norwich Chamber of Commerce, 35 Main Street, Norwich, CT 06360, 887-1647.

Rites of Spring on Nantucket

Spring comes late to Nantucket, bursting in at last near the end of April in a rush of blue skies, golden forsythia, and thousands of bright yellow daffodils.

Weather-weary islanders celebrate the long-awaited end of winter gray with their own special spring rite, the annual late-April Daffodil Festival, which fills the town with golden blooms and features two island traditions: a parade of antique cars and a tailgate picnic. Though it's a local party, everyone is welcome, and there are few more gala ways to usher in the season.

Preseason visitors to the island are rewarded with a glimpse of a Nantucket often obscured by the boatloads of summer tourists. In the mild and breezy sunshine of springtime, Nantucket town is not a bustling resort at all, but a quiet and beautiful community of 7,000 where everyone says a friendly hello. Cobbled streets and sea captain's mansions become not backdrop for the beach but focal points of delightful walks into the past.

This is, after all, the historic island outpost 30 miles at sea that once was the third-largest city in Massachusetts, sending brave seamen to the far corners of the globe for the whale oil that lit the lamps of the world. Weathered-shingle cottages still mark the original farming settlement of the 1600s and the austere Quaker era of the early 1700s that preceded the prosperous whaling days.

Both simple cottages and stately homes remain, perfectly preserved by a turn of fate that seemed disastrous 140 years ago. A destructive business district fire in 1846, coupled with the discovery of kerosene and the resulting dwindling demand for whale oil that followed in the 1850s, sent Nantucket into an economic decline that lasted for years. Hard times meant that no one could afford to "modernize," so while the rest of the mainland was changing, Nantucket remained untouched, becoming America's largest living Colonial town.

Toward the end of the last century visitors discovered that this beach-rimmed island was also a perfect vacation spot. New hotels went up and islanders began to open their great shingled houses to paying guests.

But world wars and the Depression slowed things, and the island's real renaissance did not come until the 1960s. It began with the efforts of Walter Beinecke, a wealthy summer resident who formed a corporation named Sherburne, after Nantucket's first settlement, to rescue and renovate the decaying wharves. Sherburne went on to acquire large portions of island real estate and to take over and renovate some of the better hotels. Though Sherburne has sold its holdings, the development movement goes on—too much so, in fact, to suit many who loved the old island.

Despite all the modernization, the original look of the island has been maintained and strict ordinances have been passed to ensure that all new construction conforms to the simple shingled architecture of the original homes. The church steeples and lighthouses remain the tallest structures on Nantucket, and nothing has been allowed to spoil the island's remarkably preserved past.

The pamphlet, "Rambles," provided by the Nantucket Information Bureau takes you back to the people and events of that rich past, reminding you for starters that the cobblestones that seem so picturesque today were put down originally for a very practical reason: to keep heavy whale oil drays from sinking into the mud.

The walking tour takes you past the Pacific Club, whose membership was limited to shipmasters who had whaled in the Pacific, and brings you to upper Main Street, where you pass the brick mansions of the ship-owning Coffin family, aboard whose vessel *Charles and Mary* Herman Melville once went to sea. The Coffins were responsible for planting the stately elms on Main Street as well as for importing and planting the pines, larches, and heather that have spread throughout the island landscape.

A few doors down on Walnut Lane is the Nathaniel Macy House, built in 1723 and now open to the public. Next comes one of the most fascinating sections of street in New England—twelve magnificent whaling mansions owned by various members of the Coffin and Starbuck families, testaments to Nantucket's wealth and taste. The three brick-columned Starbuck mansions, all in a row, are the subject of countless snapshots.

Wherever you walk, you'll run into fascinating history, and more historic homes have been opened to let you share it more intimately. There's the house where Maria Mitchell, one of the earliest female astronomers, was born, and various residences and monuments to the Folger family, including a memorial to Abiah Folger, wife of Josiah Franklin and mother of Benjamin Franklin. Facing Main on Pleasant, the Hadwen-Satler mansion with its beautiful rear garden has been maintained for the public by the Nantucket Garden Club.

Walk far enough in any direction, however, and you're back to the ever present sea that made Nantucket the great whaling town it was in the past as well as the popular spot it is today. Early in the year you can have the endless beaches to yourself, and if the spring temperatures aren't warm enough for swimming, they are frequently perfect for beachcombing and tanning in blissful solitude.

Biking is another ideal spring pastime, taking you away from the cobblestones to the wide-open vistas of cranberry bogs and low-lying moors of bayberry and scrub pine that also help to give Nantucket its faraway feel.

If you come for the Daffodil Festival, you'll find Nantucket's cobbled Main Street festooned with yellow flowers in every store window and doorway, bountiful and original arrangements devised to compete for the coveted blue ribbons for best window displays. Even the local cigar store Indian is holding a basket full of golden blooms.

Prizes are awarded for contestants in Saturday morning's antique auto parade as well. The procession of some 75 classic cars from Model As to MGs stops right in the middle of Main Street, so that bystanders can mill around for a closeup look at the autos and the bright yellow bouquets that adorn them. Ninety-five percent of the cars are owned by island residents, who eagerly await this chance to show off their prize possessions each year. Many of them come in vintage costume to match the era of their cars.

The best part of the day comes when everyone follows the procession of contestants down the daffodil-lined road to the picturesque fishing village of 'Sconset for the annual tailgate picnic, which just may be the most elegant event of its kind anywhere. Prizes are the lure once again, this time for the most artistic food display, and you'll see everything from a picnic for Raggedy Ann and Andy to a caviar-and-champagne feast served to diners on velvet-seated gilt chairs brought outdoors for the occasion. All the spreads are lavishly laden with daffodils, as are many of the diners. At last year's event, even a dog arrived wearing a yellow bonnet to mark the day.

The picnic ends before 3 P.M., leaving you time to walk along 'Sconset's magnificent beach and through the twisting lanes of one-time fishermen's shanties that have been transformed into charming summer cottages. Or, if you prefer, you can take a look at the village shops. There are very few gewgaw souvenirs to be found here. Most of the shops have high-quality merchandise, much of it handmade, so browsing is a pleasure. One special place to watch for is Nantucket Looms, with its handwoven mohair scarves and other lovely woolens. In stores throughout town you'll find examples of the island's best-known craft, Nantucket Lighthouse baskets. Each hand-painted ivory top is different, and since the price tags run into the hundreds, if you plan to indulge you ought to have the fun of looking at the full selection.

If you have time on Sunday, there are plenty of museums and historic houses to visit. The Peter Foulger Museum, with its memorabilia of old Nantucket, and the famous Whaling Museum are both of special interest. If you can stay on until Monday, you can see the annual Daffodil Show sponsored by the Nantucket Garden Club in cooperation with the American Daffodil Society. You needn't be a flower worshipper to appreciate the unusual varieties and the handsome arrangements on display.

In the past, incidentally, the festival weekend has chalked up an admirable record of above-average weather, sending happy visitors home with an early tan.

Off-season lodgings used to be sparse on Nantucket, but the Daffodil Festival has begun to attract visitors, and at least two of the major hotels are open all year. The historic Jared Coffin House, a long-time winter haven, has been joined by the Harbor House, an imaginative complex of small gray-shingled buildings on lanes that are almost indistinguishable from their neighboring residential streets. Ship's Inn, a tiny charmer, and several attractive guest houses are also now open most of the year.

Nantucket is distinguished among summer resorts for the large number of fine restaurants on the island. The Mad Hatter, one of the long-time favorites, is open year round, and many other fine establishments are starting early for weekends now instead of waiting for Memorial Day, traditionally the official start of the season. The Boarding House, 21 Federal, Obadiah's, and India House are some of the better choices that may be open for Daffodil Festival weekend.

There's a happy spirit of anticipation in the air in springtime Nantucket. Like the local homeowners, who can be seen outdoors putting fresh coats of paint on their shutters, shopkeepers and hotel and restaurant operators are busy sprucing up after the long winter. Hammers and paintbrushes are in evidence everywhere, and on Main Street merchants are busily arranging new stock, awaiting the coming rush of customers.

There are some who love off-season Nantucket best in the fall, after the summer crowds have left. But though the island is handsome in its autumn hues, there's a feeling of renewal in the spring that is missing in the winding-down days at season's end. From its daffodil-strewn roadsides to its cobbled downtown lanes, Nantucket comes alive in spring, and it is a guaranteed tonic for early birds.

Nantucket Area Code: 508

DRIVING DIRECTIONS Nantucket Steamship Authority, PO Box 284, Woods Hole, MA 02543, 540-2022, runs boats to the island from Hyannis year round, for both cars and passengers. The trip is approximately 2½ hours. Hy-Line, Pier 1, Ocean Street Docks, Hyannis, MA 02601, 775-7185, has service for passengers only from Hyannis during warm months. Both provide parking facilities if you want to leave your car. Peter Pan, (413) 781-3343, and Bonanza, (800) 556-3815, offer bus service to Hyannis from New York, Hartford, and Providence; Plymouth & Brockton Street Railway Co., (508) 588-2228, runs bus service from Boston and Logan Airport. Island parking is not a problem in spring but cars really are not necessary on Nantucket. Most of the activity centers in town, which is easily walkable; bike rentals are plentiful, and you can rent a car or hire a taxi for a day's exploring. Hyannis is just over 80 miles from Boston, 271 miles from New York, 187 miles from Hartford.

PUBLIC TRANSPORTATION PBA (Provincetown–Boston Airways) reservations are made through Continental Airlines, (800) 525-0280. Delta Business Express, from Boston only, (800) 345-3400.

ACCOMMODATIONS *Jared Coffin House,* 29 Broad Street, 228-2405, a restored 1845 sea captain's mansion, $$$–$$$$$ ● *Harbor House,* South Beach Street, 228-1500, attractive complex with rooms in main house or cottages, $$–$$$$ ($$$$$ in season) ● *Ships Inn,* 13 Fair Street, 228-0040, a tiny, charming sea captain's home, $$–$$$ ● Several guest houses are also open off season, including the *Periwinkle,* 7–9 North Water Street, 228-9267, $$ ($$$–$$$$ in season), and *Island Reef Guest House,* 20 North Water, 228-2156, $$ ($$$ in season). Since opening times vary, it's best to contact the Chamber of Commerce for a current list of what is available in April and May.

DINING These are restaurants that have been open recently preseason. Almost all serve excellent, reasonably priced lunches. Most are small, so reserve ahead ● *India House,* 37 India Street, 228-9043, fine food in a historic Colonial house, $$$ (prix fixe dinner) ● *Mad Hatter,* 72 Easton Street, 228-9667, informal atmosphere, beef specialties, $$–$$$ ● *The Boarding House,* 12 Federal Street, 228-9622, charming cellar café, $$$ ● *Obadiah's,* 2 India Street, 228-4430, seafood, $$$ ● *Harbor House,* South Beach Street, 228-1500, large dining room, good food, lively, dancing, $$–$$$ ● *Jared's,* Jared Coffin House (see above), $$$–$$$$ ● *21 Federal Street,* 21 Federal Street, 228-2121, $$$ ● *The Brotherhood,* 23 Broad Street, for overstuffed sandwiches, inexpensive dinners, chowder, $ ● *Downeyflake Donut Shop,* just off Main Street, is a local favorite for breakfast.

SIGHTSEEING A visitor's pass, good for all the following, is available at all locations. Adults, $6.50; 5 to 14, $2.50. ● *Peter Foulger Museum,* Broad Street. Hours: 10 A.M. to 5 P.M. daily in season; off-season weekends, 11 A.M. to 4 P.M. (double-check for exact current spring schedule). Adults, $1.50; under 12, $.75 ● *Whaling Museum,* Broad Street. Hours: same as above. Adults, $2.50; under 12, $1.25 ● Other historic sites and open houses: *Fair Street Museum, Old Mill, Maria Mitchell Home, Macy-Christian House,* Liberty Street; *Hadwen House,* Main Street; *Greater Light,* Howard Street. Check for off-season hours and rates at Nantucket Historical Association, Union Street, 228-1894.

BIKE RENTALS *Cook's Cycle Shop,* 6 South Beach Street ● *Holiday Cycle Shop,* 4 Chester Street ● *Nantucket Bike Shop,* Steamboat Wharf ● *Young's Bicycle Shop,* 6 Broad Street.

INFORMATION Nantucket Information Bureau, 25 Federal Street, Nantucket, MA 02554, 228-0925. Nantucket Chamber of Commerce, Main Street, Nantucket, MA 02554, 228-1700.

A Miracle Mile in Providence

Each year on the first weekend in June, everyone is cordially invited to view a miracle in Providence, Rhode Island.

The Festival of Historic Houses, presented annually by the Providence Preservation Society, shows off one of the nation's most outstanding restoration efforts—and one that rightfully qualifies as miraculous. For this one weekend only, visitors are able to view the exceptional private homes and gardens of the College Hill Historic District, the area that has been dubbed locally "A Mile of History."

The district, which lies between the Brown University campus and downtown, was the earliest settlement in the state and served as the civic, commercial, and residential center of the city for its first two centuries. It is widely recognized for one of the most notable displays of Early American homes in the country, one that is even more remarkable because these houses have been lived in continually for more than 200 years.

Yet in the 1950s, like Providence itself, College Hill was in serious decline. The old industrial city was run-down, and many of the older homes, which had turned into slum dwellings, were being torn down to make room for the expansion of Brown's campus. The preservationist group that formed to restore College Hill faced a formidable task, but today its efforts are a model of what can be accomplished when a community cares about preserving its heritage. On Benefit Street alone, the core of the restoration efforts, there are now more than 100 handsomely restored historic houses. The owners, who open their homes to the public for this special weekend, do so to help raise funds to further the continuing preservation efforts, which have now spread to many other portions of the city.

The festivities usually begin on Friday night with a candlelight tour, which is repeated on Saturday. Typically, the tour includes a dozen private residences on Benefit Street. Their carefully restored exteriors present fine examples of Federal, Greek revival, and early Victorian detailing, while the interiors may be traditional or contemporary.

The House and Garden Tour on Saturday extends over several blocks of Benefit Street as well as adjacent side streets, offering an even richer array of architecture that includes residences, house museums, churches, and grand mansions adapted for use as offices. Some of the mansions date back to the China Trade era following the American Revolution, the time when many Providence traders made their millions. Among the gardens are authentic Colonial planting arrangements and urban courtyard settings.

The tour borders the Brown campus, so visitors can also view the school's handsome quadrangles and stately buildings. In many ways Brown's emergence as one of the most sought-after Ivy League colleges has paralleled the reblooming of its neighborhood.

Those who take the Friday night tour can use Saturday evening to get acquainted with another special part of Providence, the Federal Hill area that is this city's thriving "Little Italy." Here, too, there are Old World street lamps and fountains, plus a wealth of good eating. Camille's is the restaurant recommended first by most of the locals.

The success of the College Hill project has been contagious, and on Sunday attention turns to downtown Providence and the wealth of nineteenth-century architecture that was recently added to the National Register of Historic Places. This new historic district is currently undergoing extensive restoration and remodeling.

To add to the pleasures of the weekend, try to snag one of the ten rooms at the Old Court, a bed-and-breakfast inn perfectly located on Benefit Street. The elegant Omni Biltmore Hotel, a downtown landmark, offers special package rates for house-touring visitors.

Though the house festival makes early June a particularly desirable time to visit Providence, the city has real pleasures to offer any time you come. The city is compact, so a walking tour is the best way to see the sights. Pick up the free pamphlet "A Stroll Through Providence" at the Visitors Bureau, or rent the taped tour from the bureau or the Providence Preservation Society and trace the history of the town founded by one of the great champions of modern democracy, Roger Williams, as a model of religious tolerance.

The eighteenth-century buildings along the waterfront reflect the early history of the city as a Colonial capital, a bustling China Trade seaport, and an early hub of industrial development. The historic downtown area includes the Customs House district's striking Victorian architecture and the 1878 City Hall, among the finest French Second Empire halls in the country. A recent restoration has returned

the patterned marble floors, mahogany and oak paneling, and elaborately painted walls to their original grandeur.

You can learn more about the city's remarkable founder at the Roger
Williams National Memorial, currently being developed in a 4½-acre
park on North Main, the site of his original settlement. The First Baptist Meeting House on North Main, with a 185-foot steeple inspired by
Christopher Wren, was founded by Williams and his followers in
1638; the existing building was constructed in 1775. Step in especially
to see the massive Waterford crystal chandelier.

A statue of Williams guards his burial place on Prospect Terrace, a
favorite spot of photographers for its panoramic view of the city and
the countryside beyond. If you have children along, you'll also want to
visit the Roger Williams Park, three miles south of the city, for its zoo,
children's nature center, and Japanese garden, as well as for its 430
acres of woods, waterways, and winding drives.

Kennedy Plaza, the central square of the city, has undergone extensive renovation, with the old Union Station converted into a visitors'
center and a new transportation hub being developed. Some other important downtown landmarks are the ornate terra-cotta Majestic Theater, now home to the highly regarded Trinity Repertory Company,
and the Arcade, a recently renovated 1828 shopping mall built in
Greek revival style.

Brown University, at the summit of College Hill, is another recom-
mended touring spot for its historic and picturesque campus. The 1770
University Hall, the John Hay and Rockefeller libraries, and Wriston
Quadrangle are some of the high spots, and the David Winton Bell
Gallery in the List Art Building across from the main gate presents
changing art exhibits that are often worthwhile.

There are also exhibits at the Providence Art Club's studios and
galleries in two eighteenth-century houses off Benefit Street. The
city's finest art collections, however, belong to the highly regarded
Rhode Island School of Design (RISD), whose campus is just below
Brown and whose museum on Benefit Street is first rate, with collections ranging from Oriental art to French impressionism. The Pen-
dleton House next door offered the nation's first American Wing, a
collection devoted entirely to Early American furniture and decorative
arts.

Another RISD gallery is the Woods-Gerry, in a nineteenth-century
Federal mansion, which presents the work of talented faculty, students, and alumni, many of them world leaders in the designing arts.
The gallery is on Prospect Street, which has many other splendid mansions, most of them still private residences.

Other noteworthy stops include the Rhode Island State House, modeled after the U.S. Capitol; the John Brown House, which John Quincy
Adams called ''the most magnificent and elegant private mansion that I

have ever seen on this continent''; the 1707 home and garden of Governor Stephen Hopkins, a signer of the Declaration of Independence; the Museum of Rhode Island History at Aldrich House, the former residence of U.S. Senator Nelson W. Aldrich; and the Providence Athenaeum, an 1838 Doric structure that was one of America's first libraries as well as the place where Edgar Allan Poe courted Sarah Helen Whitman, a resident of Benefit Street.

Another example of the virtues of preservation can be seen at Davol Square, where a former rubber tire factory has been converted into an attractive complex with shops and restaurants of all kinds in atmospheric surroundings. If you want to take time out for some bargain hunting, pick up the Visitors Bureau guide to factory outlet stores in nearby Woonsocket and Pawtucket.

One of the best features of Providence is the fact that it is truly, as the brochures proclaim, a "walkable city," and most of the sights can be covered easily on foot over a weekend, with pleasant discoveries waiting almost literally at every turn.

Long an industrial town in the shadow of Boston, its worldlier neighbor, Providence has rescued the treasures of its rich past and come into its own as a livable and charming city. For those who knew it in older days, its transformation is indeed a miracle—and one that merits discovering.

Rhode Island Area Code: 401

DRIVING DIRECTIONS   From north or south take I-95; from west take Routes 44 or 6; from east take I-195 to the center of Providence. It is 49 miles from Boston, 187 miles from New York, 77 miles from Hartford.

PUBLIC TRANSPORTATION   Amtrak trains, most major airlines, and Greyhound, Peter Pan, and Bonanza buses serve Providence.

ACCOMMODATIONS   *The Old Court,* 144 Benefit Street, 351-0747, 1863 home turned bed and breakfast in the historic district, $$$ CP ● *Omni Biltmore Hotel,* Kennedy Plaza, (800) 225-7654, inquire about weekend packages, particularly for the Festival of Historic Houses, $$–$$$ ● *Marriott Providence,* Charles & Orem streets, 272-2400, $$$–$$$$ ● *Holiday Inn Downtown,* 21 Atwells Avenue, 831-3900, $$.

BED AND BREAKFAST   *Bed and Breakfast of Rhode Island,* PO Box 3291, Newport, RI 02840, 849-1298.

DINING *Al Forno*, 7 Steeple Street, 273-9760, best in town, but no reservations so expect to wait, $$$ ● *Left Bank*, 220 S. Water Street, 421-2828, old warehouse, stone walls, continental menu, $$–$$$ ● *Raphael's*, 207 Pine Street, 421-4646, northern Italian in converted factory, $–$$$ ● *La Serre*, 182 Angell Street (on College Hill), 331-3312, American and continental, $$ ● *Blue Point Oyster Bar*, 99 North Main Street, 272-6145, seafood, $$–$$$ ● *Panache*, 125 North Main Street, 831-2660, continental, good for lunch or late supper as well as dinner, $–$$$ ● *Pot au Feu*, 44 Custom House Street, 273-8953, French, prix fixe $$$, and entrées $$–$$$ in formal upstairs dining room; $$ downstairs ● Old-fashioned southern Italian restaurants on Federal Hill include: *Camille's Roman Gardens*, 71 Bradford Street, 751-4812, $$–$$$; *Grotta Azurra*, 210 Atwells Avenue, 272-9030, $$; and *Old Canteen*, 120 Atwells Avenue, 751-5544, $–$$ ● *L'Elizabeth*, 285 South Main Street, 621-9113, Victorian decor, popular for cocktails and desserts, $ ● *In-Prov*, Kennedy Plaza, 351-8770, tapas bar for lunch, drinks, or light fare, $–$$.

SIGHTSEEING *Providence Festival of Historic Houses*, early June; for tickets and schedule, contact Providence Preservation Society, 24 Meeting Street, Providence, RI 02903, (401) 831-7440. Lower rates for advance purchase, which is always advisable for this very special event ● *Rhode Island School of Design Museum of Art*, 224 Benefit Street, 331-3511. Hours: Tuesday to Saturday, 10:30 A.M. to 5 P.M. (except Thursday, 12 noon to 8 P.M.), Sundays from 2 P.M. mid-June to August, Wednesday to Saturday, 12 noon to 5 P.M. Adults, $1; 5 to 18, $.25 ● *Woods-Gerry Gallery*, 62 Prospect Street, 331-3511. Hours: during school year, daily except Tuesday, 11A.M. to 4 P.M., Sunday from 2 P.M. June and July, Monday to Friday, 11 A.M. to 4 P.M. Free ● *Providence Art Club*, 11 Thomas Street at Benefit Street, 331-1114. Hours: September to June, Monday to Friday 11 A.M. to 3 P.M., Saturday from 12 noon, Sunday 3 P.M. to 5 P.M. Closed weekends rest of year. Free ● *Brown University Bell Gallery*, 64 College Street in List Art Building, 863-2421. Hours: Monday to Friday, 11 A.M. to 4 P.M., weekends from 1 P.M. Free ● *John Brown House*, 52 Power Street at Benefit Street, 331-8575. Hours: guided tours available March 1 to December 31, Tuesday to Saturday 11 A.M. to 4 P.M., Sunday from 1 P.M. Adults, $2.50; children, $1; family maximum, $7 ● *Roger Williams National Memorial*, 282 North Main Street, 528-4881. Hours: daily June to August, 9 A.M. to 5 P.M., September to May, Monday to Friday only. Free ● *First Baptist Church*, 75 N. Main Street at Waterman. Hours: Monday to Friday, June to August 10 A.M. to 3 P.M., spring and fall to 2 P.M., Saturday to 12 noon. Tour on Sunday after 11 A.M. service. Free ● *Rhode Island State House*, Smith Street. Hours: guided tours, Monday to Friday 9 A.M. to

3:30 P.M. Free ● *Providence Athenaeum,* 251 Benefit Street, 421-6870. Hours: Monday to Friday, 8:30 A.M. to 5:30 P.M., Saturday from 9:30 A.M., mid-September to mid-June. Free ● *Governor Stephen Hopkins House,* Benefit & Hopkins streets, 831-7440. Hours: Wednesday and Saturday, 1 P.M. to 4 P.M., April to November. Free.

INFORMATION   Greater Providence Convention and Visitors Bureau, 30 Exchange Terrace, Providence, RI 02903, 274-1636. Hours: Monday to Friday, 8:30 A.M. to 5 P.M.

A Whale of a Time on Cape Ann

Some places people watch eagerly for the first robin or the first signs of green on the trees after a cold winter. On Cape Ann, the arrival of spring means just one thing: The whales are back.

"The other cape," as some call the lesser-known northern Massachusetts strip eight miles out to sea, inspired one-time summer resident T. S. Eliot to write about "those who are in ships/whose business has to do with fish." This is fishing country, all right, especially Gloucester, where 150.8 million pounds of fish come in each year, the biggest catch of any port on the East Coast.

But fish aren't the whole story, by any means. Gloucester shares its cape with Rockport, an art town whose seven-mile boulder-strewn coastline, harbor full of sailboats, and picturesque cove packed with shops and galleries bring out both lovers of beauty and thousands of strolling shoppers.

In spring, it's the beauty that takes precedence—and it's also spring when Cape Ann takes on the title of "whale-watching capital of the world." Sign on for a cruise and sign up at one of the lovely inns in the area, and you're ready for a rare weekend. If you're a chamber music buff, make it in June and you'll be able to attend the annual Rockport Chamber Music Festival as well. The fine Gloucester Stage Company, which offers many premieres at its headquarters in an old warehouse, is also well worth a visit.

Just like clockwork every year, humpback, Minke, finback, and right whales return to the offshore feeding grounds of Jeffreys Ledge and Stellwagen Bank. They put on quite a display, especially the humpbacks. These showoffs breach the surface, flinging the entire length of their 50-foot, 40-ton bellies out of the water into the air, and then crash down with mammoth belly flops, sending out shock waves around them. They slap their flippers and bang their massive tails and blow clouds of bubbles into the air.

There are several whale-watching boats to choose from, all about equal by most accounts. You may have more trouble deciding among the many nice places to stay in the area. One excellent choice is Sea Crest Manor, an antiques-filled home once owned by a governor of Massachusetts. Set away from town off Route 127A, with a view of the sea from its second-floor sundeck, it's the sort of place where tea is served at 4 P.M. each day.

The Yankee Clipper is a complex of three handsome Colonial houses, two of them on a curving lawn that runs right down to the water. The rooms vary, with the more traditional furnishings located in the Bullfinch House across the road. The owners of the Yankee Clipper also run the Ralph Waldo Emerson Inn. Both are on Route 127 North in the area known as Pigeon Cove, and both have pools for guests in warmer weather.

The Inn on Cove Hill is an attractive eighteenth-century home in town, done in informal country style. Another small in-town charmer is the Addison Choate Inn, which also has its own small, secluded pool.

A personal favorite is the Eden Pines Inn, a simple clapboard Colonial perched smack on the water on a secluded road away from town, off Route 1A in the direction of Gloucester. This is an airy, summery hideaway with spectacular views from the oversize rooms. Another delightful inn facing the sea and the beach is Blue Shutters in Gloucester.

Rockport was never a major early trading port like some of its coastal neighbors because its broad harbor was unprotected from the elements until a breakwater was built at the turn of this century. It was named for the granite beds in the surrounding hills of Rockport, which became the chief industry of the town and attracted a large colony of Scandinavians, who worked as stonecutters. As the Scandinavians were arriving, so were the artists, drawn by Cape Ann's combination of rugged coastline and woodland beauty. Indeed, the terrain and its luminous light have been a magnet for painters and sculptors since the early eighteenth century, when Fitz Hugh Lane first began capturing the scene from his granite studio atop Duncan's Point in Gloucester. The Museum of Cape Ann History has a comprehensive collection of his paintings and drawings. Winslow Homer also painted here.

As often happens when artists congregate in scenic spots, summer visitors followed. Gloucester maintained its fishing fleet, but with the completion of a major highway into town in the 1950s, tourism became Rockport's major industry. Even though the town is being developed rapidly and can be uncomfortably packed in the center on a summer day, it retains much of its salty charm.

Most of the visitors head directly for Bearskin Neck, a spit of land extending out to sea that is lined with fishing shacks now transformed into shops of every imaginable kind. You'll need no guide—just join the throngs and make the rounds of the stores and their scrimshaw, hand-blown glassware, pewter, leather, T-shirts, crafts, and clothing.

Take note of one of the shanties on an extension of Bearskin Neck, known as Motif Number One because it has been painted by so many area artists. The Rockport Art Association, housed in a restored tavern on Main Street, is the year-round center of the current art scene, which continues to flourish even though the colorful shacks and ship's riggings have given way to shops and ice cream stands. There are a number of interesting art galleries here as well.

There is more art to be seen in Gloucester, where the North Shore Arts Association has its headquarters in summer. Another artists' group congregates at the Rocky Neck Art Colony in East Gloucester, said to be the oldest such colony in the country; here you can watch artists at work as well as visit galleries and dine in the area's most picturesque restaurants.

From Gloucester it's a lovely ride by car or bike to the Beauport Museum way out on the water on Eastern Point Boulevard. This 26-room mansion, the home of Henry Davis Sleeper, a prominent antiques collector and interior designer of the 1920s, is a feast of decorative arts, with each room dedicated to a particular type of decor, from Oriental to Paul Revere.

Hammond Castle Museum in Magnolia is an unusual find in these simple seafaring environs. Mr. Hammond, it seems, was so taken with what he saw in Europe that he decided to build his own castle at home, complete with drawbridge and Roman, medieval, and Renaissance pieces. The Great Hall here is worthy of a cathedral, with magnificent stained-glass windows at either end, a huge fifteenth-century fireplace, and an 8,600-pipe organ rising eight stories high.

You could easily spend two days viewing the whales, the shops, and the museums, but do leave some time to appreciate the rich natural beauty of the area. Take a walk south of town along Atlantic Avenue to the Headlands, dramatic outcroppings of rock where you can look out to sea and back at the harbor and homes. Then drive to Pigeon Hill at the end of Landmark Lane, a small park atop one of the highest elevations around, for a soaring view. This is the site of the annual Midsummer's Day celebration held in mid-June by the local Swedish community, an event that features maypole, costumes, music, and dancing. Check the Chamber of Commerce for this year's date.

Turn off Route 127 just before Old Farm Inn for Halibut Point, Cape Ann's furthest outpost to sea—a 69-acre state park at the northern end of the peninsula, with its own boulder-rimmed shoreline view, accessible via a path through the woods.

The Eastern Point Sanctuary in East Gloucester is prime hiker's territory, with many guided walks from the Coast Guard lighthouse. And then there are the beaches, two of them in town, more off Route 127A between Rockport and Gloucester. In between it all, you can feast on the freshest seafood to be found, everything from local cod and haddock to good old New England lobster. Make a note that Rockport is dry, so you'll have to bring your own wine for dinner.

With that exception, Cape Ann serves you everything you need for a seaworthy weekend—with whales as an unbeatable main course.

Cape Ann Area Code: 508

DRIVING DIRECTIONS Cape Ann is on Route 127, off Route 128, on the north shore of Massachusetts, just 38 miles north of Boston, 246 miles from New York, and 136 miles from Hartford.

PUBLIC TRANSPORTATION Regular train service from Boston to Rockport via Boston and Maine Railroad. It's possible to manage in the center of Rockport without a car.

ACCOMMODATIONS *Seacrest Manor*, 131 Marmion Way, Rockport, 546-2211, $$–$$$ CP ● *Yankee Clipper Inn*, 96 Granite Street, Route 127, Pigeon Cove, Rockport, 546-3407, $$$ CP, $$$$$ MAP ● *Ralph Waldo Emerson Inn*, Phillips Avenue (Route 127), Pigeon Cove, Rockport, 546-6321, $$–$$$ ● *The Inn on Cove Hill*, 37 Mt. Pleasant Street, Rockport, 546-2701, $$ CP ● *Addison Choate Inn*, 49 Broadway, Rockport, 546-7543, $$–$$$ CP ●*Eden Pines Inn*, Eden Road, Rockport, 546-2505, $$$ CP ● *Blue Shutters Inn*, 1 Nautilus Road, Gloucester, 281-2706, good value, $–$$ CP ● Motels with ocean views: *Twin Light Manor*, Atlantic Road, Gloucester, 283-7500, $$$–$$$$; *Bass Rocks Motor Inn*, Atlantic Avenue, Gloucester, 283-7600, $$$; *Cape Ann Motor Inn*, 33 Rockport Road, 281-2900, $$$; *Seafarer*, 86 Marmion Way, Rockport, 546-2648, $$ CP.

DINING *Oleana by the Sea*, 27 Main Street, Rockport, 546-2049, seafood with sea view, $–$$ ● *Peg Leg*, Beach Street, Rockport, 546-3038, informal, $–$$ ● *The Lobster Pool at Folly Cove*, 332 Granite Street (Route 127), Rockport, 546-7808, informal, deck on the bay, $–$$$$ ● *White Rainbow*, 65 Main Street, Gloucester, 281-0017, 1830 landmark, excellent continental cuisine, entertainment, $$$ ● *Rhumb Line*, 40 Railroad Avenue, Gloucester, 283-9732, ship decor,

$–$$ • *Gloucester on the Waterfront,* 17 Rogers Street, Gloucester, 281-4416, creative menus, excellent, $$ • *Outrigger,* 77 Rocky Neck Avenue, E. Gloucester, 281-4999, unbeatable for picturesque harbor views, $$ • *Farina's,* 51 Washington Street, Gloucester, 281-2918, small gem for Mediterranean food, $$ • For clams drive to Essex on Ipswich Bay, where some say the fried clam was invented and where *Woodman's,* on the causeway, is a local institution worth the mob scene.

SIGHTSEEING Whale watching off Cape Ann, usually half-day cruises averaging $15; contact any of the following for current schedules and prices (all are zip code 01930) • *Cape Ann Whale Watch,* Main Street, Rose's Wharf, Gloucester, 283-5110; *Captain Bill and Sons Whale Watching,* 9 Traverse Street, Gloucester, 283-6995; *Gloucester Whale Watch,* Cape Ann Marina, Gloucester, 283-6089; *Seven Seas Whale Watch,* Seven Seas Wharf, Gloucester, 283-1776 • *Rockport Chamber Music Festival,* PO Box 312, Rockport, 01966, concerts by Manhattan String Quartet, Bach Chamber Soloists, and others for four weekends in June at Hibbard Gallery of Rockport Art Association. Write for current season dates and prices • *Museum of Cape Ann History,* 27 Pleasant Street, Gloucester, 283-0455. Hours: Tuesday through Saturday, 10 A.M. to 5 P.M. Adults, $2; under 12, free • *Rockport Art Association,* 12 Main Street, 546-6604. Hours: Monday to Saturday 9 A.M. to 5 P.M., Sunday from 1 P.M. Free • *Gloucester Stage Company,* 267 Main Street, Gloucester, 281-4099. Hours: mid-May to October, phone for current schedule and ticket prices • *Beauport,* Eastern Point Boulevard, Gloucester, 283-0800. Hours: May 15 to October 15, Monday to Friday, 10 A.M. to 4 P.M., open weekends September and October only, 1 P.M. to 4 P.M. Adults, $5, children, $2 • *Hammond Castle Museum,* 80 Hesperus Avenue, Gloucester, 283-7673. Hours: May to October, 10 A.M. to 4 P.M. daily, closed Wednesdays, November to April. Adults, $3.50; children, $2.

INFORMATION Cape Ann Chamber of Commerce, 33 Commercial Street, Gloucester, MA 01930, 283-1601. Rockport Chamber of Commerce, Route 127, Box 67, Rockport, MA 01966, 546-6575.

The Three Bs:
A Maine Education

The time is 3 A.M. on a chilly spring night, a good time to be snuggled in bed under a New England patchwork quilt. So why are all those cars still out in a parking lot in Freeport, Maine?

They belong to sports enthusiasts, savvy shoppers, insomniacs, tourists, and the just plain curious from every part of the country, part of some 2½ million people who stop day and night year round at one of America's shopping phenomenons: L. L. Bean, the nation's only 24-hours-a-day, 7-days-a-week retail store.

Mr. Bean's enterprise has developed into a major tourist attraction and a Maine institution. Two nearby neighbors, Bowdoin College in Brunswick and the Maritime Museum in Bath, are also long-standing institutions, each reflecting another facet of the state. Put the Bs together for a weekend that is a varied and pleasure-filled Maine education.

Leon Leonwood Bean never dreamed what lay ahead in 1912 when his intense dislike for cold, wet feet led him to create a new kind of hunting shoe with leather uppers and rubber overshoe bottoms. Armed with a mailing list of Maine hunting-license holders, he advertised that with his new product their feet would be "properly dressed for hunting bear or moose." He guaranteed "perfect satisfaction in every way," a promise that proved expensive when 90 of the first 100 pairs sold were returned with the rubber bottoms separated from the leather boots.

But Bean was true to his word. He gave refunds, borrowed more money, perfected his product, and started mailing out more catalogs—and this time things went well. Under Bean's grandson, Leon Gorman, the company now exceeds $193 million in annual sales.

Today's mammoth store, complete with granite paths, pine beams, and an 8,500-gallon indoor pond stocked with trout, has been described as "a cross between Bloomingdale's and a forest glen." You'll find anything for the outdoors, from camp stools to canoes to well-styled traditional clothing, as well as luggage, outdoor furniture, and cooking paraphernalia ranging from lobster pots to outdoor grills. There's everything from the catalog and more—plus a factory store stocked with irregulars and markdowns at bargain prices.

Bargains, in fact, have become the watchword in Freeport, as more and more discount stores have opened to take advantage of the crowds drawn to Bean. Dexter shoes, Hathaway shirts, Frye boots, and Cannon towels are among the goods sold in discount outlets nearby, and recently Polo/Ralph Lauren, Dansk, and Bass shoes joined the parade.

The bigger the array of stores and shops, the bigger the crowds, it seems, so now boutiques and arts and crafts galleries are beginning to appear. Praxis, a co-op featuring the work of Maine artisans, is one of the most interesting. So far Freeport has managed to absorb them all without losing the look of a New England town. Even the new McDonald's is housed in a white clapboard structure, without benefit of golden arches.

L. L. Bean can be visited any time of day or night, but some of the rest of the shops close at 7 P.M., so schedule your time in Freeport accordingly.

Freeport lodgings are increasing, but the town is busy, and you may find the atmosphere more pleasant if you make your headquarters in nearby Brunswick or Bath. Crane's Fairhaven Inn, a 1790s country house on the river in Bath, Brunswick Bed and Breakfast, an attractive old home in town, and the Harriet Beecher Stowe House in Brunswick are worth noting.

The last is the home where Stowe lived and wrote *Uncle Tom's Cabin* during the 1850s while her husband, Calvin Ellis Stowe, taught religion at Bowdoin College. The house itself is now part gift shop and part long-term lodgings, mostly occupied by people connected with the college. Visitors stay in the motel wing, but they can still enjoy the atmosphere of the 1807 home and its Common Room, done in comfortable overstuffed Victorian, and can dine in the converted barn that is now an attractive restaurant.

Brunswick is filled with fine homes—and history. Much of it centers on Bowdoin College, Maine's proudest educational institution, whose heritage goes back to 1794 and whose alumni include Henry Wadsworth Longfellow, Nathaniel Hawthorne, Admirals Peary and MacMillan, and president Franklin Pierce. Free campus tours during the school year are given hourly from 10 A.M. to 4 P.M. from Moulton Union, but you can easily stroll the handsome 40-building campus and see the main sights on your own.

The Walker Art Building collections span the centuries and the globe; most notable are the American paintings by Copley and Eakins and Gilbert Stuart's portrait of Thomas Jefferson. Among the many Gilbert Stuart works is a portrait of James Bowdoin III, son of the Massachusetts governor for whom the school was named. Bowdoin commissioned a number of works and then bequeathed them to the school in 1811, giving it one of the earliest college art collections in America.

Bowdoin's second museum, the Peary-MacMillan Arctic Museum, honors the exploits of the two adventurous alumni explorers who were the first to reach the North Pole. If you've ever wondered what it took to make this historic trip, here is the place to find out. The museum features almost life-size painted cutout figures of Peary and MacMillan in Eskimo dress and interesting artifacts from the expedition, including the odometer, telescope, and navigational instruments they used. Another section of the museum details the life of the inhabitants of the Arctic in the first half of this century—their clothes, tools, carvings, and paintings.

Both the college and the area between Federal and Maine streets are National Historic Districts, and a walking tour will reward you with a look at some of the finest of the remaining homes. Among the beauties are 63 Federal Street, site of the Stowe House, and 25 Federal, the residence of Longfellow and his wife when he taught at Bowdoin in 1829. Lincoln Street is lined with Greek revival homes, unchanged since they were built in the 1840s. One exception is the house at 3 Lincoln, a 1772 structure that was moved from another site and altered. It is considered the oldest house in the village.

Park Row homes date from 1798 to the mid-1800s, with the Italianate brick double house at 159–161 Park Row deserving special note. Guided tours from the Pejepscot Historical Museum, at 159 Park Row, take you through the building next door, the Skolfield-Whittier House, furnished just as beautifully as it was in 1863. Also of interest is 6–8 College Street, a one-time station on the underground railroad that shielded slaves en route to Canada; 26 College Street was the boyhood home of Pulitzer Prize–winning poet Robert Peter Tristram Coffin.

Finally, Civil War buffs should note the 226 Maine Street home of General Joshua L. Chamberlain, who was also a governor of Maine and president of Bowdoin. It is now a museum with restored rooms and many original furnishings tracing the life and career of Chamberlain.

The pleasant contrast of a few peaceful hours in Brunswick and a visit to the bustling shops in Freeport makes for a full and varied day— and leaves you time for further exploration in Bath on Sunday. Bath and boats have been synonymous ever since the first 30-ton vessel, the *Virginia,* was launched here in 1607. More than 4,000 other ships have followed suit.

The sign over the gates of the Bath Iron Works proclaiming "Through these gates pass the world's best shipbuilders" is no idle boast for a company that celebrated its centennial in 1984 and that has many employees who come from a long line of shipbuilding ancestors. The boats of Bath, from sleek racing yachts to military vessels, have long been noted worldwide for their fine craftsmanship. During World War II, 82 U.S. destroyers were built here—more than the number assembled by the entire empire of Japan. The iron works still makes commercial boats and U.S. Navy ships.

The Maine Maritime Museum in Bath celebrates this long seafaring heritage in a living museum complex that also includes an internship program to keep the art of building wooden boats alive. In warm weather, you can even travel between the several parts of the museum by boat along the Kennebec River.

Park at the visitors' center at the Percy and Small Shipyard, beyond the iron works on Washington Street, and begin by touring the only surviving shipyard in America where large wooden sailing vessels were once constructed. One, the six-masted *Wyoming,* was the largest wooden sailboat ever built in the United States.

Signs in the buildings and shops of the museum complex explain the steps involved in creating a boat, from laying out patterns and cutting frames to making sails and caulking. The tour is self-guided, but if you have any questions about the shipbuilding process, you'll get ready answers from the bright young apprentices who are at work in the Apprentice Shop, learning the intricacies of constructing traditional Maine wooden crafts. From the catwalks here, you can see the actual construction of some of the old boats that are now in the process of restoration. The 18-month apprenticeship program is free for volunteers, who exchange their labor for learning. The program is partially supported by the sale of their boats.

If the museum boat *Sasanoa* is running, hop aboard; otherwise drive back to town to reach the Sewall House, an 1844 columned and shuttered mansion that contains the furnishings and memorabilia of the wealthy Sewall family as well as ships' models and a history of the Bath Iron Works. Among the models is a 12-foot mahogany-and-brass replica of J. P. Morgan's 343-foot yacht *Corsair,* built by the iron works in 1930.

A few blocks down Washington Street at the Winter Street Center are three floors of old photos, logs, and dioramas telling the story of Bath's maritime history and an exhibit showing a century of Maine steamboats. The walk along Washington puts you in the heart of Bath's historic district, past Federal, Greek and Gothic revival, and Italianate mansions once owned by wealthy shipbuilders and sea captains.

Between the museum and town, you can easily while away a day in Bath. Besides the mansions, have a look at restored nineteenth-century Front Street, with its brick sidewalks and old-fashioned lampposts, starting with the attractive City Park. The statue in the pond is appropriately known as *Spirit of the Sea.* At the top of Front Street is City Hall and the Old Customs House, and Waterfront Park will give you a view of the river.

End the day with a Maine seafood dinner, and you've completed your Three Bs tour, hopefully with a bonus B to take home—all those bargains you picked up in Freeport. And in case you want one last shot, remember that L. L. Bean will be open no matter how late you linger over dessert.

Maine Area Code: 207

DRIVING DIRECTIONS Freeport is on I-95, 20 miles north of Portland. It is 125 miles from Boston, 335 miles from New York, and 225 miles from Hartford. Follow US 1 north for Brunswick and Bath.

PUBLIC TRANSPORTATION Greyhound Bus service to Brunswick and Bath, air service to Portland (see page 48).

ACCOMMODATIONS *Harraseeket Inn,* 162 Main Street, Freeport, 865-9377, bed and breakfast just two blocks from L. L. Bean, $$$ CP ● *Stowe House,* 63 Federal Street, Brunswick, 725-5543, $$ ● *Brunswick Bed and Breakfast,* 165 Park Row, Brunswick, 729-4914, pleasant home near the college, $$ CP ● *Crane's Fairhaven Inn,* North Bath Road, Bath, 443-4391, $–$$ ● *New Meadows Inn,* Bath Road, West Bath, 443-3921, motel and cottages on the river, $–$$.

BED AND BREAKFAST *Bed and Breakfast of Maine,* 32 Colonial Village, Falmouth, ME 04105, 781-4528 ● *Bed and Breakfast Down East Ltd.,* Box 547, Eastbrook, ME 04634, 565-3517.

DINING *Jameson Tavern,* 115 Main Street, Freeport, 865-4196, Colonial home, $$–$$$ ● *Harraseeket Lunch and Lobster Company,* South Freeport, 865-4823, lobster pound on the docks, usually open from mid-May, $–$$ ● *22 Lincoln,* 22 Lincoln Street, Brunswick, 725-5893, town's most elegant, $$–$$$ ● *The Bowdoin House,* 115 Maine Street, 725-2314, popular, dependable, pleasant, $–$$ ● *The Omelette Shop Café,* 111 Maine Street, Brunswick, 729-1319, for breakfast or lunch, burgers too, $ ● *New Meadows Inn* (see above), shore dinners, lobster, $–$$ ● *Second Course,* 1 Elm Street, Bath, 442-7422, airy decor, interesting menu, $$–$$$.

SIGHTSEEING *Maine Maritime Museum,* 263 Washington Street, Bath, 443-1316. Hours: mid-May to mid-October, daily 10 A.M. to 5 P.M., check for current off-season hours. Adults, $5.50; children, $2.25; family maximum, $15 ● *Bowdoin Museum of Art.* Hours: September to May, Tuesday to Saturday 10 A.M. to 5 P.M.; Sunday 2 P.M. to 5 P.M. Free ● *Peary-MacMillan Arctic Museum,* Hubbard Hall, Bowdoin campus. Hours: same as Museum of Art. Free.

INFORMATION Freeport Merchants Association, 1 Mechanic Street, Freeport, ME 04032. Brunswick Area Chamber of Commerce, 59 Pleasant Street, Brunswick, ME 04011, 725-8797. Bath Area Chamber of Commerce, 45 Front Street, Bath, ME 04530, 443-9751.

Antiquing in Old Connecticut

Nobody knows quite how it happens. First one antiques shop springs up, then another, and before you know it a whole town is wall-to-wall antiques.

There are a few such towns in New England—Sheffield, Massachusetts, and Searsport, Maine, among them—but none with choicer shops or scenery to offer than the historic town of Woodbury, Connecticut. Woodbury has become an "antiques capital" of the state, and in combination with its beautiful Colonial neighbor, Washington, it is a prime weekender's destination.

You'll need no guidebook to find the shops—Woodbury's long Main Street along Route 6 is filled with them. They range from museum quality at Kenneth Hammett to Canadian pieces at Monique Shay to country French at Country Loft, which also offers Oriental and kilim rugs. British Country Antiques offers seven big rooms and a barn full of pine and oak, painted armoires and other English specialties. The names may change as shops change hands, but the variety and number of stores is constant.

Two unusual shopkeepers to visit are Harold Cole, who sells architectural salvage such as eighteenth-century hand-hewn beams and old doors as well as pewter, paintings, and folk art, both at Woodbury Barn and in his shop at 266 Washington Road; and Craig Farrow, a Woodbury cabinetmaker, who will create a masterful copy of your favorite unaffordable seventeenth- or eighteenth-century antique.

Between the Main Street shops, you'll spy more Woodbury trademarks: the white spires of no fewer than four fine New England churches, and the 1754 Curtis House, the oldest hostelry in the state. Stop off for a lunch of flaky chicken pot pie and the house specialty, French onion soup, in a historic setting of old beams and fireplaces. Woodbury is also filled with early Colonial homes, the most notable being the Glebe House, which dates from the late 1600s and is credited as the birthplace of the American Episcopal Church.

When you've exhausted the shops or your spending money, follow Route 47 about eight miles north to Washington to discover one of the prettiest New England villages in this or any other state. The host of two prestigious prep schools, Washington is a haven of old homes and old money. The big village green, dominated by the tall Congregational church and surrounded by glistening white Colonial homes set off with dark shutters, is all but perfect. Even the drugstore here is tucked into a Colonial home.

Though this is a very private town, there is enough to see and do to keep you occupied. The Museum of the Gunn Memorial Library on the green is a period house furnished with pieces dating as far back as 1695. Among the many displays are toys, dollhouses and dolls, thimbles, military relics, and letters from George Washington and Thomas Jefferson. If you want to be sure to get inside, note that the house is open only on Saturday from 12 noon to 3 P.M.

The most interesting of Washington's sights takes you back even further than Colonial times. The American Indian Archaeological Institute promises and delivers "10,000 years in Quinnetukut" (Connecticut), with exhibits that range from a mastodon and simulated archaeological sites to a reconstructed Indian village and longhouse. Don't forget to look into the gift shop for a fine selection of baskets, jewelry, and pottery.

Other local shops are clustered in little Washington Depot, just above the green. They are few, but what is there is choice—antiques, jewelry and fine china, and classic country clothes. The Hickory Stick Book Shop, a local landmark, has a stock that many a larger city would envy; the Pantry, the local gourmet lunching spot, has interesting kitchenware and foods for sale; and Ragazza is the place for designer clothing at discount prices.

You have your choice of interesting places to stay in this area. Curtis House will let you sleep in a four-poster bed in a simply furnished Colonial room at a most reasonable price. A few miles to the south in Southbury, the Harrison Inn offers modern and most attractive resort facilities with swimming, tennis, and golf. Best of all are the lodgings above Washington at Lake Waramaug in New Preston, where The Boulders is the best of four excellent inns, all with water views.

You might spend Sunday just checking out the sights or the shops you missed, or getting back to nature in the 95 acres of Lake Waramaug State Park or the Flanders Nature Center in Woodbury, a 1,000-acre sanctuary with many lovely nature trails. Or you can continue either antiquing or gazing at prize Connecticut architecture in two lovely towns nearby: Kent and Litchfield.

Die-hard antiquers should head for Kent and another cache of stores. Route yourself from Washington south to New Milford on Route 109 for a magnificent backcountry drive, uphill and downhill past white farms, red barns, stone walls and split-rail fences, and signs that may cause you to detour for the farm-fresh eggs for sale. At Route 7, turn north and pass through the little town of Gaylordsville, where you may choose to stop again for the local antiques stores. Another interesting spot a few miles farther north on Route 7 is Steven Fellerman's Bull Bridge Glass Works, where you'll have a chance to meet Mr. Fellerman and see the exquisite hand-blown glass he creates here.

In Kent, the current guide lists 11 antiques shops on or near Route 7, and there are plenty of other places to explore as well—the Kent Art Association gallery, the restored railroad station now known as Kent Station Square, and a complex behind it with an art gallery in an old railroad car and an antiques shop.

You'll see Kent Falls State Park right on Route 7 as you come into town, and if you want to stretch your legs, the easy trail up beside the falls will reward you with a series of scenic views, complete with roaring sound effects. Another very special stop in Kent is the Sloane-

Stanley Museum, the late artist Eric Sloane's collection of handcrafted Early American wooden tools that are truly works of art.

If you prefer architecture to antiques, follow Route 109 north from Washington to Route 63 and Litchfield, a town that is on every list of "most beautiful towns in America." Litchfield is considered by many to be the finest unrestored, unspoiled Colonial town in New England. This is a town for walking, and it's easy to see the sights since the magnificent houses here are concentrated on two long blocks, North and South streets, coming off the green. For outdoor lovers, Litchfield offers the White Memorial Foundation, the state's largest nature center and wildlife preserve, with almost every kind of outdoor activity, plus Bantam Lake, 11 ponds, and the Bantam River. There are miles and miles of trails and a unique bird-watching facility, as well as nature exhibits in the Conservation Center.

You need not be a real flower fancier to appreciate Litchfield's White Flower Farm. May and June are the peak bloom months for the eight acres of exotic display gardens in a nursery that is one of the nation's outstanding breeding grounds for perennial plants. Besides the gardens there are 1,200 varieties of flowers in 20 acres of growing fields. Delphiniums are a specialty, as are the tuberous begonias in the greenhouse.

It is less than 25 miles between any two points in this area—Litchfield to Kent or either town from Woodbury or Washington—so you'll find it easy to spend several days in this beautiful section of old Connecticut, enjoying the many sights. But if you never manage to tear yourself away from Woodbury and the shops, you needn't apologize. You won't be the first to have fallen prey to the lures of the antiques capital of Connecticut.

Connecticut Area Code: 203

DRIVING DIRECTIONS   Woodbury is on Route 6, west of Waterbury, at exit 15 off I-84. It is about 140 miles from Boston, 85 miles from New York, and 45 miles from Hartford.

PUBLIC TRANSPORTATION   Bonanza buses to Southbury, New Milford, or Kent, Metro North trains to Danbury.

ACCOMMODATIONS   *Curtis House,* Main Street, Woodbury, 263-2101, $–$$ • *Harrison Inn,* Village Green, Southbury, 264-8255, $$$–$$$$ • *Boulders Inn,* Route 45, New Preston, 868-7918, $$$$ MAP • *Hopkins Inn,* Hopkins Road, New Preston, 868-7295, open May to October, $ • *Inn on Lake Waramaug,* New Preston, 868-0563, $$$$–$$$$$ MAP • *Birches Inn,* West Shore Road, New Preston,

868-0229, $$$$ MAP • *Fife 'n' Drum,* Route 7, Kent, 927-3509, spacious, well-decorated rooms in lodge adjoining restaurant, $$$ • Some small choice Kent bed-and-breakfast inns: *Saltbox Inn,* Route 7, Kent, authentically restored early Colonial, $$$$ CP • *Flanders Arms,* Route 7, Kent, 927-3040, Laura Ashley decor, $$$ CP • *The Country Goose,* Route 1, Kent, 927-4746, eighteenth-century Colonial, $$ CP • *Constitution Oak Farm,* Beardsley Road, Kent, 354-6495, a working farm in the country, $$ CP.

BED AND BREAKFAST *Nutmeg Bed and Breakfast,* 222 Girard Avenue, Hartford, CT 06107, 236-6698 • *Covered Bridge Bed and Breakfast,* PO Box 447, Norfolk, CT 06058, 542-5944.

DINING *Curtis House* (see above), $$–$$$ • *The Bistro,* 107 Main Street North, Woodbury, 263-0466, continental, $$–$$$ • *Portofino,* Route 6, Woodbury, Italian, $$ • *Hopkins Inn* (see above), $$–$$$ • *Boulders Inn* (see above), $$–$$$ • *Inn on Lake Waramaug* (see above), $$–$$$ • *Le Bon Coin,* Route 202, Woodville, 868-7763, excellent French bistro, $$$$$ • *Wickets,* The Commons, Route 202, Litchfield, 567-8744, attractive decor, innovative menu, $$–$$$ • *Toll Gate Inn,* Route 202, Litchfield, 482-6116, 1745 landmark house, $$–$$$ • *Fife 'n' Drum,* Route 7, Kent, 972-3243, fine piano bar, $$–$$$ • For lunch, *The Pantry* in Washington is excellent.

SIGHTSEEING *Glebe House,* off Route 6, Woodbury, 263-2855. Hours: April to October, Saturday to Wednesday 1 P.M. to 5 P.M. $2 • *American Indian Archaeological Institute,* off Route 199, Washington, 868-0518. Hours: Monday to Saturday 10 A.M. to 4:30 P.M., Sunday from 12 noon. Adults, $2; children, $1 • *Gunn Historical Museum,* on the green (Route 47), Washington, 868-7756. Hours: April to December, Tuesday and Thursday 1 P.M. to 4 P.M., Saturday 12 noon to 3. Free • *Tapping Reeve House and Law School,* South Street, Litchfield, 567-4501. Hours: May 15 to October 15, Thursday to Monday 12 noon to 4 P.M. Adults, $1, children, free • *White Flower Farm,* Route 63, Morris (outside Litchfield), 567-0801. Hours: mid-April to October, weekdays, 10 A.M. to 5 P.M., weekends 9 A.M. to 5:30 P.M. Free • *White Memorial Foundation,* Route 202, Litchfield, 567-0857. Hours: daily dawn to dusk year round. Free • *White Memorial Conservation Center* (same as above), 567-0015. Hours: April to November, Tuesday to Saturday 9 A.M. to 5 P.M. Sunday 11 A.M. to 5 P.M. Adults, $1; children, $.50 • *Flanders Nature Center,* Church Hill Road off Route 6, Woodbury, 263-3711. Hours: trails open daily dawn to dusk.

INFORMATION Litchfield Hills Travel Council, PO Box 1776, Marbledale, CT 06777, 868-2214.

Greeting Spring in Sandwich

The oldest town on Cape Cod is just about the loveliest. There are few places on the Cape that can match the quiet Colonial charm and serenity of Sandwich. Beach-bound traffic tends to pass this historic village by, leaving it to those who enjoy meandering down peaceful Colonial lanes, sitting beside a mill pond, antiquing, or exploring gardens and fascinating, little-heralded museums, one of them featuring a collection of famous Sandwich glass.

If you fit the bill, you'll find this special town at its very best late in May, when the wide lawns are still wearing their fresh coats of green, and gracious homes and spired New England churches are framed in pastel clouds of crab apple, laurel, and dogwood blossoms. That's the time, too, when thousands of prize rhododendrons begin their annual spring spectacular at Heritage Plantation, a remarkable 76-acre complex with showplace gardens and museums.

Though the shore is nearby, you'll almost be grateful if it isn't warm enough for sunbathing, because there's so much to see and do in Sandwich besides the beach.

Good lodging choices right in the center of old Sandwich include the landmark Daniel Webster Inn on Main Street and any of the town's small bed-and-breakfast inns. The original historic inn dating back to 1692 is long gone, but the current version is most attractive; be forewarned, though, that it often draws tour groups for lunch. The choicest (and quietest) rooms are in the new wing or in the recently restored historic house next door. Ask for a wing room looking out at the garden or, if you want to splurge a bit, for one of the handsome suites with fireplaces in the Fessenden House. Of the bed-and-breakfast places, the Captain Ezra Nye House, a 1792 home right across the street from the inn, and the Quince Tree, just down the block, are good choices, or you can try Wingscorton Farm Inn, a beautifully furnished retreat in East Sandwich, or one of the many inns not far away off Route 6A.

Founded in 1637 by ten men from Saugus, Massachusetts, who made their way to the top of Cape Cod, the town is named after Sandwich, England. There are still many monuments to attest to this long history. The columned Sandwich Town Hall dates back to the 1630s, and the Dexter Grist Mill on Shawme Pond near the center of town is a restoration of the mill that operated here in 1640. Next door is the restored Hoxie House, one of the oldest on the Cape. It is open to the public from mid-June to September. Another source of local pride is the exquisite Wren-style steeple of the 1848 First Church of Christ, containing what is said to be the oldest church bell in America, dating to 1675.

You'll probably want to begin your stay just by taking a walk and enjoying the graceful ambience of the town, with its central green and mill pond. And since Sandwich is only a village, you'll have no problem finding your way along the central arteries—Main and Water streets—or onto the side roads with their handsome homes. You'll find many worthwhile detours along the way.

Near the old mill and also on the pond is the Thornton Burgess Museum, dedicated to the author of the Peter Rabbit stories, who grew up in Sandwich. Web-footed creatures of all kinds stroll the lawns here, and you can visit Peter's own house.

One of the most historic buildings in town is the 1638 First Parish Meeting House, which currently boasts the Yesteryear's Doll Museum. The dolls are the private collection of Mr. and Mrs. Ronald Thomas of Sandwich, who created the museum to house a lifetime of acquisitions, most of them rare dolls from Germany and Japan. Dollhouses furnished in period style, miniatures, and other interesting toys are on display as well. Doll lovers should note that a doll doctor is on duty here to repair and restore damaged treasures, and the gift shop is chock full of dolls, doll clothing, and accessories.

The main attraction in town for most people is around the corner at the Sandwich Glass Museum, where several rooms handsomely display a comprehensive collection of the renowned glassware that was made here from 1825 to 1888.

Even if the name of Sandwich glass means little to you, you'll recognize the "lacy" designs developed here that continue to influence glassware patterns today. The museum may seem small at first glance, but it takes at least an hour to tour it properly, tracing the development of pressed glass from the factory's first experiments at mass production to the ornate pieces and glowing colors that were produced by midcentury. The museum is a sleeper, more interesting than you might expect, and it may well leave you with a new interest in the craft of glassmaking. Don't be surprised if you are inspired to pick up a paperweight or other unusual glass souvenir at the sales desk on your way out.

If you've taken your time, taken in the sights, and taken an hour or so or so out for a leisurely lunch at the Daniel Webster Inn, you may need no further activity for a pleasant Saturday than to browse the half-dozen antiques stores, the wood carver's gallery and shop, and the handful of tasteful gift shops in town, almost all near the center of the village. Antiques buffs should note the annual show held the last Saturday in May at the Henry T. Wing Elementary School to benefit the local historical society.

If you want to complete all the sights, you can take a brief driving tour to Old Cemetery Point, the town's first burying grounds, dating back to 1683; to the site of the original glass factory at Jarves and Factory streets; and to the old Quaker Meeting House and Graveyard, circa 1810, at Gilman and Spring Hill Road in East Sandwich. Also in East Sandwich off Chipman Road, you can see the Thornton Burgess Briarpath, the original Peter Rabbit country, where there are now walking trails to let you follow in Peter's footsteps. One other option is a nostalgic ride on the Cape Cod and Hyannis Railroad.

With the sights checked off and a good night's sleep, you'll be fresh on Sunday for the new barrage of attractions awaiting you at Heritage Plantation. This amazing museum complex is dedicated to the memory of Josiah K. Lilly, Jr., described in the plantation brochure as "one of the most distinguished and unassuming twentieth-century American collectors."

What did Mr. Lilly collect? Name it. There are four separate buildings filled to the brim with his antique guns and military memorabilia and miniatures, vintage automobiles, paintings and American folk art, tools and crafts, and one of the largest collections of Currier and Ives lithographs in existence.

The museum buildings themselves are attractions. The cars are housed in a round barn inspired by the Shaker structure in Hancock, Massachusetts. The military museum is in a hand-hewn building held together by oaken pins and handwrought iron, a reproduction of a Revolutionary War structure called the Temple in New Windsor, New York. The arts and crafts gallery overlooking Upper Shawme Lake features an old-fashioned 1912 carousel still in perfect running order, to give visitors a nostalgic ride. To complete the display of Americana, there's a working windmill transplanted from the nearby town of Orleans that continues to grind grain. And there are galleries for rotating art exhibits as well.

If all that weren't enough, the Lilly family has located Heritage Plantation on the former estate of Charles O. Dexter, who gained distinction for hybridizing the now-famous Dexter rhododendrons. The annual blossoming of thousands of rhododendrons and other flowering evergreens in May and June is an unforgettable spectacle. There are many other flower gardens, including a day lily garden featuring 550 varieties, as well as picnic grounds and several quiet nature trails.

Bring along a picnic lunch, and Heritage Plantation can easily occupy your whole Sunday. Or you might choose to end your weekend by taking an afternoon drive east on Route 6A—the old King's Highway—which goes through the Cape's attractive north shore towns. Since the water is colder and the beaches not quite as bountiful as they are on the southern side of the peninsula, 6A has escaped the commercial buildup that has all but spoiled Route 28 across the way. The shaded drive through the old Colonial settlements of Barnstable, Dennis, Yarmouth, and Brewster is scenic any time, but without the summer traffic, you can really appreciate the lovely old homes and the many intriguing antiques shops and other stores along the way. There are some interesting small museums and some of the Cape's best dining in this area, as well.

A drive straight through to Orleans and the intersection with the Mid-Cape Highway will take you about half an hour; if you stop to browse, it can take half a day. In the center of each town, you'll see a turnoff to the harbor and the beach—a chance to take a stroll or have a seafood dinner before you head home.

If you've given up on Cape Cod and its traffic and hassles, a springtime visit to Sandwich and its neighbors may change your mind. With history intact and without summer crowds, it is easy to see why so many people fell in love with the Cape in the first place.

Cape Cod Area Code: 508

DRIVING DIRECTIONS   Sandwich is the first town on the Cape after crossing the Sagamore Bridge, reached via the Mid-Cape Highway, Route 6 or Route 6A. It is 45 miles from Boston, 255 miles from New York, and 145 miles from Hartford.

PUBLIC TRANSPORTATION   Cape Cod and Hyannis Railroad from Boston, Buzzard's Bay, and Hyannis, mid-May to October; Peter Pan and Bonanza bus service to Hyannis.

ACCOMMODATIONS   *Daniel Webster Inn,* 149 Main Street, 888-3622, ask about MAP and weekend plans, $$–$$$$ ● *Captain Ezra Nye House,* 152 Main Street, 888-6142, $–$$ CP ● *The Quince Tree,* 164 Main Street, 888-1371, $$ CP ● *Wingscorton Farm Inn,* 11 Wing Boulevard (off 6A), East Sandwich, 888-0534, $$$–$$$$ CP ● *Isaiah Hall Bed and Breakfast Inn,* 152 Whig Street, Dennis, 385-9928, excellent mid-Cape choice, walking distance to the beach, $$ CP.

BED AND BREAKFAST   *Bed and Breakfast Cape Cod,* Box 341, West Hyannisport, MA 02672, 775-2772 ● *House Guests,* Cape Cod, PO Box 1881, Orleans, MA 02653, 896-7053.

DINING   *Daniel Webster Inn* (see above), the only first-class choice in Sandwich, $$–$$$ ● *Horizons,* Town Neck Beach, Sandwich, 888-6166, informal seafood with a water view, in season only, check dates, $–$$. The following, considered among the Cape's best, are within a half-hour's drive from Sandwich: *Café Elizabeth,* 31 Sea Street, Harwich Port, 432-1147, seems everyone's current top choice, $$$–$$$$ ● *Chillingsworth,* Route 6A, Brewster, 896-3640, $$$$ ● *Bramble Inn,* Route 6A, Brewster, 896-7644, $$$$ ● *Cranberry Moose,* 43 Main Street (6A), Yarmouth Port, $$$–$$$$. Other less pricey recommendations: *La Cipollina,* 157 Main Street, Yarmouthport, 362-4341, $$$ ● *The Dennis Inn,* Scarsdale Road (off 6A), Dennis, 385-3650, $$–$$$ ● *Mattakeese Wharf,* Barnstable Harbor, 362-4511, seafood with a view, $$–$$$.

SIGHTSEEING *Heritage Plantation,* Grove and Pine streets, 888-3300. Hours: daily 10 A.M. to 5 P.M., mid-May through mid-October. Adults, $5; children under 12, $2 ● *Sandwich Glass Museum,* Town Hall Square, 888-0251. Hours: daily 9:30 A.M. to 4:30 P.M., April to November (call for off-season hours). Adults, $2; under 12, $.50 ● *Yesteryear's Doll and Miniature Museum,* Main and River streets, 888-1711. Hours: May through October, Monday to Saturday 10 A.M. to 5 P.M., Sunday from 1 P.M. Adults, $2.50; children under 12, $1.50 ● *Cape Cod and Hyannis Railroad,* 225 Main Street, Hyannis, 771-1145. Hours: mid-May to October, daily rides to Hyannis and other Cape towns; phone for current schedule and rates.

INFORMATION   Cape Cod Chamber of Commerce, Routes 6 and 132, Hyannis, MA 02601, 362-3225.

Surprising City by the Sea: Portland, Maine

"I have this friend," the Portland native was telling us, "that everybody thought was crazy. Fifteen years ago he started buying wrecked-up buildings near the waterfront. People laughed at him and asked what on earth he was going to do with those old buildings."

The punchline, of course, is that the friend is now a millionaire. In the past decade, the redevelopment of the waterfront, now a bustling complex of attractive shops and restaurants known as the Old Port Exchange, has led the way to a remarkable renaissance in Portland, Maine. It is a development that would have been hard to predict for anyone who knew the city not so long ago.

Now young professionals from throughout New England are moving to this city that native Henry Wadsworth Longfellow once described as "The beautiful town that is seated by the sea." Portland has become an increasingly sophisticated and appealing place to live and to visit, with a thriving arts community, a magnificent new art museum designed by I. M. Pei, and some of the best food to be found north of Boston.

But it remains true that the first thing you notice in Portland is water, not buildings. The city is on a peninsula with views of deep blue sea on three sides, the vistas made more dramatic because Portland is situated on a high crest of land. The proximity to shoreline, the boat cruises, and the nearby rocky cliffs below Maine's most photographed and painted landmark, Portland Head Lighthouse, make visiting this city a double pleasure.

That the rebirth of Portland should have taken so long despite its fortunate location reflects how far the city had lagged. Once a prosperous shipping and shipbuilding port and capital of Maine, it developed early in its history into a major center for importing molasses from the West Indies. The port continued to flourish until a devastating July 4 blaze in 1866 destroyed 1,800 buildings and left 10,000 people homeless. Though the city rebuilt quickly with the sturdy stone Victorian structures still evident today, it suffered a more serious setback later in the century when the port declined, partly because of competition from the opening of the St. Lawrence Seaway.

In time, the deserted buildings near the harbor became havens for artists and craftspeople, who could get them for rock-bottom rents. They formed the Old Port Association in an effort to tempt browsers, stringing up their own lights and shoveling their own streets to make the area more enticing, since the city no longer provided such services to the decaying area. That was the start of the recent revival, abetted by the Maine Way urban renewal program.

Meanwhile, downtown Portland underwent its own facelift. Today Congress Street, the main business thoroughfare, has been spruced up with brick sidewalks and old-fashioned street lamps and a cleaning job that removed a century of grime from the old façades. New buildings abound. Monument Square, at the corner of Congress and Middle, is now a plaza with colorful food carts that offer everything from bagels to health food. Lunchtime entertainment adds to its attraction as a local gathering place.

The liveliest activity in town is centered in the Old Port, between Monument Square and the wharves. Here's where young people gather in trendy cafés and tourists shop the many offbeat stores, dozens of them selling everything from pottery to antiques to clothing. The area continues to grow as more blighted blocks are restored and has become a showcase for craftspeople from throughout northern New England.

Even with all these changes, Portland remains at heart a small city (population 65,000), in which you can easily walk to all the sights. (From June on, an old-fashioned trolley offers a lazier touring alternative.)

The old face of Portland—part dowdy, part Old World charm—is still very much in evidence among the new buildings on Congress. A walking tour of this area is an architecture buff's delight and a good place to begin your look at the city. Start at the office of the Chamber of Commerce, off Congress next to the art museum, where you can pick up printed tours for different parts of the city. The Congress guide points up the contrasts now to be found on a street whose history spans more than two centuries.

At 425 Congress you'll find the Wadsworth-Longfellow House, circa 1785, crammed between stores and banks. The hostess-guided tour of the boyhood home of the famed poet and his family is a detour not to be missed by anyone interested in American literature or history. Further on, the Federal-era First Parish Church is neighbor to the new Casco Bank Building, and beaux arts and Queen Anne structures adjoin the ultramodern library built in 1979—an unconventional yet somehow congenial blending of styles.

Switching over to the Old Port Exchange guide, you'll learn about the city's ups and downs as a shipping center, and the filling of land in the 1850s to form Commercial Street. The tour book points out the major structures dating from the 1866 rebuilding, most of them on Middle, Exchange, and Fore streets, which offer another field day for architecture buffs. The Customs House Wharf—home of Boone's, a local seafood landmark, and the departure point of the Casco Bay Line boat rides—hasn't slicked up as much as the rest of the neighborhood and gives visitors an idea of what the entire area looked like a few years ago.

You'll probably not need the printed guide to notice one of the most intriguing new additions, the *trompe l'œil* mural by Portland artist Chris Denison at Exchange and Middle, which transforms a blank brick wall into what looks for all the world like a period building. The open corner in front of the mural now serves as a gathering place for informal summer concerts.

There's no question that you'll be tempted to interrupt your building gazing to look into the shops here, so allow yourself plenty of time. Among the many crafts shops, look out for the Maine Potters Market at 9 Moulton, a cooperative displaying the work of a dozen of the state's artisans. A bounty of art galleries and antiques shops beckon as well in the Old Port and on Congress. Shipwreck and Cargo, on Moulton, may be of special interest for its marine antiques, hardware, and salvage, which sometimes yield rich finds for decorators and renovators. Names and owners do change, so check the current list of local antiques stores, available in most of the shops.

Between the landmarks and the looking, you can while away a very pleasant day in Portland, but before your energy flags, one hour of your day should be saved for the glorious Portland Art Museum. At the moment, the prize permanent display here is the collection of Winslow Homer donated by Charles Shipman Payson, the same patron who was principally responsible for the new $11.6 million building. There are works by other artists associated with Maine or Maine subjects, such as John Singer Sargent, Stuart Davis, and Edward Hopper, that are part of the growing State of Maine Collection. While the museum's own collection builds, it is working hard to bring in visiting shows of high caliber, including past exhibits of Lachaise sculpture and paintings by both Andrew and Jamie Wyeth.

Perhaps the most stunning work of art here is the building itself, done in red brick and designed using shapes such as circles, squares, and arches deliberately planned to work with the traditional architecture of the city and the adjoining original museum landmark buildings of the 1900s. It is rightfully one of Portland's prides.

When hunger pangs strike, you're surrounded by possibilities. Evening entertainment is also plentiful and to every taste. For night music, some best bets are Top of the East at the Sonesta for the view; Horsefeathers, Deli One, and the Bridgeway for jazz or folk; the hotel lounges and DiMillo's for mellow dance music; Moose Alley, Genos, and the Old Port Tavern for rock.

On the cultural side, check for performances by the Portland Symphony, the Ram Island Dance Company, the Portland Ballet, the Portland Lyric Theater, and the resident theater groups: the Portland Players, the Portland Stage Company, and the Russell Square Players of the University of Southern Maine.

Another sign of the influx of educated young people is the number of art cinemas in Portland. If you want to catch up on foreign films, this is the place.

And if you want really late night entertainment or you have insomnia, remember that L. L. Bean is open all night in Freeport, just 15 minutes away.

Come Sunday, you might choose either to head for the wharf and board a cruise boat or to take a driving tour and see some of the city's prime water views. With planning, you can even manage both.

For the views, follow Congress Street east past the Portland Observatory and Monjoy Hill (once the site of a tent city housing survivors of the 1866 fire) to the Eastern Promenade overlooking Casco Bay. The homes here are bordered by a breezy park with benches to sit on and enjoy the sights; in the warmer months the observatory, a historic signal tower, can be climbed for an even more panoramic perspective.

Ft. Allen Park boasts a cannon straight from the USS *Constitution,* and the Eastern Cemetery, near Monjoy Hill on Congress and Washington, is a fascinating site dating back to 1639 that is full of centuries-old headstones embellished with angels and curlicues. The Western Promenade, another neighborhood of lovely homes, offers its own special view. On a good day you can see the White Mountains from here.

Back in town, follow State Street across the bridge to South Portland and watch for further Route 77 signs to Cape Elizabeth. (Turn left at the first school if the sign is missing, as it was recently.) The route will take you to Ft. Williams Park and the famous Portland Head Lighthouse, built for George Washington in 1791, a site that is even more imposing on its steep rocky perch than all the countless photos can convey.

Farther on is Two Lights State Park, with 40 acres along the shore, and the Lobster Shack at Two Lights, a prime stop for lobster or clams served at picnic tables with an unbeatable ocean view. If the weather is conducive to beachcombing, drive farther on Route 77 to Crescent Beach State Park or Higgins Beach or Scarborough Beach State Park in Scarborough. At Ferry Beach off Route 207 in Prouts Neck, you can view the community whose rugged cliffs were the inspiration for many of Winslow Homer's works. The artist's studio remains here, much the way he left it.

You can have your driving tour and still get back to Portland in time for an afternoon or sunset cruise from the wharf and a final seafood dinner—a fitting close to a visit to a city by the sea.

Maine Area Code: 207

DRIVING DIRECTIONS   I-95 to I-295 and US 1 both lead into downtown Portland, located on the southern Maine coast 105 miles north of Boston, 315 miles from New York, and 205 miles from Hartford.

PUBLIC TRANSPORTATION   Portland is served by Delta, Eastern Express, U.S. Air, United, Continental, and Continental Express airlines, and Greyhound Bus service. Downtown is easily manageable without a car.

ACCOMMODATIONS   Within walking distance of downtown sights are: *Sonesta Hotel,* 157 High Street, 775-5411, gracious landmark, $$$–$$$$ • *Portland Regency,* 20 Milk Street, 774-4200, restored armory building in Old Port, $$$ • *Holiday Inn Downtown,* 88 Spring Street, 775-2311, $$$ • An inn alternative is *The Inn at Park Spring,* 135 Spring Street, 774-1059, $$$ CP • Best buy: *Susse Chalet Motor Lodge,* 1200 Brighton Avenue, 774-6101, $.

BED AND BREAKFAST   *Bed and Breakfast Down East Ltd.,* Box 547, Eastbrook, ME 04634, 565-3517 • *Bed and Breakfast of Maine,* 32 Colonial Village, Falmouth, ME 04105, 781-4528.

DINING   In a city that now is bursting with restaurants, some recommendations by the natives may be helpful • Seafood: *The Galley* at Handy Boatyard, 215 Foreside Road, Route 88, Falmouth, 781-4262, $$–$$$; *Snow Squall,* 18 Ocean Avenue, South Portland, 799-2232, $$; *Cap'n Newick's,* 740 Broadway, South Portland, 799-3090, $–$$;

Seamen's Club, 375 Fore Street, 772-7311, $–$$; *DiMillo's Floating Restaurant,* Long Wharf, 772-2216, on a boat, $$–$$$ • Italian: *Roma Café,* 789 Congress, 773-9873, $–$$; *Raphael's,* 36 Market Street, $$–$$$ • Chinse: *Hu Shang,* 7-13 Brown, 774-2030, and 29 Exchange, 773-0300, among the most popular eateries in town, $–$$ • Miscellaneous: *Alberta's,* 21 Pleasant Street, 774-5408, and 27 Forest Avenue, 774-4165, young crowd, interesting off-beat dishes, mesquite grill, $$; *Café Always,* 47 Middle Street, 774-9399, innovative menu, $$; *F. Parker Reidy's,* 83 Exchange Street, 773-4731, steaks and late-night activity, $–$$; *The Madd Apple,* 24 Forest Avenue, 772-6606, is a best bet for ribs and luscious Sunday brunch, $–$$ • Informal light meals or lunch: *Deli One,* 106 Exchange Street, 772-7115; *The Art Gallery,* 121 Center Street, 772-2866; *Horsefeathers,* 193 Middle Street, 773-3501; and *Dock Fore,* 336 Fore Street, 772-8619. All $ • Finally, that all-important question, where to go for lobster? The consensus says *Boone's,* Custom House Wharf, 774-5725; *DiMillo's* (see above); *The Lobster Shack,* at the entrance to Two Lights State Park in Cape Elizabeth (*note:* they stop boiling lobster at 8 P.M.); or *The Seamen's Club* (see above). Prices vary with the season's catch.

SIGHTSEEING *Wadsworth-Longfellow House,* 487 Congress. Hours: June to mid-October, Tuesday to Saturday 10 A.M. to 4 P.M. Adults, $2.50; children, $1; family admission, $5 • *Portland Museum of Art,* 7 Congress Street, 775-6148. Hours: Tuesday to Saturday 10 A.M. to 5 P.M., Sunday from 12 noon, Thursday until 9 P.M. Adults, $3; children, $1 • *Portland Observatory,* 138 Congress Street, 774-5561. Hours: Wednesday to Sunday 1 P.M. to 5 P.M., Friday to Sunday only in June. Adults, $1; children, $.35 • Boat trips: *Eagle Tours, Inc.,* Long Wharf, 799-2201 • *Casco Bay Lines,* Custom House Wharf, 774-7871; *Longfellow Cruise Lines,* Long Wharf, 774-3578. The above three have a variety of cruises several times daily, including sunset and evening sails, with different starting dates in the spring. Call for specifics. *MS Scotia Prince,* International Terminal, (800) 341-7540 or (800) 482-0955 in Maine, (775-5616 in Portland) leaves Portland nightly for Nova Scotia, with 22- and 46-hour minicruises available. Phone for current schedules and prices.

INFORMATION Greater Portland Chamber of Commerce, 142 Free Street, Portland, ME 04101, 772-2811.

Savoring the Shore in Connecticut

Early in June, when ringing cheers send off the annual Yale-Harvard regatta on the Thames River in New London, the oarsmen will be following the same historic river route that once took clipper ships out to sea.

Connecticut's upper shoreline, the focal point for much of the state's early history, is a treasury of Early American charm and of seafaring lore spanning three centuries, from the days of masted schooners to today's atomic submarines.

But despite its attractions and the presence of America's prime maritime destination, Mystic Seaport, much of the shoreline from Old Lyme north has remained unspoiled. Quaint Old Lyme still owes as much of its flavor to its Colonial heritage as to its proximity to the sea. And such nautical lures as New London's Whaling Museum and Stonington's lighthouse and fishing fleet are delightfully overlooked by tourist crowds.

Cruising the shore by land is a perfect outing for early June, when the old Ivy League rowing rivalry is replayed as it has been for well over 100 years.

Typically, crew races are scheduled for three starting times between 11 A.M. and 12:30 P.M., and spectators can cheer on the Crimson or the Blue from riverside viewing areas along the four-mile course. For those wishing a closer look at the excitement, an observation boat offers brunch and Dixieland music as well as a better view. Other festivities take place all day along the New London pier, which is the scene of many special events throughout the spring and summer.

The pier and its activity are a symbol of the new New London, a city fighting hard to recoup some of its illustrious past as a wealthy whaling outpost. The city fell upon hard times, but recently local preservationists began a determined revitalization effort. Today the town's historic walking tour, prominently posted along the refurbished, pedestrians-only main street known as Captain's Walk, begins with the city's pride, its lovingly restored nineteenth-century train station, designed by Henry Hobson Richardson, the architect of Boston's Trinity Church.

Other stops along the tour include the restored schoolhouse named for native son Nathan Hale, the 1930s Customs House, whose front door was once part of the frigate *Constitution,* the Shaw Mansion, which served as U.S. naval headquarters for Connecticut during the Revolutionary War, and four imposing columned whaling merchant's mansions known collectively as Whale Oil Row.

As you proceed south from Whale Oil Row, you'll come to Hemp stead Street, with several fine old homes, including one of Connecticut's oldest, the 1637 Hempstead House, the only one that escaped the town's burning by the British in 1781.

One of New London's oldest landmarks is the Old Town Mill, built in 1650 and restored in 1981. It's on the Thames and offers picnic grounds as well as a look at a working water wheel. An even more recently restored shrine is the boyhood home of Eugene O'Neill, located on Pequot Avenue on the way to Ocean Beach Park, a beach and seaside amusement area. The house is open to the public only on weekday afternoons; phone ahead for an appointment if you want to see it on weekends.

New London's Coast Guard Academy, a cluster of handsome, traditional red brick buildings on 100 acres high above the Thames, has inviting grounds, a well-endowed museum, and a multimedia center at river's edge that gives a comprehensive picture of the Coast Guard's role in the nation's history. There is a bonus for visitors when the *Eagle* is in port. The 295-foot square rigger that led the nation's Bicentennial parade of tall ships serves each summer as a magnificent floating classroom for cadets. When it is in home port, however, it is open for boarding.

Across the road from the academy is the Lyman Allen Museum, named after a whaling captain, and a repository for collections from the days of the pyramids to Picasso. The Deshon-Allyn House, a Federal-era whaling captain's home, is part of the museum complex.

Groton, just across the Thames from New London, is the home of the U.S. Navy submarine base, the largest of its kind in the world, providing yet another perspective on America's maritime traditions. The world's first nuclear submarine, the 320-foot *Nautilus*, was launched here in 1954. At the USS *Nautilus* Memorial at the base you can trace the progress of submarines from those days to our own nuclear age and board that first nuclear-powered sub. Working periscopes, an authentic submarine control room, and minitheaters are part of the exhibits.

Ft. Griswold State Park in Groton marks some of the town's older historic moments. The site of an important Revolutionary War battle in 1781, the Memorial Tower and statue on a hill overlooking the Thames make an impressive picture. There is a small museum at the base of the tower, and the view from the top is worth every step of the climb.

New London and Groton can take one day or two, depending on your interest in nautical affairs. If you have never been to Mystic Seaport Museum, you really need another whole day for the feast of sights there: majestic wooden sailing vessels, a complete nineteenth-century village with working shops, museum buildings filled with rare boats, ship models, figureheads, scrimshaw, and marine art, and a "please touch'' children's museum filled with the toys a sea captain's young-sters might have played with.

In any event, do not omit a visit to Stonington, a tiny hamlet at the very tip of the shoreline that is for many the favorite destination on the shore. This wonderfully picturesque town has a Greek revival center, a green surrounded by white-spired churches, narrow streets lined with eighteenth- and nineteenth-century sea captain's homes, and a light-house dating to 1823 that houses a museum of village history. You can pick up a printed walking tour of the town at the museum. The view of the Long Island Sound from the tower on a clear day is not to be missed.

Stonington's harbor is still crowded with working fishing boats, and many of the fishermen can trace their ancestry back to the whaling men recruited from the Azores in the 1830s. Their tradition of the blessing of the fleet continues here with a colorful ceremony in mid-July.

New London's best lodging is the Lighthouse Inn, the Victorian mansion of steel baron Charles S. Guthrie, near Ocean Beach Park. It has been renovated into an elegant enclave just a block from a private beach. Rich paneling and a carved spiral staircase lead to lavish guest rooms, including four huge front bedrooms with canopy beds and water views. There are also rooms in an adjacent carriage house and an excellent dining room. In town, the Radisson Hotel offers attractive modern quarters within a walk of the pier, and there is a pleasant, modest bed-and-breakfast inn in a Victorian home a short drive from the town's center. If you want a real Colonial inn, there are two good bets in Old Lyme, just a few miles down the coast. Whether you select the Bee and Thistle, an informal yellow Colonial house, or the Old Lyme Inn, an 1850s mansion with an elegant French menu, you will find yourself in a very special town whose wide, shaded Main Street has been declared a National Historic District.

One of the finest residences on the street was the home of a pioneer-ing American art colony. The columned Georgian mansion is known as Florence Griswold House, named for ''Miss Florence,'' who housed, fed, and nurtured a group of American Impressionist painters, including Willard Metcalf and Clark Voorhees, developers of the ''ideal Lyme landscape'' that brought much attention to the area. The house now serves as headquarters for the Lyme Historical Society and contains paintings and panels left by the early artists, an extensive china collection, and completely furnished period rooms—the front parlor is circa 1830, and a lady's bedroom dates from the early 1900s.

The Lyme Art Association next door was founded in 1914 as a showcase for the many artists who continued to be attracted to the town, and it remains a prestigious gallery, with changing exhibitions of current work.

Old Lyme's third attraction can rightfully be called nutty. It may well be the world's only Nut Museum, featuring the world's tallest nutcracker as well as all manner of nut art, music, and lore.

If time allows, continue a few miles farther south for lunch in Old Saybrook at one of the informal seafood stands near the harbor, with open-air decks for watching the boats come and go. From Old Saybrook, you can board the train for the nine-mile ride inland to Essex for a combination steam train–riverboat ride.

But Essex, like Mystic, really deserves a weekend to itself. Maybe the best plan is just to return to the nautical sights you missed on Saturday and then head home to plan a return visit to the scenic seafaring coast of Connecticut.

Connecticut Area Code: 203

DRIVING DIRECTIONS   All of the towns mentioned are on I-95, north of New Haven. New London is 113 miles from Boston, 125 miles from New York, and 45 miles from Hartford.

PUBLIC TRANSPORTATION   Amtrak trains, Bonanza and Greyhound buses serve New London.

ACCOMMODATIONS *Lighthouse Inn,* 6 Guthrie Place, New London, 443-8411, $$$–$$$$$ CP ● *Radisson Hotel, 35* Gov. Winthrop Boulevard and Union Street, New London, 443-7000, $$$ CP ● *Queen Anne Inn,* 265 Williams Street, New London, 447-2600, serves afternoon tea, $$–$$$ CP ● *Bee and Thistle Inn,* 100 Lyme Street, Old Lyme, 434-1667, $$$ ● *Old Lyme Inn,* 85 Lyme Street, Old Lyme, 434-2600, $$–$$$$ CP. Also see page 202 for Mystic.

BED AND BREAKFAST   *Seacoast Landings Bed and Breakfast Registry,* 133 Neptune Drive, Groton, CT 06340, 442-1940. ● *Nutmeg Bed and Breakfast,* 222 Girard Avenue, Hartford, CT 06105, 235-6698.

DINING   *West Bank Bistro,* 52 Bank Street, New London, 444-0803, stylish café with water views, $$–$$$ ● Bulkeley House, 111 Bank Street, New London, 443-9599, Colonial tavern, $$ ● *Thames Landing Oyster House,* 2 Captain's Walk, New London, 442-2650, popular for seafood, $–$$ ● *Lighthouse Inn* (see above), elegant, water views, $$ ● *Two Sisters Deli,* 300 Captain's Walk, New London, 444-0504, is a favorite local spot for lunch, $ ● *Bee and Thistle* (see above), $$$ ● *Old Lyme Inn* (see above), $$–$$$$ ● Also see Mystic, page 202.

SIGHTSEEING   *Yale-Harvard Regatta,* early June, contact either school for dates or the Southeastern Connecticut Tourism office for dates and current information on special events ● *Shaw Mansion,* 11 Blinman Street, New London, 443-1209. Hours: Tuesday to Saturday, 1 P.M. to 4 P.M. Adults, $1; children, $.50 ● *Nathan Hale Schoolhouse,* Captain's Walk next to City Hall, New London, 269-5752. Hours: mid-June to August, Monday to Friday, 10 A.M. to 3 P.M. Free ● *Hempstead House,* 11 Hempstead Street, New London, 443-7949. Hours: mid-May to mid-October, Tuesday to Sunday, 1 P.M. to 5 P.M. Adults, $2; 16 and under, $.25 ● *U.S. Coast Guard Academy,* Mohegan Avenue, New London, 444-8270. Hours: grounds open daily; Visitor's Pavillion and Museum, May to October, 9 A.M. to 5 P.M. Free ● *Lyman Allyn Museum,* 625 Williams Street, New London, 443-2545. Hours: Tuesday to Sunday 1 P.M. to 5 P.M. Donation ● *Monte Cristo Cottage,* 325 Pequot Avenue, New London, 433-0051. Hours: Monday to Friday 1 P.M. to 4 P.M., weekends by appointment. Adults, $2; children, $.50 ● *USS Nautilus Memorial,* U.S. Submarine Base Route 12, Groton, 449-3558. Hours: daily mid-April to mid-October, 9 A.M. to 5 P.M., rest of year to 3:30 P.M. Free ● *Fort Griswold State Park,* Monument Street and Park Avenue, 445-1729. Hours: Monument and Museum open daily, Memorial Day to Labor Day, 9 A.M. to 5 P.M., weekends only September to mid-October. Free ● *River Queen Cruises,* 193 Thames Street, Groton, 445-8111, sightseeing cruises, sunset cruises; phone for schedule and rates ● *Mystic Seaport,* Route 27, Mystic, 572-0711. Hours: daily 9 A.M. to 6 P.M., exhibits close at 5 P.M. Adults, $10; children, $5, under 5 free ● *Lighthouse Museum,* 7 Water Street, Stonington, 535-0711. Hours: May to October, Tuesday to Sunday 11 A.M. to 4:30 P.M. Adults, $1; children, $.50 ● *Florence Griswold Museum,* 96 Lyme Street, Old Lyme, 434-5542. Hours: June to October, Tuesday to Saturday, 10 A.M. to 5 P.M., Sunday from 1 P.M.; November to May, Wednesday to Sunday, 1 P.M. to 5 P.M. Adults, $1 ● *Lyme Art Association,* Lyme Street, Old Lyme, 434-7802. Hours: May to mid-October, weekdays 12 noon to 5 P.M., Sunday from 1 P.M. Donation ● *Nut Museum,* 303 Ferry Road, Old Lyme, 434-7636. Hours: May to November, Wednesday, Saturday, and Sunday 2 P.M. to 5 P.M. Admission: one nut, $2 contribution.

INFORMATION   Southeastern Connecticut Tourism District, Ye Olde Town Mill, 8 Mill Street, New London, CT 06320, 444-2357.

Exploring Blooming Boston

Boston keeps getting better. From the cobbled streets of Beacon Hill to the Victorian boulevards of Back Bay to the gleaming marble monu-

ment to affluence known as Copley Place, this is a town that has retained the best of the old while keeping up with the new in a blend of
vivacious harmony few cities anywhere can match.

No city offers more diversity. Some of 350-year-old Boston remains
a citadel of conservatism—quiet charm and tradition, perfectly preserved red brick townhouses, fifth-generation Brahmins, tea at 4 P.M.,
and swan boats gliding on the lake in the Public Garden as they have
since 1877.

Yet today's Boston is also nonstop action—sculls and sailboats on
the Charles, joggers and skaters on the Esplanade, crowds converging
on the food stalls in Quincy Market, shoppers nudging to get at the
bargains in Filene's basement.

It is a city of culture—of a world-renowned symphony and Museum
of Fine Arts—and a maelstrom of rabid Red Sox and Celtics fans, Irish
and Italian politicos, marathoners, camera-toting tourists, and schoolchildren walking the red line of the Freedom Trail, plus thousands of
young people who attend 150 area colleges and universities and make
an indelible mark on the city.

You can't really begin to know this complex city in a weekend; but
you can sample its multiple pleasures more easily than you might
imagine, because central Boston is essentially a compact, walkable
area where a little energy aided by an occasional bus or "the T"—the
efficient transit system—can take you a long way. Cars are only a
nuisance, since there is no place to park them.

So "pahk your cah," as the Bostonians really do say, stop at the
Boston Common information booths on Tremont Street or the Prudential Center to arm yourself with a city map and information, and plan a
walking tour of the neighborhoods that will show you the fascinating
facets of this urban gem. If your footpower lags, just board the "the
T" or the double decker shuttle bus that makes continuous loops of the
city center.

Boston Common, the oldest public park in America, is a beautiful
introduction to the city's sights. In spring it is resplendent with magno-
lias in bloom.

You might begin by following Tremont Street west from the information booths, turning left on Park Street to Beacon Street and the
State House at the top of that bastion of old Boston, Beacon Hill.
Samuel Adams laid the cornerstone for Charles Bullfinch's gold-
domed architectural masterpiece.

To appreciate the ambience of the Hill, you need only stroll its cobbled, gas-lit streets lined with rows of fine brick townhouses adorned
with gleaming brass door knockers, overflowing flower boxes, and
finely detailed iron work. Take Joy Street and go left on Mt. Vernon to
reach the perfect hushed pocket of the past called Louisburg Square.
You can visit the inside of a typical home at the Nichols House on Mt.

Vernon. A left turn on Pinckney behind Louisburg Square and a walk downhill will bring you down to Charles Street, a choice row of antiques shops and tempting cafés and coffee houses leading back to Beacon.

The corner of Beacon and Charles is of special note, both as the departure point for the British on their fateful expedition to Lexington and Concord and as the very spot where Officer O'Malley held up traffic to make way for the eight ducklings of Mrs. Mallard on their way to the Public Garden in Robert McCloskey's timeless children's tale. A detour to see the garden in its springtime prime, with a ride on the famous swan boats on the pond, is highly recommended.

Walk right two blocks on Beacon beside the garden to Arlington and across the Arthur Fiedler Memorial Bridge to reach the Esplanade, and pause to watch the activity on the Charles River and the promenade beside it. The Hatch Memorial Shell is the site of summer serenades by the Boston Pops, and the area around it is the favored spot for joggers, skaters, and people watchers. You can see the domes of MIT just across the Charles in Cambridge, the town that is also the home of the splendid Harvard campus.

From here you can tour another handsome side of Boston by returning past Beacon to Marlborough or Commonwealth and turning right to follow the eight alphabetical streets from Arlington to Hereford through the Back Bay.

Boston was a lot hillier before the Back Bay was developed. Henry James once used the word ''odiferous'' to describe this 450-acre oozy swampland that was later filled with soil leveled off from some of the hills. What emerged over a period of some 125 years was a model of nineteenth-century architecture in a green setting by Frederick Law Olmsted. Commonwealth, a parade of stately stone Victorian row houses with a wide grassy mall in the center, is the grandest street of all. Marlborough is simpler and greener, and some like it even better.

The alphabetical streets stop past Hereford at Massachusetts Avenue. A couple of blocks beyond is Kenmore Square, a gathering place for students from Boston University, which runs farther southwest along the river. To the east, near a park called the Fenway and the better-known Fenway Park, home to Boston's beloved Red Sox, are Simmons and Northeastern colleges. The Boston Museum of Fine Arts, which houses one of the nation's outstanding collections, is in the same neighborhood. Emerson College, another Back Bay institution, occupies some of the townhouses on Beacon, closer to the Public Garden.

On the other side of Commonwealth Avenue are Newbury and Boylston, the city's traditional shopping streets. At Boylston and Hereford you'll come to the Prudential Center, built over what was once the Boston trainyard and what is now the Massachusetts Turnpike. The

Prudential Tower Skywalk offers a stunning 360-degree view of the city.

The "Pru" is now connected by an overpass across busy Huntington Avenue to Copley Place and its lineup of posh stores. Walk through the Copley Place arcade and out through the Westin Hotel lobby and you will emerge on Copley Square, another city landmark, surrounded by the Boston Public Library, Trinity Church, and one of the city's grande dame hotels, the Copley Plaza. Don't fail to stop into the Boston Public Library to see the art treasures and the glorious courtyard in this beaux arts treasure by the renowned architectural firm of McKim, Mead, and White. There is another soaring city view to be had at the top of the John Hancock Tower off Copley Square.

From Copley Square follow Dartmouth Street west two blocks to Newbury for the best of the shops and galleries, stretching four blocks back to the Public Garden at Arlington. The Bonwit Teller store in the former Museum of Natural History is among the local landmarks. There are many sidewalk cafés on Newbury to provide a resting place for weary sightseers.

This is more than enough to fill a wonderful day, with stops at the many shops and sights along the way, but the Downtown Crossing must be squeezed in on Saturday if you want to have a look at another Boston institution, Filene's basement. It is a 15-minute walk or just a hop if you board "the T" at Arlington and Boylston. Get off at Park Street, turn right when you emerge, and cross Tremont to Winter Street and the stores. Filene's and Jordan Marsh are both one block away on the corner where Winter and Summer streets intersect with Washington, a pedestrians-only crossing that is the busiest intersection in New England. The scene is further enlivened by colorful wooden pushcarts filled with street wares and impromptu entertainment by street musicians. Lafayette Place, an enclosed shopping area next to Jordan Marsh, adds to the crowds.

The famous Filene's bargain basement is frequently a madhouse. The longer merchandise remains, the lower the markdowns; aficionados watch the action day by day like brokers on Wall Street, waiting for the perfect moment to buy. On any given day, a new batch of bargains—anything from designer clothing to Oriental rugs—may be fought over by eager customers. There are no dressing rooms, but that doesn't stop anyone from trying on the merchandise. Even if you don't want to participate, it's definitely a major only-in-Boston sight.

On Washington Street to the right of all this shopping activity is the "combat zone," Boston's adult entertainment district. Go left on Washington, and at the intersection of School Street you run into history: the Old South Meeting House, a center of pre-Revolutionary agitation; the Old Corner Bookstore, once a gathering place for Emerson,

Hawthorne, and other literary greats; and the Old City Hall and the Old State House, the seat of Colonial government.

Less than a block away on the left is the Government Center, a curving red brick plaza, and its showpiece, the new Boston City Hall, opened in 1969. Some consider the center controversial for its modernity; others find it pleasingly blended with its historic neighbors. You be the judge.

You can combine this last group of historic sites with a leisurely look at the waterfront and North End on Sunday, either by following the orderly red lines of the Freedom Trail—the road marking events leading up to the American Revolution—or by making your own way and watching for the sights. On your own, take "the T" or walk from the Boston Common information booth west on Tremont and north past the Granary Burying Ground and Park Street Church. Either route will take you to the Government Center. A walk down the steps and across the street brings you to Faneuil Hall, site of many town meetings at which impassioned patriots planned their fight for liberty.

Beyond is the Faneuil Hall Marketplace, with its three 500-foot buildings. You can literally eat your way through the domed Quincy Market in the center, which is filled with a heavenly assortment of food stands offering just about every edible you can imagine. The food market is flanked by cafés and the North and South Market buildings, with shops of all kinds plus lots of pushcart wares, a flower market, and the Haymarket, an open-air produce exchange. All of this occurs in a festive setting of cobbled walks, bright banners, and clowns, mimes, and musicians that attracts more than a million people a month. You'll find lots of places here for a pleasant brunch.

The shopping area keeps spreading, and there are more things to see and do on the booming Boston waterfront, including the fun-filled New England Aquarium and cruises in the harbor. A special Harbor Walk has been laid out with blue lines, and you can pick up pamphlets to guide you at any of the city information booths. For more details on some of the harbor attractions and other city sights, see "Bringing the Kids to Boston," page 192.

To complete a look at the city, you'll want to proceed beyond Quincy Market via a pedestrian tunnel under the Fitzgerald Expressway at Hanover Street into the North End. There is a European feeling to this old residential area of brick houses and narrow streets, and dozens of tempting stops in Italian bakeries, coffee shops, and restaurants. A few blocks from the start of Hanover Street, a right on Richmond brings you to the Paul Revere House, and a few blocks farther is the Old North Church, the city's oldest, where lanterns in the steeple were the signal for Revere's famous ride.

If you follow the Freedom Trail all the way to Charlestown, you can board "Old Ironsides," otherwise known as the USS *Constitution,* the oldest commissioned warship afloat in the world, and wind up at the site of Bunker Hill, the first battle of the Revolution, marked by a 220-foot monument with a stunning city view from the top. Going from the Old North Church to Bunker Hill adds 2½ miles to your route.

Having seen most of Boston, you still haven't explored its cultural treasures, such as the Museum of Fine Art, the exceptional Isabella Gardner Museum set in a virtual palazzo, the excellent Museum of Science, and the special architecture of the Christian Science Center. Nor have you visited the very moving Kennedy Memorial Library on Dorchester Bay, or had the unforgettable experience of hearing the fanatic fans at Fenway Park or Boston Garden, or paid a visit to Cambridge. And one weekend can't begin to take in all the nighttime attractions—theater, ballet at the beautiful, newly renovated Wang Performing Arts Center, symphony and opera, sports, and all the other forms of music and entertainment that a city full of sophisticates and young people regularly attracts.

There is always something more to do in Boston and, in recent years, something new to see almost every time you go back. But top among its many pleasures is the activity that never palls no matter how many times you repeat it—strolling the unchanging neighborhoods that preserve the bouquet of the past in a blooming contemporary city.

Boston Area Code: 617

DRIVING DIRECTIONS   From north or south, take I-93/3 or I-95, also from the north, Route 1, 1A, or 128. From the west, take Route 90, the Massachusetts Turnpike, or Route 2, 9, or 20. Boston is 98 miles from Hartford and 208 miles from New York.

PUBLIC TRANSPORTATION   Boston can be reached by Amtrak, most major bus lines, and most airlines. Cars are only a nuisance in the city. Cabs, subways, a water ferry, and shuttle buses serve the airport, and the downtown transit system is excellent.

ACCOMMODATIONS   So many possibilities, so few low prices! Almost all hotels do offer weekend packages at reduced rates. These change, so this is a listing of normal rates in descending order of price. Call or write for current packages, and check to see whether prices include parking, which can up the tab ● The old luxury standbys (all $$$$$): *Ritz Carlton,* 15 Arlington Street, 536-5700 or (800) 225-7620, still the epitome of Boston graciousness; *Parker House,* School and Tremont streets, 227-8600 or (800) 228-2121, America's oldest continuously operated hotel; *Copley Plaza,* Copley Square,

267-5300 or (800) 255-7654, full of Old World atmosphere but sometimes busy with conventions ● The best of the new luxury contenders
(all $$$$$): *Meridien,* 1 Post Office Square, 451-1900 or (800)
223-7385, a stunning modern hotel retaining the traditional architectural features of its premises, the old Federal Reserve Bank; *Four
Seasons Hotel,* 200 Boylston Street, 338-4400, elegance overlooking
the Public Garden; *Bostonian,* Fanueil Hall Marketplace, 523-3600,
handsome tasteful hotel on the waterfront; *Marriott Long Wharf,* 296
State Street, 227-0800, striking contemporary on the water; *The
Colonnade,* 120 Huntington Avenue, 424-7000, small, low-key, elegant; *Boston Harbor Hotel,* 70 Rowes Wharf, 437-7000, striking
water views; *Lafayette,* 1 Avenue de Lafayette, 451-2600, Swiss elegance near Downtown Crossing ● Other possibilities: *Embassy Suites,*
400 Soldiers Field Road, 783-0090, suites for the price of a room,
$$$$ CP; *Boston Park Plaza,* 50 Park Plaza, 426-2000, $$$$–$$$$$;
Lenox Hotel, 710 Boylston at Prudential Center, 536-5300 or (800)
225-7676, $$$–$$$$$; *Copley Square,* 47 Huntington Avenue,
536-9000 or (800) 225-7062, $$$–$$$$; *57 Park Plaza,* 200 Stuart
Street, 482-2800, $$$–$$$$ ● *Howard Johnson* has two locations,
$$$–$$$$, with one of the city's most reasonable weekend packages,
both reached toll free (800) 654-2000: *Howard Johnson Motor Lodge
Fenway,* 1271 Boylston Street, 267-8300, and *Howard Johnson's
Kenmore Square,* 575 Commonwealth Avenue, 267-3100 ● Cheaper
rates at motels in outlying areas, especially *Susse Chalet,* 800 Mor-
rissey Boulevard, Dorchester, 287-9100, $. Finally, for young people,
American Youth Hostels, 12 Hemenway Street, 536-9455, dorm ac-
commodations, $.

BED AND BREAKFAST *Bed and Breakfast Cambridge and
Greater Boston,* Box 665, Cambridge, MA 02140, 576-1492 ● *Bed
and Breakfast Associates, Bay Colony Ltd.,* PO Box 166 Babson Park,
Boston, MA 02151, 449-5302 ● *Bed and Breakfast Brookline/Boston,*
Box 732, Brookline, MA 02146, 277-2292 ● *Greater Boston Hospi-
tality,* PO Box 1142, Brookline, MA 02146, 277-5430 ● *Host Homes
of Boston,* PO Box 117, Newton, MA 02168, 244-1308 ● *New Eng-
land Bed and Breakfast,* 1045 Centre Street, Newton, MA 02159,
498-9819.

DINING Once again, starting from the top, a group of Boston hotels
are considered among the city's very best, all expensive: *Seasons* at the
Bostonian Hotel, *Julien* at the Meridien, the *Ritz Carlton* dining room,
Aujourd'hui at the Four Seasons, *Le Marquis* at the Lafayette, *Café
Plaza* at the Copley Plaza, and *Parker's* at the Parker House ● More of
the best: *Café Budapest,* 90 Exeter Street at Huntington Avenue,
734-3388, Hungarian, $$$–$$$$; *Locke Ober,* 3–4 Winter Street,

542-1340, Old World and an institution since 1875, $$$–$$$$; *Maison Robert*, 45 School Street, 227-3370, French menu in old city hall, $$$–$$$$; *Jasper*, 240 Commercial, 523-1126, owned by noted former Seasons chef, $$$$; *L'Espalier*, 30 Gloucester, 262-3023, French in an old home, $$$$; *Devon at the World Trade Center*, Commonwealth Pier, 439-5800, harbor views, $$$–$$$$ ● Not so pricey: *Another Season*, 97 Mt. Vernon Street, 367-0880, continental, $$$; *Dartmouth Street*, 271 Dartmouth Street, 536-6560, gourmet pizza to formal Italian, $–$$; *Back Bay Bistro*, 565 Boylston Street, 536-4477, popular for fine wine by the glass, $$–$$$ ● In and around Quincy Market: *Wild Goose Rotisserie*, 227-9660, $$–$$$; *Cricket's*, 742-8728, $$; *Lily's*, 227-4242, $$–$$$ ● In the Italian North End: *Café Paradiso*, 255 Hanover Street, 742-1768, for capuccino and cannolis as well as dinner, $–$$; *Villa Francesca*, Hanover and Richmond streets, 367-2948, $$; *Felicia's*, 125A Richmond Street, 523-9885, celebrity favorite, $$ ● Some local institutions: *Legal Seafood*, in Park Plaza Hotel (see above), almost too popular—be prepared for long waits, $–$$$; *Durgin Park*, 340 North Market Street, Faneuil Hall Marketplace, 227-2038, roast beef and baked beans the specialties, served family style in hectic but historic surroundings, $–$$$ (don't go to the new one in Copley Place—it isn't the same); *Union Oyster House*, 41 Union Street, 227-2750, oldest in town, great chowder, $$–$$$; *Thompson Chowder House*, 300 Faneuil Hall Market, 227-9660, in the original granite basement of the hall, $–$$$; ● Two longtime tourist standbys are *Anthony's Pier 4*, 140 Northern Avenue, 423-6363, $$–$$$$, and *Jimmy's Harborside*, 242 Northern Avenue, 423-1000, $$–$$$$, both for seafood on the waterfront ● For bargains in good food: *Jacob Wirth*, 33–37 Stuart Street (across from Wang Center), long bar, German, no-frills in same spot since 1868, also known for Boston baked beans, $–$$; *No Name*, 15½ Boston Fish Pier, 338-7539, casual, good prices for top seafood, go early to avoid long lines, $–$$ ● Informal: *J. C. Hilary's*, 793 Boylston Street, 536-6300; and *Cityside*, 262 Quincy Market, 742-7390 ● For lunch or snacks: *Harvard Bookstore Café*, 190 Newbury Street, or *Rebecca's*, 21 Charles Street. For afternoon tea, a favored Boston tradition, try the *Ritz*, the *Copley Plaza*, *Four Seasons*, or the *Colonnade* ● Popular watering holes: The sophisticated *29 Newbury* (at that address); the classy *Ritz Carlton* bar (address above); *Commonwealth Brewing Company Ltd.*, 85 Merrimac Street; *Allegro*, 939 Boylston; *Rachel's* at the Marriott Long Wharf; *Bull & Finch* downstairs at the Hampshire House, 84 Beacon Street (the bar of "Cheers" TV fame), and *Top of the Hub* atop the Prudential Tower, for the view ● Singles action: *Rachel's* (see above); *Jason's*, 131 Clarendon Street; *Friday's*, at Exeter and Newbury; and *Daisy Buchanan's*, 241 Newbury Street ● For drinks with music: *Copley's* at the Copley Plaza, and the *Hampshire*

House, 84 Beacon Street; piano bars can be found at the *Park Plaza* and *Lenox* hotels ● For dancing there is *Jason's,* 131 Clarendon; the bar at *Zachary's* at the Colonnade; *Café Fleuri* at the Meridien; *The Last Hurrah* at the Parker House; *Snifters,* 65 Chatham near Fanueil Hall; and the most romantic spot in town for dancing and a city view, the *Customs House Lounge* at the Bay Tower Room, 60 State Street. The two big discos are *Metro* and *Axis,* both on Landsdowne Street, near the Fenway.

SIGHTSEEING *Old State House,* 206 Washington Street, 242-5655. Hours: May to October, daily 9:30 A.M. to 5 P.M., rest of year, weekdays 10 A.M. to 4 P.M., Saturday 9:30 A.M. to 5 P.M., Sunday 11 A.M. to 5 P.M. Adults, $1.25; children, $.50 ● *State House,* Beacon and Park streets, 727-3676. Hours: Tours weekdays, 10 A.M. to 4 P.M. Free ● *Nichols House Museum,* 55 Mt. Vernon Street, 227-6993. Hours: Monday, Wednesday, and Saturday 1 P.M. to 5 P.M. $2 ● *Prudential Center Skywalk,* 800 Boylston Street, 236-3318. Hours: Monday to Saturday, 10 A.M. to 10 P.M., Sunday from 12 noon. Adults, $2; children, $1 ● *John Hancock Observatory,* Copley Square at Trinity Place and St. James Avenue, 247-1976. Hours: May to October, Monday to Saturday, 9 A.M. to 11 P.M. Adults, $2.75; children, $2 ● *Museum of Fine Arts,* 465 Huntington Avenue, 267-9300. Hours: Tuesday to Sunday, 10 A.M. to 5 P.M., Wednesday to 10 P.M.; West Wing only, Thursday and Friday to 10 P.M. Adults, $5 (West Wing only, $4); children, free; everyone free Saturday 10 A.M. to noon ● *Isabella Stewart Gardner Museum,* 280 The Fenway, 566-1401. Hours: Tuesday to Sunday, 12 noon to 5 P.M., Tuesday to 9 P.M. Adults, $3; children, $1 ● *Museum at the John Fitzgerald Kennedy Library,* I-93 south, exit 17 at Columbia Point, Dorchester, 929-4523. Hours: daily 9 A.M. to 5 P.M. Adults, $2.50; children, free ● *Paul Revere House,* 19 North Square, 523-2338. Hours: daily 9:30 A.M. to 5:15 P.M., winter to 4:15 P.M. Adults, $1.50; under 17, $.50 ● *USS Constitution,* Boston National Historical Park, Charlestown, 241-9078. Hours: daily 9:30 A.M. to 3:50 P.M. Free. Museum hours: 9 A.M. to 5 P.M. Adults, $2; children, $.50 ● *Boston Harbor Cruises,* daily sightseeing cruises; phone 227-4321 for current departure schedule and prices. For more Boston attractions, see page 195.

ENTERTAINMENT *Bostix Ticket Booth,* Faneuil Hall Marketplace, half-price theater, music, and dance tickets on day of performance. Hours: Monday to Saturday, 11 A.M. to 6 P.M., Sunday from 12 noon.

TOURS Best to phone all of these for current schedules, rates, and pick-up points or check Visitors Information booths ● *Boston by Foot,*

77 North Washington Street, 367-2345, walking tours ● *Uncommon Boston*, 437 Boylston Street, 731-5854, special interest tours ● *Hub Bus Lines, Inc.*, 321 Washington Avenue, 776-0630, narrated, double-decker shuttle bus tours of the Freedom Trail; riders may get off and reboard as often as they wish ● *Beantown Trolleys*, 109 Norfolk Street, 287-1900, Freedom Trail shuttle.

INFORMATION Boston Common Visitor Information Booth, Tremont Street, and Prudential Center Visitors' Center, both operated by Greater Boston Convention and Tourist Bureau, open 9 A.M. to 5 P.M. daily; National Park Service Visitors' Center, 15 State Street, also open 9 A.M. to 5 P.M. daily. For written information, contact Greater Boston Convention and Tourist Bureau, Prudential Plaza, PO Box 490, Boston, MA 02199, 536-4100; $2 for official guidebook, map, and Freedom Trail guide.

SUMMER

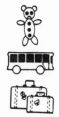

Flying High in Quechee

Summer arrives with a whoosh in Quechee, Vermont.

For more than a decade now, at 6 P.M. on a Friday late in June, the village green is crowded with people waiting to view the season's most colorful sendoff.

By then, the green has already been transformed into a patchwork of giant striped and star-spangled balloons spread flat on the ground, waiting to soar on the favorable evening breeze. One by one, the balloons are filled with flaming gusts of hot air. First they grow big and round, then stand erect, and eventually sail aloft to the loud cheers of admiring bystanders.

It was an inspired idea to stage an annual balloon festival in this classic New England setting on the green. Colorful hot-air balloons astride the wind always cause people to gaze with pleasure and a bit of envy, but there is something special about the combination of bright soaring balloons and pastoral hills and farms that makes it well worthwhile to arrive early in Quechee—and to bring along several rolls of film.

Since the winds are also right at 6 A.M., early risers can see the spectacle repeated on Saturday. Even those who watch the Friday night liftoff are likely to rise early on Saturday morning to get another angle with their cameras or to watch their favorite balloon make a new ascent. And in case they still miss the perfect shot, there's always Saturday night and Sunday morning to try, try again.

If you become curious about what it takes to get the balloons aloft or how they ever get down again, the free festival program will fill you in on everything—riding the wind and handling propane tanks, tether ropes, and burners—so you'll learn just how it's done.

Between launchings, the green is filled with down-home music and entertainment, sky-diving demonstrations, crafts booths, and food stands—all adding to the air of gaiety inspired by the balloons. The smell of chicken and roast beef on outdoor grills may well tempt you to stay for lunch or return for an economical outdoor dinner.

The festival is usually slated for the first weekend of summer, in a town that is photogenic even without benefit of balloons. Quechee is best known for the river gorge that can be seen on Route 4 outside of town on the way to Woodstock. Not all visitors make the detour into the village, where the Ottauquechee River provides the town with a scenic natural backdrop of swirling downhill rapids and a waterfall.

To miss Quechee means missing a fascinating mill restoration, historic homes, two fine country inns, and a tasteful, tucked-away condominium community with all kinds of recreational facilities. Concerts and Saturday afternoon polo matches are other Quechee summertime lures.

If you stay at the Quechee Inn at Marshland Farm, you'll be within walking distance of the green but safely away from the crowds. The two-story inn was the 1793 home of Colonel Joseph Marsh and one of Vermont's most distinguished families, whose members included a governor, a university president, and a U.S. ambassador to Italy. Those who visited here in the past may miss the taste and warmth of the former owners, but this remains a handsome inn.

The brick-floored timbered living room, equipped with a bar, offers a comfortable sitting area, there's a pleasant outdoor terrace and lawn for sunning, and an attractive Colonial dining room.

Bikes, canoe rentals, and fly-fishing school are right at the inn, and guests also have access to the clubhouse, pools, sandy lake beach, children's recreation area, golf course, and tennis, squash, and racquetball courts that are part of the Quechee Lakes resort community on 5,000 acres of woods and meadows in the nearby hills. It's also possible to rent one of the very attractive condominiums for the weekend.

Another quite elegant little lodging is the Parker House, a handsome Victorian house in the village, recently redone with flair, and with a fine dining room.

Right next door is the prime sightseeing attraction in town, the workshop and gallery of glassblower Simon Pearce, an Irishman who took over the red brick woolens mill on the dam in Quechee and harnessed the hydroelectric power to provide energy for his glass furnace. Pearce and his workers still make every piece painstakingly by hand, and the public is welcome to watch them at their labors, as well as to inspect the hydroelectric plant.

The showroom and shop are stunning, with great arched windows looking out on the river. In addition to Pearce glassware, pottery and handwoven Irish woolens are for sale. Bargain hunters can also pick up some Pearce glasses and pitchers at reduced rates, though the price for "seconds" of such meticulously made items is still high. There's also a restaurant where you can have lunch or dinner with a river view.

At the turnoff to Route 4, a stylish little complex called Waterman Place offers a cache of 16 shops and a change of dining pace at Rosalita's Southwestern Bar and Grill. Farther west on Route 4, heading toward Woodstock you'll find Scotland by the Yard, which offers tartan and tweed fabrics and handsome woolen clothing and sweaters. Continue into Woodstock, and you'll have your fill of shops.

If you need further diversion, you can see polo played every Saturday at the Quechee Polo Club. For evening activity, take a drive across the New Hampshire border to Hanover, where something is almost always happening at Dartmouth's Hopkins Center.

Add the sporting possibilities and the color of the balloons to the peace of the Quechee countryside, and you'll need little more to lift the summer season off to a good start.

Vermont Area Code: 802

DRIVING DIRECTIONS Quechee is located four miles from I-89 on Route 4 midway between Woodstock and White River Junction, Vermont. It is about 143 miles from Boston, 255 miles from New York, and 161 miles from Hartford.

PUBLIC TRANSPORTATION See Woodstock, page 6.

ACCOMMODATIONS *Quechee Inn* at Marshland Farm, Clubhouse Road, Quechee, 295-3133, $$$$$ MAP ● *Quechee Lakes Rental Corporation,* PO Box 85, Quechee, VT 05050, 295-7525, $$$$ ● *Parker House,* Quechee Village, 295-6077, attractive small Victorian inn, $$$ CP ● Also see Woodstock, page 6, and Hanover, page 206, for both lodging and dining suggestions.

DINING *Quechee Inn* (see above), pleasant atmosphere, $$–$$$ ● *Parker House* (see above), prix fixe $$$$ ● *Simon Pearce*, at the Mill, 295-2711, continental menu, $$–$$$ ● *Rosalita's Southwestern Bar and Grill,* Waterman Place, 259-1600, tacos to tequila shrimp, $–$$.

SIGHTSEEING *Quechee Balloon Festival,* Village Green, Quechee, Vermont, usually late June, sponsored by Quechee Chamber of Commerce. Admission $2. Call for schedules and information.

INFORMATION Quechee Chamber of Commerce, Quechee, VT 05050, 295-7900.

A Fourth of July Fling in Connecticut

Come the Fourth of July each year, a steady procession of cars can be seen bypassing beach and barbecue to head for a high school in Norwalk, Connecticut.

Their purpose? To see the Round Hill Scottish Games, one of the

most unusual Independence Day festivities in the country, where fireworks give way to the whirring of bagpipes and more than 700 contestants between the ages of 7 and 70 take part in the piping, dancing, and
sporting competitions that have been part of Scottish tradition for as
long as anyone can remember.

It's not the usual midsummer holiday festivity—and this suburban
commuter territory in Fairfield County is hardly an area you would
ordinarily choose for a Fourth of July destination. Yet it offers all the
elements needed for a uniquely pleasant outing, including both beach
and wooded beauty, good shopping, summer theater, and a number of
excellent restaurants nearby. If you know where to look, you may even
find some old New England atmosphere here in the suburbs.

The games, which draw well over 10,000 spectators each year, are
patterned after the famed Highland Games in Scotland. The event orig-
inated early in the twentieth century in nearby Greenwich when a
group of Scottish immigrants joined forces to provide an occasion to
wear their native Highland dress and preserve a bit of their heritage for
their children. Proceeds in the early years were used to help other
newly arrived Scots.

As word of the occasion spread, the participants began to multiply
and the spectacle became such an attraction that the Round Hill Scottish Games Association was formed in 1923 to oversee the event and
disperse the profits to a number of charities. The location has been
moved twice to accommodate ever growing crowds.

There are three categories of events—athletics, dance, and music—
all taking place at once to create something of the feeling of a three-
ring circus. The highlight of the athletic games, which include such
events as track and soccer, is the incredible "tossing of the caber." A
caber looks much like a telephone pole, measuring 16 feet in length
and weighing over 150 pounds. Heaving the heavy pole is a feat to try
even the halest, and many contestants find they can hardly *lift* the
caber, much less toss it anywhere. Yet each year a few stout lads
emerge who seem to have inherited the prowess of their ancestors, and
a husky contender inevitably comes forward to give the king-size mis-
sile a prodigious toss that sets off wild cheering from the sidelines.

While the sportsmen are having at each other, more than a hundred
dancers are competing in another area of the grounds. Gaily decked out
in plaid knee socks, kilts, tunics, and caps, the dancers are judged by
their skill in executing the carefully prescribed steps of the Highland
fling, the sailor's hornpipe, and the sword dance. The youngest contestants begin in the morning, followed by big brothers and sisters and
finally by the adults. Spectators are often mesmerized for hours as the
graceful dancers perform their nimble steps.

To give the bystanders stamina, strategically placed refreshment
stands serve regional fare such as Scottish meat pies and fish and chips

as well as the more usual Fourth of July menu of hot dogs and sodas. There are souvenir stands as well, with tiny plaid tams for tots, Celtic jewelry and other crafts, and a selection of beautiful wool tartan plaids of the clans, for sale by the yard.

The last (and far from least) of the events is the bagpipe competition, with pipers and drummers in full regalia vying individually as well as in groups. The bagpipe bands in their colorful plaids come from all over the Northeast and from as far away as Canada and Bermuda.

The pipers and bands march one by one to perform four different categories of music: a march, a reel, a strathspey, and the tongue-twisting piobaireachd. Then, when the judging is done and the winner declared, the musicians gather for one last spectacular parade across the grounds, an unforgettable finale of sound and color. No further fireworks are necessary to make this a memorable Fourth of July. (If you check the local paper, you'll probably find that the town of Norwalk has scheduled the more traditional sparkling festivities at Calf Pasture Beach, on either the night preceding or the night of July 4.)

For those who are making a weekend of it, built-up Norwalk has some unexpected pleasures to offer. Silvermine Tavern is no longer the stagecoach stop it was in 1767, but is now an inn with great Early American charm in a picturebook location overlooking a waterfall and a duck-dotted pond. Be sure to ask for one of the three choicest rooms—those that have balconies overlooking the falls. Even if you don't stay here, do have at least one meal—not so much for the food as for the cozy low-ceilinged dining room filled with antique tools and the deck overlooking the ducks and geese on the pond. It's a perfect choice for Sunday brunch, which features a generous buffet spread.

The Silvermine section of Norwalk, a pre-Revolutionary township settled beside the Silvermine River, is picturesque country. It emerged as a noted art colony when sculptor Solon Borglum set up his studio there in 1895; other artists soon followed suit. In 1922, a group got together to buy land and an old barn just across from the tavern and formed the Silvermine Guild of Artists. The barn is both school and gallery, with changing exhibits and a permanent section of original art and handicrafts for sale, many at reasonable prices. Silvermine Guild is also the scene of a summertime chamber music series, so check the current year's performance dates if you are in the neighborhood.

The main part of Norwalk dates back to 1649, but only the village green has retained its original character, since a British assault during the Revolutionary War all but wiped out the town. South Norwalk, a formerly run-down area now known locally as SoNo, is in the midst of a facelift that has brought in brick sidewalks, antique street lamps, and lots of interesting crafts shops, galleries, and restaurants to Washington Street. If you decide to take a look, be sure to check the schedule at the SoNo Theater, which features film classics.

Due to open in spring 1988 is a maritime center at the foot of Washington Street that will include an aquarium, an Imax Theater, and lots of hands-on maritime exhibits.

The chief sightseeing gem in town is the Lockwood-Mathews Mansion. Legrand Lockwood was a poor local boy who struck it rich and decided to show off for the hometown folks. A quarter of a century before the Vanderbilts and the Astors began building their opulent "cottages" in Newport, Lockwood came back to his native Norwalk to build a 60-room mansion the likes of which had never been seen before. For the then-exorbitant sum of $2 million, he brought in European architects to create soaring turrets, sweeping staircases, a three-story skylit octagonal rotunda, wall frescoes, inlaid woods and marbles, carved cherubs and nymphs, and such revolutionary devices as a hot-air furnace, hot and cold running water, and 14 full baths. A children's theater was tucked away under the eaves, and wine cellars and two bowling alleys were installed in the basement. In 1873, the *New York Sun* pronounced Mr. Lockwood's dream house "perhaps the most perfect and elegant mansion in America."

Though it later came on hard times, the mansion was saved by a group of local preservationists, and today the restoration is a community project supported by local volunteers and the Norwalk Junior League. The mansion is well on the way to its former magnificence, and really should be visited.

Since the house is closed on Saturday, you can spend the day shopping for bargains, another of Norwalk's claims to fame. On West Avenue is Loehmann's, the well-known women's fashion outlet, and farther down the street is Decker's, a haven for men's clothes. Gant shirts here sell for half the department store prices, as do many other fine labels such as Polo and Robert Bruce.

Right next door is an outlet store for brand-name sheets and towels, and there are other good buys in shoes and housewares in the shopping center just around the corner. The big bargain outlet these days is on East Avenue (exit 16 on the Connecticut Turnpike, south of the turnpike past the Howard Johnson's), where some two dozen dealers have come together in one location, with all manner of wares for sale at great savings.

If you'd rather go boating than bargain hunting, hop aboard the *Lady Joan,* a Mississippi riverboat replica at Norwalk Cove Marina, and take a cruise around the Norwalk Islands. One of the islands became the subject of controversy when a power plant went up on it some 25 years ago, but conservationists have won out, keeping most of the remaining 22 islands as nature preserves. It makes for a pleasant outing, and the cruise director offers some little-known lore about points of interest on the islands—celebrity homes, bird sanctuaries, Indian campgrounds, even the site where Nathan Hale left on his last and fatal mission for his country.

Back on shore, antiquing is another favorite pastime in these parts. Head north on Route 7 beyond the Merritt Parkway and the newer shopping centers to the road that used to be known as Antique Row. Watch on the right for the sign to Cannon's Crossing, a one-time railroad junction that has been restored and expanded into a shopping complex by actress June Havoc. Detour on Route 33 for country scenery, a few more shops, and a visit to Ridgefield, a delightful Colonial town with an avant-garde art museum, a Revolutionary War tavern for touring, and four top restaurants. It's good to plan your arrival just in time for lunch or dinner.

If chic boutiques are more to your taste than antiques, you may prefer to make your way to Westport, Norwalk's eastern neighbor on Long Island Sound. It is home to countless advertising and entertainment biggies, and has interesting shops to explore along its two-block Main Street as well as in small complexes running for several miles along US 1, known in town as State Street.

Westport lodgings are more expensive than those at Norwalk, but they are choice. The Inn at Long Shore, a former country club on the sound, has been converted into the town recreational center with attractive Colonial guest rooms upstairs in the clubhouse and tennis courts and a golf course right outside the door. If you want to splurge, the tiny Cotswold Inn, tucked on a side street near the center of town, is an elegant establishment in gracious Old World style, with each pastel bedroom elaborately decorated with antique copies and canopied or four-poster beds. The windows of the breakfast room face a lush garden.

If you don't want to miss out on the beaching that most people associate with the Fourth of July, you can visit Westport's Sherwood Island, a state park with more than a mile and a half of sandy beach on the sound and facilities for cookouts and picnicking. It is one of the few public beaches in Fairfield County, and though it shares the pebbles that plague all Long Island Sound beaches, it is one of the best on the Connecticut shore.

Any of the back roads off Route 33 in Westport heading north to the Merritt Parkway will take you into magnificent wooded residential sections that are a sightseeing tour in themselves, and if you want to get a little closer to nature, Westport's Nature Center has wooded trails along a 53-acre sanctuary.

Come evening, Westport has more than its share of fine restaurants and is also host to one of America's oldest and best summer theaters, the Westport Country Playhouse, where you'll most likely find the biggest names among the performers out on the summer circuit. And free concerts from jazz to rock to classical music are scheduled almost every summer night at the Levitt Pavilion on the banks of the Saugatuck River right in the middle of town.

What with the beaching, browsing, and sophisticated dining these wealthy commuter communities offer, you're likely to find that your few days in Fairfield County whiz by. Taken in combination with the Scottish Games, it can provide a star-spangled Fourth of July weekend.

Connecticut Area Code: 203

DRIVING DIRECTIONS Norwalk and Westport are reached via I-95, the Connecticut Turnpike, or by Route 15, the Merritt Parkway. Norwalk is 160 miles from Boston, 50 miles from New York, and 60 miles from Hartford.

PUBLIC TRANSPORTATION Metro-North train service to Norwalk and Westport.

ACCOMMODATIONS *Silvermine Tavern,* Silvermine and Perry avenues, Norwalk, 847-4558, $$–$$$ • *Holiday Inn,* 789 Connecticut Avenue, Norwalk, 853-3477, $$$ • *Inn at Longshore,* 260 Compo Road South, Westport, 226-3316, $$$$ • *Cotswold Inn,* 76 Myrtle Avenue, Westport, 226-3766, $$$$$.

DINING *Silvermine Tavern* (see above), traditional American, $$–$$$ • *50 Water Street,* at that address, Norwalk, 854-9530, seafood specialties, $$ • *The Pier,* 144 Water Street, 838-8200, overlooking Norwalk Harbor, seafood, outdoor deck, $–$$$ • *Pasta Nostra,* 116 Washington Street, Norwalk, tiny very popular Italian, expect lines, $$ • *Jaspers,* 2–4 South Main Street at Washington Street, Norwalk, 852-1716, Oyster bar, seafood, $$ • *Allen's Clam and Lobster House,* 191 Hills Point Road, Westport, 226-4411, gracious seafood restaurant on the water, $$–$$$$ • *Le Chambord,* 1572 Post Road East, Westport, 255-2654, French, elegant old-timer, $$$ • *Dameon,* 30–32 Railroad Place, Westport, 226-6580, bistro, $$ • *Francine's,* 8 Sconset Square, Westport, 454-9531, Continental, $$–$$$ • *Pompano Grill,* 1460 Post Road East, Westport, 259-1160, continental, grill specialties, $$ • *Stonehenge,* Route 7, Ridgefield, 438-6511, charming farmhouse setting, prix fixe $$$$$ • *The Inn at Ridgefield,* 20 West Lane, Ridgefield, 438-8282, Colonial decor, nouvelle menu, prix fixe $$$$$ • *The Elms,* 500 Main Street, Ridgefield, 438-2541, 1799 Colonial inn, continental menu, $$$–$$$$ • *Le Coq Hardi,* Big Shop Lane, Ridgefield, 431-3060, French, $$$

SIGHTSEEING   *Round Hill Scottish Games,* Cranbury Park, Kensett Street, Norwalk. Every Fourth of July starting at 9 A.M. and continuing all day. Adults, $5; 6 to 15, $2. Advisable to phone to check on current rates and information at 324-1094 ● *Lockwood-Mathews Mansion Museum,* 295 West Avenue, Norwalk, 838-1434. Hours: Tuesday to Friday 11 A.M. to 3 P.M., Sunday 1 A.M. to 4 P.M.; Closed July 4. Adults, $3; under 12, free ● *Silvermine Guild of Artists,* 1073 Silvermine Road, Norwalk, 966-5617. Hours: Tuesday to Saturday 11 A.M. to 5 P.M., Sunday from 12 noon. Free ● *Norwalk Harbor Cruises,* Shoreline Boating Service, Beach Road, East Norwalk, 838-9003. Check for current times and rates. ● *Nature Center for Environmental Activities,* 10 Woodside Lane, Westport, 227-7253. Hours: Monday to Saturday 9 A.M. to 5 P.M., Sunday 1 P.M. to 4 P.M.; closed holidays. Adults, $1; children, $.50 ● *Westport Country Playhouse,* 25 Powers Court, Westport, 227-4177. Write or phone for current schedule and ticket rates.

INFORMATION   Norwalk Chamber of Commerce, PO Box 668, Norwalk, CT 06854, 866-2521. Westport Chamber of Commerce, 15 Imperial Avenue, Box 30, Westport, CT 06880, 227-9234.

Crafts Spectacular in Springfield

You can hardly find a good orrery nowadays.

In case you don't know, an orrery is a mechanical reproduction of the solar system, named for Charles Boyle, Fourth Earl of Cork and Orrery, who had the first known such contrivance made about 1710.

Handmade orrerys were sold last year at the American Craft Council's Craftfair in West Springfield, Massachusetts—unbelievably intricate devices with enough gears to make three separate clocks. Which just goes to prove there's very little you can't find at this superbowl of craft shows, a gathering of America's top craftspeople in a spectacular event that is the largest of its kind in the country.

Some 600 artisans take part, selected from almost four times that many who apply to the show's jury of master craftsmakers and store buyers. The potters, metalsmiths, candle molders, glassblowers, basket weavers, leather cutters, quilters, zither makers, wood carvers, weavers, and creators of orrerys and other wares so diverse as to defy description come to sell to buyers from stores around the country for the first part of the week and to the public on the weekend.

The Craftfair was originally held in outdoor tents in Rhinebeck,

New York, but by 1984 the crowds had grown so large that a move was necessary, and the big Eastern States Exposition Center in West Springfield won the prize. The fair seems to be bigger and better than ever now, with sales topping $6 million and many thousands of people turning out for the three-day public event.

The main displays offer everything from a ceramic toothbrush holder to a handmade rolling pin, from casseroles and cannisters to large sculptures and exquisite furniture, with price tags anywhere from $25 to $25,000. In fact, if there is anything to complain about at this mammoth exhibition, it is the huge number of displays. Don't buy until you've covered everything.

Crafts supplies of all kinds are also for sale at Storrowtown Village, a group of restored Early American buildings nearby. The crafts are absolutely top quality, and again, though the quantity can be exhausting, it's still a treat to see what the top people in the country are turning out.

There will be plenty of food stands to refuel your energy along the way, plus the traditional taverns and New England wine gardens on the center grounds, which are also the annual site of the largest fall fair in New England.

When you've had your fill of browsing, you'll find plenty more to see and do in the Springfield area. This old New England town has recently spruced up its historic downtown area around Court Square, a charming urban park, and is a surprisingly pleasant place for a stroll and a bit of sightseeing. In one complex at State and Chestnut streets known as the Quadrangle, you can choose among four free museums around a green. The George Walter Vincent Smith Art Museum offers European and Oriental decorative arts; the Connecticut Valley Historical Museum features period rooms and antiques plus collections of glass, pewter, and silver; the Museum of Fine Arts has paintings and sculpture by American and European artists; and the Science Museum has an African hall, a dinosaur hall, an aquarium, and a planetarium along with nature exhibits.

One of Springfield's favorite museums is the Basketball Hall of Fame on the grounds of Springfield College, with a replica of the gym where the sport was first played in 1891, movies and photographs, a parade of changing uniforms, and all manner of memorabilia sure to fascinate lovers of the game.

The Springfield Armory, the inspiration for Longfellow's poem "The Arsenal at Springfield," is a national historic site, with a unique collection of small arms through the centuries. And if you want to stroll an urban pocket of choice Victoriana, walk over to Mattoon Street, two blocks east of Main. The tree-shaded, cobblestone block with its old-fashioned street lights has been listed in the National Register of Historic Places.

If you stay overnight, you can save some of the sights for Sunday, unless it's such a fine day that you'd rather be out of doors. If that's the case, head for the picnic grounds or nature trails in Springfield's Forest Park, or the Laughing Brook Education Center and Wildlife Sanctuary, a 260-acre complex that was the former home of children's author Thornton Burgess. This is a great place for the kids, with live animal exhibits of many of Burgess's characters, a nature center, and four miles of trails to get you back to nature.

Springfield is also the perfect starting point for a driving tour to the Pioneer Valley and its well-known Five Colleges. You get a real cross-section of college architecture on these handsome campuses. In Amherst, there's Amherst College, with its traditional halls of ivy and picture-book green, plus the mammoth, modern University of Massachusetts and the rustic buildings of Hampshire College. Old and new manage to mix nicely along the quadrangles of Smith College in Northampton and Mount Holyoke in South Hadley. Both of these fine women's colleges have excellent art galleries, as does the Amherst campus.

There is some interesting shopping in this area, particularly around Northampton, though Sunday hours may be erratic. American Indian products are the specialty at a gallery called White Star at 46 Green Street, just off the Smith campus. There are a couple of antiques shops on the same block. Most of the dealers will be able to give you a free guide to 18 other shops in Northampton and neighboring Hadley, with current data on exactly who is open where.

The Pioneer Valley has developed into a crafts center in its own right, with more than 100 working artists in the area. Northampton is the gallery center, and there are interesting wares to be found at shops in the Thorne's Market complex on Main Street, Old School Commons on New South, and in many individual shops in town. At the Springfield Craftfair (or by mail) you can also get a map showing homes of artisans who welcome visits by appointment and other shops such as Craftsmen & Artists, Inc., in Leverett, offering the very best local work. For a copy of the map, contact: Arts Extension Service, Division of Continuing Education, University of Massachusetts, Amherst, MA 01003, (413) 545-2360.

It's a weekend to send you home with a new appreciation of the fine craftsmen and craftswomen who are keeping the art of American handwork alive and well. And if you don't return with an original souvenir, it certainly won't be for lack of choice. You might even turn out to be the first on your block with an orrery.

Springfield Area Code: 413

DRIVING DIRECTIONS Springfield is located in southwestern Massachusetts. It can be reached from north or south via I-91 and from east or west via the Massachusetts Turnpike, Route 90. The Eastern States Exposition Center is off I-91 at exit 3. Springfield is about 75 miles from Boston, 140 miles from New York, and 30 miles from Hartford.

PUBLIC TRANSPORTATION Amtrak serves Springfield and may be offering special fares to the Craftfair with bus shuttle service from the station. United, Delta, and several other lines fly into Bradley International Airport serving Hartford-Springfield. Greyhound, Peter Pan, and Vermont Transit provide bus service.

ACCOMMODATIONS *Sheraton Inn West,* 1080 Riverdale Street, West Springfield, 781-8750, $$$ • *Howard Johnson,* 1150 Riverdale Street, West Springfield, 739-7261, $$ • *Susse Chalet Motor Lodge,* Johnnycake Hollow Road, Chicopee, 592-5141, $ • *Marriott Springfield,* 1500 Main Street, Springfield, 781-7111, $$$–$$$$ • *The Beeches,* Hampton Terrace, Northampton, 586-9288, is former Calvin Coolidge home turned bed and breakfast, $$ CP • *Lord Jeffrey Inn,* on the Common, Amherst, 253-2576, classic college inn, recently refurbished, $$–$$$.

BED AND BREAKFAST *Berkshire Bed and Breakfast,* PO Box 211, Main Street, Williamsburg, MA 01096, 268-7244.

DINING *Old Storrowtown Tavern,* Eastern States Exposition Grounds, Exposition Road off Route 147, West Springfield, 732-4188, Colonial atmosphere, $–$$$ • *Ciro's,* 870 Main Street, 736-9626, Italian, $–$$ • *Monte Carlo,* 1020 Memorial Avenue, West Springfield, 734-6431, Italian, located opposite Exposition grounds, $–$$$ • *Student Prince and Fort,* 8 Fort Street, 734-7475, German, with interesting collection of beer steins, $–$$ • *Orient Express,* 1441 Main Street, Center Square, Springfield, 734-2318, Vietnamese, known to many for its popular original location in the Berkshires, $–$$ • *Beardsley's Café,* 140 Main Street, Northampton, 586-2699, Beardsley artwork, French menu, $–$$$ • *Eastside Grill,* 19 Strong Avenue, Northampton, 586-3347, trendy menu, $–$$ • *The Depot,* 124A Pleasant Street, Northampton, 586-5366, stylishly renovated train station, $$$ • *Lord Jeffrey Inn* (see above), $$$ • *Yankee Pedlar,* 1866 Northampton Road, at US 5 and Route 202, Holyoke, 532-9494, Colonial, $$–$$$ • *Log Cabin,* Easthampton Road, Route 141, Holyoke, 536-7700, lovely valley view, $–$$$ • A few informal lunch or light meal places in the college towns: *Fitzwilly's,* 23 Main Street, Northampton; *Greenstreet's,* 8 Green Street, Northampton; *Judie's,* 51 North Pleasant Street, Amherst; *Plumbley's Off the Common,*

30 Boltwood Walk, Amherst; *Black Sheep Deli,* 79 Main Street, Amherst.

SIGHTSEEING *American Craft Council Craftfair,* Eastern States Exposition Center, West Springfield, 736-3003, late June or July. For current dates and rates, contact American Craft Enterprises, PO Box 10, 256 Main Street, New Paltz, NY 12561, (914) 255-0039 ● *The Quadrangle,* State and Chestnut streets, 739-3871, four museums. Hours: Tuesday to Sunday, 12 noon to 5 P.M. Free ● *Springfield Armory National Historic Site,* Federal Street. Hours: daily 8 A.M. to 4:30 P.M. Free ● *Naismith Memorial Basketball Hall of Fame,* 1150 West Columbus Avenue, 781-6500. Hours: daily 9 A.M. to 6 P.M. July to Labor Day; 10 A.M. to 5 P.M. rest of year. Adults, $5; 8 to 14, $3 ● *Laughing Brook Education Center and Wildlife Sanctuary,* 789 Main Street off Route 83, Hampden. Hours: Tuesday to Sunday, 10 A.M. to 5 P.M. Adults, $3; under 16, $1.50.

INFORMATION Pioneer Valley Convention and Visitors' Bureau, 56 Dwight Street, Springfield, MA 01103, 787-1548.

Scenery by the Sea in Ogunquit

Families love Ogunquit. So do singles, lovers of the opposite and the same sex, photographers, artists, nature seekers, theatergoers, weekenders without cars, teenagers, toddlers, and great-grandparents.

When you see the powdery three-mile stretch of beach curving into a backdrop of rugged cliffs you'll know instantly why Ogunquit draws such a mélange of fans. The site the Indians called Beautiful Place by the Sea is aptly named, and the bountiful beach is a special treasure in Maine, a state whose rockbound coastline yields few such open spaces.

The beach alone explains why Ogunquit has been a popular vacation haven for the past 100 years, ever since a bridge was built in 1888 across the river that once divided the shore from the town. But Ogunquit has also made the most of its cliffs, topping them with a magnificent winding path called the Marginal Way, which meanders in and out of the bayberries and brush for a scenic mile of strolling, with unparalleled views of the crashing sea beyond. It is a walk that never palls no matter how many times it is repeated.

Follow the Marginal Way to its end and you come to another facet of this delightful town. Perkins Cove is a picturesque harbor that was

discovered more than half a century ago by artists and craftspeople.
Now the one-time fishermen's shanties are filled with shops, restaurants, and galleries. The Ogunquit Playhouse is another long-time resident, a mainstay on the summer circuit since 1933.

To add to Ogunquit's special pleasures, you don't need a car here—
in fact, you're almost better off without one, since parking spaces are
at a premium and weekend traffic is a pain. Almost everything is
within walking distance, and should your energy flag, all you need do
is hop aboard *Daisy, Daffodil,* or *Petunia,* the town's old-fashioned
trolley buses that make the rounds from 8 A.M. to midnight during the
season for a minuscule 25-cent fare.

It's hardly a surprise to learn that the beach is busy on weekends,
particularly near the most popular entry at Beach Street, where there
are snack bars and dressing rooms. Both the footbridge at Ocean Street
off US 1 north of the village and the Moody Beach entrance at Eldridge
Street are less congested. Happily, however, if you are willing to walk
a bit, no matter where you enter you can still find plenty of space to
plant your blanket and do some people watching, a particularly colorful pastime given the unusual mix of beachgoers.

You hardly need an itinerary for Ogunquit. When you've had
enough sun (or if the unthinkable happens and it rains), just head down
Shore Road to Perkins Cove and check out the crafts and clothing
shops along the way. Ellen Moore on Shore Road displays her hand-
screened crafts right in her own studio, while Candlewick claims to
have the most unusual selection of candles in New England—just to
name two of many possibilities. The Strawberry Bazaar is interesting
not only for its handcrafted gold and silver jewelry but for the building
in which it is housed—the Old Ice House near the much-photographed
footbridge leading to Perkins Cove.

There are many art galleries to choose from, including the Ogunquit
Art Center on Hoyt's Lane and the Barn Gallery on Shore Road which
offers concerts, films, and lectures as well as exhibits. The Museum of
Art of Ogunquit is exceptional, a handsome building of stone and
wood with many windows to bring in the view of the rocky cove and
meadows outside, and a lovely sculpture garden and lawns that make
the most of the setting. The five galleries include works by Reginald
Marsh and Charles Burchfield.

Where you stay in Ogunquit really depends on your personal prefer-
ences and pocketbook, for there's everything from guest houses to
motels to low-key resorts, all convenient to the beach. For dining,
Jackie's and Barnacle Billy's on Perkins Cove are local favorites, and
the Ogunquit Lobster Pound, where you pick your own dinner to be
cooked on the coals out of doors, is all but an institution.

You might prefer to visit during the week, when the many Boston
families who flock here on Saturday and Sunday have returned home,

but somehow Ogunquit is a town that even weekend crowds can't spoil. As you walk the expanses of beach or contemplate the waves from the Marginal Way, the rest of the world recedes before the splendor of the Maine coast at this Beautiful Place by the Sea.

Maine Area Code: 207

DRIVING DIRECTIONS   Take I-95 to US 1 or simply follow US 1, which becomes Main Street in Ogunquit. Ogunquit is 70 miles north of Boston, 40 miles south of Portland, 275 miles from New York, and 170 miles from Hartford.

PUBLIC TRANSPORTATION   Greyhound Bus service to nearby Biddeford. Air service to Portland, about 30 minutes away.

ACCOMMODATIONS   There are dozens of choices. Here are just a few: *Ogunquit River Plantation,* PO Box 1876, 646-9611, overlooks wildlife refuge, $$$ CP; *Captain Lorenz Perkins House,* North Main Street, 646-7825, eighteenth-century home with antiques, $$ CP (shared baths) ● Guest houses: *Hayes Guest House,* 133 Shore Road, 646-2277, cozy Colonial near Perkins Cove, $$ CP ● *Blue Shutters,* 6 Beachmere Place, 646-2163, quiet secluded location yet still convenient, $$ CP ● Motels: *Norseman Motor Inn,* Ogunquit Beach, 646-7024, directly on the beach, $$$–$$$$; *Sea Chambers,* 37 Shore Road, $$$–$$$$ CP; *The Aspinquid,* Beach Street, 646-7072, modernistic complex that includes many efficiencies, $$$ ● Resort motels: *Sparhawk,* Shore Road, 646-5562, ocean views, tennis, $$$–$$$$ ● *Cliff House,* Bald Head Cliff, Shore Road, 646-5124, classic old resort, spectcular view but far from town, $$$$.

BED AND BREAKFAST   *Bed and Breakfast of Maine,* 32 Colonial Village, Falmouth, ME 04105, 781-4528 ● *Bed and Breakfast Down East Ltd.,* Box 547, Eastbrook, ME 04634, 565-3517.

DINING   *Jackie's, Too,* Perkins Cove, 646-5177, on the harbor, $–$$ ● *Barnacle Billy's,* Perkins Cove, 646-5575, informal, nautical, outdoor deck, $$–$$$ ● *Ogunquit Lobster Pound,* US 1, 646-2516, $$ ● *Clay Hill Farm,* Agamenticus Road, 646-2272, gracious country setting (car essential), $$–$$$ ● *The Old Village Inn,* 30 Main Street, 646-7088, $$–$$$ ● *Gypsy Sweethearts,* 18 Shore Road, 646-7021, $$ ● For breakfast, try *Barbara Dean's* on Shore Road.

SIGHTSEEING   *Museum of Art of Ogunquit,* Shore Road at Narrow

Cove, 646-4909. Hours: late June to Labor Day, Monday to Saturday 10 A.M. to 5 P.M., Sunday from 1:30 P.M. Free.

INFORMATION For a comprehensive directory, including complete lodgings listing, write or call Ogunquit Chamber of Commerce, PO Box 637, Ogunquit, ME 03907, 646-2939. Information Bureau, 646-5533.

On Top of the World at Mt. Washington

The first scientists who set out to measure Mt. Washington back in 1784 calculated the peak was some 10,000 feet high. They were a bit off the mark—the actual height is 6,288—but it's easy to understand their error.

The White Mountains of New Hampshire, the highest in the Northeast, have a majesty beyond their actual measure. Unlike the soft green mountains next door in Vermont, these are rugged granite peaks, stark and grand, and the view from Mt. Washington, the highest of them all, was aptly described by P. T. Barnum as "the second greatest show on earth."

Ever since Darby Field became the first to climb Mt. Washington back in 1642, adventurers have found the mountain an irresistible lure, and today scores of hikers take up the challenge or head for some of the other magnificent trails in the surrounding mountains of the Presidential Range—Mts. Adams, Jefferson, Monroe, Eisenhower, and Franklin, to name a few—New England's prime hiking territory. Many hikers stay in the Appalachian Mountain Club Lodge at Pinkham Notch or take advantage of the club's many guided walks and workshops.

But you needn't be an alpine climber to enjoy the Mt. Washington Valley. Since the first carriage roads were cut through the mountain passes in the early nineteenth century, increasing numbers of people have come every year just to be inspired by the view. Painters like Thomas Cole and writers like John Greenleaf Whittier were among the early visitors.

These days you can scale the mountain by railway or by car as well as on foot, browse in dozens of shops, and enjoy a number of fine inns—all enhanced by the ever present mountain views.

When it comes to views, there are few hotels anywhere to rival the Mt. Washington, as grand today as when it was built in 1902, with no expense spared to make it one of the nation's premiere resorts. The annals of the hotel—host to presidents, statesmen, socialites and sportsmen, and home of the Bretton Woods International Monetary Conference in 1944 when the dollar became the standard of world currency—would make a chapter in themselves.

What awes the first-time visitor is the unforgettable image of the giant, gleaming white, twin-towered, red-roofed hotel set against the mountains like a fairy-tale palace. If you can handle the tab, treat yourself to a stay here and relive the good old days when ceilings were lofty, chandeliers were grand, evenings were spent in ballrooms, and even busboys wore tuxedos. At the Mt. Washington Hotel it's all still true.

If that's not your style, there are alternatives for almost every taste. The Darby Field Inn in Conway, named for that pioneering climber, is a small, cozy farmhouse set away by itself on Bald Hill, 1,000 feet above the valley, with its own fine mountain view. Stonehurst Manor, though right off the main street in North Conway, is set back on 33 acres of pine forest and offers very attractive lodgings in a turn-of-the-century Victorian mansion. And the attractive little village of Jackson offers several excellent choices: Dana Place Inn, farmhouse simplicity with a noted dining room; Christmas Farm Inn, a minivillage of Colonial dwellings with all the facilities of a resort; Nestlenook, a cozy working farm and equestrian center; the gracioius old Wentworth Resort, and a choice of pleasant smaller inns.

The first order of business for most Mt. Washington visitors is simply to see the scenery, and Routes 16 and 302, which intersect in North Conway, lead to the best of it. Wait for the clearest and calmest of your days before you head for Mt. Washington itself, and bring along a sweater, because the summit tends to be windy and foggy much of the time. In fact, the highest wind ever recorded, 231 miles per hour, was measured at the weather station here.

The eight-mile auto toll road to the top, reached off Route 16 above Jackson, is the quick way up, with beauty filling every mile as you pass through lush greenery and wildflowers on your way above the timberline to the stark granite peak.

Allow about three hours for the 3½-mile round-trip ride on the steam-powered Cog Railway, the world's first mountain-climbing railway, built in 1869. It takes off from Route 302, east of Twin Mountain, and chugs its way slowly up a right-of-way with plenty of steep grades to take your breath away. If you want an aerial view of things, the gondola at Wildcat Mountain at Pinkham Notch, and the skimobile at Mt. Cranmore in North Conway will fit the bill.

Down in the valley, the most spectacular views are at the various "notches," the passes between the mountains. A hike, however short, is strongly recommended to make the most of the scenery. You can pick up trail maps and information near Pinkham Notch at the Appalachian Club headquarters on Route 16, and at Crawford Notch State Park headquarters on Route 302, near the Mt. Washington Hotel.

Crawford Notch is where White Mountain tourism began. Soon after the first carriage road went through, the region's most noted climber, innkeeper Ethan Allen Crawford, led a hiking party bearing a barrel of rum to Mt. Washington's bare and windy summit. There, raising their mugs in turn to surrounding peaks, they named the other mountains of the range as they toasted America's presidents. A marker shows the site of Crawford's inn, now vanished along with most of the other big turn-of-the-century wooden hotels. Only the Mt. Washington remains as a reminder of the grand old days.

If you are looking for a spot for a picnic, Echo Lake State Park near North Conway offers swimming and picnic grounds along with a scenic road to Cathedral Ledge and a panoramic view of the mountains and the Saco River Valley. Saco Bound on Route 302 in Center Conway specializes in canoeing and kayaking and offers rentals as well as lessons and guided canoe and raft trips on the river.

When you are ready for more worldly pursuits, you'll find North Conway a lively center for the region. You can hardly call it unspoiled, but it does remain a pleasant town despite a main street that is a mélange of motels, shops, fast food stops, and restaurants. Art galleries, antiques, a quilt shop, goldsmiths and silversmiths, Scottish and Irish sweater shops, clothing boutiques are all part of the eclectic mix.

The Mt. Washington Valley also has developed into a nirvana for bargain hunters, with manufacturers' outlet stores sprouting like wildflowers in the area. Among the many top labels found in North Conway are Anne Klein, Barbizon, Converse, Corning, Frye, London Fog, Oshkosh, Gorham, Manhattan, Polo/Ralph Lauren, and Timberland. And just a few miles farther in Conway, Hathaway, Bass, Cannon Mills, White Stag, and other outlet stores await.

Cross the covered bridge into the little town of Jackson for a few more shops in a picturesque country setting. Among them is the Irish Import Shop, with handknits and Celtic jewelry.

The valley is rich in activities as well as scenery in the summer. The Mt. Washington Valley Theater Company offers productions throughout the season at the Eastern Slope Playhouse on Main Street in North Conway. From late June to September, the Arts Jubilee features ballet, musical performances from symphony to jazz, and an arts and crafts exhibit at Schouler Park in North Conway.

If the kids are along, you can take them to the waterslide at Attitash and to Heritage New Hampshire, a sound-and-light journey depicting everything from a voyage from England in 1690 to a train ride through Crawford Notch in 1910. From Heritage they'll probably beg you into Story Land next door, where there are rides and life-size exhibits of children's stories. Neither attraction is cheap and neither is a must—

just a way to keep everyone occupied should you need further activities for restless small fry.

A final attraction that really should not be missed won't cost you a cent. The Kancamagus Highway (Route 112 between Conway and Lincoln) runs for 32 magnificent miles right through the heart of the White Mountain National Forest. Created by the U.S. Forest Service to provide both scenery and access to beautiful wilderness through picnic areas and hiking trails, it is one of the region's real treasures.

Take the highway across the mountains to see some of the wonders on the other side, particularly Franconia Notch with its famous Flume and the Old Man of the Mountain. Or maybe just save Kancamagus for last and go home savoring some of the best scenery New England has to offer.

New Hampshire Area Code: 603

DRIVING DIRECTIONS North Conway, the center of activity in the Mt. Washington Valley, is at the intersection of Routes 16 and 302, reached from the east via I-93 and Route 3 to Route 302 (or via Route 2 to Route 16) and from the south via I-95 or I-495 to Route 16. North Conway is 145 miles from Boston, 335 miles from New York, and 225 miles from Hartford.

PUBLIC TRANSPORTATION Vermont Transit bus service to North Conway. Closest air service is via Portland, Maine, or Lebanon, New Hampshire.

ACCOMMODATIONS *Mount Washington Hotel,* Bretton Woods, 278-1000 or (800) 258-0330 outside New Hampshire, $$$$$ MAP ● *Stonehurst Manor,* Box 1900, North Conway, 356-3113, gracious estate, $$–$$$$ ● *Buttonwood Inn,* Mt. Surprise Road, PO Box 3297, North Conway, 356-2625, bed and breakfast convenient to town but tucked on five private acres, $$ CP ● *Cranmore Mt. Lodge,* Kearsage Road, North Conway, 447-2181, modest country inn with modernized barn, pool, tennis, hiking trails, $$ CP. ● Darby Field Inn, Bald Hill, Conway, 447-2181, $$$$ MAP ● *Dana Place Inn,* Route 16, Pinkham Notch, Jackson, 383-6822, $$–$$$ CP ● *Christmas Farm Inn,* Box 176, Jackson Village, 383-4313, $$$$–$$$$$ MAP ● *Inn at Thorn Hill,* Jackson Village, 383-4242, gracious home with excellent dining room, $$$ or $$$$–$$$$$ MAP ● *Village House,* Route 16A, Jackson, pleasant bed and breakfast with a pool, $$ CP ● *Wentworth Resort Hotel,* Jackson Village, 383-9700, old-time resort, golf and tennis, recently refurbished, $$–$$$$.

BED AND BREAKFAST   *New Hampshire Bed and Breakfast*, RFD 3, Box 53, Laconia, NH 03246, 279-8348.

DINING   *Stonehurst Manor* (see above), $$$ • *Scottish Lion*, Main Street, North Conway, 356-3000, English-Scottish specialties, $$–$$$ • *Dana Place Inn* (see above), $$–$$$ • *Christmas Farm Inn* (see above), $$–$$$ • *Mt. Washington Hotel* (see above), prix fixe $$$$$ • *The Bernerhof*, Route 302, Glen, 383-4414, excellent Swiss fare, $$–$$$ • *Wildcat Inn and Tavern*, Jackson Village, 383-4245, informal atmosphere, good food, $$ • *Inn at Thorn Hill* (see above), $$$ • *Horsefeathers*, Main Street, North Conway, 356-2687, informal, popular for lunch or dinner, $–$$

SIGHTSEEING   *Mt. Washington Cog Railway,* Route 302, Twin Mountain, 846-5404. Hours: late June to Labor Day, hourly 9 A.M. to 5 P.M.; September to Columbus Day and late May to mid-June, runs as needed. $25 • *Mt. Washington Auto Road*, Route 16, Pinkham Notch, 466-3988. Hours: mid-May to late October, daily 7:30 A.M. to 6 P.M. weather permitting. Car and driver, $10; each additional adult passenger, $4; children, $3 • *Wildcat Mountain Gondola*, Route 16, Pinkham Notch, Jackson, 466-3326. Hours: late May to mid-October, daily 9 A.M. to 4:30 P.M. in season; weekends only in spring and fall. Adults, $5; children, $3 • *Cranmore Skimobile*, Routes 16 and 302, North Conway, 356-5544. Hours: late June to mid-October, daily 9 A.M. to 5:30 P.M. Adults, $5; children, $3.75 • *Attitash Alpine Slide*, Route 302, Bartlett, 374-2369. Hours: 10 A.M. to 5 P.M., daily in summer, weekends only from late May to Mid-June and from September to mid-October. Rides, $4.50; under 4, free • *Heritage New Hampshire*, Route 16, Glen, 378-9776. Hours: mid-June to Labor Day, daily 9 A.M. to 6 P.M.; after Labor Day to mid-October to 5 P.M. Adults, $5.50; 4 to 12, $3 • *Story Land*, Route 16, Glen, 383-4293. Hours: 9 A.M. to 6 P.M. $9 for all.

INFORMATION   Mt. Washington Valley Chamber of Commerce, PO Box 385, Route 16, North Conway, NH 03860, 356-3171.

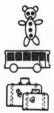

Looking for the Real York

Pick your favorite York—historic village, rocky Maine peninsula, beach resort, or yachtsmen's haven.

Until a few years ago, each one was a separate village, known respectively as York Village, Cape Neddick, York Beach, and York Harbor. Though officially they've been combined into a single community, they're still commonly called "The Yorks," plural because each part has such a distinct personality. Together, they offer a mini-sampler of the Maine coast.

For history buffs, York Village is the chief lure. The onetime Indian settlement of Agamenticus has the distinction of being not only the oldest surviving English settlement in Maine, dating back to 1624, but America's first chartered city, established in 1642. Its name at that time was Gorgeana, after Sir Ferdinando Gorges, an English soldier and mariner who was then proprietor of the Province of Maine.

It was given the name York and reduced to mere township when it was seized by Massachusetts along with the whole Province of Maine in 1652. In spite of frequent Indian attacks threatening its existence in the 1600s, York survived, and by the eighteenth century it had become a prosperous provincial capital and an important warehousing center and way station between Portsmouth and points east.

One of the many warehouses on the York River was owned by John Hancock, the well-known signer of the Declaration of Independence. It has been restored and is now maintained by the Society for the Preservation of Historic Landmarks as a museum displaying tools of Colonial times as well as ship models and other relics of York's seafaring days.

As York diminished in commercial importance with the years, it gained new prominence late in the nineteenth century as a seaside resort. Many wealthy easterners, including one Samuel Clemens, bought up the fine Colonial residences of the village as summer homes. A number of the historic houses in town never changed hands, however, and even today they are occupied by descendants of their builders, making York Village something of a living museum with an unusual sense of its past and a determination to preserve it.

Six buildings in the village now comprise Historic York and are open to the public. The most fascinating of them is the Old Gaol, the oldest remaining English public building in the country. Stone dungeons with walls three feet thick and separate cells for criminals, women lawbreakers, and debtors were actually part of the gaoler's home. Kids love poking through the cells and peeking through the window in the children's bedroom, where the prisoners were once passed their meals. Young or old, almost everyone poses outside in the pillory.

Another interesting stop is the 1742 Emerson-Wilcox House, which has served as home, tavern, and post office over its long history. Now it offers period rooms, a chimney passage, and some exquisite eighteenth-century crewel bed hangings.

Other stops with tales of the past to tell are the 1745 Old Schoolhouse, where children learned navigation, bookkeeping, and surveying along with their three Rs, and Jefferd's Tavern, where weary stagecoach passengers found refreshments after their dusty ride in the late 1700s.

Besides touring, over the course of the summer you can see all kinds of Colonial crafts demonstrations in historic York houses, including the making of candles, weaving, spinning, and whittling. Fishermen's crafts such as tying nets and crafting lobster traps are shown at the Hancock Wharf, and cooking demonstrations are given on the open hearth.

The town walking tour will take you to all these attractions and more—the restored Elizabeth Perkins House, the Old Burying Ground, the Green, handsome private homes, and a couple of prize New England churches. Stop at the town information booth on Route 1 for the walking tour pamphlet and summer schedule of special events.

If York Village has the monopoly on local history, Nubble Light on Cape Neddick takes the prize for scenery. From the south, follow Route 1A past Long Sands Beach to Nubble Road; from the north, take 1A to Broadway. Either way, you'll reach the lighthouse, one of Maine's most photographed landmarks. You'll understand why when you see the spectacular rocky promontory that gives this coast its special character.

Continuing on 1A north past Short Sands Beach, you'll find Cape Neddick Harbor, fed by York's second river, the Cape Neddick. The small, sheltered beach at the river's mouth is a good place for small children or picnickers. Another prime picnicking spot along River Road is Cape Neddick Park for the Arts, 100 acres of woodland set aside by Brenda Kuhn as a memorial to her parents. In the park are the Walt Kuhn Gallery, featuring the well-known Maine landscapes and circus drawings of the late artist as well as works by other regional artists, and the Vera Spier Kuhn Sculpture Garden, where contemporary sculpture is displayed in a natural setting. Musical entertainment is presented in the summer in an amphitheater in the woods.

York Beach, with its two main town beaches, is most likely to have appeal if you prefer a lot of action and people around or if you have teenage children. The town of York Beach is filled with tourist shops, food stands, and an amusement park. It won't be to all tastes, but it does offer the advantage of having varied activities within walking distance of lodgings, so it's easy for you and your family to go off in different directions.

There are lots of reasonably priced Victorian rooming houses in this area, but the choicest lodgings in York are in the remaining section, York Harbor.

This is boating territory, and the picturesque harbor is filled with boats of all kinds, from sleek yachts to fishermen's dories. The inns make the most of the scene. At Dockside Guest Quarters, you can sit on the porch and watch skippers navigating around the tricky 90-

degree turn where the York River comes into the sea. The Maine House dates from the late 1800s and retains the flavor of a sea captain's home, filled with model sailboats, paintings of clipper ships, scrimshaw, and bookcases lined with books on lighthouses and sailing. Five rooms are in the house, the rest in pine cottages along the shore, done in rustic nautical decor.

Harborside Inn has a sun porch overlooking the harbor, where you can see the lobster boats setting out, and Stage Neck Inn, on a spit at the entrance to the harbor, is a full scale resort with tennis, boating, and an 18-hole golf course. The elegant dining room with three-sided water views is especially attractive. York Harbor Inn lacks the direct water view, but makes up for it with a lot of Early American charm.

York Harbor has its own beach, pebbly but more peaceful than the others, and its own historic home—the Sayward House, an eighteenth-century mansion high above the York River. And it's in York Harbor that you'll find the start of a mile-long cliff walk beside the sea, one of the pleasantest strolls to be found anywhere on the coast.

Go to the beach end of Harbor Beach Road, on the left just after a weathered building that is part of a private swim club, and left again along a boardwalk parallel to the beach for the beginning of this path hugging the shore. Outcroppings of rock for scrambling and gazing at the waves of foam spewing against the cliff are on one side, wildflowers and evergreens and handsome seaside homes on the other. Eventually the path ends at a rocky beach just short of Cow Beach Point. You can head back here or pick your way onward until you reach a sheltered rocky beach adjacent to Norwood Farms Road, which leads back to Route 1A.

What with beach and boats and all the Yorks to explore, you may not need further activities, but if you have a long weekend, there's a lot to see and do just south of York in Kittery and then just over the bridge in Portsmouth, New Hampshire, only 12 miles away.

Kittery's Ft. Clary State Memorial, with its restored hexagonal blockhouse and view across to Nubble Light, is high on the list. Also of interest in this once-wealthy shipbuilding town is the Kittery Naval Museum and a number of historic houses, including the exquisite Lady Pepperell House and the John Bray House, the oldest dwelling in Maine. Kittery Mall offers a number of outlet stores for bargain goods, Dansk pottery and Dexter shoes among them.

Portsmouth deserves at least half a day for viewing Strawbery Banke, an outdoor museum of 30 buildings representing Early American life in a seacoast village. Five of the buildings are fully restored and furnished; others hold exhibits. This village from the past ties itself firmly to the present by giving working space to contemporary craftspeople in some of its historic houses.

There are many more fine homes to be seen in Portsmouth, includ-

ing the one-time residence of naval hero John Paul Jones, as well as a
wealth of interesting shops to explore. Portsmouth harbor cruises
aboard the *Viking Sun* to the Isle of Shoals and Star Island are also
highly recommended. There are nightly dinner cruises too, and weekend evening cruises with dancing and entertainment.

None of these will ease the task of selecting your favorite York—
but they may just add to your conclusion that Maine's southernmost
coastal resort has more than its share of reasons for a visit.

Maine Area Code: 207

DRIVING DIRECTIONS   York is on the southern coast of Maine,
on Route 1A off US 1 or off the York exit of I-95, the Maine Turnpike.
It is 62 miles from Boston, 267 miles from New York, and 157 miles
from Hartford.

PUBLIC TRANSPORTATION   Greyhound provides bus service
to nearby Portsmouth, NH. Limo service is available from Boston and
Portland airports.

ACCOMMODATIONS   Expect minimum stays in season ● *Dock-
side Guest Quarters*, PO Box 205, York Harbor, 363-2868, $$ ● *Ed-
wards' Harborside Inn*, PO Box 866, York Harbor, 363-3037, $$ ●
York Harbor Inn, PO Box 574, York Harbor, 363-5119, $$–$$$ ●
Stage Neck Inn, York Harbor, 363-3850, $$$$ ● *Nirvana by the Sea*,
Nubble Road, 363-3628, modest guest house with a view, $ CP ●
Nubble Cove Cottages, PO Box 39, Nubble Point, Cape Neddick,
363-3624, has housekeeping facilities with a choice vantage—first pri-
ority here goes to week-long reservations, $–$$$ ● Many unpreten-
tious, moderately priced almost look-alike Victorian guest houses are
lined up across from the beach on Long Beach Avenue—send for local
listings.

BED AND BREAKFAST   *Bed and Breakfast of Maine*, 32 Colonial
Village, Falmouth, ME 04105, 781-4528 ● *Bed and Breakfast Down
East Ltd.*, Box 547, Eastbrook, ME 04534, 565-3517.

DINING   *Dockside Dining Room* (see above), $–$$ ● *York Harbor
Inn* (see above), $$–$$$ ● *Nubble Light Restaurant*, Nubble Road,
363-4054, food not quite up to the location, which is great, $–$$$ ●
Cape Neddick Inn and Gallery, Route 1, Cape Neddick, $$$ ● *El's
Fried Clams*, Route 1, Cape Neddick, 363-2101, local favorite, infor-
mal, mostly moderate, $–$$ ● *The Lobster Barn*, Route 1 north of

town, 363-4721, $–$$ • *Cape Neddick Lobster Pound,* Route 1A, 363-5471, $$.

SIGHTSEEING *Historic York*—All buildings in York Village open mid-June to September and Columbus Day weekend, daily 10:30 A.M. to 5 P.M. Combined admission to all: Adults, $6; 6 to 15, $2.50; individual admissions: Adults, $2; children, $1.

INFORMATION The Yorks Chamber of Commerce, Box 417, York, ME 03909, 363-4422.

Away from It All on Block Island

It's more than the 12-mile distance to the mainland that separates Block Island from the rest of the world. Block Island is a trip to yesterday.

Despite the ferry boats that bring more visitors every year, this exquisite island somehow manages to retain its wild beauty and the look and serenity of a time long gone by. Around every bend, flower-splashed meadows and pond-dotted moors come into view, open and unspoiled, with nothing but crisscrossing stone fences and an occasional weathered clapboard house to show that anyone has been there before you.

The beaches bend for miles around the edges of the island, some of them easily accessible, some reached only by narrow sandy paths descending down bluffs as much as 200 feet above the ocean. The tallest of the cliffs, known as Monhegan Bluffs, is as spectacular a sight from below as from the top, where you can see forever out to sea.

Bicycles outnumber cars a hundred to one here, adding to the tranquillity. The islanders are so upset by the recent intrusion of mopeds that they have threatened to secede from Rhode Island if a law is not passed banning the hated motorbikes from their quiet lanes.

Though some of the old Victorian hotels have been spruced up in recent years, there's been no attempt to build resorts or amusements on Block Island, so the visitors who board the ferry boats from mainland Rhode Island, Connecticut, and Long Island are precisely those who want to get away from all that. Even a weekend visit is enough to leave you refreshed, better able to cope with the pressures of the real world when you get back.

Most of the boats arrive at the pier in Old Harbor opposite a row of century-old, gingerbread-trimmed Victorian hotels now listed on the

National Register of Historic Places. The most impressive is the spanking-white National Hotel, meticulously restored to its original 1888 lines and resplendent with its dark green shutters, shiny black mansard roof, and elaborate cupola.

For faraway views, you'll want to climb the hill up Spring Street to the recently renovated Spring House or the neat and trim 1661 House, where a seat on the porch or the deck can keep you mesmerized for hours, gazing at that deep and unbelievably blue sea. Atlantic Inn, not far away on High Street, is another old-time beauty with a fine view.

With its wraparound porch and wide lawn, Narragansett Inn, nearer to the New Harbor piers, has its own special views of the Great Salt Pond marinas and the boats going in and out of the harbor.

Except for the National and a few spots now going condo, few Block Island lodgings are fancy by mainland standards, and most island lovers like it that way. One visitor, in fact, complained that the pleasant 1661 House was too nice—"too much like home." Like many regulars, she prefers the simpler island look of the older Victorian hotels.

To get your bearings on a first visit, you'll want to circle the island—not too difficult a task, since it is only seven miles long and three miles wide. There are a dozen taxis that will gladly take you around if you've wisely left your car on shore, and bike shops all over the place that will equip you to pedal your own path, poking down those tempting side roads as you ride to the beach. It's easy to get by on foot as well, especially with the beaches as tempting rest stops all along the way.

The island is shaped like a lamb chop, with Old Harbor situated just where the meatiest portion might begin. Heading north, you'll come to Crescent Beach, which is really a whole string of beaches along the Atlantic with the dunes growing steeper as you proceed farther north. State Beach is the most crowded, since it has changing facilities and a lifeguard, but all it takes is a short walk down the beach to find space to yourself.

The island is almost bisected at this point by the Great Salt Pond, with New Harbor sitting at the pond's most sheltered inland spot. Here's where the sailors and yachtsmen drop anchor at nearby marinas.

Continuing on the main (and only) highway, Corn Neck Road, you'll come to Sandy Point with its historic 1867 granite lighthouse in the dunes and a wildlife sanctuary that is a favorite spring nesting ground for seagulls as well as one of the prime destinations for bird watchers on the East Coast.

Corn Neck Road was named for the crop grown there by the Narragansett Indians, Block Island's original inhabitants, who called their home Isle of the Little God. They were spotted in 1524 by Giovanni da

Verrazano, then in 1624 by Adrian Block, the Dutchman for whom the island was named. He was probably the first but by no means the last to sail over by yacht from Long Island.

Settler's Rock at Sandy Point marks the arrival of the English, who created the first real colony. Block Island abounds with legends of shipwrecks and tales of ghosts and eerie lights, passed on by long generations of seafaring residents.

Sandy Point and its environs are flat. As you turn back to the south past Old Harbor, the hills begin and the dips and turns on Spring Street, Southeast Light Road, and the Monhegan Trail yield glorious views on all sides. It's at the southernmost end that you'll find the dramatic view from Monhegan Bluffs and the Southeast Light, a quaint brick building that has stood as a beacon to sailors for over 100 years. Wooden stairs in the sea grass make it easy to descend to the rocky beaches below and to gaze back at the bluffs and perhaps find a suitable perch on sand or rocks for basking on the beach.

The main road here cuts back inland past Rodman's Hollow, another of the island's five wildlife refuges, a great natural ravine left by a long-ago glacier. Once again, many paths wind through the meadows and marshes to the sea.

Once you've found your favorite spots, you'll want to spend most of the time occupying them and enjoying the beauty around you. If you want more activity, you can rent a sailboat at the Block Island Club or charter a fishing boat at Old Harbor Dock. If you want to try wind surfing, Andy's Way on Corn Neck Road offers rentals and instruction.

Shopping is definitely not a major occupation on Block Island, though there are a few worthwhile stops in Old Harbor, where almost everything is right on Water Street across from the docks. The Ragged Sailor is a combination clothing store, gift and antiques shop, and upstairs art gallery with the most interesting buys on the island. Sea Breeze Gallery at the crest of Spring Street Hill is another place to see island art and photographs.

When the sun begins to set, the best view in town is off the deck at the Oar at Block Island Boat Basin in New Harbor. For dining, there is no shortage of places to enjoy Block Island swordfish, bluefish, and the other fresh seafood that is a specialty at this fishermen's paradise. If you want evening action, go to Ballard's, a boating hangout that is by far the noisiest and most popular place around.

And if you want an island souvenir, you might think of having Finn's Fish Market in Old Harbor pack up fresh fish or lobster for your trip home. It may prove some small consolation for having to leave this extraordinary getaway at sea.

Rhode Island Area Code: 401

DIRECTIONS AND TRANSPORTATION Block Island is 45 minutes by ferryboat from Port Judith on the Rhode Island shore, 2 hours from New London, Connecticut, and about 2 hours from Montauk, Long Island. There are also boats from Providence, stopping at Newport on the way, a 4-hour ride. For schedules and rates, contact Nelesco Navigation, PO Box 482, New London, CT 06320, (203) 442-7891; Interstate Navigation Company, Galilee State Pier, Point Judith, RI 02882, (401) 789-3502. Bonanza buses from Providence connect to local bus service to Galilee. Amtrak trains stop at Westerly, Rhode Island, where there is air service via New England Airlines. Plane service is also available from New London and Providence.

ACCOMMODATIONS Expect minimum stays in season ● *1661 House,* Spring Street, 466-2421, buffet breakfast and cocktails served on a wonderful deck overlooking the water, $$$–$$$$$ CP ● *Spring House,* Spring Street, 466-2633, $$$$ CP ● *Atlantic Inn,* High Street, 466-2006, room 22 on top is prime, $$$$–$$$$$ CP ● *Manisses House,* Spring Street, 466-2421, same owners as 1661 House, elegant little restored hotel but no views, $$$–$$$$$ CP ● *Narragansett Inn,* New Harbor, 466-2626, $$$$ MAP ● *National Hotel,* Water Street, 466-5577, $$$$ CP ● For guest houses near town, there is the very pretty *Blue Dory,* Dodge Street, 466-2254, $$$$–$$$$$ CP, and the more modest *Gables* and *Gables II,* Dodge Street, 466-2213, $$. To obtain a list of the many other adequate hotels on the island, send $4 to the Chamber of Commerce.

DINING *Manisses House* (see above), attractive dining room with continental menu, $–$$$ ● *Atlantic Inn* (see above), excellent seafood, $$$ ● *Harborside Inn,* Water Street, 466-5504, view of harbor from the porch, $$–$$$ ● *Ballard's,* Old Harbor, 466-2231, a madhouse, but the best lobster prices in town, $–$$ ● *Finn's Seafood Bar,* on the piers near Ballard's, Old Harbor, 466-2473, informal, attached to local fish market, $–$$.

INFORMATION Block Island Chamber of Commerce, Drawer D, Block Island, RI 02807, 466-2982.

High Notes
near Mt. Monadnock

They call it the "Quiet Corner" of the state, a world of apple orchards, covered bridges, mountain views, and tiny towns all but untouched by time.

But come summer each year, New Hampshire's southwestern Monadnock region comes alive with music. You can follow the melody from town to town—Schubert in Antrim tonight, Haydn at Jaffrey tomorrow, Mozart in Dublin the day after.

In all, more than a dozen hamlets and villages in this green and rolling region took part last year in the annual six-week traveling chamber music festival known as Monadnock Music. The concerts, mostly free, move from white-spired village church to meeting house to town hall in different small-town locales four nights each week.

Add to the scene the Apple Hill Chamber Players in Nelson, the Temple Town Band, a local tradition since 1799, folk concerts at Folkway in Peterborough, and the Monadnock Chorus and Orchestra, and there's music in harmony with every taste, strategically placed to help you get acquainted with one of New England's quaintest and least spoiled regions.

Besides all the music, there are three long-established summer theaters in the area. The Peterborough Players have performed classics for over 50 years in a converted barn, and the American Stage Festival in Milford has been known for over a decade as a spawning ground for new talent.

The wonder is that the area remains unspoiled and relatively uncrowded, especially since Mt. Monadnock, the peak that Ralph Waldo Emerson called "the new Olympus," is, according to state authorities, the most-climbed mountain in the United States. A conservative estimate puts the number of climbers at 125,000 each year.

Part of the reason is that an ascent to the 3,165-foot summit is an accomplishment within reach of even novice hikers, who can then enjoy the soaring view of five states that is worthy of a far loftier peak. On a really clear day, the White Mountains to the north, the Green Mountains to the west, and the tops of Boston skyscrapers to the east are all in sight.

The view of the mountain from below can be equally impressive, for again it looms majestically out of all proportion to its size, visible from almost every town in the region. During the late nineteenth century, it attracted writers like Emerson, Hawthorne, and Thoreau, who spent their summers here in sight of the inspiring peak. In the twentieth century many of America's most famous writers, artists, and composers have also come here to be inspired at the MacDowell Colony, the famous retreat on a 450-acre estate in Peterborough. Most of the time the privacy of the colony's residents is carefully guarded. But on Medal Day in late August, when the MacDowell medal is presented to distinguished men and women in the arts—recent winners include sculptor Isamu Noguchi and author John Updike—everyone is invited for the ceremonies, a picnic lunch, and the chance to follow the wooded paths to the studios of the current artists-in-residence.

With all the music and theater in the area, the only problem you'll have filling your evenings in the Monadnock region is choosing among the many offerings.

By day, the choices are equally tempting. If you're at all active, you'll want to head for Mt. Monadnock. Stop at the State Park Eco-center at the base to see a model of the mountain, pick up a trail map, and get some firsthand hiking pointers from the helpful staff members of the Society for the Protection of New Hampshire Forests. There are thirty miles of trails and paths ranging from one to ten miles long, for every ability level. A two-hour walk will take an average hiker to the top.

The society also offers guided walks on Saturday following a variety of themes, from rhododendrons and wildflowers to hunting for rocks and mushrooms.

With or without a guide, don't miss the early to mid-July riot of color at Rhododendron State Park on Route 119 in Fitzwilliam. There are some 16 acres of the showy wild shrubs, one of the largest tracts in the Northeast. The park offers a walking path around the entire glen, plus picnic grounds in shaded pine groves—and, of course, more of those ever present views of Mt. Monadnock.

If you want to remain out of doors, there are five more parks to explore and a number of local swimming holes. Among the highlights of the parks are the auto road to the summit of Pack Monadnock Mountain in Miller Park on Route 101 in Peterborough, the swimming area on Otter Lake in Greenfield Park off Route 136 in Greenfield, and the ghost town and abandoned mines and potholes of Bear Den Geological Park in Gilsum. More swimming possibilities are the Otter Brook Dam on Route 9 in Keene, and the Surry Mountain Dam on Route 12 in Surry.

There are also any number of lakes and rivers for swimming as well as canoeing or sailing, and with the necessary state fishing license, this is good country for anglers. Just ask wherever you are staying for directions to the nearest water. And this is excellent golfing territory, with three public 18-hole golf courses available in Francestown, Hillsboro, and Keene. Those who want to be at the first tee bright and early can stay at Tory Pines Resort, which is built around a golf course.

If indoor diversions such as antiques and art galleries are more to your taste, you'll still not lack for choices. The best plan is to make a tour of the pretty little towns to see what each has to offer. Fitzwilliam, strong contender for the title of prettiest town in the area, has a block-long green lined with fine white Colonial homes and several antiques shops, including one in a restored schoolhouse. Picture-postcard Hancock offers The Barn, which is filled with furniture, crafts, and paintings by local artists.

Francestown, another front-runner in the local town beauty derby, has more shops in its small town center, and flea market enthusiasts can treasure-hunt to their hearts' content at the event held regularly on weekends at the Cheshire Fairgrounds on Route 12 in Swanzey.

When it comes to art, you can see fine work from throughout New England at the Thorne-Sagendorph Art Gallery at Keene State College and the Killian Gallery at the Sharon Arts Center.

Crafts are even more plentiful. The Sharon Arts Center includes a branch of the fine League of New Hampshire Craftsmen shops, and the Country Artisans Gallery in Keene is an outlet for 300 craftsmakers. In Peterborough, Folkway Crafts Shop features work by local artisans, Joseph's Coat sells handmade clothing, and Tewksbury's Art Gallery and Handicrafts Shop has a large selection of unusual wares of all kinds. A different but equally interesting stop in town is Brookstone, a retail outlet for the catalog people with all those intriguing tools.

Bacon's Sugar House in Jaffrey Center is one of several places to find locally produced maple syrup.

If you are still searching for more to do, just about every little town has its own historic house museum. Peterborough has something unique, the Game Preserve, containing over 850 Early American board games. Dublin is notable as the home of *Yankee* magazine and of Friendly Farm, a place where youngsters can pet tame farm animals and see eggs being hatched. Both Hancock and Milford boast Paul Revere bells in local steeples. One other notable home for President watchers is the restored Franklin Pierce Homestead in Hillsboro. You can also check out the local covered bridges, four of which are to be found around Swanzey.

One final place you may want to see is Cathedral of the Pines in Rindge, an outdoor shrine with a panoramic view and an altar honoring American war dead. Nondenominational services are held on Sundays.

Except for Keene, a small city, and Peterborough, whose new malls have created a central shopping area for neighboring communities, all the towns in the Monadnock region are tiny and little touched by time, so you'll hardly go wrong wherever you roam.

Nor are you likely to go wrong picking among the growing number of small country inns in the area. The Victorian Monadnock Inn is simple and pleasant, the Colonial John Hancock is cozy and historic, and the Amos Parker House is a charmer that does justice to its pretty hometown of Fitzwilliam.

But first choice for lodging has to go to the Inn at Crotched Mountain, and you'll know why as soon as you drive up the long hill and see the 40-mile view. There is one hazard, however, if you manage to snag one of the 12 rooms: Once you settle beside the pool with that vista before you, you may never be able to tear yourself away.

New Hampshire Area Code: 603

DRIVING DIRECTIONS The Monadnock region is in the southwestern corner of New Hampshire near the Vermont and Massachusetts borders. It can be reached from the west via I-91, taking the Route 119 exit to Hinsdale and on to Fitzwilliam; from the north off I-89 to Route 202; from the south via Route 2 to Route 202, which runs directly into Jaffrey and Peterborough. From the east, take Route 3 to Route 101 and go west to Route 202. The region is about 75 miles from Boston, 205 miles from New York, and 95 miles from Hartford.

PUBLIC TRANSPORTATION Vermont Transit bus service to Keene and Fitzwilliam. Eastern Express air service to Keene.

ACCOMMODATIONS *Monadnock Inn*, Box B, Jaffrey Center, 532-7001, $$ ● *John Hancock Inn*, Hancock, 525-3318, $$ ● *Tory Pines Resort*, Route 47, Francestown, 588-6352, $$$ ● *Inn at Crotched Mountain*, Mountain Road off Route 42, Francestown, 588-6840, $$–$$$. ● *Amos A. Parker House*, Route 119, Fitzwilliam, 585-6540, delightful, $$ CP ● *Thatcher Hill Inn*, Thatcher Hill Road, Marlborough, 876-3361, country farmhouse, $$ CP ● *Stepping Stones Bed and Breakfast*, RR 1, Box 78, Wilton Center, 876-3361, nineteenth-century home, artisan hostess, $$ CP ● *Grassy Pond House*, Rindge, 899-5166, restored 1831 homestead on 150 acres, $$ CP ● *Mill Pond Inn*, 50 Prescott Road, Jaffrey, 532-7687, 1800s Colonial murals on the walls, $$ CP ● For full list of smaller area inns, write to Monadnock Region Bed and Breakfast Association, PO Box 236, Jaffrey, NH 03452.

BED AND BREAKFAST *New Hampshire Bed and Breakfast*, RFD 3, Box 53, Laconia, NH 03246, 279-8348.

DINING *Fitzwilliam Inn*, on the green, Fitzwilliam, 532-8342, historic, cozy dining room, $$ (some lodgings upstairs, too, $—but sparse) ● *Monadnock Inn* (see above), well recommended, $$ ● *Inn at Crotched Mountain* (see above), $$ ● *Petite Maison*, Bennington

Square, Bennington, 588-6655, French in a country house, $$ ● *Maitre Jacq,* foot of Crotched Mountain, Francestown, 588-6655, country French and American, $$ ● *The Boilerhouse at Noone Falls,* Route 202 South, Peterborough, 924-9486, picturesque views, $$–$$$ ● For lunch, try *The Folkway,* Grove Street, Peterborough, Greek salad, tostadas, and more, $.

SIGHTSEEING *Monadnock Music,* PO Box 255, Peterborough, NH 03458, 924-7610, six-week summer season. Write for schedule of four free concerts each week, and prices and dates of Saturday Peterborough Town House opera series ● *Peterborough Players,* Middle Hancock Road, Peterborough, 924-7585, changing repertory July and August; call for details ● *American Stage Festival,* Route 13 North, Milford, 673-7515. Check for this year's plays and prices ● *Mt. Monadnock State Park,* off Route 124, Jaffrey, 532-8862 ● *Sharon Arts Center,* Route 123, Sharon, 924-7256. Hours: Monday to Saturday, 10 A.M. to 5 P.M., Sunday from 1 P.M. Free ● *The Game Preserve,* 110 Spring Road, Peterborough, 924-3235. Hours: open all year "by chance or appointment" ● *The Friendly Farm,* Route 101, Dublin, 563-8444. Hours: daily 10 A.M. to 5 P.M. May to Labor Day; weekends through mid-October. Adults, $3; children, $2.25 ● *Cathedral of the Pines,* Route 110, Rindge, 899-3300. Hours: daily May to October, 9 A.M. to 4 P.M.

INFORMATION Monadnock Region, c/o Greater Keene Chamber of Commerce, 12 Gilbo Avenue, Keene, NH 03431, 352-1303.

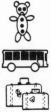

Visiting Martha's Vineyard

If you're wealthy and/or a celebrity, chances are you already have your own place on Martha's Vineyard, along with the likes of Carly Simon, Walter Cronkite, Jacqueline Onassis, Katherine Graham, William Styron, and Beverly Sills.

The next best thing to owning is renting a place here, with time to get into the rhythm of the island and discover its private places and pleasures. More than most places, the Vineyard has two personalities, public and private, and though it's a perfectly lovely spot for a weekend, be forewarned that you'll get only a superficial look at the reasons so many people fall totally in love with the island.

First of all, Martha's Vineyard is by far the biggest of the major vacation islands on the New England coast—108 square miles compared with roughly 30 for Block Island and 52 for Nantucket, its not-so-near neighbor off the Massachusetts shore. It takes a while to learn the ins and outs.

Martha's Vineyard is also very easy to get to—just a 45-minute boat ride from Cape Cod. That attracts lots of summer vacationers, bringing the population from 10,000 people year round to a summer glut of 70,000. Add hordes of day-trippers who also find it easy to get here and want to see everything in a tour bus in a few short hours, and you can understand the problem.

But with all of that, the Vineyard still has magnificent beaches, seaside cliffs, woodlands, ponds and wildlife preserves, and several diverse and interesting little towns to explore. What many like best about the island is its ambience, an unusual blend of country retreat and beach resort, with great sailing waters thrown in as a bonus.

Among the towns, Edgartown, with its handsome sea captain's homes and ready supply of inns, is the first choice for lodgings among most weekend visitors, though some prefer the more isolated charm of the little fishing village of Menemsha. Getting to either is no problem. Shuttle buses make regular rounds from the ferry docks at Vineyard Haven and Oak Bluffs to the courthouse in Edgartown, and taxis are readily available for transportation anywhere on the island.

To get around on your own and really see the variety of the island's offerings, you can bring or rent a car or rent a bicycle or moped when you get off the ferry. Like most islands, this is ideal biking country, with few cars on the main roads and many bike paths. There is a protected paved path for bicycles all the way from Oak Bluffs to Edgartown, and many miles of paths in the state forest connecting Vineyard Haven, Oak Bluffs, Edgartown, and West Tisbury.

However you make the trip, one of the first orders of business to understand the makeup of Martha's Vineyard is to visit each of its disparate communities. There are six of them, those already mentioned plus Chilmark, Gay Head, and Tisbury (which includes Vineyard Haven). Most people also make a separate ferry trip from Edgartown to Chappaquiddick Island.

The big island was dubbed Martha's Vineyard by an early explorer, Bartholomew Gosnold, who landed there in 1602 and named it to honor one of his daughters as well as the wild grapes he found growing in profusion. The first permanent Colonial settlement on the island came 40 years later at Edgartown, known then as Great Harbor.

With its rich farms and the whaling expeditions leaving from its harbors, the island prospered until the Revolutionary War. In 1778 the British fleet arrived to burn ships and raid more than 10,000 sheep and 300 head of cattle from local farmers. In the 1820s the whaling industry revived and the fine homes in Edgartown were built by sea captains and merchants. Now a center for yachters instead of whalers, Edgartown still has the look of a nineteenth-century seaport. A walk around the little town, whose Water Street runs right beside the harbor, is a tour past Greek revival homes that still display their dark shutters, fan lights, and "widow's walks" where worried wives watched for their husbands to return safely from sea.

One of the houses on South Water Street belonged to Captain Valentine Pease, master of the ship on which Herman Melville made his only whaling voyage. Two other notable homes now serve as museums and another is the office of the *Vineyard Gazette*. The Federated Church, built in 1828, remains a local landmark along with the massive six-columned Old Whaling Church, which dominates Main Street and now serves as the local performing arts center. Next door is the home of Dr. Daniel Fisher, once the richest man on the island, a physician who was also the largest manufacturer of spermaceti candles and who held the contract to supply all the nation's lighthouses with whale oil.

Behind the Fisher House is the oldest remaining residence, the 1672 Vincent House. It has been preserved with the original brickwork, hardware, and woodwork to allow visitors to see how buildings were constructed 300 years ago. The 1765 Thomas Cooke House, now headquarters of the Dukes County Historical Society, is also worth a stop to see the antique furniture, scrimshaw, ship models, and costumes, and gear used by the early whalers and farmers on the island.

From Edgartown, the drive along the north shore takes you past the Windfarm Museum, a reflection of the island's future rather than its past. Many visitors are attracted to this modern solar-heated, wind-powered home with an organic garden in operation.

Drive on to Oak Bluffs and you'll find a totally different kind of island history awaiting. Just about the time the golden age of whaling was coming to an end, a new "industry" grew up: religion. It all began in 1835, when the Edgartown Methodists held a camp meeting in an oak grove that later became known as Wesleyan Grove, on the bluffs at the northern end of town. The meeting, with worshippers and preachers living in improvised tents and speakers standing on a driftwood platform, became a yearly affair of growing popularity. By 1859 the Martha's Vineyard Camp Meeting had become the largest in the world, with 12,000 people attending. Within 40 years of the first meeting, crowds of 30,000 gathered regularly for Illumination Night, which marked the end of the summer season with mammoth Japanese lanterns and fireworks displays. The event is still celebrated each year in August.

According to island history, many who attended the meetings found the seashore and lovely surroundings "as uplifting as the call to repent"—and thus began Martha's Vineyard's new era as a summer resort. The tents gave way to wooden cottages, with the owners often trying to outdo one another in gaudy Victorian gingerbread. Wesleyan

Grove turned first into Cottage City and then, as tourism grew, into Oak Bluffs, a town of 1,000 cottages plus boarding houses and stores.

Religion remained a drawing card. In 1879 a new steel tabernacle was built to replace the old circus tent. The building and the remaining old cottages give a unique flavor to the present-day town of Oak Bluffs. The town also claims to own the oldest carousel in the country, the Flying Horses, which delights children today as it did in the 1870s.

Ironically, pious Oak Bluffs, along with Edgartown, is one of the only places on Martha's Vineyard that offers bar service with meals. Otherwise, it's BYOB in island restaurants.

A drive farther along the coast to Tisbury and Vineyard Haven will bring you to seafaring territory again and to the busy dock where most of the island ferries pull in. The Seamen's Bethel, once a refuge for sailors far from home, has been restored and is now a chapel and museum. The Tisbury Museum in the 1796 Ritter House on Beach Road shows life as it was in this town in the nineteenth century. The Town Hall, once a Unitarian church, is one of the island's handsome architectural legacies from whaling days.

Follow Lambert's Cove Road and North Road through part of West Tisbury and into Chilmark, an area of rolling green hills and exceptional private coastline that is a choice location for summer homes. Next you'll come to Menemsha, a tiny quintessential fishing village, and, following Lighthouse Road, to the brilliantly colored cliffs of Gay Head and its lighthouse, one of the first revolving lighthouses in the country, built in 1799.

You can vary your route back to Edgartown by taking South and West Tisbury roads into town. For a scenic detour off West Tisbury, take Deep Bottom for two miles and follow the sign to Long Point, a 580-acre preserve on the south shore with frontage on Tisbury Great Pond, as well as a couple of coves and a half-mile of beach on the Atlantic.

Seeing the sights of Martha's Vineyard can take at least half a day—more if you want to do it by bike or stop for a seafood lunch. Another highly recommended approach is to pack a picnic lunch and take time off for stops at a beach or walks through some of the nature preserves along the way. Besides Long Point, there are Felix Neck off the Vineyard Haven–Edgartown Road and Cedar Tree on the north shore down Indian Hill Road off State Road. These are places to see wildflowers, birds, and all manner of island pond life.

As for beaches, despite all those residents-only locations, there are many fine ones left to choose from. One of the most beautiful of the public beaches is South Beach, also known as Katama Beach, on the south shore at Edgartown—three miles of powdery sand with surf on one side and protected salt pond on the other. Across the way in Chappaquiddick is East Beach, part of the Cape Pogue Wildlife Refuge, and

Wasque Reservation, which includes most of the barrier beaches forming the northeastern tip of Martha's Vineyard. Much of Chappaquiddick is an untouched wilderness of dunes, cedar thickets, salt marsh,
and scrubby upland, a lot of it accessible only on foot or in a four-
wheel-drive vehicle. No tour groups to contend with here.

You'll find every kind of outdoor recreation on the island—public
tennis courts in Vineyard Haven, Oak Bluffs, Edgartown, Chilmark,
and West Tisbury and an 18-hole golf course in Oak Bluffs. Fishing
boats go out of all the main island docks, sailboats are for rent in
Vineyard Haven, and both sailboats and powerboats are available in
Edgartown.

There are enough standard resort gift shops in Edgartown to keep
die-hard shoppers occupied for a bit. Among the most interesting are
the Golden Door, with treasures from the Far East, and the Charlotte
Inn, with its art gallery and shop on the main floor.

But shopping is the least of the reasons to come to Martha's Vineyard. Once you spend a weekend getting acquainted with the special
combination of country and seashore this lush island offers, with its
exceptional beaches and unspoiled natural beauty, you may well find
you're one of the many who come back for more.

Martha's Vineyard Area Code: 508

DIRECTIONS AND TRANSPORTATION   Passenger and car ferries to Martha's Vineyard run year round from Woods Hole on Cape
Cod (45 minutes), and ferries for passengers only run in the warm
months from the Cape towns of Falmouth (40 minutes) and Hyannis (1
hour, 45 minutes) and from New Bedford, Massachusetts (also 1 hour,
45 minutes). Woods Hole is 85 miles from Boston, 271 miles from
New York, and 187 miles from Hartford. For ferry information, contact Steamship Authority, Woods Hole, Cape Cod, MA 02543,
540-2022. For current information on other ferry services, contact the
Martha's Vineyard Chamber of Commerce. For air service, PBA
(Provincetown-Boston Airways) reservations through Continental Airlines, (800) 525-0280. For information on smaller airlines currently
serving the island, phone Martha's Vineyard Airport, 693-0550. For
new catamaran service from Boston, phone (617) 723-7800.

ACCOMMODATIONS   Best known of Edgartown's many early
American inns and guest houses are *Charlotte Inn*, South Summer
Street, 627-4751, elegant, antique-furnished 1820 home with gallery
and fine restaurant downstairs, $$$$–$$$$$ CP ● *Daggett House*,
North Water Street, 627-4600, snug historic sea captain's home with
garden on the harbor, $$$–$$$$ CP ● *Edgartown Inn*, North Water

Street, 627-4794, an 1800 Colonial inn, $$–$$$$; with a more modest annex, $ ● Victorian Inn, South Water Street, Edgartown, 627-4784, $$–$$$$ CP ● *Beach Plum Inn,* Basin Road, Menemsha, 645-9454, a breezy country inn overlooking the sea with excellent dining room, $$$$–$$$$$.

LODGING RESERVATIONS SERVICES *Dukes County Reservation Service,* 1 Lake Avenue, Oak Bluffs, MA 02557, 693-6505 ● *Martha's Vineyard Reservations,* PO Box 1769, Vineyard Haven, MA 02568, 693-4111.

DINING *L'Etoile,* in Charlotte Inn, 627-8947, French, best and most expensive in town, prix fixe $$$$$ ● *Warriners,* Post Office Square, Edgartown, 627-4488, gracious, elegant, $$$ ● *The Wharf,* Main Street, Edgartown, 627-9966, seafood in former blacksmith shop, $–$$$ ● *Seafood Shanty,* Dock Street, Edgartown, 627-8622, for outdoor dining on the harbor, $–$$$ ● *Home Port,* Menemsha Road, Menemsha, 645-2679, nautical, informal, on picturesque harbor, $$–$$$ ● *Louis' Tisbury Café,* 102 State Road, Vineyard Haven, 693-3255, highly regarded by island regulars, $$–$$$ ● *Black Dog,* Beach Road, Vineyard Haven, 693-9223, longtime informal waterfront favorite, $$–$$$ ● Carly Simon's *Hot Tin Roof* at the Edgartown Airport, 693-1137, is the most popular island nightspot.

SIGHTSEEING *Vincent House and Old Whaling Church,* Main Street, Edgartown. Hours: June 25 to August 31, Monday to Friday, 10 A.M. to 2 P.M. Free. ● *Dukes County Historical Society,* Cooke Street, Edgartown, 627-4441. Hours: mid-June to mid-September, Tuesday to Saturday, 10 A.M. to 4:30 P.M. Adults, $2; children, $.50 ● *Windfarm Museum,* Edgartown–Vineyard Haven Road, 693-3658. Hours: late June to Labor Day, daily except Wednesday, 10:30 A.M. to 4:30 P.M. Adults: $4; children, $2 ● *Tisbury Museum,* Beach Road, Vineyard Haven. Hours: July through September, Monday to Saturday, 1 P.M. to 5:30 P.M., Sunday from 2 P.M. Adults, $1; 13 to 18, $.50; under 13, free ● *Seamen's Bethel,* Union Street, Vineyard Haven, 693-9317. Hours: daily 10 A.M. to 4 P.M. Free.

INFORMATION Martha's Vineyard Chamber of Commerce, Beach Road, PO Box 1698, Vineyard Haven, 02568, 693-0085.

Moonlight and Mozart in Vermont

The sun was setting to the strains of Bach. While the concert played, listeners sat on the lawn and watched the sun dip behind the billowy profiles of the Adirondack Mountains across Lake Champlain in a progression of pinks, roses, and smoky grays that were mirrored in the stillness of the water.

There are many summer music festivals in sylvan settings, and many larger and more famous such affairs than the Vermont Mozart Festival. But few can rival the beauty or the intimacy of this very special event. Since 1974, this three-week festival beginning in mid-July has been a movable musical feast in and around Burlington, switching locations from Shelburne Farms and other estates bordering Lake Champlain to college campuses and churches or to the ferry boat on the lake.

It is the lakeside lawn concerts, particularly those on the grounds of Shelburne Farms, that provide the most memorable moments. The music and the change in scene from spectacular sunsets to intermission views of moonlight on the water provide a rare harmony of sights and sounds.

And the music is first rate, with the New York Chamber Soloists and the Festival Winds performing along with many guest artists. The high caliber of the musicians is even more evident because the audiences are so small that even at the outdoor performances no amplification comes between listeners and performers.

For anyone who loves music, the Mozart Festival is the perfect reason for a trip to Vermont's largest city. As an encore, you'll have a chance to get acquainted with one of New England's most remarkable collections of folk art.

Not that Burlington (population 38,000) feels anything like a big city. With Lake Champlain as its western border, the Adirondacks across the water, the Green Mountains to the east, and the University of Vermont and several smaller college campuses adding green space to the center, Burlington has the feel of a cosmopolitan college town blessed with enviable surroundings.

Burlington was not much of a tourist city until big industries such as IBM and GE moved in about 20 years ago and things began to look up. There is scant evidence that this is a town dating back to 1773, but the downtown business area has been transformed into a pleasant four-block pedestrian mall with colorful banners overhead and interesting shops and sidewalk cafés along the way. There are scenic boat rides on the lake, and city restaurants have taken on greater sophistication. All these help to make a visit to Burlington a growing pleasure.

A good way to get acquainted with the city is to spend Saturday morning on a walking tour. Burlington developed into a shipping center when the Champlain Canal, built in 1823, connected the lake to the Hudson River. One tour route will take you through the King Street neighborhood near the waterfront, the site of one of the earliest settlements, and then downtown. The unexpected discoveries along the tour range from the City Hall, designed by the famous architectural firm of McKim, Mead, and White, to Burlington Square Mall, a high-tech center done in the 1970s by Mies Van Der Rohe.

Another pleasant stroll is in the Hill section through the Champlain College and University of Vermont campuses and prosperous residential neighborhoods dating back to the city's heyday. The university, incidentally, was founded by Ira Allen, brother of Revolutionary War hero Ethan Allen.

The $7 million mall that transformed Church Street in 1982 houses dozens of merchants, from shops selling clothing, crafts, and books to Sweetwater's, a former bank converted into a restaurant. You'll have no trouble spotting an outdoor café for lunch. Leunig's Old World Café, to name just one of the possibilities, is the place for a capuccino or an iced espresso and a recommended choice for breakfast or Sunday brunch.

The Déjà Vu Café is the downtown restaurant with the most interesting decor, but the Ice House takes the prize for location, with two terraces overlooking the lake. If you can't make it for dinner, have a drink here at sunset. Two other excellent choices south of town on Route 7 are Pauline's and Francesca's. And if you want to taste the ice cream that *Time* magazine rated the best in America, Ben and Jerry's at 169 Cherry is the place.

The afternoon offers many pleasant possibilities. If you want a summery diversion, there are town beaches as well as a boat ride on Lake Champlain, an unusually scenic cruise thanks to the mountain views on the far side. A bike and jogging path along Lake Champlain also is accessible from the city's four lakeside parks.

If shopping is your thing, Burlington has a growing number of outlet stores. The Outlet Center on Route 7 south of town has Bass Shoes and Kidsport, which offers Healthtex clothing, among its 20-plus stores. TenneyBrook Square includes Aileen, Van Heusen, and Timberland outlets. There is even a cheese outlet on Pine Street that advertises a third off on Vermont cheese. Champlain Mill in neighboring Winooski is another shopping mecca, offering all kinds of shops and crafts in an atmospheric restored mill. The Waterworks Restaurant here is a top choice for Sunday brunch on the deck overlooking the Winooski River rapids.

Shelburne Farms is the principal site of the Mozart Festival concerts, but this unusual estate is also worth touring in the daytime, when you can really see the grounds. The 1,685-acre farm is a rolling landscape of open fields and woodlands laid out by Frederick Law Olmsted, with striking views at every curve of the road through the property. It was the home of Dr. and Mrs. William Seward Webb (she was a Vanderbilt), who had architect Robert Henderson Robertson design the magnificent buildings in shingle, slate, and limestone to blend with the landscape. Both the mansion, whose porch serves as main stage for the summer concerts, and the coach barn, where smaller concerts are held, are exceptional buildings.

The Webbs began their farm as an experimental agricultural showplace, and Webb descendants have continued it as a model of progressive cattle and dairy farming, as well as a demonstration bakery and cheese-making operation. Little or no fossil-fuel fertilizers, herbicides, or pesticides are used on the farm. The two-hour tour includes the manor house, the great barns and dairy building, exhibits of Vermont agriculture, and a small store featuring farm products, including some of the tastiest Vermont cheese to be found. There are walking trails here also, with stupendous water views.

The main house has been restored and is open for dining and lodging. Reserve well in advance, and you'll learn how it feels to live like a lord of the manor.

You may well be back on the lawn at Shelburne for an evening concert, though the locations vary from night to night. If you have an evening to spare, you may also want to take in a performance at the Champlain Shakespeare Festival, held annually on the University of Vermont campus. There are matinees on Saturday, in case it turns out to be a rainy day.

Do pray for sun, however, because rain sends the evening concerts indoors, often to the Burlington High School auditorium, a poor substitute for the outdoor settings.

On Sunday, drive back to Shelburne to see another of the Webbs' legacies, the Shelburne Museum. There is no way to take in all of this amazing complex of Americana in a day, for this is the nation's foremost showcase of folk art. There are more than 40 buildings on the 45-acre site, which is probably best described as a "collection of collections." The beautifully landscaped grounds are set up like a New England village, and some of the buildings are simply homes furnished in period antiques. But within many of them are unmatched exhibits of quilts, decoys, cigar store Indians, and carousel figures, weather vanes, trade signs, primitive drawings and paintings, and painted furniture.

There seems to be no end to the variety of displays—dolls and dollhouses, Toby jugs and luster pitchers, clocks, valentines, penny banks and puppets, embroidery, scrimshaw, and so on—all in prodigious numbers. Among the more unusual exhibits are a 525-foot hand-carved model of a circus parade and the big-as-life *S.S. Ticonderoga*, the last vertical-beam sidewheel passenger steamer intact in the United States. You can go right on board to see the handsome paneling and elegant interiors.

Meanwhile, the pleasant little town of Shelburne has some interesting shops to bring you back to reality—everything from a delightful country store to products of Scotland. Or you can continue driving south for another half-hour or so to Middlebury to see a picture-book college town that is also the home of the Vermont State Crafts Center at Frog Hollow, a shop filled with the highest quality handicrafts made by state residents.

The Dog Team Tavern, just off Route 7 about four miles north of Middlebury, is a traditional New England country inn with such regional specialties as sticky buns, country fried chicken, and baked ham with fritters. What nicer way to end a weekend in Vermont?

Vermont Area Code: 802

DRIVING DIRECTIONS   Burlington is in northwestern Vermont. I-89 goes directly into the city, as does Route 7. It is 225 miles from Boston, 300 miles from New York, and 200 miles from Hartford.

PUBLIC TRANSPORTATION   Burlington is served by several airlines, including Eastern Express, Continental, and U.S. Air, as well as by Amtrak rail service and Vermont Transit bus lines. Ferry service is available from New York State across Lake Champlain.

ACCOMMODATIONS   *Shelburne House,* Shelburne, 985-8498, palatial lodgings in estate mansion with superb lake views, exceptional, $$$–$$$$$ ● *Sheraton Burlington Inn,* 870 Williston Road, 862-6576, pleasant, offers tennis, health club, indoor and outdoor pools, $$$ ● *Radisson-Burlington,* Burlington Square, 658-6500, downtown with a lake view, $$$–$$$$ ● *Lindenwood,* 916 Shelburne Road, 658-1125, the only inn in town, but unfortunately on a main road—still the people are nice, the breakfast muffins are good, and there is a quieter motel in back, $$ CP ● *Econo Lodge,* 1076 Williston Road, 863-1125, $$ ● Two pleasant places within half an hour's drive: *Waybury Inn,* East Middlebury, 388-4015, cozy inn featured on "The Bob Newhart Show," $$–$$$, and *North Hero House,* North Hero, 372-8237, charming, away from it all in the Champlain Islands, on the lake with beach, tennis, boating, $$–$$$.

BED AND BREAKFAST   *American Collection of Bed and Breakfasts,* 984 Gloucester Place, Schenectady, NY 12309, (518) 370-4948 ● *Vermont Bed and Breakfast Reservation Service,* PO Box 1, East Fairfield, VT 05448, 827-3827.

DINING   *Deja Vu Café,* 185 Pearl Street, 864-7917, striking decor, light and regular menu, crepe specialties, $–$$$ ● *Ice House,* 171 Battery Street, 864-1800, varied menu, unbeatable harbor view, $–$$

● *Pauline's,* 1834 Shelburne Road (Route 7), 862-1081, attractive and one of the town's best, $–$$$ ● *Sweetwater's,* 120 Church Street, 864-9800, on the mall, informal, snacks to meals, big Sunday brunch, $–$$ ● *Francesca's,* Jelly Mill Common, Route 7, Shelburne, 985-3373, Italian, $–$$ ● *Village Pump House,* Shelburne Village, Shelburne, 985-3728, continental, well recommended locally, $$–$$$ ● *Waterworks,* Champlain Mill, Winooski, 655-2044, terrific location overlooking rapids, creative menu, $–$$.

SIGHTSEEING *Vermont Mozart Festival,* PO Box 512, Burlington, VT 05402, 862-7352, three weeks mid-July to August. Write or phone for current schedule and concert prices ● *Champlain Shakespeare Festival,* UVM Royall Tyler Theater, Burlington, 862-2144. Contact for current information ● *Shelburne Museum,* Route 7, Shelburne, 985-3344. Hours: daily mid-May to late October, 9 A.M. to 5 P.M., winter usually Sunday only, 11 A.M. to 4 P.M.; best to check. Adults, $9.50; 6 to 17, $4 ● *Shelburne Farms,* Shelburne, 985-8686. Hours: June through September, several tours daily. Adults, $5; 6 to 12, $2.50 ● *Spirit of Ethan Allen Cruises,* Lake Champlain, 862-9685. Hours: summer day and dinner cruises, $6 to $17.95; phone for exact rates and schedules ● *Burlington Ferry,* King Street Dock, one-hour trips across Lake Champlain, mid-May to late October. Round trip car and driver, $20; additional adults, $5; 6 to 12, $1.50; maximum car fare, $25 ● *Vermont State Craft Center* at Frog Hollow, Mill Street, Middlebury, 388-3177. Hours: spring through fall, Monday to Saturday, 9:30 A.M. to 5 P.M., also Sunday 12 noon to 5 P.M. Free.

INFORMATION Lake Champlain Regional Chamber of Commerce, PO Box 453, 209 Battery Street, Burlington, VT 05402, 863-3489.

Scaling the Heights at Acadia

Mother Nature created many wonders along the coast of Maine, but when she got to Mt. Desert Island she pulled out all the stops.

The heart of this ultimate "down east" destination, the easternmost point on the Atlantic coast, is Acadia National Park—32,000 spectacular acres that encompass everything from rugged rockbound coastline to green hills, 26 lakes and ponds, and 18 mountains. One of the latter, Mt. Cadillac, is the highest point on the eastern seaboard.

Mt. Desert (accent on the last syllable), a 16-by-13-mile retreat just across a causeway from the mainland, also includes Bar Harbor, once a mecca for the wealthy and now a thriving little waterside resort town of shops, restaurants, and lodgings, including lavish summer homes that have been transformed into attractive inns.

For boaters, or for anyone who appreciates peerless water views, there is Somes Sound, which splits the far end of the island almost in half. This deep arm of the sea between mountainsides is the only fjord on the East Coast. The two sides provide ample coastline for scenic resorts in the peacefully removed fishing village of Southwest Harbor and in Northeast Harbor, a yachting town with just a bit more action. It is closer to the park but still far away from Bar Harbor's busy streets.

As if all that weren't enough of a lure, these are also absolutely prime lobstering waters, and almost all the restaurants on Mt. Desert, as well as a couple of very reasonably priced "lobster pounds," offer the very best of Maine's most famous culinary treat.

The focal point for visitors is Acadia, one of the nation's most popular national parks. To make the most of your visit, start at the Visitors Center, just off Route 3 at Hull's Cove north of Bar Harbor, for a film on the park, information, park maps, and schedules of the many activities conducted by park rangers during the summer months. These include nature walks, mountain hikes, naturalist sea cruises, and evening activities such as a "beaver watch," a night prowl to observe life in the forest after dark, and on clear nights "Stars of Acadia," a look at the heavens from a heavenly perspective.

Armed with maps and, if you wish, an information tape available for rent or sale at the Visitors Center, you're ready for the 26-mile Park Loop Road. Stopping points include Sieur de Monts Spring, featuring the Wild Gardens of Acadia with their profusion of native wildflowers, and the views along Ocean Drive, where the road becomes one-way, a plan no doubt wisely devised to make it easier to wonder at the views and pull over to the lookouts without causing traffic problems. Crescent-shaped Sand Beach is a favorite sunning spot off the drive, and there is always a crowd at Thunder Hole, named for the deafening thump of the surf as it roars into caverns carved in the cliffs.

When you get to Jordan Pond House, make a stop for a meal or the famous tea served with popovers on the lawn in midafternoon. The house is a contemporary edition of the landmark original that burned down a few years ago. It is a handsome structure with glass walls to take in the noted view of the pond and the two round peaks behind known as "The Bubbles." The melt-in-your-mouth popovers and legendary homemade ice cream can be had with lunch or dinner as well as with tea—and they're worth a wait in line.

Near the end of the Park Loop is the side road to the top of Mt. Cadillac and awesome views from every side of the 1,532-foot summit. As the first place where the sun reaches the nation each morning, the peak inspires some unique rituals, including the annual Fourth of July square dance at 12:01 A.M. followed by a sunrise breakfast.

At the park exit on Route 3 you'll come to Seal Harbor, another popular beach and a village that gained some note as the summer home of Nelson Rockefeller. It was his father, John D., along with Edsel Ford and some of the other early summer residents, who recognized the fragile beauty of the area and moved to preserve it for public use. They bought up nearly a third of the park's total acreage and turned it over to the government in 1919 as the basis for the first national park in the East.

Because cars were banned on Mt. Desert for a time, the park contains some 50 miles of pathways—once the province of the horse-drawn carriages of the wealthy—that are ideal for hikers, bikers, horseback riders, and cross-country skiers in the winter.

Route 3 ends in Northeast Harbor, a yachtsmen's haven and an elegant summer colony of large "cottages," special inns, and exclusive village shops. The big Asticou Inn, with an incomparable view of the harbor, is the most elegant of all Mt. Desert hotels, though the atmosphere is a bit staid. Two quite exceptional inns are in wooded settings on a steep hill across from the harbor: the Grey Rock Inn, a Victorian mansion where you'll sleep in an enormous room in a canopied bed, and, almost next door, the gracious shingled Harbourside Inn, a homier place where the hostess takes particular pride in serving her guests homemade blueberry muffins for breakfast.

To complete an island tour, follow Sargeant Drive, an enclave of secluded, lavish summer homes that parallels Somes Sound, and at the end of the drive take Route 198, which curves around the head of the sound into Somesville, a well-preserved village of white Colonial homes that is the island's oldest settlement. The drive south from Somesville on Route 102 along Echo Lake will bring you to Southwest Harbor, a shipbuilding and fishing village that is also a placid and popular summer community. The rooms at the 100-year-old Claremont Inn aren't anything special, but the location on Somes Sound most definitely is. A bit farther on is the Moorings, a snug and cozy berth with nautical motifs and a popular restaurant looking out on the harbor. Every kind of boat, including a canoe, can be rented right next door.

While you're in Southwest Harbor, take time for two special attractions that are easy to overlook. The first is the tiny Wendell Gilley Museum, showing off the work of a local artist who became known for his extraordinary wooden bird carvings. The second is the Mt. Desert Oceanarium, a great place for kids, with its "touch tanks" and other hands-on exhibits, including phones for listening in to the songs of whales. In the Lobster Room, a local fisherman is on duty to fascinate you and your youngsters with a zillion little-known facts about how these tasty crustaceans live and how they are caught. He illustrates his narrative with live lobsters, including a mother carrying several dozen babies on her bottom.

Appropriately, one of the best lobster pounds in the area is nearby on the docks. At Beal's Lobster Pier, you can buy fresh lobster at very reasonable prices, wait for your choice to be boiled up, and eat it on the spot at outside picnic tables beside the water. Fisherman's Landing, a similar establishment on the pier in Bar Harbor, offers a rustic enclosed eating pavilion with water views in case of rain. The Landing closes by 8 P.M., Beal's even earlier, so if you want a relatively inexpensive lobster feast, plan for an early dinner.

"Bah Hahba," as the natives call it, is filled with restaurants that offer lobster specials and other fine seafood, and enough shops to keep you browsing for quite a while. Amidst a glut of typical tourist offerings on West Street you'll find the Lone Moose, a Maine artisans collective selling high-quality weaving, pottery, metalwork, jewelry, and stained glass.

The most gracious of Bar Harbor's many present-day lodgings are in the summer showplaces that line West Street and the shore path east of the municipal pier. They include Ledgelawn, Cleftstone Manor House, and Thornhedge. For location alone, however, you really can't beat the Bar Harbor Motor Inn, a motel with a dining room and pool deck directly overlooking the harbor and the bay.

Bar Harbor can become clogged with tourists, but it is lively and attractive and offers visitors much to see and do within an easy stroll. There are a number of special events in the area during the summer, ranging from a seafood salute to a dulcimer festival. The Acadian Scottish Festival in mid-July in neighboring Trenton, the Bar Harbor Festival, and the Arcady Chamber Music Series featuring special musical events in late July and early August are worth noting. The local drama group is the Acadia Repertory Theatre, which performs at the Masonic Hall in Somesville—a good evening out combined with an early lobster dinner at Beal's.

And should you want to get out on that deep blue water while you are here, you'll find a number of ways to do so. Besides the fascinating and informative naturalist cruises sponsored by Acadia National Park, the Frenchman Bay Boating Company next to the Municipal Pier in Bar Harbor offers daily sightseeing cruises and deep-sea fishing boats. Sailing sloops go out from the Golden Anchor Pier, and the Bluenose Ferry offers a day-long "Sea Fun" outing to Yarmouth, Nova Scotia, with all the meals and trappings of a lavish ocean cruise. There are still more cruises to view lobstering, seals, and osprey, whale-watching cruises, fishing charters, windjammers, and a variety of ferry boat and mailboat cruises to nearby islands out of Northeast Harbor, plus the ferry to Swan's Island at Bass Harbor.

The Island Information Bureau on Route 3 just past the causeway leading to Mt. Desert and the Bar Harbor Chamber of Commerce Information Center at the Blue Nose Ferry Terminal on the harbor will have all the current schedules.

If you find yourself facing a rainy day, don't despair. Take the opportunity to check out those museums in Southwest Harbor and to have a look at the College of the Atlantic's Natural History Museum, another place where visitors get involved with hands-on exhibits and live talks. Special participatory programs are held every morning at 10:30. The Bar Harbor Historical Museum in the basement of the Jesup Memorial Library displays photos and clippings of what it was like in the lavish old days of the grand hotels and steamers.

Sun is preferable, of course, to make the most of the natural beauty of the area, but whatever the weather and whatever you like in the way of getaways—bustling or serene settings, fishing boats or yachts, active exercise or sitting back and gazing at the view—Mt. Desert is an unbeatable destination. It's the place for unsurpassed "down east" scenery—and just about the best lobster dinners that Maine has to offer.

Maine Area Code: 207

DRIVING DIRECTIONS   Take I-95 to Augusta, then Route 3 east to Mt. Desert or the Maine Turnpike to Bangor; follow Route 1A to Ellsworth and then Route 3 across the causeway. On Mt. Desert, Route 3 leads to Bar Harbor, Route 102 to Southwest Harbor, and Route 198/3 to Northeast Harbor. Bar Harbor is 276 miles from Boston, 482 miles from New York, and 372 miles from Hartford.

PUBLIC TRANSPORTATION   Eastern Express to Bar Harbor; Delta and other airlines serve Bangor. There is also Greyhound bus service to Bangor and Bar Harbor.

ACCOMMODATIONS   *Asticou Inn,* Northeast Harbor, 276-3344, $$$$–$$$$$ MAP ● *Grey Rock Inn,* Northeast Harbor, 276-9360, $$$–$$$$ CP ● *Harbourside Inn,* Northeast Harbor, 276-5526, $$–$$$ CP ● *The Claremont,* Southwest Harbor, 244-5036, $$$$ MAP ● *The Moorings,* Shore Road, Southwest Harbor, 244-5523, $–$$ CP ● *Cleftstone Manor,* 92 Eden Street, Bar Harbor, 288-4951, $$–$$$$ CP ● *Ledgelawn,* 55 Mt. Desert Street, Bar Harbor, 288-4596, $$$–$$$$ CP ● *Manor House Inn,* West Street, Bar Harbor, 288-3759, $$–$$$$ CP ● *Thornhedge Inn,* 47 Mt. Desert Street, Bar Harbor, 288-5398, $$–$$$$ CP ● *Bar Harbor Motor Inn,* 7 Newport Drive, Bar Harbor, 288-3351, $$$–$$$$. For more old homes, ask the Chamber of Commerce for a listing of "The Inns of Bar Harbor."

BED AND BREAKFAST   *Bed and Breakfast Down East Ltd.*, Box 547, Eastbrook, ME 04634, 565-3517 ● *Bed and Breakfast of Maine*, 32 Colonial Village, Falmouth, ME 04105, 781-4528.

DINING   *The Moorings* (see above), $–$$$ ● *The Reading Room* at Bar Harbor Motor Inn (see above), elegant, super view, $$–$$$ ● *Testa's*, 53 Main Street, Bar Harbor, 288-3327, old-timer, Italian and seafood, serves all three meals, $–$$$ ● *Brick Oven Restaurant*, 21 Cottage Street, 288-3708, interesting decor, $–$$ ● *Duffy's Quarterdeck*, 1 Main Street, Bar Harbor, 288-5295, sit upstairs for the view, $–$$ ● For informal fare, families: *Island Chowder House*, Cottage Street, Bar Harbor, 288-4905, *West Street Café*, West Street, Bar Harbor, 288-5242; *The Snack Station*, 112 Main Street, Bar Harbor ● For lobster by the pound: *Beal's Lobster Pier*, Clark Point Road, next to Coast Guard Base and Oceanarium, Southwest Harbor, 244-3202; *Fisherman's Landing*, West Street on the Pier, Bar Harbor, 288-4632. Prices vary by the season, but these are always the best around.

SIGHTSEEING   *Acadia National Park*, PO Box 177, Bar Harbor, ME 04609, 288-3338. Hours: open year round; Visitors Center open May to October, 8 A.M. to 8 P.M. Park headquarters on Route 233 has information on the rest of the year; write for specific information, schedules of naturalist sea cruises, and special events ● *Wendell Gilley Museum*, Southwest Harbor, 244-7555. Hours: April through December—summers, Tuesday to Friday, 10 A.M. to 5 P.M. (also 7 to 9 P.M. on Tuesday), weekends 12 noon to 5 P.M.; spring and fall, 10 A.M. to 4 P.M. weekdays, 12 noon to 4 P.M. weekends; off season, weekends only. Adults, $2.50; children, $.50 ● *Mt. Desert Oceanarium*, Clark Point Road, Southwest Harbor, 244-7330. Hours: mid-May to mid-October, Monday to Saturday 9 A.M. to 5 P.M. Adults, $3.25; 4 to 12, $2 ● *Natural History Museum at the College of the Atlantic*, Route 3, Bar Harbor, 288-5015. Hours: mid-June to Labor Day, daily 9:30 A.M. to 4 P.M. Adults, $1.50; children, $.50 ● *Bar Harbor Historical Society*, Jesup Memorial Library, Route 3, Bar Harbor. Hours: mid-July to mid-September, Monday to Saturday, 1 P.M. to 4 P.M. Free.

INFORMATION   Bar Harbor Chamber of Commerce, 93 Cottage Street, PO Box 158, Bar Harbor, ME 04609, 288-5103.

Supping with the Shakers in Hancock

Was it brown sugar? Honey? Maybe a touch of apple cider? No one at the long dinner table in the Believers Dining Room was sure of the secret ingredient from the old Shaker recipe. The guests knew only that cabbage, nobody's favorite vegetable, had been transformed into a treat that had everyone asking for more.

At the World People's Dinners held during the Shaker Kitchen Festival at Shaker Village in Hancock, Massachusetts, you quickly discover that the industrious people who lived here a century ago definitely did not include good food among the worldly pleasures they disdained. From their earliest years, the Shakers paid careful attention to food and its preparation, and as the skill of the "Kitchen Sisters" became known, city excursionists began arriving to share the Shakers' Saturday and Sunday dinners.

They still do. The summer week of dinners made from the original Shaker recipes is a sellout, with many people driving all the way from Boston or Albany for the night just to sample menus that include traditional fare such as roast lamb with ginger and cider, turkey with sage dressing, Eldress Bertha's summer squash casserole, and Mother Ann's birthday cake with rosewater ice cream. The chocolate bread pudding is a favorite, along with the rich caramel-flavored gingerbread, but even "calico cabbage" takes on added flavor from the seasonings and surroundings of the village. The week includes daily daytime cooking demonstrations as well, with recipes and tastes for visitors.

The Kitchen Festival is an added treat in the Berkshire region of western Massachusetts, which regularly serves up one of New England's most overflowing platters of summer pleasures. The Boston Symphony concerts at Tanglewood, the dance festival at Jacob's Pillow, the top-notch summer theater at Stockbridge and Williamstown, and the Shaker Village are only the start of a true smorgasbord of weekend delights.

With all of this, it should come as no surprise that summer reservations are hard to come by, and when the Boston Symphony arrives for a weekend, prices almost double. Even for the many motels on Route 7, several months in advance is none too soon to secure a room, though things are eased somewhat for last-minute planners by the advent of bed-and-breakfast listings and a Lenox Chamber of Commerce referral service. Because weekend rooms are at such a premium, if you'll settle for student concerts at Tanglewood during the week, this is one area that is definitely worth considering for a middle-of-the-week break.

The region known as the Berkshires actually runs the entire length of Massachusetts from its southern to northern borders along Route 7. Sheffield, the first of the towns, is an antiquer's haven, along with its western neighbor, Ashley Falls. Next comes Great Barrington, a local commercial center, and Stockbridge, the quintessential New England village immortalized by its most famous resident, Norman Rockwell. To either side are South Egremont, New Marlboro, Lee, Becket, and

West Stockbridge, the first four slightly removed from the crush of summer visitors, the latter a boutique-strewn shopping town filled with strollers.

Lenox, the home of Tanglewood, was known as the Inland Newport for its fine summer homes occupied both by the wealthy and by literary greats of the last century. It is the most gracious of the towns—and the most crowded in summer. Farther on are Pittsfield, another local shopping center, and Williamstown,the handsome hometown of Williams College with a fine small museum known for its Impressionist paintings and other noted collections.

There are dozens of lodgings in these towns for every taste and pocketbook—historic inns, resorts, and two particularly lavish retreats: Wheatleigh, where you'll enjoy all the luxury of an Italian palazzo built by a contessa, and Blantyre Castle, a summer mansion that is every bit as regal as the name implies. The wonderful old Red Lion on the corner in Stockbridge, a classic Colonial inn, is the place where everyone seems to show up eventually for a drink on the porch or the patio. The Apple Tree Inn, a 22-acre retreat conveniently set at the gate of Tanglewood, shares with Wheatleigh the distinct advantage of allowing guests to walk to the concerts. It's a benefit you'll appreciate more when you see the lines of traffic.

For dining, the Gateways in Lenox, the Old Mill and Weathervane in Egremont, the Federal House in Lee, and Williamsville Inn in West Stockbridge currently get the nod from most Berkshire gourmets. Also in West Stockbridge The Orient Express, a Vietnamese restaurant in an old house by the river, has become such a local institution that the owners recently opened another place in Springfield. The Shaker Mill Tavern is a good bet for its informal and varied menu, outdoor decks, and lively evening entertainment.

With the basics out of the way, you can now begin the difficult task of choosing among the rich arts offerings throughout the area. Tanglewood, of course, tops the list. It has been a major Northeast attraction since 1936, when it became the summer home of the Boston Symphony. The 6,000 seats in the open-air shed, which is noted for its acoustics, are frequently sold out; as many as 10,000 more people may congregate on the big lawn in back, enjoying elegant picnics along with a symphony concert under the stars. The grounds can be seen best on Sunday afternoons, when visitors have a chance to stroll some of the 210 acres of William Aspinwall Tappan's former estate, past the formal gardens and the re-creation of the red house where Nathaniel Hawthorne once worked.

Tanglewood is not the only attraction for music lovers in the Berkshires. There is chamber music at South Mountain in Pittsfield on the spacious grounds of the handsome summer home of Elizabeth Sprague Coolidge. (Bring a cushion for this one—the setting is lovely, but the benches are hard.) Some 150 voices accompanied by the Springfield Symphony are the feature at the Berkshire Choral Festival in a shed on the campus of the Berkshire School in Sheffield, and Aston Magna presents early music on original instruments at the St. James Church in Great Barrington. The Berkshire Opera Festival, the newest addition to the roster, has its home at the Cranwell Resort in Lenox.

For fans of the dance, Martha Graham, Merce Cunningham, and other major troupes from around the world can be seen at the Jacob's Pillow Dance Festival in Becket, the oldest event of its kind in the country, and the most prestigious. The theater also offers jazz concerts on Sunday. The Berkshire Ballet has a six-week summer season at the Arts Center of Berkshire Community College in Pittsfield.

Theater buffs have the happy choice of the long-established and ex- cellent Berkshire Theater Festival in Stockbridge, with three arenas showing drama, musicals, and children's plays, or the highly ac- claimed experimental productions at the Williamstown Theater Festi- val. If the Bard's the thing, there is Shakespeare & Company, performing in a natural amphitheater on the grounds of the Mount, Edith Wharton's former estate high above Laurel Lake, and the Berk- shire Public Theater presents regional repertory in Pittsfield year round.

All these performances benefit from their sylvan settings.

In addition to the arts, there are enough sightseeing attractions in the mountains and woodlands and lovely towns of the Berkshires to keep you busy even if you had nothing else to do. Priority goes to two special places. The first is Norman Rockwell's Corner House on Main Street in Stockbridge, a museum featuring the well-known illustrations of the artist in the town where he spent his last 25 years. The second is Hancock Shaker Village, the most elaborate of all the Shaker mu- seums, where 20 buildings have been restored of the original 100 structures in a settlement that was established in 1790 and reached its height in the 1830s.

You'll learn a lot about the ingenious Shaker people, whose faith was founded on four fundamental principles: separation from the world, common property, confession of sin, and celibacy, meaning separation in living quarters but equality in privileges for the sexes. The name Shaker came from the lively dance that worshippers prac- ticed to drive evil away.

The Shakers had a genius for finding the most functional way of doing things, exemplified by their classically simple tables and chairs and pegs, precursors of modern design. Their legacy to us includes the first packaged garden seeds and herbal remedies and such practical inventions as the circular saw, the flat broom, and the clothes pin.

The trilevel round stone barn in Hancock is the most striking re- minder of Shaker ingenuity, with a shape as practical as it is beautiful, a shape that enabled as many as 54 head of cattle to be fed by a single farmhand from a single middle core. Among the other buildings to be toured are the Brethren's and Sisters' Shops, where you'll see the chair, broom, carpentry, cobbling, and clockmaking industries that were run by the men and the dairy, medical, and weaving facilities that were the province of the women. Costumed craftsmen, on hand to demonstrate these various occupations, reproduce Shaker small goods, wooden objects, tinware, and furniture for sale to visitors.

One of the most important buildings is the Brick Dwelling, which housed 100 and contained the communal dining room and meeting room used for weekday worship. Here is where the World People's Dinners are held, and where food-making demonstratioins are offered throughout the Kitchen Festival week in the Great Cook Room in the basement. Samples of homemade bread, chutneys, preserves, and other foods made from Shaker recipes are for sale in the appropriately named Good Room.

If you want to check out the best of the area shops, head for West Stockbridge, where you'll find leather, jewelry, stained glass, pottery, clothing, and a new Oriental gallery run by the Orient Express. It's touristy, but the shops are attractive, particularly the interesting G/M Galleries, a combination of new and antique jewelry and ethnic arts.

To forget about sights or shops and enjoy a swim, try York Lake in New Marlboro, Benedict Pond in Beartown State Forest near Great Barrington, or Pontoosue Lake on Route 7 south of Pittsfield, which offers boat rentals as well as a little beach. For hikers, there are several choices, including Monument Mountain between Great Barrington and Stockbridge and Mt. Greylock, the highest in the state. Serious hikers or anyone who is on a budget and is willing to put up with Spartan furnishings and shared rooms can stay on top of Greylock in the Bascom Lodge, run by the Appalachian Mountain Club. The club sponsors many guided walks and programs. You can pick up a schedule at the visitors' center, just off Route 7 in Lanesboro north of Pittsfield. The road is plainly marked.

Should you have the time, there are more places of interest to be visited, two of them monuments to famous sculptors. Chesterwood, an estate set beside the Housatonic River overlooking the mountains, was aptly described as heaven by its former owner, Daniel Chester French, the sculptor of the Lincoln Memorial in Washington. Tyringham Art Galleries is a curiosity. The studio of Sir Henry Kitson, best known for his minuteman statue at Lexington, it is a Hansel and Gretel affair appropriately called the Gingerbread House, with a "thatched roof" that is itself a sculpture, weighing 80 tons. The stained-glass windows inside are lovely and the sculpture garden includes a pond and flowers.

Flower lovers will also enjoy Bartholomew's Cobble, a 200-acre world of meadows and woods and wildflowers in Ashley Falls, and the

Berkshire Garden Center, a 15-acre show garden in Stockbridge. Then there's the Clark Art Institute in Williamstown, a prize small museum that shouldn't be missed by anyone who is interested in art. And don't overlook Herman Melville's Arrowhead, in Pittsfield, the home where he wrote *Moby Dick.*

All these attractions simply can't be seen in one weekend, which is probably a very good thing. The Berkshire mountainsides are beautiful in autumn, offer skiing in the winter, and take on a special glow in the bloom of spring—which gives you lots of excuses to come back and see what you've missed.

Hancock Area Code: 413

DRIVING DIRECTIONS   Lenox, the heart of Tanglewood country, is on Route 7, about 146 miles from Boston, 163 miles from New York, and 53 miles from Hartford. Hancock Shaker Village is about 15 minutes away in Pittsfield; make a left turn off Route 7 in Pittsfield to Route 20, which takes you directly to the village.

PUBLIC TRANSPORTATION   Bonanza and Arrow Lines provide bus service to the area; Amtrak serves Pittsfield from Boston. Closest major airports are Springfield, MA, 70 miles, or Albany, NY, 37 miles. If you stay near Tanglewood, you can manage without a car, but you'll miss a lot of the sights.

ACCOMMODATIONS   Rates given are for weekends in July and August concert season and foliage season; all are less on weekdays and in September, much less after October. All inns have minimum stays in season. • Starting with the very top: *Wheatleigh,* West Hawthorne Road, Lenox, 637-0610, Italian-style villa, $$$$$ MAP • *Blantyre Castle,* East Street, Lenox (on the road to Lee), 637-1728, palatial indeed, $$$$$ MAP • *Cranwell Resort and Conference Center,* Route 20, Lenox, 637-1364, Tudor mansion with views, pool, tennis, health club, golf, center of a condo community, $$$$$ • Back to reality, though few of these qualify as budget: *Williamsville Inn,* Route 41, West Stockbridge, 274-6580, charm, pool, tennis court, excellent dining room, $$$–$$$$ CP • *Weathervane Inn,* South Egremont, 528-9580, attractive converted farmhouse, pool, $$$$ MAP • *Apple Tree Inn,* 224 West Street, Lenox, 637-1477, fabulous mountaintop location, $$$–$$$$ CP • *Merrell Tavern,* Route 102, South Lee, 243-1794, authentically restored 1800 home, $$$$–$$$$$ CP • *Red Lion Inn,* Main Street, Stockbridge, 298-5545, $$–$$$$ • Some other possibilities: *Haus Andreas,* Stockbridge Road, Lee, 243-3298, tennis court and pool, $$$$ CP; *Milhof Inn,* Route 43, Stephentown, NY, just 500 feet across the state line from Hancock, (518) 794-9345, cozy and secluded mountain chalet with a pool, about 20 minutes from Lenox, $$; *Colonial Ashley Inn,* Bow Wow Road (off Route 41), Sheffield, 229-2929, tiny charmer out in the country, pool, $$$ CP; *The Orchards,* 222 Adams Road, 458-9611, elegant Colonial decor, pool, $$$$–$$$$$ • Some of the mansions-turned-inns in Lenox: *Birchwood Inn,* 7 Hubbard Street, Lenox, 637-2600, spacious, canopy beds, handsome garden, $$–$$$$ CP; *Cliffwood Inn,* 25 Cliffwood Street, Lenox, 637-3330, Belle Epoque showplace, veranda overlooking grounds, $$$$ CP; *Underledge,* 76 Cliffwood, Lenox, 637-0236, manor house on four acres, $$$$$ CP; *Seven Hills,* Lenox, 637-0060, lovely grounds, pool, tennis, music-student waiters perform, $$$–$$$$ CP.

BED AND BREAKFAST *Berkshire Bed and Breakfast,* PO Box 211, Williamsburg, MA 01096, 268-7244 • *Covered Bridge Bed and Breakfast,* PO Box 447, Norfolk, CT 06058, (203) 542-5944.

DINING *Paolo's* at Wheatleigh (see above), prix fixe $$$$$ • *Williamsville Inn* (see above), also for Sunday brunch, $$$ • *Federal House,* Route 102, South Lee, 243-1824, highly rated, $$$ • *Gateways Inn,* 71 Walker Street, Lenox, 637-2532, gracious mansion, longtime local favorite, $$$ • *Apple Tree Inn* (see above), continental with an Italian accent, great views, $$–$$$ • *The Orient Express,* off Main Street, West Stockbridge, 232-7110, $ • *Shaker Mill Tavern,* Routes 102 and 41, West Stockbridge, 232-8565, also for entertainment, Sunday brunch, $–$$ • *The Old Mill,* Route 23, South Egremont, 528-1421, eighteenth-century gristmill, charming, $$–$$$ • *The Painted Lady,* 285 South Main Street, Great Barrington, northern Italian, $$–$$$ • *20 Railroad Street,* same address, Great Barrinton, 528-9345, burgers to dinners, $–$$ • For lunch: in Stockbridge, *The Café* in the Mews near the Red Lion; in Lenox, *Café Lucia,* 90 Church Street, or *The Quiet Corner,* 104 Main Street. • For Tanglewood picnics, it's *The Elegant Picnic,* 637-1621, or *A Moveable Feast,* 637-1785.

SIGHTSEEING *Hancock Shaker Village,* Route 20, Pittsfield, 443-0188. Hours: Memorial Day through October, 9:30 A.M. to 5 P.M. Adults, $6.50; children, $2.50. Kitchen Festival held annually for one week in late July or early August; World's People's Dinners held nightly, $16; advance reservations required. Send stamped, self-addressed envelope for current annual calendar of special events, dates, and prices. For all of the following listings, it is wise to write for current schedules and prices • *Tanglewood,* West Street (Route 183), Lenox, 637-1940, symphony concerts July and August. Hours: Friday

9 P.M. (preludes at 7 P.M.), Saturday 8:30 P.M., Sunday 2:30 P.M. Open rehearsal on Saturday at 10:30 A.M., recitals and chamber music most Thursday evenings and some Tuesday concerts. Tickets from $6 to $50; $7.50 for the lawn ● *Berkshire Music Center,* concerts at Tanglewood by students at the Boston University Tanglewood Institute on Monday, Tuesday, Wednesday, and Sunday at 8:30 P.M., Saturday at 2:30 P.M., and Sunday at 10 A.M. in the Theatre–Concert Hall or Chamber Music Hall; unreserved seats available one hour prior to concerts, $5 to $6. For schedules write to Tanglewood Brochures, Symphony Hall, Boston, MA 02115 ● *Jacob's Pillow Dance Festival,* off Route 20 on George Carter Road, Becket, 243-0745, performances Tuesday to Saturday evenings, Saturday afternoons, free concerts and tours 90 minutes before performances, $17.50 to $23.50; Sunday jazz concerts, $13.50 and $14.50 ● *Shakespeare & Company,* The Mount, Route 7, Lenox, 637-3353, July to Labor Day, Tuesday to Sunday, 8 P.M. $8 to $15 (The Mount can be toured Tuesday to Friday, 11 A.M. to 5 P.M., Saturday and Sunday 9:30 A.M. to 5 P.M. $3.50.) ● *South Mountain Concerts,* Route 7, one mile south of Pittsfield, 442-2106, August to early October, summer performances Saturdays 3 P.M., fall performances Sundays, $15 ● *Aston Magna,* Great Barrington, 528-3595, three Saturday evening chamber concerts; phone for dates and rates ● *Berkshire Theater Festival,* Main Street, Stockbridge, 298-5576, performances Monday 8 P.M., Tuesday to Friday 8:30 P.M., Saturday 5 P.M. and 9 P.M., Thursday at 2 P.M. $11 to $23 ● *Berkshire Choral Festival,* Berkshire School, Route 41, Sheffield, 229-7926, performances 7:30 P.M. on selected Saturdays in July and August ● *Williamstown Summer Theater,* Park and Main (intersection of Routes 7 and 2), Williamstown, 597-3400, performances late June to August, Tuesday to Friday 8:30 P.M., Saturday 5 P.M. and 9 P.M. ● *Norman Rockwell Museum,* Main Street, Stockbridge, 298-3822. Hours 10 A.M. to 5 P.M. daily except Tuesdays in winter. Adults, $3; 5 to 18, $1 ● *Chesterwood,* Route 183, Stockbridge, 298-3579. Hours: May to October, 10 A.M. to 5 P.M. Adults, $4; children, $1 ● *Tyringham Art Galleries,* at Routes 102 and 20, Tyringham, 243-3260. Hours: weekdays 10 A.M. to 5 P.M., weekends to 6 P.M. $.50 ● *Bartholomew's Cobble,* off Route 7A, Ashley Falls. Hours: museum open April 15 to October 15, 9 A.M. to 5 P.M.; grounds open year round. Adults, $2; children, $.75 ● *Berkshire Garden Center,* Routes 102 and 183, Stockbridge. Hours: open daily, admission charged mid-May to mid-October. Adults, $3; children, $.50. ● *Sterling and Francine Clark Art Institute,* 225 South Street, Williamstown, 458-9545. Hours: Tuesday to Sunday, 10 A.M. to 5 P.M. Free. ● *Arrowhead,* 780 Holmes Road, Pittsfield, 442-1793. Hours: Memorial Day through October, Monday to Saturday, 10 A.M. to 4:30 P.M., Sunday 11 A.M. to 3:30 P.M. Closed Tuesday and Wednesday after Labor Day; by appointment only

in winter. Adults, \$3; children, \$1.50. Tickets to all area events can be purchased at the Berkshire Ticket Booth at the Lenox Chamber of Commerce on Main Street, open daily 1 P.M. to 5:30 P.M..

INFORMATION   *Lenox Chamber of Commerce,* Lenox Academy Building, 75 Main Street, Lenox, MA 01240, 637-3646, for general local information and lodging referral service. *Berkshire Visitors' Bureau,* The Common, Pittsfield, MA 01201, (800) BERKSHR (except in MA, 443-9186), for information and lodging listings in the entire area.

Show and Tell
at Lake Sunapee

I almost hate to tell about New London, New Hampshire. After all, if too many people find out about this classy little college town at the top of Lake Sunapee, the congenial and reasonably priced inns in town may be booked solid when I want to go back.

There's no problem, however, talking about the annual summer show of the League of New Hampshire Craftsmen Foundation at Mt. Sunapee State Park, because it is already one of the region's most eagerly awaited annual events, so popular that it has grown from a weekend affair to a full nine days.

Fine crafts seem to flourish best in the country, where artisans still take time and pains with handwork, and in New Hampshire, a state that remains largely rural with lots of country to go around, the crafts tradition is strong and still growing. Much of the impetus is largely due to the efforts of the League, which began holding the nation's first crafts fair more than 50 years ago.

The dozen big, brightly striped tents set up in front of the grassy ski slopes host a range of artisans—from potters and silversmiths to basket makers and bird carvers. One of the most popular features of the fair is the unique "Living with Crafts" exhibit in an adjoining building, a display showing off handicrafts in model-room settings, giving everyone new ideas and inspiration to take back home. The handmade furniture, which includes modern versions of that old cabinetmaker's work of art, the highboy, are real showstoppers—the priceless antiques of the future.

But this lively affair is more than booths and displays. There are lots of demonstrations by talented men and women from various guilds around the state—a blacksmith laboring at the forge, a tinsmith hamering at metal, and a seamstress turning flax into yarn at a spinning wheel—much to the delight of an audience of fascinated children.

The kids have their own Children's Tent for supervised creative play, art activities, and special entertainment—and many of them manage to coax their parents into a ride on the Mt. Sunapee chair lift, which allows everyone a bird's-eye view of the mountains and lakes of the area.

The big lake is Sunapee, and there's a public beach right in the state park to make the most of it. It is pleasant, albeit crowded. Boating is another favorite pastime. You can either rent your own small crafts at Lake Sunapee Harbor or go out for a two-hour cruise on the big motor vessel *Mt. Sunapee II.* Cruises are also offered on the *Kearsarge,* featuring buffet suppers and beautiful sunsets.

Two pleasant Sunapee lodgings are also favored dining spots. Seven Hearths might be called rustic-sophisticated. Rooms vary in size and decor and are quite pricey for this area; however, there's a pool and an elegant menu. The Inn at Sunapee is a homey farmhouse on a spectacular site with views of lake and mountains, and it also offers a pool and tennis court. Dexter's is another delightful hideaway, tucked high up on a hill with a choice of views—lake on one side, mountain on the other. There's a lot of emphasis on tennis here, and the pool is situated perfectly to make the most of the views.

But there's no getting away from it—you can't really talk about the Sunapee area without mentioning New London, though many generations of Dartmouth students who made their way here to date the women at Colby-Sawyer College certainly will need no introduction to the town.

Don't expect anything big or flashy. The New London Barn Players have been resident summer performers here since 1933, and there are summer concerts on the Colby campus as well. Even so, New London is light years away from being a tourist town—and that's part of its charm. The real pleasure of New London is simply strolling the pretty and unspoiled streets and savoring the relaxed small-town ambience that can make workaday pressures seem a faraway illusion.

The traditional red brick buildings of the Colby campus are right in the center of things on Main Street, and they lead on to a row of handsome white Colonial homes and the requisite white-spired New England church. There are a few crafts and antiques shops for browsing—nothing fancy, but enough to pass the time. You can stop at the New London Creamery for an ice cream cone or a lemonade, and eventually you'll find your way to the New London Inn, either for a meal or for lodgings at night.

The inns in town are not sophisticated resorts, but homey and simple lodgings with down-to-earth rates. The New London Inn is the most historic: The new wing was built in 1806; the rest of the building dates back to 1792. It's a warm and unpretentious place with a fine dining room whose creative menus are among the area's best. Guests at the inn are given passes to the residents-only beach at Little Sunapee, which is about a mile and a half away and much less crowded than the big beach at the big lake.

Past Little Sunapee at the end of a dirt road is an aptly named inn called the Hideaway, an old country house with a big porch spilling over with brightly blooming geraniums. Another hideaway, though not quite so hidden, is the Pleasant Lake Inn, an eighteenth-century farm-house with a view of Pleasant Lake on one side and Mt. Kearsarge on the other. Once again, it's not elaborate, but it's reasonable, attractive, and comfortable, and it has a dining room overlooking the lake and guest privileges at the private beach club just across the way.

One last lodging of special interest to golfers is the Lake Sunapee Country Club and Inn, with rooms within a putt of the starting green and tennis and a pool as well.

The crafts fair, the boating and swimming, some backroads explor-ing and antiquing in other unspoiled little towns nearby like George's Mill and the Suttons, plus a stroll or two down New London's Main Street should easily fill a pair of peaceful country-style days. The eve-nings hold a choice of the New London Players or the Dartmouth Play-ers Repertory Company at Hanover, just half an hour away, as well as the music at King Ridge summer concerts held on the Colby campus.

A highly recommended end to the weekend is a detour north on Route 12A to Cornish and the late-afternoon Sunday concerts at Saint-Gaudens National Historic Site. This is the magnificent home, garden, and studio of Augustus Saint-Gaudens, one of America's greatest sculptors, whose famous *Standing Lincoln* and other works led the way toward realism in sculpture. The mansion is a showplace, and the many-acred grounds are even more spectacular, with a soaring view of hills and mountains beyond. The chamber music series is held in the sky-lit studio, but many people prefer staying out on the lawn to listen while they contemplate the beauty around them.

Lovers of Colonial homes may want to stay over at nearby Chase House, a beautifully restored national landmark. Built in 1775, the Federal-period house was once the home of Salmon Portland Chase, a Chief Justice of the Supreme Court and founder of the Republican Party. If you have a $10,000 bill handy, you'll recognize him there.

Saint-Gaudens is another little-heralded treat in an area filled with unexpected pleasures, not the least of them the no-longer-hidden charms of New London.

New Hampshire Area Code: 603

DRIVING DIRECTIONS   To reach the Lake Sunapee area from the east, take I-93 to I-89 west to exit 12 for New London, south on Route

11 to Mt. Sunapee State Park. From the west, take I-91 to exit 8, go about 13 miles east on Route 103 to the park, then north on Route 11 to New London. New London is 110 miles from Boston, 260 miles from New York, and 150 miles from Hartford. Mt. Sunapee Park is about 10 miles away.

PUBLIC TRANSPORTATION Vermont Transit bus service to Mt. Sunapee and New London.

ACCOMMODATIONS *New London Inn,* Main Street, New London, 526-2791, $$ CP ● *Pleasant Lake Inn,* Box 1030, Pleasant Street, New London, 526-6271, $–$$ ● *Hideaway Lodge,* New London, 526-4861, $$$ MAP ● *Lake Sunapee Country Club and Inn,* Route 11 East, New London, 526-6040, ask about golf packages, $–$$ ● *Dexter's Inn and Tennis Club,* Stagecoach Road, Sunapee, 763-5571, $$$$ MAP ● *The Inn at Sunapee,* Box 336, Sunapee, 763-4444, $$–$$$ CP ● *Seven Hearths,* Old Route 11, Sunapee, $$$$$ MAP ● *The Chase House,* Route 12A, Cornish, 675-5391, $$–$$$ CP.

DINING *The Inn at Sunapee* (see above), good food, unbeatable view, $$ ● *Seven Hearths* (see above), excellent, prix fixe $$$ ● *New London Inn* (see above), tops in town, $$ ● *Pleasant Lake Inn* (see above), $–$$ ● *Hideaway Lodge* (see above), $$–$$$ ● *Millstone,* Newport Road, New London, 526-4201, extensive continental menu, good Sunday brunch, $$ ● *Gray House,* King Ridge Road, New London, 526-6603, mountain views, wide range of foods, reasonable, $–$$ ● *Drummer Boy,* New London, light meals, breakfast served all day, $.

SIGHTSEEING *League of New Hampshire Craftsmen's Fair,* Mount Sunapee State Park, Route 103, Newbury, held annually in early August. Adults, $4; under 12, free. For dates, contact the league at 205 North Main Street, Concord, NH 03301, 224-1471 ● *Mount Sunapee State Park Beach,* 763-2356, June 16 to Labor Day. $2 per car ● *MV Mt. Sunapee II* sails from Sunapee Harbor. Call 763-4030 for current schedules and rates ● *Saint-Gaudens National Historic Site,* Route 12A, Cornish. Hours: late May through October—buildings 8:30 A.M. to 4:30 P.M.; grounds until dark. Adults, $1; under 12, free. Write for current concert schedule.

INFORMATION Lake Sunapee Business Association, PO Box 400, Sunapee, NH 03782, 763-5592; out of state (800) 258-3530.

Smooth Sailing in Boothbay Harbor

Picture postcards of Boothbay Harbor, Maine, resemble paintings of a perfect seacoast village. Views from the land show shimmering light on the water, a montage of masts and deep blue sea studded with pine-rimmed islands. From the sea, you can see the harbor backed by a row of wharves and tiny shops, with trim New England homes, church steeples, and green hills in the distance.

The pictures don't lie. This is as idyllic a spot as you'll find on the Maine coast—or any coast. It is also a lively community full of crowds in summer, a town that can rightfullly boast of being the "boating capital of New England." Boothbay becomes even more picturesque in mid-July during Windjammer Days, when a fleet of many-rigged tall ships makes a stately procession into the harbor. Parades, band concerts, and fireworks also mark the occasion.

But this is one place that needs no special occasion to make your visit an event. You need only board one of the many crafts waiting in the harbor to appreciate just why this is a perennial favorite spot for sailors and yachtsmen. The trip from Boothbay to Monhegan Island in particular is a not-to-be-missed experience for anyone who appreciates untouched natural beauty.

But first you'll want to settle on land, and that can be a pleasantly difficult decision. There are four parts to Boothbay—the village and three fingerlike peninsulas jutting out to sea. Each has its own attractions.

If you want to be within walking distance of the village piers, shops, and restaurants but a bit removed from the bustle, the top choices are just up the steep hill on McKown Street, where simple lodgings come with an unbeatable water view. Topside, which offers both home and motel units with balconies, is the top (and most expensive) choice. Welch House gives you the same view with simpler accommodations in a nineteenth-century sea captain's home or a more modern motel section, known as the Sail Loft. Hilltop House, a guest house, also shares the view.

Spruce Point, a scenic rocky peninsula about five minutes' drive from the village, offers the area's most elegant resort, Spruce Point Inn (coat and tie for dinner), as well as a rustic retreat known as Spruce-wold Lodge, with knotty-pine and fieldstone decor, tennis courts, and a heated pool—not a small matter given the temperature of Maine waters and the scarcity of beaches in the area.

Ocean Point is a bit farther out and a bit more rugged, with a classic rocky shoreline to explore. Ocean Point Inn is off by itself at the entrance to Linekin Bay, a complex of inn and lodge, motel and cottages, with its own dining room, boat excursions, and again that handy heated pool.

But if you really want the sense of being away from it all, head across the bridge from Boothbay to Southport Island. Two rustic inns here have water views to stop you in your tracks, so dazzling you may never want to return to town at all. Don't expect fancy decor at Newagen Inn but do expect an extraordinary site in the middle of a nature preserve jutting directly into the Gulf of Maine. Albonegon Inn (accent on the *nee*), a cozily cluttered little place that calls itself "determinedly old-fashioned," has an equally smashing site on its own tiny island off the mainland with a view of harbor islands, forested peninsulas, and the fishermen's passage that is the gateway to the Atlantic.

These are places where you could easily settle in not just for a relaxing weekend but for a quiet, rejuvenating week or two contemplating the view.

One thing to do as soon as you get to Boothbay Harbor is to head straight for the wharf and make your reservation for an outing on the water. There is a wide choice of boat rides—more than 30 kinds—from an hour's sail to a 41-mile cruise up the Kennebec River to see the ships being built at the Bath Iron Works. Whichever you choose, you'll be gloriously out to sea among picturesque pine-covered islands and lighthouses, where ospreys soar and herons skim, dolphins and seals are at play, and (with a little luck) whales can be sighted in the distance.

For the most extraordinary trip of them all, board the *Balmy Days* for Monhegan Island. Jamie Wyeth, one of the many artists who summer on Monhegan, described the island to a reporter as "like living on a ship, out of sight of land."

The living here is primitive—few telephones, little electricity—and that's just the way those who love the place want to keep it. Part of Monhegan's beauty is its wildness, and the amazing variety of terrain—200-foot cliffs jutting into the sea, virgin forests, ponds and coves, and sighting places along the way for bird and seal watchers with binoculars in hand. The harbor seals are seen best at half-tide on Seal Ledge, and sometimes they can be spied at Lobster Cove and off Fish Beach as well.

You'll be given a map as you come on the island to guide you on your way. There are a few sights to visit—a museum, a lighthouse, and many artists' studios—but the island's most fabulous exhibit is itself. Walking trails are clearly marked on the map for distance and difficulty. The Cathedral Woods are pleasant, cool, and shady and strewn with wildflowers, ferns, and "fairy houses" of sticks and bark, built (according to the guide) to entice woodland fairies to set up housekeeping. The most spectacular walks go straight across the top of the cliffs, offering high-up views of crashing waves on rocky head-lands that may well remain your favorite memories of Maine.

Monhegan takes up an entire day. The *Balmy Days* ships out at 9:15 A.M., arrives at 10:50, and allows you four hours on shore before heading back for a 4:30 P.M. arrival in Boothbay Harbor. Lunch is available at both of the island's laid-back hotels, the Island Inn and the Trailing Yew, and if you are so taken that you want to come back to stay a while, you can make your reservation now for next season—the hotels are often booked a full year ahead.

You'll be back on land in plenty of time to try some of the many restaurants for dinner, and to make the rounds of the shops, most of which are conveniently open in the evening. If you wander the winding narrow streets of town, you'll find some worthwhile stops tucked among the souvenir emporiums. The Custom House on Wharf Street is headquarters for crafts by natives of the state, including original blue-berry pottery. Working metalsmiths are on hand at Silver Lining, and hand-carved puffins are among the offerings at Harbor Decoys.

There are many art galleries for pleasant browsing, including the community-supported Boothbay Region Art Gallery, which displays some of the better work of area artists in changing shows each season. The gallery is housed in the Old Brick House, circa 1807, built by a well-known early builder, John Leisman Jr., who had the bricks im-ported from England. Mark it down for a visit before 5 P.M. The other odd museums in town are recommended only for a rainy day, though kids may enjoy the steam train ride at the Boothbay Railroad Museum and the Aquarium on McKown's Point.

The town of Boothbay Harbor extends across the river via a foot-bridge, but there's little incentive to cross over to East Boothbay unless you want to dine on the deck of the Rocktide, with its postcard view of the harbor on the other side, or eat at Brown Brothers Wharf or the Lobstermen's Cooperative.

Evening entertainment is informal, mostly just live music in places such as Fisherman's Wharf. The Boothbay Dinner Theater offers Broadway shows, as does the Carousel Music Theater, but remember that you're very far off Broadway.

If you spend your Saturday at sea, you might relax on Sunday and enjoy the scenery, try another kind of boat excursion, check out the art gallery, or perhaps make the half-hour drive to Pemaquid Point, an-other of those convoluted peninsulas that mark this part of the coast. This one is reached through the neighboring town of Damariscotta, back on US 1.

One of the lesser-known gems of Maine's shoreline, Pemaquid is a prime example of that much vaunted "rockbound coast," with a pho-togenic old lighthouse, a little fishermen's museum and art gallery, and descending shelves of granite into the sea that are special fun for rock clamberers. The area around the lighthouse has been turned into a park, and the crescent-shaped beach around the bend is open to the public for a fee.

Not only is Pemaquid as dramatic a vantage point as any you'll encounter on the coast, but it offers a bonus for history and archaeology buffs at Ft. William Henry in the new state park that has been developed by the beach. This is where the English held off the French in four successive forts built between 1605 and 1729. The Old Fort House, built for the last battles, has been restored and shouldn't be missed, even if all you want to do is take a scenic snapshot.

North of the fort are the remains of a once-thriving settlement dating back as early as 1620. Archaeologists have unearthed many of the old cellars here, including that of the Customs House, where clearance was required of all ships. Some 40,000 artifacts have been recovered, and a tremendously interesting small museum nearby known as Colonial Pemaquid holds the results of the digs—tools and pottery shards and all manner of possessions reflecting the lives of those who settled on this spot more than 350 years ago.

If you want to have a meal on Pemaquid Point, there's the New Harbor Co-op on the harbor for lobster served indoors or on the deck; Small Brothers, a restaurant that's a bit more expensive and formal than its co-op neighbor; and the Bradley Inn, a pleasant Colonial-style inn on Route 30. The inn, by the way, is a bargain, something to keep in mind if you decide to come back to Pemaquid. Like Monhegan and Southport Island and all the beautiful coast around Boothbay Harbor, it seems to beg for a longer visit.

Maine Area Code: 207

DRIVING DIRECTIONS Boothbay Harbor is 12 miles off US 1 on the midcoast of Maine, 55 miles east of Portland. Turn south off US 1 onto Route 27 about a mile north of Wiscasset and follow it into town. It is 164 miles from Boston, 374 miles from New York, and 264 miles from Hartford.

PUBLIC TRANSPORTATION Greyhound to Wiscasset or plane to Portland; taxi service available from either into Boothbay. You can manage without a car if you stay right in town.

ACCOMMODATIONS *Topside,* McKown Hill, Boothbay Harbor, 633-5404, $$$ ● *Welch House,* McKown Hill, 633-3431, $–$$ ● *Hilltop House,* McKown Hill, 633-2942, $–$$ ● *Spruce Point Inn,* Boothbay Harbor, 633-4152, $$$$$ MAP ● *Sprucewold Lodge,* Boothbay Harbor, 633-3600, $–$$ ● *Ocean Point Inn,* PO Box 409, Shore

Road, East Boothbay, 633-4200, $–$$$ ● *Albonegon Inn,* Capitol Is-
land, 633-2521, $ CP ● *Newagen Inn,* Southport Island, Cape New-
agen, 633-5558, $$–$$$ CP ● *Rocktide,* in town across from the
harbor, 633-4455, $$–$$$ ● *Ocean Gate,* 633-3321, $$$–$$$$, and
Lawnmeer, on Southport Island, 633-2544, $, are among the nicest of
the motels.

DINING   First things first: Lobster! Prices vary with the year and are
less at these informal outdoor eateries ● *Boothbay Region Lob-
stermen's Cooperative,* Atlantic Avenue, East Boothbay, 633-4900, a
working lobster pound serving no-frills lobster and steamers at water-
side picnic tables ● *Seth's Old-Fashioned Lobster Fest,* 633-5490,
cruise to Southport at 5 P.M. daily on the boat *Argo* and go ashore for a
clambake dinner, $$$ ● *Robinson's Wharf,* Route 27 at the bridge,
Southport, full menu as well as lobster, dine outside and watch the
boats go by, $$. Other recommended restaurants ● *Rocktide,* 45 Atlan-
tic Avenue, 633-4455, good seafood, buffets, great view, $–$$$.
They have a free bus that runs regularly to and from the village. Note
that jackets are required in the Dock Room, but not in the Chart Room,
$–$$ ● *Chowder House,* at the footbridge, Boothbay, 633-4074, infor-
mal, outdoor deck on the water, also good for breakfast and lunch, $–
$$ ● *Lawnmeer Inn,* Southport, 630-2544, pleasant atmosphere and
view of inlet, good food, $–$$ ● *Tugboat Inn,* on the pier overlooking
the harbor, 633-4434, seafood, $$–$$$ ● *Black Orchid,* on the By-
Way, 633-6659, interesting menu, $–$$$ ● If your lodging serves
coffee and you want something to go with it, join the line for the 45
varieties at *Sappy's Donuts* in town.

BED AND BREAKFAST   *Bed and Breakfast Down East Ltd.,* Box
547, Eastbrook, ME 04634, 565-3517 ● *Bed and Breakfast of Maine,*
32 Colonial Village, Falmouth, ME 04105, 781-4528.

SIGHTSEEING   Boat trips: *Argo and Linekin II,* Pier 6, 633-4925,
sightseeing cruises daily in season; *Balmy Days to Monhegan,* Pier 8,
leaves 9:15 A.M. daily, 633-2284; *Cap'n Fish's Goodtimes Sightsee-
ing Boat Trips,* daily one-hour excursions from Pier 1, also sunset
cruises, lobster fishing, and nature cruises, 633-3244; *Maranbo II,*
Pier 8, 638-2284, daily cruises; *Miss Boothbay,* Fisherman's Wharf,
633-4925, lobster boat cruises; Sailboat cruises: *Bay Lady,* Pier 1,
633-3244, and *Eastward,* 633-4780. For any new additions and fishing
boat schedules, contact the Chamber of Commerce ● *Boothbay Rail-
way Village,* Route 27 outside of Boothbay, 633-4727. Hours: daily 9
A.M. to 5:30 P.M., mid-June to September. Adults, $4; children, $2 ●
Brick House Gallery, off Townsend Avenue near the footbridge,

Boothbay, 633-2703. Hours: Monday to Saturday, 11 A.M. to 5 P.M., Sunday 2 P.M. to 5 P.M.. Adults, 25 cents; children, free.

INFORMATION Boothbay Harbor Region Chamber of Commerce, Route 27, Boothbay Harbor, ME 04538, 633-2353.

Discovering the Other Nantucket

The day-trippers hardly know it exists. For most of the passengers pouring off the ferry, Nantucket Island means the quaint cobblestoned village with its whaling captain's mansions, rose-covered cottages, shops, beaches—and crowds.

But just a few miles away there's another Nantucket to be found, Siasconset and Wauwinet, two tiny settlements that still miraculously match one eighteenth-century visitor's description: "perfectly unconnected with the real world and far removed from its perturbations."

The better know of the two, universally called 'Sconset, is a beguiling village set between the cranberry bogs and the rose-grown bluffs overlooking the Atlantic. The miniature cottages winding along 'Sconset's lanes suggest its seventeenth- and eighteenth-century origins as a whaling outpost. They are fishermen's shanties that have been altered and added to over the centuries, remnants not only of early America but of a building style that goes back to medieval Wales. Many are unique, built with used wood brought from town or retrieved from shipwrecks, giving rise to the town's nickname of "Patchwork Village."

'Sconset's special flavor began to attract visitors as early as the 1800s. By the end of the century, when the Nantucket Central Railroad extended its narrow-gauge tracks to provide a fast 35-minute ride from town to the village, the passengers included a "who's who" of the American stage. Stars like Lillian Russell and Joseph Jefferson came to vacation in what had become a summer haven for Broadway luminaries.

With the rise of Hollywood, the actors' colony moved westward, leaving 'Sconset's glorious beaches in peace. With the exception of one pleasant little café and a spot for gourmet box lunches, the village square, marked by the antique water pump that once served the entire community, offers little more than basics—food, papers and magazines, liquor, and gasoline.

Tucked behind hedges and a garden down the lane, however, is the

Chanticleer, the island's best (and most expensive) restaurant, where chef Jean-Charles Berruet has held sway for more than a decade creating delicacies such as scallops poached in madeira sauce with truffles and gratin de homard in a lobster sauce with cognac. For lunch, tables are set in a vine-covered arbor outside. Dinner is served in a summery dining room overlooking the garden.

Though many people rent houses here during the summer, there are few lodgings in 'Sconset for transient visitors, one reason the village retains its peaceful air. Summer House, on a bluff at the southeastern edge of the island, is the best of the choices, offering cottage accommodations with access to the beach plus its own pool and cheerful dining spaces. The other possibility is Wade Cottages, a former estate perched on a magnificent seaside bluff. You can rent an entire cottage or a single room here.

Wauwinet, Nantucket's more undiscovered area, is even less developed. It consists of miles of ocean and bayfront beach to tempt strollers, sun worshippers, and fishermen; there are a few houses, one hotel, and not another commercial establishment in sight.

Fishermen were originally attracted to Wauwinet because of the strand of land they dubbed "the Haulaway," a strip separating the calm inner harbor from the open Atlantic where they could literally haul their dories across from one to the other. As in 'Sconset, the fishermen built huts that were expanded over the years, but this community soon centered on Wauwinet House, a rambling gray-shingled beach house opened by James Buckus in 1897 to serve meals for fishermen on its big screened porch. People began asking to stay overnight, and Wauwinet House soon became a thriving summer hotel.

New owners took over recently, keeping the historic exterior of the building but completely gutting the inside to create a 28-room superluxury hotel and cottages, which they call simply The Wauwinet. They've tried to retain a casual feel even while upgrading the decor and adding niceties such as afternoon tea on the front porch.

One thing that has not changed is unending vistas of blue sea. You can play tennis or rent a boat, but this is really the place to do absolutely nothing—just appreciate the rare tranquillity ensured for years to come by the Backus family's bequest of more than 500 acres of surrounding land to the Massachusetts Trustees of Preservation, a conservation group.

Almost everyone here eventually takes off along the four-mile curved beach to Great Point and its lighthouse, rebuilt after a recent storm and now solar powered.

If you want more action, drive or bike the eight or so miles and join the tourists on the cobbled lanes in Nantucket Village, where there are good restaurants, a movie theater, nightspots, and plenty of shops to keep you occupied. The Whaling Museum is just the thing for a cloudy day, as are the elegant homes of the old whale oil merchants. The Information Bureau will provide a brochure of walking tours to the most interesting historic sights, including the lightship *Nantucket*, moored in the harbor.

When you've had your fill of the sights, you can come back to 'Sconset or Wauwinet, leaving crowds and cares behind for the company of the gulls and the sea.

Nantucket Area Code: 508

DIRECTIONS AND TRANSPORTATION   See pages 19–20.

ACCOMMODATIONS   *Summer House*, PO Box 313, Siasconset, 257-9976, May 25 to October 15, $$$$$ CP ● *Wade Cottages*, Siasconset, 257-6308, late May to early October, $$–$$$$ ● *The Wauwinet*, Wauwinet, 228-0145, April to October, $$$$$. A three-day minimum may be required in season; all accommodations are less in May–June and September–October.

DINING   *The Chanticleer*, Siasconset, 257-6231, reservations essential, open late May to mid-October, lunch served June through September, $$$–$$$$; for dinner, prix fixe $$$$$ ● *Summer House* (see above), $$$–$$$$ ● *'Sconset Café*, on the square, Siasconset, 257-4008, $–$$ ● *Claudette's Box Lunches*, on the square, Siasconset, 257-6622, ● *The Wauwinet*, (see above), $$$–$$$$. For additional Nantucket suggestions, see page 20.

SIGHTSEEING   See pages 20–21.

INFORMATION   Nantucket Information Bureau, 25 Federal Street, Nantucket, MA 02554, 228-0925. Nantucket Chamber of Commerce, Main Street, Nantucket, MA 02554, 228-1700.

FALL

Indian Summer in Kennebunkport

Kennebunkport, Maine, is picturesque, posh—and packed with people and cars in midsummer. There's every good reason for all the cars clogging the village center, but since the special pleasures of this seafaring town are not limited to July and August, there's no reason to put up with the crowds.

Instead, mark Kennebunkport down for a warm Indian summer weekend after Labor Day. You can still live in a sea captain's mansion, see the lovely shuttered Colonial homes and enormous summer "cottages," walk the cliffs and the wide beaches, watch the foam spout at Blowing Cave and the sun set at Porpoise Point, and eat all the fresh-caught lobster you can hold—without having to fight for space to do it all.

Kennebunkport has always been a desirable place to be. Even Maine's Indians chose to set up their campgrounds along the beautiful beaches here, and countless artists and writers have been inspired by the views. Kenneth Roberts, a native, immortalized the town in his novel *Arundel* (the name of the village until 1821), and Booth Tarkington wrote his novels from aboard his schooner *Regina,* which was moored on the Kennebunk River for years.

The village became a favorite summer resort for the wealthy in the late 1800s and even now boasts prominent summer residents like former Maine Senator Edmund Muskie and Vice President George Bush, an adopted son who is so much a local favorite that photos of his inauguration adorn postcards sold in the local stores.

In the 1700s, Kennebunkport grew into a port and shipbuilding center second only to Portland on the Maine coast. Eight hundred vessels were launched from its wharves in less than 80 years. The unusual profusion of fine Colonial residences in the central Historic District are testament to the fortunes that were made in the shipbuilding trade.

Though there are lodgings of every kind to be found, one of the particular pleasures of Kennebunkport is to stay in one of the old mansions that now serve as elegant inns. The best known (and for good reason) is the Captain Lord Mansion, built by a wealthy shipbuilder who kept his carpenters occupied during the British blockade of the harbor in 1812 by putting them to work constructing the town's most imposing residence. And grand it remains, a three-story, creamy yellow Federal-style clapboard structure with rows upon rows of tall shuttered windows and an octagonal cupola on top. The three-story stairway, many fireplaces, and ornate Victorian furnishings in the inn's 16 rooms are exceptional.

Needless to say, your odds for getting a reservation are better off season, but do write well ahead anyway. Incidentally, ten of the rooms here have working fireplaces, making this a perfect hideaway all year round. If Captain Lord is full, all is far from lost, for the Captain Jefferds Inn, circa 1804, is another beauty built by an affluent merchant captain, and its antique-filled interior is also exceptional. Less formal but still charming are the 1802 House and the Captain Fairfield House. All of these are open year round.

The Lower Village, the heart of Kennebunkport, is a short stroll from any of these inns. It is a compact area best appreciated on foot. The 1824 South Congregational Church across the way from the shopping area, with its 100-foot white steeple and weathervane-topped Christopher Wren cupola and belfry, is a quintessential New England sight and the subject of many photographs.

Across the way, in the Temple Street post office, you can see a Gordon Grant mural depicting the harbor as it was in the old days, when the air was filled with the clang of shipbuilders' hammers and the cries of crews unloading cargo from around the world. Dock Square, where square-riggers once were moored, is no less busy today as a complex of weathered buildings housing all manner of shops and restaurants. The Dock Square Market Building, moved here in 1849, once housed a Baptist church and a school. The Bookport Building started life as a rum warehouse for Perkins's West India Goods. You'll find almost every kind of clothing and craft for sale here; lots of the fashions are on the preppy side, but the prices are surprisingly fair for a resort town.

From Dock Square, walk down Ocean Avenue past more shops and turn left on Pearl Street, then right on Pleasant to view some of the finest of the sea captain's homes. Green and Maine streets offer more architectural delights.

You'll find art galleries almost everywhere you go, since Kennebunkport remains a magnet for artists. The Art Guild brochure available in most inns and shops lists almost two dozen galleries and studios.

Return to Ocean Avenue and take a very long walk or a drive around rocky Cape Arundel and you'll begin to see what inspires the artists. The rugged coastline here is superb, and there's a bonus if you clamber down the rocks to Spouting Rock and Blowing Cave, where the waves perform a leaping foam dance in rhythm with the tide. Keep going, and you'll see St. Ann's Episcopal Church, built of sea-washed stone just beyond reach of the waves, with the ocean in sight beyond the altar of an outdoor chapel.

There is a beach off Ocean Avenue in town, but the better bet is Goose Rocks Beach, about a ten-minute drive along King's Highway off Route 9. The beach is near Cape Porpoise, whose pier is a center for lobstering and much of the commercial fishing activity of Kennebunkport. It is a scenic spot for photos, especially near sunset.

Two of the best places in town for lobster are in Cape Porpoise. At Nunan's Lobster Hut and Tillie's, both informal eateries on the water, you can have lobsters brought in fresh from the nearby pier. Another eating experience that shouldn't be missed is breakfast at the Green Heron Inn, a many-course delight with wonderful fresh fruits and baked goodies that has become a local institution—as the long waiting lines outside the inn on weekend mornings suggest.

If the shops and galleries pall and the weather isn't conducive to beach walks, visit the Seashore Trolley Museum, which houses one of the largest collections of electric and railway cars in the country, for a bit of nostalgia and an old-fashioned trolley ride. If bargains are more interesting than trolleys, head for Wells and its array of discount stores, which include Dunham and Bass footwear and Hathaway shirts.

Another possibility is the short drive to Kennebunk to see still another magnificent early New England church, the First Parish Unitarian Church, built in 1772. The Christopher Wren steeple was added when the church was enlarged in 1803–04 and a Paul Revere bell was hung at the same time. Kennebunk's tiny Brick Store Museum on the main street offers interesting exhibits from the town's early days, including furniture, paintings, and ship models. Kennebunk lacks its seaside sister's charm, but it does have some interesting historic homes and some fine beaches of its own.

In truth, though, it's hardly likely you'll stray far from Kennebunkport. Ensconced in your own sea captain's quarters with magnificent seascapes, historic homes, and half a hundred shops and galleries just around the corner, why on earth would you want to leave?

Maine Area Code: 207

DRIVING DIRECTIONS Kennebunkport is on the southern coast of Maine, about 25 miles below Portland. From I-95 or US 1, follow Route 35 east into town. Route 9, closer to the shore, also leads to Kennebunkport. It is 88 miles from Boston, 298 miles from New York, and 188 miles from Hartford.

PUBLIC TRANSPORTATION   Greyhound bus service to Bidde-ford, 7 miles. Nearest air service from Portland.

ACCOMMODATIONS   *Captain Lord Mansion,* Box 527, Pleasant and Green streets, 967-3141, $$$–$$$$ CP (less from January 1 to April 30, and the rooms have fireplaces!) ● *Captain Jefferds Inn,* Pearl and Pleasant streets, Box 691, 967-2311, $$$ CP ● *Captain Fairfield House,* Box 202, Ocean Avenue, 967-4454, $$$ CP ● *1802 House,* Box 774C, Locke Street, 967-5632, $$$ CP ● *The Colony,* Ocean Avenue and King's Highway, 967-3331, the big, staid classic hotel in town, $$$$–$$$$$ AP ● *Old Fort Inn,* Old Fort Avenue, 967-5353, secluded and rustic, with pool and tennis court, $$–$$$$$ CP.

BED AND BREAKFAST   *Bed and Breakfast of Maine,* 32 Colonial Village, Falmouth, ME 04105, 781-4528. ● *Bed and Breakfast Down East Ltd.,* Box 547, Eastbrook, ME 04634, 565-3517.

DINING   *Tillie's,* Pier Road, Cape Porpoise, 967-2410, lobsters, chowder, seafood, $–$$ ● *Nunan's Lobster Hut,* Route 9, Cape Porpoise, another lobster spot, $–$$ ● *White Barn Inn,* Beach Street, 967-2321, charmingly restored barn, excellent fare, $–$$ ● *Kennebunkport Inn,* Dock Square, 967-2621, gracious, $$–$$$ ● *The Olde Grist Mill,* Mill Lane off Route 9, 967-4781, New England fare in a real old mill, $$–$$$. Almost any of the cafés in Dock Square are safe bets for an informal meal, and the ice cream parlor has terrific apple strudel.

SIGHTSEEING   *Seashore Trolley Museum,* Log Cabin Road, Box 220, Kennebunkport, 967-2712. Hours: daily, mid-June to Labor Day, rides every half hour 10 A.M. to 5 P.M.; late April to mid-June, and Labor Day through October, 12 noon to 5 P.M. weekends, from 1:30 P.M. weekdays. Adults, $3.50; under 16, $2 ● *Brick Store Museum,* 117 Main Street, Kennebunk, 985-4892. Hours: Tuesday to Saturday, 10 A.M. to 4:30 P.M. Adults, $2; children, $1.

INFORMATION   Kennebunk–Kennebunkport Chamber of Commerce, 105 Main Street, Kennebunk, ME 04043, 985-3608.

Inns and Arts of Vermont

Inn fever is an epidemic that strikes thousands in New England, and it is highly contagious. You'll find victims in small towns and on back roads everywhere, ready to travel any lengths to track down a new and choice country inn.

If you share this delightfully incurable affliction, you'll find the southwestern corner of Vermont a happy inn-hunting grounds. Within a wiggly scenic rectangle roughly 30 by 21 miles with Dorset, Bennington, Wilmington, and Jamaica as the corners, there are dozens of inns to be found. Ten among them, both modest and extravagant, can rightfully be called exceptional, each in its own way.

To make the quest even more rewarding, the route is rich in art, with prize galleries as well as one of Vermont's major annual exhibitions, the month-long fall Stratton Arts Festival. Add the scenery of an area with four major ski mountains, lots of opportunity for hikes and canoeing, and more shops than you can fit into a month of weekends, and you have a year-round destination that becomes absolutely unbeatable in foliage season.

The major commercial center is Manchester, a town that likes to call itself Manchester and the Mountains to underscore its role as the heart of this cluster of villages. Since it is within easy reach no matter where you choose to stay, Manchester makes an ideal starting point for an inns-and-arts tour.

There's plenty to see and do right here, and you'll find lots of information and guidance at the Visitors Booth on the Green on Route 7 in Manchester Center. You'll also find cars—long lines of them—clogging the intersection of Routes 30, 11, and 7. The lure is Manchester Commons, a shopping complex that includes outlets for Polo/Ralph Lauren, Benetton, and many other upscale labels. Right across the street is Battenkill Plaza where Anne Klein, Kidsport USA (Healthtex), and Van Heusen stores beckon.

There are some area old-timers to the south on Route 7 as well, stores that can help keep you warm in winter, like Landau for Icelandic sweaters, the Overland Sheepskin Store, and Herdsmen Leathers. The usual Vermont shoe outlets—Bass, Dexter, and Dunham—are also in residence.

If shopping is not your sport, outdoor enthusiasts should note that there are three golf courses plus public tennis courts in town, and more facilities not far away at Stratton Mountain. For more outdoor activity, bikes are for rent at Battenkill Sports and Vermont Pedal Pushers, both on merged Route 11/30, and there's plenty of hiking in the area, with both the Long Trail and the Appalachian Trail nearby. Stop at the U.S. Forest Service headquarters on the way to Bromley Mountain, north of Manchester on Route 11/30, for maps and guidance.

There are two main sightseeing stops around Manchester, both offering expansive hilltop views as well as a chance to get out and walk. The Southern Vermont Art Center, a gracious mansion on 375 sylvan acres, has changing exhibits of art, sculpture, and photography and also offers nature walks, including a botany trail with 67 varieties of wildflowers. The Garden Café here is a highly recommended stop for lunch or brunch with a view.

Hildene is the Georgian mansion built by Robert Todd Lincoln, Abraham's son, and occupied by descendents of the Lincoln family until 1975. It is one of the more fascinating historic houses to visit and offers a wagon ride and a demonstration of the mansion's 1,000-pipe organ. Hildene sits on 412 acres with formal gardens and walking trails, and you can picnic here with the valley below spread before you in its best autumn colors.

When it comes to inns, drive six miles northwest to Dorset, the northern tip of your driving tour, for three lovely lodgings in a tranquil Colonial oasis. Barrows House is a world of its own, a collection of houses centered by a 1784 mansion, all set amid towering trees and well-groomed gardens. This is one of the most exquisite inns around and offers its guests tennis courts, a pool, a croquet court, and a gazebo for sitting and enjoying the setting. The excellent restaurant is prettier than ever with a recently added greenhouse wall. The rooms are on the small side for such exclusive lodgings, but Barrows remains among the handful of inns generally considered to be the region's finest.

Village Auberge, a small and elegant Dorset farmhouse, is best known as a restaurant with fine continental cuisine; but the rooms are charming as well. By now there will be even more of them if a recent expansion has been completed.

The Dorset Inn is still another very attractive possibility, located right on the pretty little Main Street of town. The inn offers lots of Colonial atmosphere and a highly regarded dining room.

The fighting-mad Green Mountain Boys signed their personal declaration of independence in Dorset, an event remembered by a marker in the center of town. In the peaceful moneyed Dorset of today, a more significant claim to fame may be what is reputedly the oldest nine-hole golf course in the country, the Dorset Field Club course open to guests of local inns. The Dorset Playhouse is one of the few summer theaters that remains open into the foliage season, and the town has several stops for antiquers.

Though you'll spy plenty of antiques shops in Manchester and all the way along your drive, avid antiquers may want to add a detour a few miles farther north on Route 7 to Danby, where the Danby Antiques Center has 24 dealers under one roof. A detour for apples instead of antiques will take you to the other side of Route 7 to Mad Tom's Orchard in East Dorset, where you can pick your own delicious Vermont apples to go with the Vermont cheese and maple syrup you'll probably acquire in a country store en route.

Returning to Manchester and heading south, take historic Route 7A to Manchester Village. This was a posh resort during the pre-Civil War days when its Equinox House was a well-known summer retreat, and it still boasts the marble slab sidewalks and handsome homes from those glory days. The village is looking very spiffy once again since restoration of the grand old hotel was completed, and it now has many upscale shops to tempt the upscale visitors. The hotel itself offers golf, tennis, and a well-equipped spa.

Two really choice smaller inns are just a stone's throw from the Equinox. The Reluctant Panther, a 150-year-old house, is on the whimsical side with lots of lavender paint and eclectic decor, while the 1811 House is as elegant a country inn as you'll find, beautifully furnished and sitting on three acres of lawn and gardens.

Continuing south, one of those ubiquitous country stores awaits on Route 7A in Arlington, as well as a shop and museum featuring the works of Norman Rockwell, a one-time village resident. Detour onto Old Mill Road for Candle Mill Village, eight shops in a former gristmill beside a waterfall. The specialty here is candles—some 50,000 of them—and if none of them please, you can dip your own. There are also shops that offer 1,000 kinds of cookbooks and more than 600 kinds of music boxes.

The Arlington Inn on Route 7A is a most impressive cream-colored mansion done in high Victorian style and graced with big, airy rooms. Take the road just opposite the mansion to see the West Mountain Inn, with simpler rooms but a warm country ambience and an unbeatable mountain view.

On the way to West Mountain, you'll pass the Battenkill River and a rental outlet for canoes as well as tubes for floating downriver, an increasingly popular sport in the summer in these parts.

When you come into Bennington, turn right on Route 7 to historic Old Bennington, a stately beauty of a village with a host of magnificent eighteenth- and nineteenth-century homes. On the way you'll pass the impressive columned Bennington Museum, which offers free walking tour pamphlets of the old part of town and a delightful gallery devoted to one of the region's better-known painters, former resident Grandma Moses, who captured the surrounding Vermont landscapes with so much color and naïve charm. There are 32 of her works on display, and if perchance you've never seen an original Grandma Moses, you have a treat in store. The museum also contains a military gallery, an excellent and comprehensive collection of American pressed glass, including pieces by Louis Comfort Tiffany, and examples of the well-known brown-glazed Bennington pottery.

Continuing west on Route 9, turn right on the main street of Old Bennington and drive up the hill to the impressive 360-foot stone obelisk commemorating the famous Battle of Bennington, a major turning point in the Revolutionary War. It was here that General John

Stark turned back the British, saying, "There are the Redcoats and they are ours, or this night Molly Stark sleeps a widow." The tall monument on the hill can be seen for miles around, and the elevator ride to the top affords an unforgettable view of the countryside. There is also a diorama depicting the battle, done by Vermont artist Paul Winters.

Take a walk down the hill from the monument to really appreciate the details of the gracious houses on both sides of the road, with the walking tour as a guide to each home's history. At the bottom on the green is the Walloomsac Inn, said to be the oldest continuously oper-ated inn in Vermont. It's doubtful you'll want to stay in this inn, which is looking rather the worse for its 220-plus years of wear, but it is definitely worth a visit.

Another place to visit in town is the Potter's Yard. Follow Route 7 two lights north of Route 9, then turn on County Street to the place where Bennington pottery was founded more than three decades ago on the site of a former gristmill. Though the pottery works are still very much in operation, most of the pieces now are modern rather than copies of the originals. There is a tremendous collection of pottery pieces in an attractive shop that also includes a small section selling woven goods and baskets from around the world. A store next door features fine glassware, and another adjoining shop carries cooking wares.

Time your visit for lunch to sample the gourmet fare at the Bras-serie, founded by the late chef Dione Lucas and still an outstanding restaurant. Only lunch and Sunday brunch are served here, from a menu that lists 12 kinds of omelettes, great onion soup, and dis-tressingly tempting desserts.

From Bennington proceed west on Molly Stark's Route 9, a heavily wooded and very scenic road along a river that will bring you to Wilmington. Once a sleepy village, Wilmington has had an infusion of energy from all the skiers who come to town for Haystack Mountain or nearby Mt. Snow, and is now pleasantly alive with restaurants, inns, and shops that make for a half-hour of very pleasant browsing. Check out Quaigh Design Center for top Vermont crafts and Down in the Valley for quilts and good prices on ski wear. There's another shot at a country store here too.

Turn left on Route 100 north and then make another left at Cold-brook, the road to Haystack Mountain, for the Hermitage, a gracious old inn above the mountain, set on 24 acres of woods and fields that make for prime ski touring in winter and provide a view that goes on forever. Prize game and fowl, raised by the owner, are a specialty of the inn dining room, along with trout from a pond on the property. The rooms here are big and handsome, the inn warm and welcoming.

But you've saved the very best inn for last. Come back to Route

100, continue north a few miles to West Dover, and cross the bridge to the Inn at Sawmill Farm, to see a hideaway straight from the pages of a magazine. This one-time barn and stable is now an antique-filled inn making the best use of the soaring heights and beams of the old barn. The rustic setting is softened with warm brick and fieldstone, and all manner of attractive and comfortable upholstered pieces with mellowed brass accent pieces. It's sophisticated and elegant yet country in feel, and the fare in the beautiful dining room does justice to its surroundings. It goes almost without saying that the inn is expensive, but if you can afford the tab for one of the 20 rooms (10 of them with fireplaces), you may have found the ultimate inn.

Having completed the inn circuit, you may be able to sample more arts at Mt. Snow, farther north on Route 100, where a crafts fair is held in early October. For the best of the arts, however, continue north to the intersection of Route 30 at Jamaica (last chance for a country store), and then turn west to the mammoth show at Stratton Mountain. The Stratton Arts Festival, which began in 1964 as a Columbus Day art show with 30 participants, has grown into the state's largest and finest display of local talent. Today it is a kaleidoscope of textures and colors, with more than 300 carefully chosen exhibitors showing oils and watercolors, metal and stone sculpture, prints and photographs, and handcrafted clay, metal, and fiber pieces. Exhibitors are present on weekends to demonstrate their work and talk about their craft.

The performing arts also share the weekend Stratton spotlight. More than 15,000 people came last year for music, drama, and dance performances, many of them commissioned especially for the festival.

It might be possible to do all this in a day—but it's not probable, or advisable. You'd do better to head back to your inn when your energy flags and save half the route for a second day, allowing plenty of time for enjoying the views, the out of doors, and your own discoveries along the way.

In fact, you could spend many a happy weekend exploring the varied pleasures of this rich section of southern Vermont. When you've gotten back home, stored the apples and cheese and maple syrup, settled on a spot for your newly bought finds, and taken the film to be developed, you can begin figuring out which of those wonderful inns to try when you come back for a repeat performance.

Vermont Area Code: 802

DRIVING DIRECTIONS Manchester is on Route 7 at the intersections of Routes 11 and 30. It is 160 miles from Boston, 248 miles from New York, and 138 miles from Hartford.

PUBLIC TRANSPORTATION   Vermont Transit provides bus service to Manchester; closest air service is Eastern Express to Rutland, 30 minutes away.

ACCOMMODATIONS   *Reluctant Panther Inn,* Box 678, Route 7, Manchester Village, 362-2568, $$$–$$$$ CP • *1811 House,* Route 7A, Manchester Village, 362-1811, $$$$ CP • *Equinox Hotel,* Route 7A, Manchester Village, 362-4747, $$$$–$$$$$ • *The Barrows House,* Dorset, 867-4455, $$$$–$$$$$ MAP • *Village Auberge,* Dorset, 867-5715, $$–$$$ • *The Dorset Inn,* Church and Main streets, Dorset, $$$$ MAP • *Arlington Inn,* Route 7A, Arlington, 375-6532, $$–$$$ • *West Mountain Inn,* Route 313, Arlington, 375-6516, $$$$ • *The Hermitage,* Cold Brook Road off Route 100, Wilmington, 464-3759, $$$$$ MAP • *The Inn at Sawmill Farm,* Box 367, Mt. Snow Valley, West Dover, 464-8131, $$$$–$$$$$ MAP. For less expensive inns, motels, and ski lodges, try the Manchester Chamber of Commerce and the Stratton Mountain Reservation Service, (800) 843-6867.

BED AND BREAKFAST   *Vermont Bed and Breakfast Reservation Service,* PO Box 1, East Fairfield, VT 05448, (802) 827-3827 • *American Country Collection of Bed and Breakfasts,* 984 Gloucester Place, Schenectady, NY 12309, (518) 370-4948.

DINING   All of the above inns, mostly $$–$$$. • *The Brasserie,* Bennington, lunch only, $ • *Garlic John's,* Routes 11/30, Manchester, 362-9843, cheerful spot for pasta and spaghetti, $–$$ • *The Black Swan,* Route 7A, Manchester, 362-3807, continental fare in an old farmhouse, $$–$$$ • *Chantecleer,* Route 7 north of Manchester, 362-1616, Swiss and Provençal specialties, $$–$$$ • *River Café,* Bondville, 297-1010, sandwiches, salads, pasta, $.

SIGHTSEEING   *Stratton Mountain Arts Festival,* Stratton Mountain Base Lodge, Route 30, Bondville, 297-2200. Hours: mid-September to mid-October, daily 9:30 A.M. to 5 P.M.; contact for current admission and dates • *Historic Hildene,* Route 7A, Manchester Village, 362-1788. Hours: mid-May through October, daily 9:30 A.M. to 5:30 P.M. Adults, $5; children, $2 • *Southern Vermont Art Center,* off West Road, Manchester, 362-1405. Hours: early June to mid-October, Tuesday to Saturday and Monday holidays, 10 A.M. to 5 P.M., Sunday from 12 noon. Adults, $3; under 13, free; free to all on Sunday • *Bennington Museum,* West Main Street, 447-1571. Hours: March 1 to November 30, daily 9 A.M. to 5 P.M. Adults, $4; 12 to 16, $3; under 12, free. Family rate, $10.

INFORMATION **INFORMATION**   Manchester and the Mountains Chamber of Commerce, PO Box 928, Manchester Center, VT 05255, 362-2100. Bennington Chamber of Commerce, Route 7, Bennington, VT 05201, 442-5900. Stratton Mountain, Bondville, VT 05155, 297-2200 or (800) 843-6867.

Back to Nature on Cape Cod

For true beach and nature lovers, the real Cape Cod does not begin until you reach the "elbow," the bend that marks the break from the calm waters of Nantucket Sound to the rough surf of the Atlantic.

The wide, sandy dune-backed ocean shores beginning here and stretching for 40 unbroken miles from Chatham and Orleans to the tip of Provincetown are as fine as any beach area in the country. Thanks to the National Park Service, which took over when most of the area was declared a National Seashore in 1961, not only the beach but the fragile 27,000 acres of marshes, meadows, and ponds around it have been protected to provide recreation and beauty for swimmers, surfers, hikers, bikers, and horseback riders as well as for anyone who just wants to sit on an uncrowded beach and contemplate the hypnotic rhythms of the sea.

But ask anyone who knows the Cape and its seasons and you'll learn that the seashore is at its most glorious in September, just when most of the tourists leave. The days are generally bright and sunny, but not too hot for outdoor activity; the evenings are cool and breezy, the better to enjoy the indoor pleasures of dining in good restaurants now relieved of their summer crowds. As a special bonus, it is during these cooler and calmer days of early fall that the many artists on the Cape hold their annual open houses and special shows.

This is ideal bed-and-breakfast territory, since private home accommodations often allow you to stay in wooded settings in towns like Truro that don't offer inns or hotels.

When it comes to inn lodgings, the Bradford Inn in Provincetown and the Duck Creeke in Wellfleet are pleasant possibilities, but the choicest accommodations are in East Orleans near Nauset Beach, the first major public beach within the National Seashore. Ship's Knees Inn is a trim, snug nautical haven right up the hill from the beach, with a pool and tennis court. About a mile farther up is Nauset House, a delightfully renovated and antique-filled farmhouse boasting a plant- and wicker-filled glass conservatory that is cheerful even on the gloomiest day.

As the shopping center for the lower Cape, Orleans has been invaded recently by discount stores and fast food outlets, but outside the commercial center it remains a placid and attractive town with some of the best restaurants in the area. It also provides necessary shops and diversions in the unhappy event of rain (The Artful Hand is the pick of the crafts galleries), and such worldly pleasures as gourmet ice cream in a branch of Boston's Emack and Bolio's as well as a local outlet known as the Sundae School in East Orleans.

Once you've settled in, begin your explorations with a stop at either the Salt Pond visitors' center at Eastham or the Province Lands center near Provincetown, both right off the main highway (Route 6) and clearly marked. Both are well supplied with excellent maps of hiking, biking, and riding trails and beach locations, as well as schedules of ranger-guided walks and talks at the National Seashore.

The well-tended trails of the National Seashore are designed to show the variety of the terrain as well as the ever changing effects of wind and water on this fragile land, where one place is often torn down while another is built up. The power of erosion is clearly seen at the Marconi Wireless Station at Wellfleet, where the Cape is only a mile wide. Much of the cliff has disappeared along with the towers that Guglielmo Marconi built there to transmit the first wireless communication from America to Europe in 1903. Both sites are victims of the relentless tides that take away an average of three feet of coastline each year.

The Marconi site leads into the Atlantic White Cedar Swamp Trail, where lush green vegetation surrounds walkers as they thread their way through the swamp on an elevated boardwalk. There are many other trails for taking in the salt ponds, forests, and dunes. On any of the paths, you are also liable to find yourself suddenly in a clearing with pond or sweeping ocean views, a scenic bonus that often appears in unexpected places.

There are still more nature trails to be found at the Massachusetts Audubon Society headquarters in Wellfleet. And when you've had enough nature for one day, there are two more worldly visitors' paths away from the seashore for a pleasant change of pace. One afternoon will do nicely for the galleries in Wellfleet and the historic narrow streets of Provincetown, particularly since even the museums stay open late in lively Provincetown.

Wellfleet, a small, no-longer-sleepy town of church spires and white Colonial homes, has developed into an art center. The local printed guide, available in any of the shops, lists a dozen or so galleries and shops offering paintings, crafts, and sculpture, and handicrafts or antiques. The shops are easy to find, since most are right on Main Street or around the bend on Commercial Street. The Spectrum is worth a special look. In mid-September, Wellfleet joins the rest of the lower

Cape in the Fall Arts Festival, with performances, workshops, concerts, and readings as well as open studio demonstrations by many local artists. The town adds its own "Bygone Day," offering house tours, parades, boat races, and other fun.

An hour or two of browsing should suffice in Wellfleet, and another 10-minute drive to the tip of the Cape will bring you to Provincetown. With its spectacular dunes and open beach, this is the most beautiful area of the seashore, and the view from the deck of the Visitors Center should not be missed.

It was at Provincetown, not Plymouth, that the Pilgrims first landed in 1620. The Mayflower Compact, drawn up during their five-week stay before heading for more sheltered waters, is considered the root of democratic government in America. A bronze plaque set into a boulder at the west end of Commercial Street on the present-day harbor marks the landing place. The tallest granite structure in the United States, the 255-foot Pilgrim Monument, was added in 1910 as a memorial and landmark for fishermen, sailors, and tourists alike. If it is open when you come (off-season hours are erratic), climb to the top for a view of the entire Cape and across the bay to Plymouth. On a clear day you can even see Boston.

Provincetown itself is a town with several distinct personalities. The Provincetown Heritage Museum, a national landmark, houses both reminders of the nineteenth-century whaling and fishing village and works that reflect the town's later emergence as an art colony. Local luminaries include Hans Hofman and Edward Hopper.

The Provincetown Art Association and Museum, established in 1914, has an outstanding permanent collection of 500 works and features emerging artists as well. Its membership is a "who's who" of the American art world. There are two other galleries to be visited: the Provincetown Group Gallery, a showcase for 25 artists living and working in the town, and the summer gallery at the Fine Arts Center, a working retreat for artists and writers from October to May.

Provincetown plans a leading role in the annual Fall Arts Festival, usually running for two weeks in September. Contact the Lower Cape Arts and Humanities Council for this year's exact dates.

Writers and poets were also inspired by the beauty of Provincetown. The list is an eminent one, boasting Eugene O'Neill, John Dos Passos, Tennessee Williams, and Sinclair Lewis among others. Many famous actors also appeared at the Provincetown Playhouse early in their careers.

Present-day Provincetown retains some of the flavor of the past. The artists and writers are still present, poet Robert Kunitz and painter Robert Motherwell among them. Fishermen can still be seen at work at MacMillan Wharf, and their presence adds the bonus of good Portuguese food in town. And the waterfront along Commercial Street remains as beautiful as ever, despite the crowds that clog the sidewalks. The Dolphin Fleet at the Wharf is the best known of the groups offering a taste of the past on whale-watching cruises.

Commercial Street has become a kind of outdoor theater for the arty and the showy, and for couples of the same sex and the opposite sex. Some find it fascinating; others consider it a turnoff. Whatever your reaction, you'll find things considerably calmer off season—and if you have dinner at the Red Inn, rest assured you'll have no quibble about the view.

Cape Cod Area Code: 508

DRIVING DIRECTIONS   Cape Cod is reached via Route 3 south from Boston or via I-195 or I-495 from the west. The Mid-Cape Highway, Route 6, goes directly to Orleans and is the only main road continuing from there to the tip at Provincetown. Orleans is 86 miles from Boston, 296 miles from New York, and 186 miles from Hartford.

PUBLIC TRANSPORTATION   PBA (Provincetown-Boston Airlines—reservations through Continental Airlines) and Peter Pan and Bonanza buses serve Provincetown and Hyannis; Bonanza also makes stops in Orleans, Eastham, and Wellfleet. There is also boat service from Boston to Provincetown; contact the Cape Cod Chamber of Commerce for current schedules.

ACCOMMODATIONS   *Nauset House Inn,* Beach Road, PO Box 774, East Orleans, 255-2195, $$–$$$ ● *Ship's Knees Inn,* Beach Road, East Orleans, 255-1312, $$ CP ● *The Inn at Duck Creeke,* E. Main Street, Wellfleet, 349-9333, $$ ● *Bradford Gardens,* 178 Bradford Street, Provincetown, 487-1616, $$–$$$ CP ● A motel worth noting is *Nauset Knoll,* East Orleans, 255-2364, directly across from Nauset Beach. Besides having fabulous views of beach and ocean, you save $10 on beach parking fees on weekends, $7.50 during the week. There are dozens of additional motels all along Route 6, and one pleasant Victorian inn, the *Overlook Inn,* just off the highway in Eastham, 255-1886, $$ CP.

BED AND BREAKFAST   *Bed and Breakfast Cape Cod,* Box 341, West Hyannisport, MA 02672, 775-2772 ● *House Guests,* PO Box 1881, Orleans, MA 02653, 896-7053 ● *Orleans Bed and Breakfast Associates,* Box 1312, Orleans, MA 02653, 255-3824.

DINING   *Captain Linnell House,* Skaket Road, Orleans, 255-3400, 1840s mansion, excellent continental food, $$–$$$ ● *The Barley Neck*

Inn, Beach Road, East Orleans, 255-6830, Colonial decor, longtime local favorite, $$–$$$ ● *Sweet Seasons,* at the Inn at Duck Creeke (see above), especially good for seafood, $$ ● *The Arbor,* Route 28, Orleans, 255-4847, attractive, continental menu, good value, $–$$ ● *The Red Inn,* 15 Commercial Street, Provincetown, 487-0050, fabulous water view, $$–$$$ ● *The Moors,* Beach Road and Bradford Street, Provincetown, 487-0840, Portuguese, $$ ● *Napi's,* 7 Freeman Street, Provincetown, 487-1145, delightful eclectic menu, $$ ● *Gene Greene's Terrace,* 133 Bradford Street, 487-0558, on the elegant side, $$$ ● Definitely worth a drive is *Café Elizabeth,* 31 Sea Street, Harwich Port, 432-1147, one of the Cape's best, $$$–$$$$ ● For lobster, *The Eastham Lobster Pool,* Route 6, Eastham, and in Wellfleet, the *Bayside Lobster Hutt,* on Commercial Street, where you order at the window, eat family-style, and get good food at good prices ● Other places to note in Orleans: *Cap'n Cass* on Rock Harbor, a tiny place with the best lobster roll to be found; *Philbrick's* at Nauset Beach, a beachside stand with amazingly good fried clams and onion rings; and the *Brown Bag,* Old Colony Way for terrific breakfasts. For evening entertainment, try the *Barley Neck* in Orleans or the *Tavern* at the Inn at Duck Creeke in Wellfleet.

SIGHTSEEING *Cape Cod National Seashore,* five public beaches, ten guided nature trails, three bicycle trails, riding trails, ranger lectures, and walks. Salt Pond Visitors' Center, Route 6, Eastham, 255-3421. Hours: 9 A.M. to 5 P.M. in fall, 6 P.M. in summer. Ten-minute orientation film, much free literature; Province Lands Visitor Center, off Race Point Road, Provincetown, 487-1256, same hours, 20-minute orientation film, free literature, great view from the deck ● *Provincetown Heritage Museum,* Commercial and Center streets, 487-0666. Hours: daily 10 A.M. to 8 P.M. Adults, 2; under 12, free ● *Provincetown Art Association and Museum,* 460 Commercial Street, 487-1750. Hours: Memorial Day through September, daily 12 noon to 4 P.M. and 7 P.M. to 10 P.M. Adults, $2; children, $1 ● *Provincetown Group Gallery,* 286 Bradford Street (upstairs at Provincetown Tennis Club), 487-0275. Hours: June through October, daily 11 A.M. to 4 P.M., and 6 P.M. to 8 P.M. Free. ● *Dolphin Fleet,* MacMillan Pier, Provincetown, 255-3857, whale-watching cruises mid-April to October; phone for rates and schedules.

INFORMATION Cape Cod Chamber of Commerce, Routes 6 and 132, Hyannis, MA 02601, 362-3225. Provincetown Chamber of Commerce, 307 Commercial Street at MacMillan Wharf, PO Box 1017, Provincetown, MA 02657, 487-3424. For information on Fall Arts Festival events, contact Lower Cape Arts and Humanities Council, PO Box 132, Provincetown, MA 02657.

Fair Weather at Fryeburg

When's the last time you saw an oxen-pull competition? How about a pig scramble or a sheep-judging show or an old-time fiddler's contest? For that matter, when did you last watch someone milking a cow?

From July to October, country fairs are in high gear all over the New England states, a harvest ritual that gives farmers a showcase for their crops and livestock, homemakers a place to exhibit their prize baking and canning, and city folks an opportunity for some old-fashioned down-on-the-farm fun.

Maine saves the best for the last—the West Oxford Agricultural Society Fair at the very end of September in Fryeburg, a town in the western part of the state near New Hampshire's White Mountains. This event celebrates its 140th year in 1990. It's the biggest fair in Maine in what just might be the prettiest fairground setting in New England, with a mountain peak as a backdrop.

To make it even better, Fryeburg is an easy drive from the heart of lake country as well as from Maine's share of the White Mountain National Forest, so you can have your pick of scenery at the height of foliage season.

At Fryeburg you'll see the traditional "pull" competitions—oxen, horses, ponies, and tractors all hauling heavy loads that make moving, much less racing, almost impossible. There's a woodmen's field day when ax-chopping contests make chips fly, a milking parlor, and all the livestock and agricultural judging you'd expect at a major event of this kind.

Some things you might not expect include a wreath maker's demonstration, sheep dog races, and a shuffleboard tournament. Of course, there is a midway with plenty of rides and games for kids big and small, plus country music, a motorcycle thrill show, and harness racing to keep things lively at night. Friday night's fun is capped with fireworks.

Assuming you are working your way west to Fryeburg from Portland on Route 302, you'll pass through Naples, the place to board for boat rides on the lakes, and Bridgton, the shopping center of the lakes area and a mecca for antiques and crafts collectors.

From the top of Pleasant Mountain in Bridgton, you can get the lay of the land, or rather the lakes, for some 50 bodies of water can be seen here. The Sebago–Long Lake chain, made up of Sebago, the state's second largest lake, plus Little Sebago, the Songo River, Long Lake, and numerous lesser lakes and streams, covers hundreds of square miles, including the 1,300-acre Sebago Lake State Park, a fine place for a picnic with a water view.

If you want an even loftier view, the ski lift at Pleasant Mountain may be open for scenic rides. And you can stay right on the base of the mountain at Pleasant Mountain Inn, a secluded rustic condo cottage resort on Moose Pond. Westways on Kezar Lake in Center Lovell is an even more appealing lakefront cottage resort, and the Noble House, a bed-and-breakfast inn in Bridgton, offers swimming privileges and boating on Highland Lakes.

But deciding where to stay is something of a dilemma because there are so many tempting possibilities. Once the peak vacation period ends, weekend reservations become available at one of the loveliest of the rustic lakeside resorts, Migis Lodge on Sebago, where a week's stay is usually required in summer. Migis is an escapist's dream, with cottages in the pines on 90 acres bordering the deep blue lake. The trees go right to the water's edge, and pine-covered islands in the lake add to the idyllic scene. Though autumn nights can be cool in lake country, you won't mind them here with your own fireplace in your own cozy cottage. And since late September days are often warm and sunny, the location is ideal for hiking the many woodland trails on the grounds or enjoying the lodge's fleets of boats.

Through September, you can also enjoy a ride on the *Songo River Queen II*, a 90-foot paddlewheeler out of Naples that offers one-hour cruises on Long Lake and longer trips through the narrow Songo River lock into the expanse of Sebago Lake.

For those who prefer to paddle their own canoe, the Saco is a popular waterway, especially the broad, flat, and scenic portion from the New Hampshire state line to Hiram. There are many places to rent canoes in the area, including Saco River Canoe and Kayak on Route 5 north of Fryeburg and the Sportshaus on Main Street in Bridgton.

North of Bridgton you'll find two other towns for possible lodging, both quaint, picture-perfect New England villages that are lovelier than ever when their white clapboard houses and church steeples stand out in sparkling relief against the bright autumn foliage.

In Bethel, the gracious Bethel Inn and Country Club faces an entire village common that has been declared a National Historic District. Golfers will enjoy the course here with its splendid views. Rockhounds too may enjoy being in Bethel, an area rich in minerals. Stop at the Gem Shop on Route 2 north of town or Perham's Maine Mineral Store in West Paris to see some of the local finds. The shops should be able to tell you where to go for your own finds. Bumpus Mine on Routes 5 and 35 is one possibility; there are other defunct mines along many hiking paths.

The second town, Waterford, is best described by its most celebrated resident, Charles Farrar Browne, better known as Artemus Ward, one of America's most famous early humorists. A favorite of Abraham Lincoln and an inspiration for Mark Twain, Ward once said: "The village . . . is small. It does not contain over 40 houses, all told;

but they are milk white with the greenest of blinds and for the most part are shaded with beautiful elms and willows. To the right of us is a mountain—to the left a lake. The village nestles between.'' There are three inns in this gem of a village, all recommended. If you stay in Waterford, you'll find Mt. Tir'em a relatively easy climb that is rewarded with a view of five lakes.

There are other pleasant small inns scattered about the area, including the Oxford House, right in Fryeburg. Add the Fryeburg fair, the lakes, and a few country walks and you've almost filled a weekend.

But be sure to block out some time for the nearby White Mountain foothills—spectacular scenery that shouldn't be missed, especially during foliage season. For a rewarding day, pack a picnic lunch and walking shoes and head north from Fryeburg on Route 113 to the White Mountain National Forest and Evans Notch. This scenic pass through the peaks offers any number of memorable views, including the Roost, a suspension bridge high above the Wild River that is a favorite of photographers. An easy half-mile trek will get you to top of the Roost. There's lots of other good hiking territory for all capabilities, with some difficult and rewarding climbs to rocky ledges overlooking the river valley. Stop in Bethel at the Evans Notch Ranger District on Bridge Street for advice and maps.

Save the picnic, however, until the views get even better farther north. Take Route 2 west to Bethel, then north on Route 26 to Grafton Notch State Park. Screw Auger Falls, the best-known spot in the park, fits its name, cascading down the mountain in a series of spirals through the rocks. If you're up for a steep hike from the falls, you can reach the scenic overlook at Table Rock.

When you can't wait another minute for lunch, head for Cascade Falls, and its prize picnic area nearby. Other sights to see are Mother Walker Falls and Moose Cave, a fascinating cavern in the rocks that is just a quarter of a mile from the main road. The trails are clearly marked off the road as you drive through. For serious hikers, there are trail heads for the Appalachian Trail and a loop trail up Old Speck, the third-highest mountain in the state.

If luck is against you and it rains, you can still while away a pleasant afternoon in area shops. In Bridgton alone, there are more than a dozen shops on Main Street and Route 302, all of them marked on a guide map available in most of the stores. The Jones Gallery of Glass and Ceramics off Route 107 in Sebago is a rarity, displaying over 4,000 pieces of glass and ceramics from 1800 B.C. to the present, and an adjacent shop sells ceramics and glassware. Bonnema Pottery is an interesting stop in Bethel, and over 150 craftspeople display work in wood, wool, flowers, clay, and fabrics at Sleepy Hollow Collectibles on Route 117 in Denmark Village. Small antiques shops dot almost all the little villages in the area, and the Oxford Common Antique Center on Route 26 offers over a dozen dealers in one location. And the Fryeburg Library has its own attraction, a room devoted to Clarence Mulford, creator of Hopalong Cassidy.

You can pick up pumpkins, apples, and other produce of the season at roadside stands beside the farms on almost any back road or at the larger Reinhardt Farms stand in Naples and Carter's Farm Market in Oxford.

But cross your fingers and hope for good weather—not only for visiting the Fryeburg fair but for making the most of the few areas where unspoiled villages, lakes, mountains, and forest wilderness come together within one superb backcountry area. Fall in western Maine forecasts a fair weekend indeed.

Maine Area Code: 207

DRIVING DIRECTIONS Fryeburg is on the western border of Maine, about 60 miles from Portland and 6 miles from Conway and the White Mountains of New Hampshire. Take Route 302 west from Portland and Route 113 to 302 east from Conway, New Hampshire. Fryeburg is 180 miles from Boston, 380 miles from New York, and 270 miles from Hartford.

PUBLIC TRANSPORTATION Air service to Portland. Fryeburg is an easy drive by rental car from the Portland airport.

ACCOMMODATIONS *Oxford House Inn,* Route 302, Fryeburg, 935-3442, comfortable Victorian, $$ CP ● *Noble House,* on Highland Lake, Box 86, Bridgton, upstairs suites perfect for families, $$–$$$ CP ● *Lake House,* Routes 35 and 37, Waterford, 583-4182, simple country charmer, $$–$$$ CP ● *Kedarburn Inn,* Route 35, Box A-1, Waterford, 583-6182, 1858 house on a brook, $$ CP ● *Waterford Inne,* PO Box 49, East Waterford, 583-4037, quiet location with a view, $$ ● Resorts: *Westways,* on Kezar Lake, Center Lovell, 928-2663, $$$–$$$$ or $$$$–$$$$$ MAP; *Migis Lodge,* off Route 301, South Casco, 655-4524, $$$$$ AP; *Bethel Inn and Country Club,* on the common, Bethel, 824-2175, $$$$. For other Bethel area lodgings, see page 234.

BED AND BREAKFAST *Bed and Breakfast of Maine,* 32 Colonial Village, Falmouth, ME 04105, 781-4528 ● *Bed and Breakfast Down East Ltd.,* Box 547, Eastbrook, ME 04634, 565-3517.

DINING *Oxford House* (see above), excellent dining room, $$$ ● *Westways* (see above), lovely view, $$$ ● *Lake House* (see above), varied cuisine, $$ ● *Kedarburn Inn* (see above), American and conti-nental, $$ ● *Bethel Inn* (see above), prime rib a specialty, $$ ● *Lobster Pound,* Route 302, Bridgton, 693-6580, informal, $–$$$ ● *Olde Rowley Inn,* Route 35 North and Route 118, North Waterford, 583-4143, 1790 stagecoach stop, charming and excellent, $–$$ ● *Epi-curean Inn,* Routes 302 and 35, Naples, 693-3839, for fine dining, $$–$$$. Lake House and Kedarburn Inn are also good choices for Sunday brunch. Also see Bethel, page 234

SIGHTSEEING *Fryeburg Fair,* Route 5, Fryeburg, runs one week in late September or early October; admission and parking charge. Write for current dates and fees to H. Ted Raymond, Box 36, Fryeburg, ME 04037, 935-2155 ● *Songo River Queen II,* Route 302, Naples, 693-6861. Hours: one-hour Long Lake Cruises, daily July to Labor Day, weekends in June and September: Adults, $4; children, $3. Two ½-hour Songo River cruises: Adults, $7; children $4. Mail-boat rides in season from Naples Causeway, phone 693-6861 for schedules and rates.

INFORMATION Bridgton Chamber of Commerce, PO Box 236, Bridgton, ME 04009, 647-3472. Greater Bethel Chamber of Com-merce, PO Box 121, Bethel, ME 04217, 824-2346.

Leafing Through the Northeast Kingdom

Anyone who despairs of making a fortune in this world can take heart from the story of Thaddeus Fairbanks.

Thaddeus is the man who invented the platform scale that registers weight at eye level when an object or a person is on the platform. Not such a remarkable notion, you say? Well, that simple invention made the Fairbanks family one of the ten wealthiest in the world back in the 1800s. And since members of the Fairbanks clan were generous with their fortune, their hometown of St. Johnsbury, Vermont, was trans-formed.

Thanks to the Fairbankses, when you visit St. Johnsbury today, you discover not just a center of the state's maple sugar industry but a town boasting one of the handsomest small town public libraries to be found, not to mention one of the most elaborate small museums. It's a surprise, way up here in rural northern Vermont—and only the first of the happy surprises awaiting in this beautiful and relatively unexplored area known as the Northeast Kingdom.

Not the least of the reasons to plan your trip here during the foliage season is the fact that not too many people have discovered the mountains and lakes and exceptional inns in this quiet corner of the state. So while the roads are clogged farther south, you can drive the scenic routes and walk the wooded trails here without ever feeling jostled by the rest of the foliage watchers of the world.

Since the inns are small and appealing to treasure seekers, you'll need to reserve early for Rabbit Hill, the warm and attractive hideaway in Lower Waterford, about ten miles east of St. Johnsbury. The elegant Inn on the Common, farther north in tiny Craftsbury Common, is also frequently filled with sophisticated travelers who want to get away from it all. Less well known is the appealing Craftsbury Inn, a handsomely furnished 1850 country home. Farther to the east, heading toward Burke Mountain, is the Wildflower Inn, a real charmer set on a ridge with views that go on forever and with lots of windows to make the most of them. And on the Mountain Access Road, the rustic little Old Cutter Inn is well known locally for its Swiss fare.

A Northeast Kingdom weekend itinerary ideally includes half a day in St. Johnsbury, with the rest of the time allotted to the scenic back roads, country walks, oohs and ahs, and photos.

Don't expect traditional rural motifs when you step inside the Fairbanks Museum and Planetarium in St. Johnsbury. The Fairbanks family wanted nothing but the best and hired Lambert Packard, one of America's great Victorian architects, to design the building. Packard did them proud, with soaring 30-foot barrel-vaulted ceilings, stained-glass windows (some by Tiffany), and lavish use of wood.

The exhibits inside are a mélange of history, archaeology, and science, with collections of dolls and Japanese Netsuke carvings and enough stuffed animals and birds to gladden a taxidermist's heart. The building also features northern Vermont's official weather station and its only public planetarium. The wacky variety of the displays adds to the fun of a visit. And downstairs you can see some of the scales that made the Fairbanks fortune—and the museum—possible.

Visiting the St. Johnsbury Athenaeum is reentering the gracious world of the nineteenth century. It was built as a public library and presented to the town in 1871 by Horace Fairbanks, a nephew of the inventor, who became president of the scale manufacturing company and eventually governor of Vermont. The cathedral ceilings, tall windows, spiral staircases, and elaborate woodwork and floors with alternating strips of oak and walnut make for a truly elegant structure.

In 1873 an art gallery was added to the main building to hold some of Horace Fairbanks's growing art collection. It is now the oldest unaltered art gallery in the country. The unusual design of the gallery was determined by the need to house Fairbanks's prize canvas, *The Domes of Yosemite*, an enormous (10-by-15-foot) painting by Albert Bierstadt. The exceptional landscape opposite the entrance to the gallery benefits from the natural light of an arched skyway, which enhances the feeling of looking down into the valley.

Another of St. Johnsbury's claims to fame has nothing to do with its illustrious benefactors. This is the heart of Vermont maple sugar country, which in a typical year produces about two thirds of the nation's supply. Maple Grove, the world's largest maple candy factory, has been operating since 1915, creating more than 200 kinds of delectable maple sweets.

For 50 cents, you are invited to tour the Maple Grove factory for a closeup view of the vats of boiling sap being poured into different kinds of candy molds, to emerge in familiar Vermont shapes from maple leaves to pine trees.

Visitors are also welcome to the Maple Cabin here to see a 15-minute film on the maple sugar process. Actual kettles of sap are boiling year round in the adjacent small Maple Museum, which features exhibitions of sugarmaking equipment, both ancient and modern.

After the tour, you can taste free samples of the final result—but be forewarned that after the tempting smells and tastes, it is almost impossible to leave without buying something in the gift shop.

A special autumn excursion from St. Johnsbury is a ride on the St. J. & L.C. Railroad, a 3-hour 57-mile round-trip journey with a spectacular vista around each of the many turns that make this known as the "Zig-Zag Railroad."

Before you leave St. Johnsbury, have a look at the fine houses to be seen along Main Street. Then, leave "city" business behind and strike out for the country roads waiting to show off their autumn colors. One prime route for scenery is the drive north from St. Johnsbury on Routes 5 and 114 to East Burke and Burke Mountain. On the way you'll pass through Lyndonville, whose claims to fame are the five covered bridges nearby and a delightful country store in East Burke. The auto road to Burke Mountain's 3,267-foot summit yields sweeping views of the countryside.

From here, head for Vermont lake country by connecting again with Route 5, which becomes 5A as you drive north to Lake Willoughby. Two cliffs, Mt. Pisgah and Mt. Hor, rise from opposite sides of this lake, making for a majestic vista. To get an even more spectacular view, take advantage of the well-maintained hiking trails in the 7,000-acre state forest surrounding the lake. The view from the cliffs is worth the climb.

There are some 15 lakes in this general area, providing recreation for boaters and fishermen and scenery for all. Almost all the lakes are surrounded by hills, and Crystal Lake back on Route 5 is another beauty set against a dramatic cliff. If you follow Route 5 north a few miles, you'll come to a pleasant change of pace, the Old Stone House in Browington Center. Run by the Orleans County Historical Society, this handsome granite museum has 11 rooms of memorabilia representing furnishings, weapons, tools, paintings, and decorative arts of the eighteenth and nineteenth centuries from the 11 towns in the county.

Turn south again and follow Route 14 to Craftsbury, another charmer. It is actually made up of a string of villages so minute that you can easily pass through before you know you have arrived—until you reach Craftsbury Common, with its picture-book green surrounded by white clapboard buildings and a church. It is an appropriate setting for The Inn on the Common, an uncommon inn where guests don jackets for dinner served on Tiffany china with heirloom silverware.

In late September each year, six of the tiny towns in the area join in the Northeast Kingdom's Foliage Festival, taking turns holding church lunches and suppers, crafts shows, and special events. These are small affairs, nothing to write home about or to drive miles out of the way for, but if you plan your driving itinerary to pass through any of the towns on the day of the festival, it may add a down-home touch and a home-cooked meal to your memories. The towns to watch for are Cabot, Plainfield, Peacham, Barnet, Groton, and Walden. A schedule of events is available from the state tourist office as well as in most towns in the area.

It was U.S. Senator George Aiken of Vermont who dubbed this area the Northeast Kingdom when he saw its untouched beauty during one brilliant fall foliage season some years ago. When you view the mountain peaks and lakes and the peaceful mosaic of unspoiled villages and farms, you may agree that this corner of Vermont is, indeed, a kingdom of its own.

Vermont Area Code: 802

DRIVING DIRECTIONS   St. Johnsbury is off I-91 at exit 20. It is 150 miles from Boston, 300 miles from New York City, and 190 miles from Hartford.

PUBLIC TRANSPORTATION   Vermont Transit bus service to St. Johnsbury. Closest air service is Eastern Express to Waterbury, VT, or Lebanon, NH.

ACCOMMODATIONS   *Rabbit Hill Inn,* Route 18, Lower Waterford, 748-5168, $$$$–$$$$$ MAP ● *The Wildflower Inn,* Star Route, Lyndonville, 626-8310, $$ CP ● *The Old Cutter Inn,* Burke Mountain Access Road, East Burke, $ ● *The Inn on the Common,* Craftsbury

Common, 586-9619, $$$$ MAP • *Craftsbury Inn,* Craftsbury, 586-2848, $$–$$$ CP or $$$–$$$$ MAP.

BED AND BREAKFAST   *Vermont Bed and Breakfast Reservation Service,* PO Box 1, East Fairfield, VT 05448, 827-3827.

DINING   Chances are you'll be eating at your inn. All the above are recommended, in addition to the following • *The Creamery,* Danville (near St. Johnsbury), seafood specialties in a charming converted creamery, $–$$ • *Willie's,* Route 114, East Burke, 626-8475, good food in a converted meeting house, $–$$ • *Harvest Sun Café,* 70 Railroad Street, St. Johnsbury, 748-9974, good lunch spot, ethnic weekend dinner menus, $ • *Rainbow Sweets,* Marshfield, 426-3531, tiny, exceptional desserts, $.

SIGHTSEEING   *Fairbanks Museum and Planetarium,* Main and Prospect streets, St. Johnsbury, 748-2372. Hours: Monday to Saturday 10 A.M. to 4 P.M., Sunday 1 P.M. to 5 P.M.; July and August, Monday to Saturday to 6 P.M. Adults, $2; children, $1; families, $5 • *St. Johnsbury Athenaeum,* 30 Main Street, 748-8291, library and art gallery. Hours: Monday to Saturday, 9:30 A.M. to 5 P.M. and Monday and Wednesday to 8 P.M. Free • *Maple Museum,* US 2 on eastern edge of St. Johnsbury. Hours: Memorial Day to late October, Monday to Friday 8 A.M. to 4:45 P.M., weekends also during foliage season; tours every ten minutes. Admission, $.50 • *The Old Stone House,* Brownington Center, 754-2022. Hours: daily July and August 11 A.M. to 5 P.M.; May 15 to June 30 and September to October 15, Friday to Tuesday only. Adults, $3; children, $1 • *St. J. & L.C. Railroad,* PO Box 636, St. Johnsbury, 748-3678 or 748-3685. Weekend excursion rides in late September and early October; contact for current schedule. Adults, $15; children, $5.

INFORMATION   St. Johnsbury Chamber of Commerce, 30 Western Avenue, St. Johnsbury, VT 05819, 748-3678.

Making a Pilgrimage to Plymouth

When the cranberries ripen to ruby red, that's the time to plan your pilgrimage to Plymouth, Massachusetts.

In case you didn't know, cranberries became part of our traditional Thanksgiving feast because the *Mayflower* Pilgrims happened to come to rest in the heart of America's cranberry-growing center. Come late September each year when the berries are ready for harvest, the countryside around Plymouth is transformed into a remarkable landscape of glowing red.

A very special steam train ride will take you right through the cranberry bogs, and there are many special harvest-time festivities, including an old-fashioned country fair. It's an extra splash of color for a trip that ought to be made anyway by anyone who is interested in how our country began.

Don't expect a dull history lesson. Plymouth Rock and a replica of the *Mayflower* are here, of course, but the real story of Plymouth is told best at Plimoth Plantation, an amazingly realistic re-creation of America's first settlement. This authentic replica of the 1627 Pilgrim village is peopled with "residents" who have been intensely trained to re-create the atmosphere of the first surviving colony in New England. You'll be entering a farming community where everyone is at work at the typical seasonal tasks, and you can see firsthand what it was like to settle in a new land where almost everything had to be grown or made on the spot. The Pilgrim residents are so authentic they even have differing accents to match the regions they left in England. You'll meet Miles Standish and John Alden and lots of other people who will tell you in the most believable way how it felt to make a home in the wilderness. They'll tell you all about life in the old country as well as the new and will describe the *Mayflower* voyage—in fact, they'll answer any question you ask as long as it doesn't involve knowledge of anything past the year 1627.

The village is so well done that you'll almost forget it isn't real, and you'll see kids eagerly approaching one after another of the residents to find out who is married to whom and which child belongs to which parent. Make Plimoth Plantation your first stop while you're fresh on Saturday morning and allow two to three hours to really make the most of this experience.

Back in Plymouth, you can get some notion of how it felt for 102 people to cross the ocean on a 104-foot boat by boarding the replica of the *Mayflower* that is the second part of the plantation's "living museum." Once again, the sailors and passengers aboard represent the real ones.

The *Mayflower* is docked at the harbor right in the heart of town, next to what is probably the best-known boulder in the country, Plymouth Rock. An elaborate columned monument has been built over the rock to protect it and to provide a viewing platform, and the waterfront area around it has been turned into a pleasant grassy promenade that is now a state park. Guides lead tours of the rock and its surroundings daily during the summer and on weekends in spring and fall.

Across the street is Coles Hill, where you can get a panoramic view of Plymouth Harbor. The Pilgrims buried their dead in unmarked graves here during their first terrible winter. Also on Coles Hill is the statue of Massasoit, chief of the Wampanoag Indians, who befriended the newcomers and helped them to survive that winter. The 81-foot Pilgrim Monument on Allerton Street was built between 1859 and 1889, at the then-enormous cost of $155,000, to commemorate the bravery of these early settlers. If you like that sort of thing, you'll also find a wax museum on Coles Hill portraying the Pilgrims' story.

Follow the signs inland a block or two for a visit to America's oldest public museum, Pilgrim Hall. You'll see John Alden's bible, William Bradford's chair, William Brewster's books, and many other possessions and furniture of the settlers, as well as paintings by Gilbert Stuart and Henry Sargent.

There are several historic houses to be seen in Plymouth, the most impressive being the Mayflower Society House, headquarters for the General Society of Mayflower Descendants. A particularly pleasant walk will take you through Brewster Gardens with its placid duck pond to see Jenney Gristmill, a working twentieth-century reconstruction of a seventeenth-century mill. The meal at the mill is for sale, and there are several other shops around.

The oldest house of all, the 1640 Richard Sparrow House, is now a pottery-making center and shop. The Harlow Old Fort House offers hands-on experience with such Colonial arts as spinning, weaving, and candle dipping. The house was built with timbers from the original fort.

All the shops are a sign that the waterfront in Plymouth is packed with tourists in season. The town has gone slightly commercial to take advantage of that fact, but so far things are not out of hand. The most extensive shopping is in a complex called Village Landing, some two dozen clapboard-and-shingle structures built to resemble a nineteenth-century village. These shops are pleasant enough, offering everything from jewelry to hand-stenciled plaques to high-quality brassware and antiques. There's also a shop with homemade ice cream and a candy store. And on Sunday afternoons, musicians entertain at the bandstand in the village square.

There are several seafood restaurants on or across from the water, as well as more modestly priced takeout stands where you can have your seafood at picnic tables with a water view—a real boon for families. Save time for a walk along the long rock jetty into the harbor for a closeup look at the many sailboats and yachts that fill Plymouth Harbor today. If you want to get out on the water, several boat outings are available through the early fall.

Come Sunday, it's cranberry time. Start at the Ocean Spray headquarters on Water Street for an excellent tour that traces how the berries have been grown and harvested throughout history. You'll see how the quality of a berry is judged by its bounce and be able to inspect the tools for both dry and wet harvesting.

After a free sample of cranberry juice, you'll be ready to head for South Carver and the Edaville Railroad for a 5½-mile steam train ride right through the cranberry bogs. The rails were originally laid to help harvest an 1,800-acre plantation, but the train soon became a tourist attraction, and eventually a "family fun park" grew up with a museum of railroading and other Americana, an old-fashioned carousel, a children's petting zoo, a horse-drawn trolley, a paddlewheel steamboat ride, and the inevitable nineteenth-century shopping village.

On weekends in late September and early October Edaville holds its Cranberry Festival, with exhibits, crafts, an annual quilt show, and lively entertainment added to the usual attractions.

If you can't make it in September, the Columbus Day weekend is also special for the annual Harvest Home celebration at Plimoth Plantation, a re-creation of the feasts and games that marked the end of the colony's successful growing season.

Whichever weekend you choose, do visit Plymouth in autumn. You'll leave with a lot more knowledge about your country and with a rosy cranberry glow as well.

Plymouth Area Code: 508

DRIVING DIRECTIONS   Plymouth is off Route 3 on Route 3A, 35 miles south of Boston, 245 miles from New York, and 135 miles from Hartford.

PUBLIC TRANSPORTATION   Plymouth and Brockton bus lines run from Boston and Hyannis; nearest airport is Boston.

ACCOMMODATIONS   *Sheraton Inn,* 180 Water Street at Village Landing, 747-4900, best in town, $$$–$$$$ ● *Governor Carver Motor Inn,* 25 Summer Street, 746-7100, walking distance to town but away from traffic, $$ ● *Governor Bradford Motor Inn,* Water Street, 746-6200, across from the water in the middle of town, $$ ● *Pilgrim Sands,* 150 Warren Avenue, 747-0900, best waterfront location, 3 miles south of town near Plimoth Plantation, $$.

BED AND BREAKFAST   *Be Our Guest Bed and Breakfast,* PO Box 1333, Plymouth, MA 02360, 837-9867 ● *Around Plymouth Bed and Breakfast,* PO Box 6211, Plymouth, MA 02360, 747-5075.

DINING   *Marina Landing,* 14 Union Street, 746-5570, seafood with a view, away from the crowds, $$ ● *Station One,* 51 Main Street,

746-6001, handsomely restored fire station, $$ • *Sante,* 320 Court Street, North Plymouth, 747-4226, country French, best in area, $$$ • *Bert's,* Warren Avenue, 746-3422, informal, seafood on the water, near Plimoth Plantation, $–$$ • *McGrath's,* Town Wharf, 746-9751, seafood, water view, busiest place in town, $–$$ • *1620 House,* Water Street, 746-9565, seafood, across the street from the harbor, not so frantic, $–$$ • *Inn for All Seasons,* 97 Warren, 746-8823, mansion on a hilltop, $$ • *Scruples,* Water Street, Village Landing, attractive, $$.

SIGHTSEEING   *Plimoth Plantation,* Route 3A, 3 miles south of Plymouth, 746-1622. Hours: April to November, daily 9 A.M. to 5 P.M. *Pilgrim Village,* adults, $7.50; children, $4.75. *Mayflower,* adults, $3.75; children, $2.75. Combination tickets for both, adults, $9.50; children, $6.50. Under 5 free • *Pilgrim Hall Museum,* 75 Court Street (Route 3A), 746-1620. Hours: daily 9:30 A.M. to 4:30 P.M. Adults, $3; 6 to 15, $1 • *Harlow Old Fort House,* 119 Sandwich Street, 746-3017. Hours: late June to early September, Monday to Saturday, 10 A.M. to 5 P.M., Sunday from 12 noon; early spring and fall, Friday to Sunday only. Adults, $1.50; 6 to 12, $.50 • *Mayflower Society Museum,* 4 Winslow Street, 746-2590. Hours: late June to mid-September, daily 10 A.M. to 5 P.M. Adults, $2; under 12, $.25 • *Edaville Railroad,* Route 58, South Carver, 866-4526. Hours: May to December, daily 10 A.M. to 5 P.M. Adults, $7.50; children, $5 • Cruises: *Capt. John Boats,* Town Wharf, 746-2643; *Plymouth and Provincetown Steamship Company,* Mayflower II Pier, 747-2400.

INFORMATION   Plymouth Chamber of Commerce, 91 Samoset Street, Plymouth, MA 02360, 746-3377.

Fall Foliage in Franconia

*Men hang out signs indicative of their respective
trades; shoemakers hang out a giant shoe;
jewelers hang out a monster watch; and a dentist
hangs out a gold tooth; but up in the mountains of
New Hampshire God Almighty has hung out a sign
to show that there He makes men.*

It was Daniel Webster who wrote these words on viewing the Old Man of the Mountain, an unmistakable craggy profile in stone carved on a mountainside by some celestial sculptor.

The rugged visage of the Old Man, now the official symbol of the

Granite State, can be seen clearly, high on a rock cliff at the end of the eight-mile mountain pass called Franconia Notch, where he presides over a panorama of peaks and valleys, awesome gorges, tumbling waterfalls, and ice blue mountain lakes, a vista that has few peers in New England.

Add the region's most scenic mountain highway, aflame in fall foliage, and a chance to view it all from a cable car that travels 4,200 feet into the sky and you have all the makings of an unforgettable fall outing.

Since this is a deservedly popular destination in the fall, it's well to begin by reserving a place early in one of the area's excellent inns. An old favorite is Lovett's by Lafayette Brook, a 190-year-old inn by the side of the road in a country setting, looking out at the mountains. There are a wide variety of rooms in the old inn and in motel-type cottages on the grounds, now being spruced up by new owners, who also plan a new pool. But accommodations have not been the chief attraction here. It's the dining room that keeps guests coming back, not only for dinners such as lamb with chutney, and chicken in brandy and cream, but for breakfast menus that include blueberry, apple, or butternut pancakes, shirred eggs with herbed tomatoes and mushrooms, and fried cornmeal mush with maple syrup. If the old chefs remain, don't expect to count calories here.

Off on a quieter road is the Franconia Inn, another longtime local mainstay, rebuilt after a 1934 fire to resemble the original Colonial inn of the 1860s. Here you have your pick of views, meadow or mountain, and there are horses for riding, tennis courts, and a hot tub for guests.

Just above Franconia, on a site with even more spectacular views, is the little town of Sugar Hill, a definite must for a visit even if you don't stay there. The Sugar Hill Inn is a tasteful 1748 Colonial with charming rooms done in traditional Laura Ashley prints with interesting antiques and hand stenciling. It's the pick of the local lodgings.

Sunset Hill House is a good alternative if the others are filled. The hilltop location and view are superb, but in recent years, the inn has been in need of some redecorating.

Once you've settled in, you're in for two days of spectacular sights. If you want to enjoy the area to the fullest, you can easily spend an entire day driving, walking, and picnicking in the fantastic beauty of Franconia State Park.

You might as well drive right to that famous profile at Franconia Notch. Profile Lake has been dubbed the "Old Man's Washbowl" for its location 1,200 feet below the outline of the Old Man himself. A parking area along the lake gives a magnificent view of mountains reflected in the deep blue water and is also the best vantage point for seeing the distinct face above, which is actually composed of five separate granite ledges. The forehead alone is a 20-foot-long granite block weighing about 30 tons. The profile is 25 feet wide and measures about 40 feet from chin to forehead.

Continuing on the main road, you'll come to a waterfall cascading into a granite pool called the Basin. It is believed that the granite was eroded by a melting glacier 25,000 years ago. Below is a water-eroded rock formation, then comes the rushing water of the Baby Flume, a forerunner of what lies ahead.

The Flume is a natural gorge whose 70- to 90-foot granite walls extend for 800 feet along the southern flank of Mt. Liberty. A bus takes you to within 500 yards of the gorge, then it's an easy two-mile round-trip hike along the paths and wooden walkways crisscrossing the stream to reach the actual Flume and the crescendo of sound that announces Avalanche Falls, a torrent of water crashing 23 feet down the canyon into a pool. A short trail leads you to the Cascades, another rush of mountain streams tumbling into a narrow valley known as Liberty Gorge. On the way back you'll pass a deep basin called simply the Pool, fed by a cascading river. In 1938 a giant pine uprooted by a hurricane fell across the river and now forms a base for the Sentinel Pine Bridge, which offers the best viewing point for the Pool.

By now you've surely worked up an appetite for lunch. The closest picnic grounds are right across from the Flume, the most scenic are back in the other direction at Echo Lake, a pool of blue in a setting of granite cliffs. There's boating and fishing at Echo Lake, and a sandy beach near the picnic area. If you're up for a one and a half mile walk, Artist's Bluff up above is a rocky palisade with fine views of the Franconia and Kinsman ranges. The name comes from yet another profile carved in the mountain, this one known as the Artist.

Now it's time for the view that beats them all, the thrilling cable-car ascent via the Cannon Mountain Aerial Tramway to the 4,200-foot peak of Cannon Mountain. This was the first such lift in America, and is still one of the most spectacular. The present tram, completed in 1980, goes a mile straight up, a five-minute ride that affords amazing views of all the White Mountain ranges in their best fall dress. There are trails at the summit up to an observation tower for a longer view.

When you come down you'll find a League of New Hampshire Craftsmen shop off the tramway parking lot, with high-quality handcrafts by the state's own artisans. If you still have energy and you're ready for more indoor activity to finish the day, you can check out the smattering of gift, clothing, and country stores in Franconia, though it's far from a shopping haven. Or you may want to take the time to visit Frost Place, the simple frame house where poet Robert Frost lived and worked. You can stand at his desk or on the front porch, sharing the mountain views that inspired him.

After a hearty breakfast at the inn, you can start Sunday by exploring one of the less heralded but no less intriguing natural attractions of the area, the strange formations known as Lost River. The river here flows through a narrow, steep-walled glacial gorge and disappears beneath immense blocks of granite that tumbled into the gorge eons ago. You can follow its course on a wooden walkway as it moves through the gorge and canyons and down Paradise Falls. There are bridges and ladders all along the way that let you wander into caves and through hidden passages in the boulders. Kids absolutely love it—but then so do the grown-ups. The walk takes about an hour.

In Lincoln you can get another bird's-eye view of the colorful mountains from the Loon Mountain Tramway, which bills itself as the state's longest aerial ride.

But the major attraction for this day is down to earth, a drive that gets my vote as the most beautiful in New England. The Kancamagus Highway (Route 112) runs for 32 miles between the villages of Lincoln and Conway through the heart of the White Mountain National Forest. It was designed by the U.S. Forest Service to make the most of the views and to give access to the magnificent wilderness on either side in picnic areas and hiking trails. Once again, it's a good idea to bring a lunch along.

The drive alone is extraordinary, especially with the added glow of autumn color, but to make the most of the highway you really should get out and investigate the scenic areas marked off on the way. One special one is the Rocky Gorge area where, over the ages, the Swift River has worn a cleft in the rock now known as Rocky Gorge. Within this area is Falls Pond, a five-minute walk over the gorge via a rustic footbridge. Some other easy walks are to Boulder Loop, which gives a spectacular view of Mt. Chocorua and the Swift River Valley from the ledges, and Sabbaday Falls, a picturesque series of cascades in a narrow flume. You can spend an hour here—or a day.

At the end of the road in Conway, you're very much back in civilization, with many shops to choose from and lots of good restaurants as well. But somehow it seems a shame to lose the glow of all that pristine beauty. A better move may be to take the return trip on the Kancamagus, seeing it all from a different perspective this time, and heading home with the glorious New Hampshire autumn recorded in your mind's eye to sustain you through the winter ahead.

New Hampshire Area Code: 603

DRIVING DIRECTIONS   Franconia is on the west side of the White Mountains in upper New Hampshire and can be reached via I-93. It is 115 miles from Boston, 325 miles from New York, and 215 miles from Hartford.

PUBLIC TRANSPORTATION   Air service to Manchester or Lebanon, New Hampshire; bus service via Vermont Transit to North Conway.

ACCOMMODATIONS   *Lovett's by Lafayette Brook,* Profile Road, Franconia, 823-7761, $$–$$$$ MAP; dinners $$$ • *Franconia Inn,* Easton Road (Route 116), Franconia, 823-5542, $$$$–$$$$$ MAP; $$–$$$ EP; dinners $$–$$$ • *Sugar Hill Inn,* Route 117, Sugar Hill, 823-5621, $$$$ CP or $$$$$ MAP • *Sunset Hill House,* Sugar Hill, 823-5522, $$$$ MAP; dinners $$–$$$ • For those on a budget: *Ledgeland,* Route 117, Sugar Hill, 823-5341, rustic lodge-style motel with a few inn rooms, $$; *Mill House Inn,* Route 112, Lincoln, 745-6261, attractive hotel; part of restoration now a shopping complex, pool, $$–$$$.

BED AND BREAKFAST   *New Hampshire Bed and Breakfast,* RFD 3, Box 53, Laconia, NH 03246, 279-8348.

DINING   Inns above serve dinner • Also excellent is *Horse and Hound Inn,* off Route 18, Franconia, 823-5501, $$–$$$ • For breakfast or lunch, *Polly's Pancake Parlor,* Route 117, Sugar Hill, 823-5525, a local legend for home-ground cornmeal and whole-wheat pancakes and waffles with luscious fillings and homemade sausages • For a takeout lunch, the choices are *Dutch Treat* or the *Franconia Dairy Bar,* both on Main Street, Franconia, or ask at your inn.

SIGHTSEEING   *Franconia Notch State Park,* Route 3/93, Franconia, 823-5563. Hours: late May through mid-October, 9 A.M. to 4:30 P.M. Free admission into park • *The Flume.* Hours: daily 9 A.M. to 4:40 P.M. Adults, $4; 6 to 12, $2.50 • *Cannon Mountain Tramway.* Hours: daily 9 A.M. to 4:30 P.M. Adults, $6; 6 to 12, $3.50; • *Frost Place,* Route 116 Franconia, 823-5510. Hours: Daily July and August, Wednesday to Monday, 1 P.M. to 5 P.M.; June, September, and early October, Saturday and Sunday only. Adults, $2.50; 6 to 15, $1.50 • *Lost River Reservation,* Route 112, Kinsman Notch, 745-8031. Hours: daily 9 A.M. to 6 P.M. Adults, $4; 6 to 12, $2 • *Loon Mountain Tramway.* Hours: Daily July to mid-October, 9:30 A.M. to 5:30 P.M.; weekends only in June. Adults, $5; 5 to 12, $3.

INFORMATION   Franconia/Easton/Sugar Hill Chamber of Commerce, Franconia, NH 03580, 823-5661.

Meandering the Mohawk Trail

In 1663 the Pocumtuck Indians invaded the lands of the Mohawks by creating a footpath from their home in Deerfield, Massachusetts, through the Berkshire Mountains to Mohawk territory in Troy, New York. This strategic route was to become known as the Mohawk Trail.

Later pioneers made this route the first toll-free interstate road, opening the Berkshires to tourists.

Today the 63-mile Mohawk Trail, known as the Highway of History, is a route through the mountains stretching from the Massachusetts–New York border to the Connecticut River just east of Greenfield, an up-and-down drive of twists and turns and amazing mountain views. One 42-mile segment connects two beautiful New England towns, Deerfield and Williamstown, as well as providing access to Greylock Mountain, the state's highest peak, with soaring views of fall foliage. There are few more rewarding autumn journeys.

Whether to base yourself at the eastern or western end of the road depends largely on whether you prefer historic homes or mountain scenery. Since the Deerfield Inn is located on one of America's most magnificent main streets, it may rate a special recommendation.

Known simply as the Street, Old Deerfield's main avenue is a mile-long row of more than 50 fine Colonial and Federal houses, each one carefully maintained in its original condition. In the dozen buildings open to the public, visitors can see more than 100 rooms filled with china, glassware, silver, pewter, fabrics, and furniture—all testaments to the good taste of our early settlers.

But this is by no means a museum town. The houses on the Street have been continuously occupied over the years, and even the museum homes have apartments in the rear for the faculty of the Deerfield Academy, the noted boys' school that has stood on the Street since 1797, giving Deerfield a rare living continuity with the past that is evident the moment you arrive. It is heightened by the fact that no modern intrusions such as telephone wires have been allowed; they are carefully buried to preserve the street's untouched beauty.

It is hard to believe this peaceful, elm-shaded village of today was once a frontier outpost, twice besieged by Indian attacks. The stubborn survivors rebuilt their town, reworked their farms, and began to prosper, replacing their original primitive homes with gracious weathered-clapboard houses in the Connecticut Valley tradition, marked by distinctively carved doorways. Though rustic compared with houses of this period in Boston or Philadelphia, their very simplicity makes them all the lovelier.

Deerfield's farmers used their new wealth to commission the finest furnishings they could find, particularly from the excellent craftsmen and cabinetmakers of their own valley. Fortunately, this era of good taste has been preserved, thanks largely to the generosity of Mr. and Mrs. Henry Flynt, who came to Deerfield in the 1930s when their son enrolled at the academy. The Flynts bought and restored the white-columned inn at the center of town, which remains a gracious Colonial lodging, and then acquired one of the old houses for themselves. One house led to another until, in 1952, they founded Historic Deerfield, Inc., to care for the properties.

Though Deerfield is only a village, it deserves a full day of touring to savor all it has to offer. Start by just strolling the Street and admiring the architecture, the handsome buildings of the academy, and the delightful post office, a replica of a 1696 meeting house. Then head for the Hall Tavern information center, where color photos will help you make the difficult choice of which houses to visit during a limited stay. Each house tour takes from 30 to 45 minutes.

One of the "musts" is Ashley House, with its elegant North Parlor, the subject of countless magazine photographs. Other excellent choices are the Sheldon-Hawks House, for its memorable bedroom with brilliant flame-stitch bed hangings and red moreen curtains and chairs; the Dwight-Barnard House, for another fancy parlor and the doctor's office behind its weathered exterior; and Frary House, a one-time tavern with a ballroom, excellent examples of country furniture, and a "touch me" room where children (and adults) can handle some of the tools that are off limits elsewhere.

Those who admire fine needlework will want to include the Helen Geier Flynt Fabric Hall, a Victorian barn housing Mrs. Flynt's exceptional collection of American, English, and European embroideries, textiles, quilts, bed hangings, and costumes.

The last weekend of September brings the annual Old Deerfield Crafts Fair, held on the front lawn of the Memorial Hall Museum—a change-of-pace bonus for visitors.

If you've given Saturday to Deerfield, plan an early start Sunday to allow for the scenery and sights awaiting along the Mohawk Trail. Take I-91 six miles north to Greenfield to connect to the trail (Route 2) and its many vistas heading west. Allow two hours for the 42-mile trip because of the dips and twists and stunning scenery along the way. You can't miss the best views because, sad to say, they've been marked by signs at local souvenir shops and restaurants adjoining scenic lookouts. The first is Whitcomb Summit, the top of the trail, an elevation of over 2,000 feet with views of mountains as far away as Vermont and New Hampshire. The most famous of the lookouts is the Hairpin Turn, opening to another soaring mountain vista.

Other than these well-visited spots, much of the trail remains wooded and unblemished, allowing you to enjoy this state's premiere autumn panoramas. There are a number of minor sightseeing stops along the way if you have the time. Among them are the unique Bridge of Flowers in Shelburne Falls, an old trolley bridge covered with a profusion of shrubs and blossoms, and Salmon Falls just downstream, a historic spot where the Mohawk and Penobscott tribes signed a fishing treaty, now best known as the site of many ancient glacial potholes. New England's only natural bridge—a white marble span over Hudson Brook—can be found in North Adams.

By the time you get to North Adams, the scenery will have given way to commercial establishments of all kinds, but if you watch for the signs and make a left turn onto Notch Road, you'll be en route to the 3,491-foot summit of Mt. Greylock, the state's highest peak, and the most stunning view of all. The road may seem bumpy at the start, but it gets better as you ascend.

At the summit in Bascom Lodge, you'll find an information center manned by the Appalachian Mountain Club, with maps covering the 35 miles of trails available here for hikers of all abilities. A favorite hiker's destination is the Hopper, a wildlife preserve of giant conifers and lush growth where the natural scene is untouched by human development. By car, follow the signs to Stony Ledge for an outlook over this heavily wooded, brook-coursed canyon.

The famous hiking route, the Appalachian Trail, also passes through Mt. Greylock Reservation, a 10,000-acre preserve around the mountain maintained by the Massachusetts Department of Environmental Management. The state agency and the Appalachian Mountain Club combine to offer many guided tours and talks on the mountain.

You can return to the bottom on Notch Road or on the road that takes you to the Route 7 information center in Lanesboro. Either way, your next stop is Williamstown, a classic New England town with a college dating back to 1793 as its center. Williams is so much a part of its hometown that it is hard to tell where campus stops and town begins, and the campus offers some interesting places to visit, including the collection of rare books at the Chapin Library (closed Sundays, unfortunately) and the Williams Art Museum.

But Williamstown's best-known art attraction is the Sterling and Francine Clark Art Institute, one of the most inviting and impressive small museums in the country. Sterling Clark had the good fortune to be heir to the wealth his grandfather amassed as a partner to Isaac Singer, the sewing machine king. He began collecting fine art around 1912, starting with works of the Old Masters, but with the encouragement of his French-born wife, he shifted emphasis in the 1920s and 1930s to nineteenth-century French painting and to American artists like Sargent, Remington, and Winslow Homer, who is represented by seven excellent oils. The real heart of the museum is the exceptional display of paintings by Rubens, Monet, Degas, and Renoir.

When the Clarks decided in the 1950s to build a museum to hold their treasures, they chose Williamstown for the beauty of the setting and designed a building to make the most of it. Tall windows in the corridors look out on natural scenery that adds immensely to the pleasures of visiting the building. The galleries are done to drawing-room scale and many are furnished with antiques, making this museum particularly enjoyable.

While you're in Williamstown, a stroll over to Water Street (Route 43) will bring you to half a dozen interesting shops. The Potter's Wheel, a gallery with picture windows overlooking a brook, has particularly attractive displays of art, glass, sculpture, and jewelry.

If you prefer to concentrate on hiking in the fine autumn weather, you might want to consider the Spartan but clean accommodations at Bascom Lodge. The rooms at $8 and the family-style meals are a real bargain, and the kitchen will also pack an inexpensive trail lunch. Williams Inn is Colonial in style and has a sauna and indoor pool, but it is new and has none of the warmth of a country inn. A far better choice is The Orchards, which is also new but offers oversize rooms and elegance. If you want cozy ambience, you can drive 12 miles from Williamstown to the Milhof, a *gemutlich* Alpine chalet hideaway just 500 feet across the New York border from Hancock, or settle for the six rooms above Le Jardin, a country restaurant just outside of town.

Whether you hike, house tour, look at art, or concentrate on the scenery, Deerfield to Williamstown is an end-to-end route that can hardly be bettered. And whether you make a return scenic trip on the Mohawk Trail or find a speedier route home, you'll be bringing back memories of the New England autumn at its very best.

Deerfield Area Code: 413

DRIVING DIRECTIONS Deerfield can be reached via I-91, exit 24 northbound and exit 25 southbound to Route 5, which leads six miles north into town. Williamstown is at the intersection of Route 7 and Route 2 (the Mohawk Trail), reached via I-91 exit 26, a few miles north of Deerfield. Though the portion designated as the trail stops at Miller's Falls, Route 2 continues east to Boston. Deerfield is about 100 miles from Boston, 187 miles from New York, and 77 miles from Hartford.

PUBLIC TRANSPORTATION Peter Pan bus service to Deerfield; Bonanza buses to Williamstown.

ACCOMMODATIONS *Deerfield Inn,* the Street, Deerfield,

774-5587, $$$ • *The Orchards,* 222 Adams Road, Williamstown,
458-9611, $$$–$$$$$ • *AMC Bascom Lodge,* Mt. Greylock, PO Box
686, Lanesboro, 743-1591 • *The Milhof,* Route 43, Stephentown, NY,
(518) 733-5606, $$ • *The Williams Inn,* on the green, Williamstown,
458-9371, $$$ • *Le Jardin Inn,* Route 7, Williamstown, 458-8125,
$$–$$$ CP.

BED AND BREAKFAST *Berkshire Bed and Breakfast,* PO Box
211, Main Street, Williamsburg, MA 01096, 268-7244.

DINING *Deerfield Inn* (see above), $$–$$$ • *Le Jardin* (see
above), converted estate, French menu, $$–$$$ • *River House,* Water
Street, Williamstown, 458-4829, varied menu, also lunch and late-
night snacks, $$ • *The Orchards* (see above), $$–$$$ • *Capers,* 412
Main Street, Williamstown, 458-9180, popular locally for all three
meals, dinners $$–$$$ • *Erasmus Café,* 76 Spring Street, Wil-
liamstown, 458-5007, light fare in a book shop, pleasant, open late
hours, $–$$.

SIGHTSEEING *Historic Deerfield,* on the Street, Deerfield,
774-5581. Hours: Monday to Saturday 9:30 A.M. to 4:30 P.M., Sunday
11 A.M. to 4:30 P.M. (to 6 P.M. July through October). Guided tours of
3 houses, $4.50; of 12 houses, $15. Individual tickets may also be
purchased at each house, varying rates • *Sterling and Francine Clark
Art Institute,* South Street, Williamstown, 458-9545. Hours: daily except Monday 10 A.M. to 5 P.M. Free • *Chapin Library,* Stetson Hall,
Williams College, Williamstown, 597-3131. Hours: Monday to Friday
9 A.M. to 12 noon and 1 P.M. to 5 P.M. Saturday 9 A.M. to 12 noon.
Free • *Williams College Art Museum,* Lawrence Hall, Williamstown,
597-2429. Hours: Monday to Saturday, 10 A.M. to 5 P.M., Sunday 1
P.M. to 5 P.M. Free.

INFORMATION The Mohawk Trail Association, PO Box J, Char-
lemont, MA 01339, 664-6256.

Breezing Through the Past in Essex

Standing on the docks at Essex, Connecticut, enjoying the sea breeze
and admiring the panorama of sleek-masted sailboats in the harbor,
you'll find it hard to believe that this placid spot was once the most
bustling landing on the Connecticut River.

With its pleasure boats, lanes of picket fences, and handsome white clapboard Colonial and Federal homes, today's Essex is the picture of Early American serenity, a mecca for sailors and strollers. But for more than 300 eventful years of history, this town has been a major port on the 410-mile river that has served as a main artery for much of New England. There's rich history to be explored as well as some special pleasures of the present, including a cruise on the majestic river, some unusual shops, and several exceptional inns.

Just up the river is a Victorian jewel box of a theater offering classic American musical comedies and Connecticut's answer to those romantic castles on the Rhine, not to mention the chance nearby to ride a puffing, chugging turn-of-the-century steam train, all adding even more incentive to make the trip.

Start your get-acquainted tour of Essex at its most significant site, Steamboat Dock, at the foot of Main Street on the riverfront. Situated in lush countryside just five miles above the spot where the Connecticut River feeds into the sea, Essex has been inextricably tied to its river from the first days in 1648 when settlers from the shore colony of Old Saybrook decided to form a farming community a bit inland. The first wharf at the site of the present Steamboat Dock was in operation as early as 1656 and trade with the West Indies had begun by the 1660s.

Shipbuilding was soon a major activity as well, and Connecticut's first warship, the *Oliver Cromwell*, was built at the Hayden Yard here in 1776. The British raided and burned the flourishing shipyards as well as 28 ships in the harbor during the War of 1812. That event is commemorated by a marker at the foot of the harbor, as well as by the Essex Fife and Drum Corps, known as the Sailing Masters of 1812, who parade down Main Street in period dress to mark most national holidays.

Things revived after the war, however, and Essex's ships and sailors were known to nineteenth-century commerce throughout the world. A new era of prominence came with the arrival of steamboat service on the river in 1823; the original Steamboat Dock was built in 1845 to accommodate the growing traffic. It was enlarged and the dockhouse built in the 1860s. The three-story clapboard structure with its graceful cupola became a well-known landmark for river passengers.

The Connecticut River Foundation has restored the exterior of the historic dockhouse and a portion of the interior as it was in its warehouse days. The building also houses a small museum with exhibits telling the story of the waterway and Essex-built ships with tools, navigational instruments, paintings, and scale-model steamboats.

An unusual display is the full-size reproduction of the *Turtle*, America's first submarine, designed in 1776 in nearby Old Sayville. Though the sub fared better in its river trials than it did once it went to war, it is still a fascinating exhibit.

Ask at the museum for a printed walking tour to lead you to the rest of the town's sights. Though they aren't on the map, you'll certainly want to check out some of the many shops on Main Street and in a little shopping complex just behind it for antiques, handicrafts, gifts, and gewgaws, many with a nautical bent.

For those who want a closer look at the river itself, there are several excursion trips offered from the dock; ask about them at the museum. Local parks with water views are located in coves on both the east and west sides of town. Bushnell Park off Bushnell Street above the boatyards and the Town Park off Main Street are ideal spots for a picnic lunch.

The official town tour leads past the gracious homes that once belonged to schooner captains and shipbuilders, and past the churches and other historic buildings that tell more about the Essex of yesterday. As you follow the tour along Main to Essex Square and up Methodist Hill to Prospect Street and West Avenue, watch for some of the distinctive fan lights, the handsome door knobs and knockers, and the unusual brick patterns and chimneys that mark many of the handsome homes in town.

The Pratt House at 20 West Avenue, restored and furnished by the Essex Historical Society, gives a glimpse of life in Essex in the mid-1800s. Inside you'll see fine oak and chestnut beams, burnished paneling, and many rare antiques originally owned by the Pratts, an important early family in town. The Essex Garden Club has planted a fragrant Colonial herb garden around the house.

The 1845 Baptist church is hard to miss, with its white steeple and gold dome. It is one of only two examples of Egyptian revival architecture in the country.

Walk to the end of Prospect and turn left on North Main and you'll be at the Riverview Cemetery, resting place of the Pratts, Haydens, and other Essex first families. This is a cemetery with a river view—a lovely panorama across the Connecticut River to the Lyme Hills.

The Griswold Inn in Essex is part of the official tour. Even the British troops who invaded in 1814 made a point of staying at "the Gris," which has been open for business on the same spot on Main Street since 1776 and has hardly changed on the outside over the years.

You'll have to call early to get one of the 20 much-in-demand rooms here, but whether you stay or not a stop is a must, at least for a meal and a visit. The Sunday Hunt Breakfast, a worthy local tradition, includes the inn's 1776 sausages, made from a recipe handed down for eight generations.

If the inn is filled, there are other inviting possibilities in the neighborhood. The Copper Beech Inn in nearby Ivoryton has elegant rooms and a restaurant that is a frequent award winner. A few miles upriver in East Haddam, in a secluded setting but within walking distance of a major local attraction, the Goodspeed Opera House, you'll find the Bishopsgate Inn, which comes highly recommended by several who have stayed there. And the Inn at Chester is a sophisticated rural charmer complete with tennis court, jogging trail, and exercise room with sauna.

Reserve ahead for all the choice inns in this popular region as well as for the Goodspeed Opera House, a highlight of a Connecticut River Valley visit. Musicals of the 1920s and 1930s are served up here in a restored Victorian theater full of frou-frous and charm. The theater is located right on the river, and the Gelston House next door is an ideal place for before- or after-theater dining and drinks. There is a newer branch of the Goodspeed in Chester dedicated to new musicals.

If you've spent Saturday on foot in Essex, you might want to begin Sunday's sightseeing with a drive along River Road, with glimpses of water and many fine houses along the way. Then it's on to a different kind of ride—or two of them, to be exact, by land and by sea. The Valley Railroad, just a couple of miles from the center of town, offers a double dose of nostalgia, a ten-mile excursion into the countryside aboard the same kind of steam train that grandpa might have ridden when he was a boy, then an optional connection to a riverboat for a half-hour cruise up the Connecticut River.

If you haven't taken a ride on the river yet, don't miss the opportunity. The pristine and beautiful woodland banks are a pleasure to behold anytime and ablaze with color in autumn foliage season. And there are just enough diversions to whip photographers into action— hilltop mansions, the gingerbread façade of the Goodspeed Opera House, and the stone turrets of Gillette Castle.

When you get back to shore, take the three-minute ride across the river from Chester to Hadlyme aboard one of the region's oldest and smallest ferryboats for a closeup view of Gillette Castle, a one-of-a-kind curiosity.

It was built by William Gillette, a somewhat eccentric gentleman who gained fame and fortune by portraying Sherlock Holmes on the stage. The castle cost over a million dollars, quite a sum when it was built in the early 1900s; complete with turrets and balconies, it was meant to re-create the feel of the castles on the Rhine that Gillette had admired in Europe.

Among Gillette's eccentricities was a dislike for metal. All the doors are fitted with wooden locks operated by hidden springs, and even the light switches are made of wood. The walls are wooden also, hand-carved of oak. To protect all that wood Gillette had fire hoses and a sprinkler system installed, safety features that were many years ahead of their time.

Whatever you think of the castle, you'll certainly admire the clifftop river view. The grounds are now a state park, and the perfect place for a picnic with a last sweeping perspective on the Connecticut River as it winds its way downstream to Essex and on to the sea.

Connecticut Area Code: 203

DRIVING DIRECTIONS Essex is reached via I-95 or I-91. From either direction, take Route 9 to exit 3, then Route 153, which becomes Main Street. Essex is about 133 miles from Boston, 118 miles from New York, and 35 miles from Hartford.

PUBLIC TRANSPORTATION Amtrak to Old Saybrook; Greyhound to Middletown. Both are just a short drive from Essex. You'll need a car to get around the area.

ACCOMMODATIONS *Griswold Inn,* Main Street, Essex, 767-0991, $$ CP • *Copper Beech Inn,* Main Street, Ivoryton, 767-0330, $$$–$$$$ • *Bishopsgate Inn,* Goodspeed Landing, East Haddam, 873-1677, $$$ CP • *The Inn at Chester,* 328 W. Main Street, 526-4961, $$$ • *Riverwind,* 46 Main Street, Deep River, 526-3047, small pleasant bed and breakfast, $$–$$$ CP • *Stonecroft Inn,* 17 Main Street, East Haddam, 873-1754, 1832 home, $$$ CP.

BED AND BREAKFAST *Nutmeg Bed and Breakfast,* 222 Girard Avenue, Hartford, CT 06107, 236-6698 • *Seacoast Landings Bed and Breakfast Registry,* 133 Neptune Drive, Groton, CT 06340, 442-1940 • *Bed and Breakfast Ltd.,* PO Box 216, New Haven, CT 06513, 469-3260.

DINING *Griswold Inn* (see above), $$ • *Copper Beech Inn* (see above), $$$–$$$$ • *The Gull,* Essex Harbor, 767-0916, informal nautical atmosphere on the docks, $$–$$$ • *Restaurant du Village,* 59 Main Street, Chester, 526-5058, excellent French bistro, $$$ • *Gelston House,* Goodspeed Landing, East Haddam, 873-9300, $$–$$$ • *Fine Bouche,* Main Street, Centerbrook, 767-1277, fine French, $$$–$$$$; prix fixe $$$$.

SIGHTSEEING *Connecticut River Foundation Museum,* Main Street, Essex, 767-8269. Hours: April to December, Tuesday to Sunday, 10 A.M. to 5 P.M. Adults, $1.50; children, $.50 • *Valley Railroad,* Essex, 767-0103; check for current hours and prices • *Goodspeed Opera House,* Route 82, East Haddam, 873-8668. Hours: season runs April through November; performances Wednesday through Saturday evenings; Wednesday, Saturday, and Sunday matinees. Check for current productions and prices • *Gillette Castle,*

Gillette Castle State Park, Route 82, Hadlyme, 536-2336. Hours: Memorial Day to mid-October, daily 10 A.M. to 5 P.M. Adults, $1; under 12, free; park admission free.

INFORMATION Connecticut Valley Tourism Commission, 70 College Street, Middletown, CT 06457, 347-6924.

Mountains and Sea in Camden

Captain John Smith (of Pocahontas fame) said it well: "Camden lies under the high mountains of the Penobscot against whose feet the sea doth beat."

In less poetic terms, Camden, Maine, is a town where the mountains meet the sea. The deep blue natural harbor fed by rushing falls reflects the wooded slopes of Mt. Battie and Mt. Megunticook in a scenic juxtaposition that has won the awestruck admiration of visitors ever since the days of Samuel de Champlain and other early explorers.

It is a winning summer destination that becomes doubly appealing in fall when the crowds recede and the harbor begins to mirror the myriad autumn colors of the mountains. Middle to late September, before the Camden windjammer fleet calls it a season, is an ideal time for a visit.

At the turn of the century, Camden's favored location attracted the wealthy, who built elaborate summer homes here and traveled up the coast by steamer to vacation. The houses still grace the town, but today Camden is a tourist magnet for everyone. The well-kept village, festooned with hanging flower pots on every available lamp post, has good reason for its boast of being "the prettiest town in Maine." The harbor scene has been made even more picturesque by the presence of New England's largest fleet of windjammers, the many-masted sailing ships patterned after clipper ships of old. The resulting influx of visitors has transformed quiet Camden into an attractive browsers' town, filled with shops, galleries, and restaurants, and has led to a bumper crop of lodgings that can't be beat anywhere on the coast.

The town's dowager hotel is the rambling Whitehall Inn, where Edna St. Vincent Millay was discovered by a wealthy patron when she read her poem "Renascence" in the parlor now named for her. The main attraction of the other old standby, the Camden Harbour Inn, is that it has the town's best harbor view—the one you see on all the postcards—though the rooms here are very small for the price.

Both inns have been outclassed by a newcomer called Norumbega, a Victorian mansion that is one of the most elegant inns on the East

Coast. It is a virtual castle with many porches and balconies overlooking the ocean. Half a million dollars reputedly were spent to bring back to mint condition the elaborate carving, golden oak paneling, and other magnificent touches that make this residence so distinctive. The luxurious furnishings in the public rooms and seven bedrooms do justice to their formal setting.

A simpler but particularly attractive country inn recently opened just across the way is the Edgecombe-Coles House, a turn-of-the-century summer home that is now a warm and tasteful lodging furnished with antiques. Fresh flowers and potpourri in the rooms reflect the attention of the caring innkeepers, who did the redecorating themselves.

Camden also has a number of attractive small bed-and-breakfast inns—the Maine Stay and Hawthorn Inn among them—and there are six rooms at the Belmont if you want to be just upstairs from the restaurant judged to be the best in town and, some say, on the coast. For an unpretentious lodge and cottage arrangement right on the water, the High Tide Inn is the choice.

Wherever you stay, it's the Public Landing that you'll want to head for first of all, to admire the sleek boats in the harbor and take in the extraordinary view—Camden Hills rising on one side, Penobscot Bay opening on the other.

Most of the tall-masted windjammers in the harbor sail off on six-day cruises on Monday, returning on the weekend in a regal display of furling sails. While some of these tall ships were built exclusively for the tourist trade, others enjoyed intriguing histories as Grand Banks fishing schooners or pilot ships before they were converted to passenger vessels.

The local tourist office is behind the parking lot at the landing, and is well stocked with information, including a walking tour map. You can't miss the shops on Bay View Avenue, at the Public Landing, and on Main Street. The town tour proceeds from the landing left past the shops to the Yacht Club, a fixture on the docks since 1906, and along the water to the Camden Harbour Inn and that special view.

Turn right on Limerock past the inn, then right again on Chestnut to see some of the town's finest homes. Number 87 is the 1800 Jacobs House, home of an early town official and the site of a fortification during the War of 1812. Number 77 is Thayercroft, a distinguished 1821 house that was a setting for the movie *Peyton Place*. The entire block is lined with historic homes from the late 1700s and early 1800s, including the Hathaway-Cushing-Millay house at number 31, which belonged to members of the family of Edna St. Vincent Millay.

Past the Baptist church, you'll be back at the village green, where you can bear left to Elm and Wood and Pleasant to see more houses or take a stroll down Main Street to view some interesting nineteenth-century town architecture while you check out the shops. You'll no doubt want to return to the many other shops around the landing as well.

Like many Maine towns that attract tourists, Camden has become a showcase for talented state artisans, and you'll be able to find everything from hand-thrown pottery to handmade fishermen's sweaters. Maine Gathering on Commercial Street has the work of over 30 Maine craftspeople. Among the many shops on Bayview, Unique 1 specializes in Maine woolen sweaters and ceramics and Ducktrap Bay Trading Company near the Public Landing has decoys and other nautical carvings. Back on Main, you'll be offered complimentary coffee or tea on a balcony overlooking the harbor at the Smiling Cow, a fine crafts and gift store that has been run by the same family on the same spot since 1940. The Admiral's Buttons and Harborside on Bay View and Maine Sport on Main are among the many clothing stores in town selling chic and practical boating attire.

When you're ready for a lunch break, Cappy's Chowder House or the Waterfront with its harbor deck should fill the bill. Or you might pick up a lunch at the Blueberry Puffin on the landing and take it to the grassy slopes of the Camden Amphitheater behind the library, scene of a Shakespeare Festival in summer and a pleasant place to sit with a harbor view anytime. Another possibility is the shoreside picnic area at Camden Hills State Park on Route 1, just north of town.

Lunch or not, take the park toll road to the top of Mt. Battie for an exceptional view of the town and harbor below. A short, steep hiking trail from Megunticook Street in Camden will also bring you to the top.

Some of Maine's most scenic hiking, in fact, is in this park. The top of Mt. Megunticook, the second-highest point on the Atlantic seaboard, can be reached in a one-hour hike from park headquarters on Route 1 that includes a stop at a natural grotto. Megunticook Lake and Megunticook River separate the several peaks in the park's 5,000 acres from the Camden Hills, making for views on all sides. Mt. Battie and Camden Snow Bowl are among the rare places where you can see the sea as you ski.

If you prefer your water views from the side of a boat, you'll find several going out on excursions from the landing into Penobscot Bay through late September. All year round you can drive north to Lincolnville and board the Maine State Ferry for the 25-minute crossing to Isleboro or go south to Rockland for the ferry ride to Vinalhaven or North Haven Island, an hour and a half and an hour and ten minutes away, respectively. Boats to Monhegan Island leave from Port Clyde. Vinalhaven is the biggest of the islands, with shops and an art gallery, and Monhegan is by far the most scenic, with dramatic clifftop vistas of the sea. Isleboro offers a state park and beaches, a Sailors Memorial Museum, a gallery, and the lovely Isleboro Inn if you want to get away from it all. All are extremely pleasant outings on a fine fall day, and there's every good chance of spotting seals cavorting in the water along the way and even dolphins and whales if you are lucky. Some of the ferries do not operate on Sunday, so plan for Saturday or check current schedules before you make the trip. There are also excursion cruises out of Rockland Harbor. Inquire at the Public Landing.

A highly recommended Sunday activity is the six-mile drive to Rockport, a tiny and totally charming fishing and shipbuilding village dating back to the early 1770s. The entire village was made a National Historic District in the mid-1970s, and there are 127 buildings listed in the inventory.

In Marine Park, overlooking the picturesque harbor, you'll find a statue of Andre the seal, a late local hero who used to swim up from Boston to spend the summer every year. Smart seal.

Rockport has become very much an artists' town, home of the Maine Coast Artists Gallery, situated in a strikingly renovated old livery station cum firehouse, and host to the respected summer Maine Photography Workshops. The restored Town Hall–Opera House at the start of Marine Park is known for its acoustics and is home to summer Bay Chamber Concerts, theater, and other cultural events.

What to do in Rockport? Visit the Maine Coast Artists Gallery, check for a last exhibition at the Photography Workshop Gallery, and wander through the handful of galleries and shops on Main Street. Admire the many fine historic homes on almost any village street, and drive out to Vesper Hill, known as the Children's Chapel, a gift to the community by a former resident, for a quiet and beautiful spot over-looking the sea. You'll understand why this is a favorite site for local marriages. The Sail Loft is the place if you want to have Sunday brunch or dinner overlooking the harbor.

To finish off the day, you might drive a few miles farther south into Rockland, not the most scenic town you've ever seen but home of the Farnsworth Art Museum, a superior regional museum of paintings and sculpture. Among the Maine collections are works by all three genera-tions of Wyeths. The handsome Victorian Farnsworth Homestead, res-idence of the museum's benefactress, adjoins the museum.

Or you may choose to return to Camden for more hiking or shop-ping—or simply a last look at that incomparable harbor scene where the mountains meet the sea.

Maine Area Code: 207

DRIVING DIRECTIONS Camden is about halfway between Port-land and Bar Harbor on US 1 on the Maine coast. From the Maine Turnpike, take Route 17 east to Route 90 to US 1. Camden is about

200 miles from Boston, 400 miles from New York, and 290 miles from Hartford.

PUBLIC TRANSPORTATION Greyhound bus service direct to Camden; air service to Bangor (50 miles away), Portland (85 miles), or Rockland (8 miles). You can manage easily without a car if you stay in town; get to the park by hike or bike.

ACCOMMODATIONS *Norumbega,* High Street (US 1 North), 236-4646, $$$$$ CP ● *Edgecombe-Coles House,* 64 High Street, 236-2336, $$$ CP ● *Whitehall Inn,* 51 High Street, 236-3391, $$$$ MAP ● *Camden Harbour Inn,* 83 Bayview Street, 236-4200, $$$–$$$$$ CP ● *Maine Stay,* 22 High Street, 236-9636, $$ CP ● *Hawthorn Inn,* 9 High Street, 236-8842, $$–$$$ CP ● *Belmont,* 6 Belmont Avenue, 236-8053, $$$ CP ● *Swan House,* 49 Mountain Street, 236-8275, pleasant small bed and breakfast, $$ CP ● *The High Tide Inn,* Route 1 North, 236-3724, $$–$$$ ● *Samoset,* at the Breakwater, Rockport, 341-1650, modern complete resort, indoor tennis and pool, golf, health club, $$$$.

BED AND BREAKFAST *Bed and Breakfast of Maine,* 32 Colonial Village, Falmouth, ME 04105, 781-4528 ● *Bed and Breakfast Down East Ltd.,* Box 547, Eastbrook, ME 04634, 565-3517.

DINING *Belmont* (see above), nouvelle French and exceptional, $$$ ● *Camden Harbour Inn* (see above), $$–$$$ ● *Whitehall Inn* (see above), $$–$$$ ● *The Waterfront,* Bayview Street, Harbor Square, 236-3747, lunch and dinner, $–$$ ● *The Sail Loft,* Public Landing, Rockport, 236-2330, $$–$$$ ● Informal fare: *Cappy's Chowder House,* Main Street ● For lobster: *Lobster Pound Restaurant,* US 1, Lincolnville (11:30 A.M. to 8 P.M.; closes Columbus Day).

SIGHTSEEING *Camden Hills State Park,* Route 1 North, Camden, 236-3109. Free except toll road to top of Mt. Battie, $.75. Shore area open May 1 to November 1, small fee. Free hiking trail maps available at Information Center on Route 1 ● Cruises from Public Landing, June to September, inquire at Camden Information Booth for current schedule and prices; among the boats operating: Sloop *Dirigo,* 236-2908, day sails; Schooner *Surprise,* 236-4325 ● *Maine State Ferry Service,* US 1, Lincolnville Beach, and 517A Main Street, Rockland, 595-5543; inquire at Camden Information Booth for current schedules and prices ● *Maine Coast Artists Gallery,* Russell Avenue, Rockport, 236-2875. Hours: May through September, daily 10 A.M. to 7 P.M. ● *Farnsworth Museum,* off US 1, Rockland, 596-6457. Hours: June 1 to September 30, Monday to Saturday, 10 A.M. to 5 P.M., Sunday from 1

P.M., after October 1, closed Monday. Free ● *Farnsworth Homestead.* Hours: June 1 to mid-September. Small fee ● *Windjammer Cruise Information,* Maine Windjammer Association, Box 317T, Rockport, ME 04876.

INFORMATION   Rockport-Camden-Lincolnville Chamber of Commerce, PO Box 919, Camden, ME 04843, 236-4404. Information booth at the Public Landing parking lot open year round.

A Bewitching Halloween in Salem

It stands to reason. Since Salem, Massachusetts, is best known for the long-ago days when witch fever swept the town, it seems only natural that Halloween is a cause for celebration here.

Not that Salem today bears much resemblance to the town that was notorious for its witch hunt. These days what comes through is a pleasant, historic New England maritime center dating back to 1626, now in the process of sprucing up its heritage, and a town as much a literary shrine for its "House of Seven Gables" complex as a reminder of witch trial terror. For a relatively small town, Salem has a large share of sights to interest visitors, including two exceptional museums and some sea captains' handsome old mansions.

But there's no question that Salem is a great place to be at Halloween, when the whole town gets into the spirit of the holiday in a big way. On the weekend before the big day, there are happenings such as a "haunted house" at Pickering Wharf, ghost story telling at the Witch Museum, "Eerie Events" at the Essex Institute, costume balls, a costume parade on the common—even a gathering of psychics ready to read your fortune. And you can join a spooky "Witch Trial Trail" walk by candlelight, or take a candlelit tour of the House of the Seven Gables.

The events change slightly from year to year, as more activities are added to the roster. The agenda offers more than can be fit into one day, so you'll have to pick and choose your activities, saving some of the sights for Sunday.

With or without kids, do take time for the Children's Costume Parade at 12:30 P.M. on Saturday, a procession of several dozen Salem children of all sizes in their Halloween finery. It's guaranteed to bring smiles and some adorable souvenir snapshots.

The highlight of a stay for most people is the Salem Witch Museum. It is crowded during Halloween weekends, so an early or late visit is a good idea. The excellent presentation here puts you in the center of a darkened room and uses spotlights to showcase life-size reenactments of the shameful 1692 hysteria.

Salem's was not the only witchcraft trial in New England, but it was by far the worst. The only thing to be said for the debacle was that the revulsion it caused finally put an end to sentencing so-called witches to death.

The Witch House in Salem turns out to be the restored home of Jonathan Corwin, judge of the original witchcraft court. Preliminary examinations of the accused were held here, but the residence is actually of far more interest as one of the oldest dwellings in the United States. Built in the early seventeenth century, it is filled with a fine collection of seventeenth-century furniture and household items. A number of other handsome historic houses have been preserved with period furnishings and made open to the public in Salem. Several of these are maintained by the Essex Institute, and four are located right next to the Institute's museum building on Essex Street.

The museum itself, containing the art and artifacts of Salem's Essex County since its beginnings, offers a well-done short movie on local history, plus displays of furniture, clocks, china, silver, paintings, and military memorabilia. It is attractively laid out on two floors around an open court, and doing justice to the exhibits can take up a worthwhile two hours of your time.

The Peabody Museum across the street began with the formation of the East India Marine Society, an organization of Salem ship's captains who had navigated the seas near or beyond the Cape of Good Hope or Cape Horn. In those days, Salem was one of the busiest seaports on the East Coast, with her ships to be found on all the world's waters. The "curiosities" brought back by the ship's captains formed the basis of the museum's first collections. It holds myriad nineteenth-century treasures from Asia and the Pacific Islands as well as some fascinating nautical exhibits of scrimshaw, figureheads, old fishing implements, and navigational instruments. There's even a full-size reconstruction of the master's saloon of *Cleopatra's Barge,* built in 1816 as America's first ocean-going vessel.

It's probably best to schedule one museum per day, to get the most of each—but even then you won't have exhausted the most important sights of Salem.

Some of the wharves used by the old sailing fleet can still be seen. Derby Wharf, stretching half a mile into Salem Harbor, has an 1800s lighthouse and a warehouse. Central Wharf still boasts the foundation of a brick warehouse dating back to 1791. Both are part of the Salem Maritime Historic Site maintained by the U.S. Department of the Interior. The original Customs House of 1819 also has been restored, with offices furnished just as they were in the old days. You can listen to a tape of the prose Nathaniel Hawthorne wrote while he worked here.

Nearby are more historic houses and a herb garden, the old Scale House where weighing and measuring equipment was kept, and the West India Goods Store, built to sell cargoes brought from Africa and the West Indies but now a coffee house and a shop selling imported spices.

Across the street is the "House of Seven Gables," made immortal by Nathaniel Hawthorne's novel. It was actually the 1668 home of ship's captain John Turner. The house with its secret stairway is a charmer, and it is easy to see why it captured Hawthorne's imagination when he came to visit his cousin, Susan Ingersoll, whose family later lived here. The Turner house is part of a small historic complex of early homes, including Hawthorne's own birthplace, an antique-filled, gambrel-roofed seventeenth-century residence that was moved to this appropriate site in 1958.

A more modern addition to the waterfront is nearby Pickering Wharf, a replica of a commercial wharf now bustling with shops and restaurants. Another recent addition to the scene is Salem Marketplace, a former open-air fruit and vegetable market that has been converted into brick stalls housing a variety of specialty shops.

As if it weren't difficult enough to fit all of Salem's sights into a weekend, there's the lure of Marblehead, one of the shore's most distinctive seaside communities, beckoning just four miles away. When George Washington visited here, he noted that Marblehead certainly had "the look of antiquity." Some 200 years later you can walk the same twisting streets and see the same mix of merchant's mansions and steep-gabled fishermen's cottages that mark this village's 350-year existence as a seaport.

A ride along the steep shoreline past the homes crowded pell-mell along the winding lanes is exceptional and shouldn't be missed. The area's loveliest inn, the Harbor Light, is here as well. If nothing else, at least plan a meal in town to give yourself a chance for the drive.

Better yet, enjoy the spooky hijinks of Halloween and then think about a return visit. After the goblins have gone, you can concentrate on the rest of the sights of this intriguing town by the sea.

Salem Area Code: 508
Marblehead Area Code: 617

DRIVING DIRECTIONS Salem is located on the Massachusetts shore 16 miles north of Boston at exit 25E off Route 128. It is 238 miles from New York and 128 miles from Hartford.

PUBLIC TRANSPORTATION MBTA bus and North Station train service from Boston.

ACCOMMODATIONS *Hawthorne Hotel,* 18 Washington Square West, 744-4080, a hotel conveniently located in the town center, $$$–$$$$ ● *Salem Inn,* 7 Summer Street, 742-0680, adjoining historic houses, pleasant rooms, and a back garden, $$$ ● *Susannah Flint House,* 98 Essex Street, 744-5281, modest bed and breakfast, central location, $$ CP ● *The Stepping Stone Inn,* 19 Washington Square North, 745-2156, bed and breakfast on the green, $$$ CP ● *The Inn at 7 Winter Street,* 7 Winter Street, 745-9520, Victorian bed and breakfast, $$$ CP ● *Pleasant Manor Inn,* 264 Pleasant Street, Marblehead, 631-5843, modest Victorian inn with a tennis court, $$$ ● *Harbor Light Inn,* 58 Washington Street, Marblehead, 631-2186, special and elegant Colonial, beams and four-posters, $$$–$$$$.

BED AND BREAKFAST See Boston listings, page 60.

DINING *The Lyceum,* 43 Church Street, 745-7665, historic building and best food in town, $–$$$ ● *Chase House,* Pickering Wharf, 744-0000, seafood, water view, $–$$ ● *Rosalie's,* 18 Sewall Street, Marblehead, 631-9888, popular Italian, in an old factory building, $$–$$$ ● *Roosevelt's,* 300 Derby Street, Salem, 745-9608, fun, Teddy Roosevelt decor, $–$$ ● *Café La Fortuna,* 107 Essex Street, Salem, 745-1044, candlelit Italian, $$–$$$ ● *Tammany Hall,* 208 Derby Street, Salem, 745-8755, political memorabilia, popular for Sunday brunch, $–$$ ● *Giancarlo's,* 261 Washington Street, Marblehead, 639-2156, excellent Italian, $$–$$$ ● *Maddee's Sail Loft,* 15 State Street, Marblehead, 631-9824, informal seafood, busy bar is the meeting place in town, $–$$ ● *The Landing,* 81 Front Street, Marblehead, 631-1878, informal, seafood, water views, $$.

SIGHTSEEING *Salem Halloween Happenings,* write to Chamber of Commerce for complete current schedule ● *Salem Witch Museum,* 19½ Washington Square North, 744-1692. Hours: daily 10 A.M. to 5 P.M., July and August to 7 P.M., during Halloween weekends, to midnight. Adults $3; children $1.75 ● *Essex Institute Museum Complex,* 132 Essex Street, 744-3390. Monday to Saturday, 9 A.M. to 4:30 P.M., Sunday and holidays, 1 P.M. to 5 P.M., shorter schedule after November 1. Adults $2.50; 6 to 16, $1.50; combination ticket, museum and three historic houses, adults $5; children, $2.50 ● *Peabody Museum,* East India Square, 745-1876, Monday to Saturday, 10 A.M. to 5 P.M., Sunday from 1 P.M., tours daily at 2 P.M. Adults, $3; children 6 to 16, $1.50 ● *Salem Maritime National Historic Site,* 178 Derby Street, 744-4323, March to November, daily 8:30 A.M. to 5 P.M., phone for winter schedule. Free ● *House of Seven Gables,* 54 Turner Street, 744-0991, guided tours daily of four historic buildings, 10 A.M. to 4:30 P.M., summer 9:30 A.M. to 5:30 P.M. Adults $4; children 5 to 17, $1.50.

INFORMATION Salem Chamber of Commerce, Old Town Hall, 32 Derby Square, Salem, MA 01970, 744-0004.

A Peak Experience at Killington

Back in 1739, Reverend Samuel Peters stood atop the 4,241-foot peak of Killington Mountain, surveyed the land around him, and christened the land "Verd-Mont," ever after to be known as the Green Mountain State.

It's probably fortunate that the good reverend made the climb in the "verd" of summer, for had he come to the top of Killington in autumn, Vermont might have gone nameless. The four-state panorama of mountains and valleys cloaked in crimson, gold, and orange has left more than one viewer at a total loss for words.

The good news is that nowadays you don't even have to climb for the view. The Killington Gondola, one of the longest ski lifts in America, is in service in the fall to bring leaf-watchers to the highest point reached by aerial lift in New England.

The ride alone is good reason to plan an early October weekend near Killington, but the area has more than its share of lures all year long. In addition to being the largest ski complex in the East, with six mountains to choose from, this is prime hiking territory, offering both the Appalachian and Long trails, which converge on Route 4 at a point near Pico, Killington's smaller ski mountain neighbor. Tennis and golf facilities are plentiful, and you'll search far to find more scenic backroading via bike, horseback, or car. The interesting sights to be seen nearby make the rides all the more rewarding.

The same rugged terrain that makes the area so attractive also prevents it from having a central village. Rutland is nearby to the west on Route 4 and Woodstock is within reach to the east on the same road. But other than the ski lodge motels on the access road, accommodations near Killington are scattered. They run the gamut from motel to condominium to cozy inn to full-scale resort, and where you stay may well depend on just how much activity you have in mind, as well as on your budget.

One major advantage to a popular winter area with over 100 lodgings in the vicinity is that even at the height of the foliage season, when all the country inns have been booked up for months, some of those motels on the access road or Route 4 may still have vacancy signs. And the Killington-Pico Lodging Bureau is available to help you find a place with just one phone call.

If you plan ahead, two of the prime inn candidates are in Chittenden, a small village with an attractive reservoir, tucked away from it all in the woods on a back road about six miles from Route 4.

For a secluded, homey country inn where meals are served family style and guests get a chance to know one another, Tulip Tree Inn is the place. This is just what many people imagine a country inn should be—tastefully done but comfortable and warm.

Not far away in Chittendon is one of the few real resorts in Vermont, Mountain Top Inn, and an attractive one it is, with a spectacular 500-acre site high above a lake surrounded by mountains. The views from the inn terrace and dining rooms are unbeatable and the rooms, both public and private, are appealing. There's everything to do here: sailing, canoeing or fishing on the lake, tennis, horseback riding, golf, and indoor exercise and recreation rooms plus sauna and whirlpool. If the tab is within your budget, you won't go wrong.

Red Clover Inn, a former 1840 summer estate, offers a gracious stay out in the country in Mendon. Vermont Inn is homey and more reasonably priced, and if you want to drive about 15 minutes west of Rutland to Fair Haven, you can stay in style at the Vermont Marble Inn, a marble mansion, circa 1860, with very reasonable rates—particularly considering that you get a six-course breakfast.

For an attractive condominium community on the mountainside with tennis, golf, lakes and ponds, and very attractive accommodations, there's Killington Village. The Villager Motel, part of the complex, offers all the recreation.

One last really luxurious possibility is Hawk Mountain, an award-winning community of fieldstone-and-wood mountain homes scattered in wooded pockets on the mountainside with picture windows to bring in the view and big stone fireplaces to warm those cool Vermont evenings. Annabelle's, the resident restaurant, is highly regarded—but some guests never get there at all. Instead, they light the fire and phone for a chef, who promptly arrives to cook and serve them dinner on the spot. Tennis, riding, and boating are all available on the grounds.

If you choose more modest accommodations, take note that you can still have access to the stables at Mountain Top and Hawk, and tennis courts can be rented at Cortina Inn, Killington Resorts, Brookside Health and Racquet Club, and the Vermont Inn.

Having settled in, you can plan your activities. If hiking is on your agenda, a popular short trek is Deer Leap Trail, which takes about half an hour up a steep winding path ending on a cliff with a panoramic view from 2,490 feet up. All the skiing trails on Killington and Pico become hiking trails off season, and the Long Trail Hiking Path, part of the famous Footpath in the Wilderness, runs from Killington Mountain to Pico and then down to Sherburne Pass on Route 4. If you start at the top, taking the gondola to the summit, the average time down is three hours.

Hike or not, the gondola ride is quite something. There is a small nature trail at the top, a cafeteria, and a deck where you can have drinks with an unforgettable view: the Green, White, Berkshire, and Adirondack mountains spread out around you.

There's no real competition for this view, though the outlook at the top of the Killington Chairlift, which is slightly less expensive, is clearly not to be sniffed at. There is another unique scenic ride in store if you take the chairlift up to the Alpine Slide at Pico and come down the trails some 3,410 feet on a sled. The sled has a control stick, so you needn't worry about descending at breakneck speed; you set your own pace.

Most people choose a more earthbound kind of ride, doing the back roads by car. It's usually pleasantest to plan a route with sightseeing stops across the way, and that's easy to do in this area. Heading north, you might want to begin by following Route 4 through Rutland and then north on Route 3 to Proctor, a town where everything is made of marble, from the schools and churches to the sidewalks and the bridge spanning Otter Creek.

Proctor is the heart of the Vermont marble industry and the largest marble production center in the country. A film at the Vermont Marble Exhibit briefly explains how the marble quarried from the Green Mountains is processed into the handsome polished slabs that mark many of the nation's best-known buildings. From the visitors' gallery you can watch huge slabs weighing up to ten tons swing through the air to the diamond-blade coping saws that slice them right before your eyes.

There are slabs and seconds for sale at the Marble Market outside, in case you want to take home a table top as a souvenir, and many smaller marble items are available inside at the gift shop.

There's yet another sight in little Proctor: Wilson Castle, a nine-teenth-century mansion on a 115-acre estate. It is quite an elaborate place, with 84 stained-glass windows, hand-painted ceilings, and priceless Oriental and European antiques as well as fine art and sculpture.

Once you've had your fill of finery, head north from Proctor to Route 7 and Pittsford, where you can learn about another backbone Vermont industry, maple sugaring, at the New England Maple Museum. This small museum doesn't look too promising at first glance, but it turns out to be quite interesting. Watch the slide show to find out how sap is turned to syrup, then inspect the tools involved—in this case, the largest collection of antique sugaring equipment ever assembled. There's also a simulation of modern techniques, complete with sap dripping from a tree into a bucket, with the wonderful smell of boiling syrup at the end of the process permeating everything. Needless to say, there is a gift shop waiting, filled with you know what.

A little farther north is Brandon, a pleasant village with some 200

historic buildings around two village greens. Among them is the Stephen Douglas Homestead, home of the famous orator who debated
Abraham Lincoln. The Brandon Antiques Center on Route 7 is a recommended stop for treasure hunters.

For views, the best bets are the roads that cut across the mountains.
Brandon Gap, running from Route 7 to Route 100, is unexcelled. If
you want to do a giant scenic loop back, follow Route 100 five miles
north to Hancock, with a detour there to Route 125 to see the cascades
at the Texas Falls Recreation Area.

Then make the drive from Route 100 back to Route 7 across the
Middlebury Gap, also known as the Robert Frost Memorial Drive.
(Frost's home was in Ripton, a town along the Gap road.) You'll come
out in East Middlebury, just four miles from the attractive college town
with its excellent Vermont State Crafts Center at Frog Hollow. Middlebury also has many shops that make for pleasant browsing.

An alternate return route is to go back to Brandon and then south on
Route 30 to Lake Bomoseen in Castleton or Lake St. Catherine in
Poultney, both in attractive state parks and ideal for picnicking.

If you've spent most of Saturday admiring nature via gondola, slide,
hiking boots, or automobile, you may be ready for a few sights and
shops in Rutland on Sunday. By Vermont standards Rutland, with a
population of 18,000, is a sizable city. It boasts the Chaffee Art Gallery, with continuous exhibits, and the Norman Rockwell Museum,
which has more than 1,000 pictures, including his famous Four Free-
doms and Boy Scouts series, Rockwell memorabilia, and all 326 of his
Saturday Evening Post covers.

Rutland also offers several discount stores. Dexter and Dunham
shoes are on Route 4 east of town. The Tennybrook Square complex
on North Main (Route 7) features Bass shoe and Hathaway shirt outlets
and Country Quilt and Fabric. Outlets for sweaters, sneakers, and canvas bags and luggage are located on Route 4 West.

The outlets are open on Sunday, but if you are interested in used and
rare books, you may want to get to Rutland on Saturday to visit
Charles E. Tuttle Company on Main Street, which maintains one of the
largest stocks in New England.

For more attractive shops, drive farther west on Route 4 to the
lovely Colonial town of Woodstock. Or, for a final dose of both scenery and history, make the 11-mile drive south on Route 100 to the
Plymouth Notch Historic District, and enjoy the view that made Calvin
Coolidge decide he'd rather return to Vermont than be President.

Vermont Area Code: 802

DRIVING DIRECTIONS   Killington Mountain is on US 4 near the
junction with Route 100. Killington is 158 miles from Boston, 250
miles from New York, and 162 miles from Hartford.

PUBLIC TRANSPORTATION: Eastern Express air service to Rutland, VT, or Lebanon, NH; Vermont Transit buses to Sherburne (Killington) or Rutland.

ACCOMMODATIONS *Tulip Tree Inn,* Chittenden, 483-6213, $$$$–$$$$$ MAP ● *Mountain Top Inn,* Chittenden, 483-2311, $$$$$ MAP ● *Red Clover Inn,* Woodward Road, Mendon, 775-2290, $$$$–$$$$$ MAP ● *Vermont Marble Inn,* on the green, Fair Haven, 265-8383, $$–$$$ CP ● *Vermont Inn,* US 4, Killington, 773-9847, $$$–$$$$ MAP ● *Killington Village* and *Villager Motel,* 718 Killington Road, 422-3101 or (800) 343-0762, condominium units, $$$$–$$$$$, motel, $$–$$$$ CP ● *Hawk Mountain,* Route 100, Pittsfield, 746-8911, condominium units in five locations, reception center at Annabelle's Restaurant, junction of Routes 100 and 107 in Stockbridge, $$$$–$$$$$ MAP. For information on last-minute vacancies, rates, and free reservations, contact Killington-Pico Areas Association, PO Box 114, Killington, VT 06751, (800) 372-2007 or 773-1330.

BED AND BREAKFAST *Vermont Bed and Breakfast Reservation Service,* PO Box 1, East Fairfield, VT 05448, 827-3827 ● *American Collection of Bed and Breakfasts,* 984 Gloucester Place, Schenectady, NY 12309, (518) 370-4948.

DINING *Hemingway's,* US 4 east of Route 100, 422-3886, continental menus, the area's best, $$$ ● *Annabelle's* (see above), 746-8911, excellent, $$–$$$ ● *Mountain Top Inn* (see above), come for the view, $$–$$$ ● *Vermont Inn* (see above), $$ ● *Red Clover Inn* (see above), $$ ● *Alpine Inn,* Killington Access Road, 422-3485, pleasant atmosphere, good Sunday brunch, $$–$$$ ● *Governor's Table,* 49 North Main Street, Rutland, 775-7277, historic home, elegant, Sunday champagne, $$–$$$ ● *Royal's Hearthside,* 37 North Main, Rutland, 774-0856, New England specialties, $–$$$ ● *Countryman's Pleasure,* Townline Road, Mendon, 773-7141, fine dining in a country home, $–$$$ ● *Vermont Marble Inn* (see above), $$.

SIGHTSEEING *Killington Gondola,* Route 4 (1 mile west of Route 100), 422-3333 Hours: daily late September to mid-October, 10 A.M. to 4 P.M. Adults, $11; children, $7 ● *Killington Chairlift* also operates from top of Killington Road, five miles from junction of Routes 4 and 100. Adults, $7; children, $5 ● *Pico Alpine Slide,* US 4, Rutland, 775-4345. Hours: Memorial Day to Columbus Day, daily (weather permitting) 10 A.M. to 5 P.M. Adults, $3.75; children, $2.75 ● *Vermont Marble Exhibit,* Route 3, Proctor, 459-3311. Hours: late May to late October, daily 9 A.M. to 5:30 P.M. Adults, $2.50; 6 to 12, $1 ● *Wilson Castle,* West Proctor Road, Proctor, 773-3284. Hours: late

May to mid-October, daily 8 A.M. to 6 P.M. Adults, $4; 6 to 12, $1 ●
New England Maple Museum and Gift Shop, US 7, Pittsfield,
483-9414. Hours: Memorial Day through October, daily 8:30 A.M. to
5:30 P.M.; rest of year, 10 A.M. to 4 P.M.; closed January and February. Adults, $1; children, $.50 ● *Chaffee Art Gallery,* US 7, Rutland,
775-0356. Hours: mid-May to December, daily 10 A.M. to 5 P.M.
Free. ● *Norman Rockwell Museum,* US 4, Rutland, 773-6095. Hours:
daily 10 A.M. to 5 P.M. Adults, $2; children, $1 ● *Plymouth Notch
Historic District,* US 100, Plymouth, 823-3226. Hours: mid-May to
mid-October, daily 9:30 A.M. to 5:30 P.M. Adults $2; under 15, free.

INFORMATION: Killington-Pico Association, Box 114, Killington, VT 05751, 775-7070. Rutland Chamber of Commerce, 7 Court
Square, PO Box 67, Rutland 05701, 773-2747.

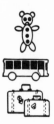

Bringing the Kids to Boston

Merlin the sea lion isn't what you would call modest. When he finishes
balancing balls on his nose, catching rings on his head, and otherwise
showing off in the water for the delighted audience at the New England
Aquarium, Merlin joins right in the applause, clapping his flippers in
appreciation of his own prowess—and causing the kids to cheer even
louder.

Merlin is just one of many things children can cheer about in Boston. From the playful sea lions and leaping dolphins at the Aquarium to
one of the country's most creative Children's Museums, the nation's
first Computer Museum, to the Boston Tea Party ship where visitors
take a turn at tossing chests of tea overboard, this town offers family
activities that are as much fun for grown-ups as for youngsters. It's
hard to imagine a better joint outing for either generation. The fact that
much of the fun is also educational is just icing on the cake.

The New England Aquarium has slightly reduced rates on Friday
nights and is literally guaranteed to start things off with a splash. The
exhibits of exotic fish from around the world are exceptional, particularly the 80-foot central tank simulating a coral reef in all its dazzling
colors and shapes. The show in the boat theater next door stars Merlin
and a chorus of dolphins who leap to amazing heights and find rings in
the water blindfolded, thanks to their built-in sonar equipment. The
loquacious dolphins also jabber ''hello'' to the enthralled audience.

Countless groups of schoolchildren have gotten a lively lesson in
American history by following the birth of America's fight for inde-

pendence along the red line of Boston's Freedom Trail. Make the trail your introduction to the city on Saturday, while everyone is still fresh. You can begin anywhere along the clearly marked lines, and any city information booth has brochures to tell you about the sights. But the best place to start is at the National Park Service's Information Center across from the Old State House, which officially maintains the major structures as Boston National Historical Park. The center has maps and guides to both the Freedom Trail and the Harbor Walk along the waterfront area, and also offers free guided tours.

If you don't think little ones can make it all on foot, there is a double-decker sightseeing bus with narration as well as trolley tours, allowing you to get on and off as often as you like all day.

From the center, the Freedom Trail runs roughly in a figure eight, with a tail leading into Boston's North End. In one loop are Boston Common, the land set aside for common use in 1634 that later served as a training ground for Revolutionary soldiers and is now the nation's oldest public park; the golden-domed State House designed by Charles Bulfinch for the new independent Commonwealth of Massachusetts; Park Street Church, where the song "America" was first sung publicly; and the Granary Burying Ground, where Paul Revere, Samuel Adams, John Hancock, James Otis, and other patriots are buried.

While you are at Boston Common, you may want to stroll over to the more formal Public Garden next door and take a ride on the famous swan boats, which have been a fixture here since 1877.

Sights on the second loop include the 1749 Kings Chapel, the first Anglican church in the United States and later the first for the Unitarian faith; the Kings Chapel Burying Ground, established in 1630; the Old State House, where James Otis aroused his countrymen when he proclaimed in 1761, "Taxation without representation is tyranny"; and the Old Corner Bookstore, a 1712 house that later became a meeting place for writers like Longfellow, Hawthorne, Emerson, Holmes, Stowe, and Whittier.

Ahead is Faneuil Hall, nicknamed the "Cradle of Liberty" by John Adams for its fiery and eloquent town meetings of Colonial patriots. Beyond, just as the younger tourers may be getting restless, is the perfect place to take a pause from history for some good food and fun—the historic world of food at Quincy Market. There's pizza, barbecue, Chinese food, shish kabob, gyros, Polish sausage, and more in the stalls. Unless you choose to pass them up to dine at one of the cafés around the market, you'll take your selection to benches outside, where there is sometimes entertainment by street musicians to go with your meal.

After lunch, continue along the trail to the North End for Paul Revere's home and the Old North Church, where he got the signal to begin his fateful ride to Lexington to warn the Colonists that "the British are coming."

The Freedom Trail ends beyond the North End in Charlestown with two historic sites that are usually favorites of young people. In Charlestown, you can board the USS *Constitution*, the oldest commissioned ship in the U.S. Navy, nicknamed "Old Ironsides" for its strong oak planking. And you can climb Bunker Hill, with its 220-foot obelisk commemorating the famous battle of June 17, 1775. The film *Whites of Their Eyes*, shown at the Bunker Hill Pavilion, will tell you the story of that historic battle. A trip up the spiral stairway to the top of the monument is rewarded with a fabulous view of the city.

If you've spent the afternoon in this part of town, dinner in one of the many North End Italian restaurants is a perfect way to end the day. At the very least, stop for a cannoli. At night, one of the exciting things to do in Boston is to get a skyscraper-high view of the glimmering city from the fiftieth floor of the Prudential Tower or from the top of the John Hancock Tower, which also has a multimedia presentation.

On Sunday, head for the Boston Children's Museum and its new upstairs neighbor, the Computer Museum in a restored warehouse on Museum Wharf on the waterfront, both a real tribute to the possibilities of creative education. The imaginative participatory displays at the Children's Museum allow youngsters to broadcast the news from their own TV newsroom and experiment with gravity by rolling balls on a series of giant ramps or by blowing bubbles. Kids learn how a house is constructed by climbing from cellar to attic in a three-story cross-section of a house whose furnishings also reveal the changes in appliances and furniture over the last couple of generations.

The world's first Computer Museum was recently installed on the top two floors of the Children's Museum building, and contains fascinating exhibits tracing the computer's development. Here, you can walk through the components of one of the early giant vacuum-tube computers, see the control room for the SAGE, America's air defense system from 1957 to 1983, and progress to the miracles of today's compact silicon-chip microcomputers, with a chance to try your hand at creating computer graphics. Some special crowd pleasers are a theater showing computer-generated cartoons, a computer that draws the outlines of the buildings it faces outside in Boston Harbor, and another that takes images of the city and whirls them into a thousand shapes and colors.

At the other end of the street is the Boston Tea Party Museum on an old clipper ship moored in the harbor. The exhibits may seem static after the extraordinary pair of museums that came before, but you will learn what the famous tea party was all about in Revolutionary days and will enjoy the famous gimmick here—the chance to toss your own case of tea overboard, just like the protesting patriots of 1773.

The historic Harbor Walk, marked out in blue lines along the rejuvenated Boston waterfront, traces the maritime history of the city and ends at the handsome waterfront park beyond the Marriott Hotel at Long Wharf. The city Information Centers have free walking tour guides. If you haven't been to the New England Aquarium yet, it's right in front of the Marriott. And the harbor cruises from the Long Wharf are quite a treat for young seafarers.

For older children, Boston's Museum of Science is a fascinating place, with everything from dinosaur bones to an explanation of how a telephone works; the museum also has its own sophisticated participatory exhibits and fine planetarium shows.

You won't find a better introduction to art than Boston's Museum of Fine Arts, one of the country's premiere art museums, even more spectacular with its recent addition, the sky-lit West Wing designed by I. M. Pei. If you plan to take in the art museum, note that it is free from 10 A.M. to 12 noon on Saturdays.

You can also introduce your youngsters to first-class ballet in Boston or attend the symphony or learn how American cities looked almost 200 years ago on Beacon Hill. You can let the children follow the time line at the John F. Kennedy Library to learn about the slain president along with the events in world history that paralleled his life. Or just forget about history and culture and go down to the Esplanade by the Charles River, stretch your legs on the promenade, and watch the skaters and joggers in action on land and the sailboats in motion on the water.

One Boston family tradition you shouldn't miss is a visit to Steve's Ice Cream, where your choice of toppings is rolled right into the ice cream before you are presented with an overloaded cone. Boston, in fact, is a city overloaded with pleasures of all kinds for all ages. It's almost guaranteed that if you and your family come once, you'll all want to come back for a second helping.

Boston Area Code: 617

DIRECTIONS AND TRANSPORTATION   See page 59.

ACCOMMODATIONS   See the medium-priced possibilities on page 60.

DINING   For family-priced dining, see Quincy Market, North End and Bargains, page 61, and Cambridge, page 245.

SIGHTSEEING   Freedom Trail information, including double-decker bus and trolley tours, at Visitor Information Booths on Tremont

Street, Boston Common, or Prudential Center Visitors' Center, and National Park Service Visitors' Center, 15 State Street, all open 9 A.M. to 5 P.M. daily. All sites free except those noted below ● *Boston Tea Party Ship and Museum,* Congress Street Bridge near Museum Wharf, 338-1773. Hours: daily 9 A.M. to 5 P.M. Adults, $3; 5 to 14, $2.50 ● *Children's Museum,* Museum Wharf, 300 Congress Street, 426-6500. Hours: daily 10 A.M. to 5 P.M., Friday to 9 P.M. Adults, $4.50; 2 to 15, $3.50; free to all Friday 5 P.M. to 9 P.M. ● *The Computer Museum,* Museum Wharf, 300 Congress Street, 426-6758. Hours: Tuesday to Sunday, 10 A.M. to 6 P.M., Friday to 9 P.M. (also open Monday, July to Labor Day). Adults, $4; children, $2; free Friday P.M. ● *Constitution Museum,* Charlestown Navy Yard, 426-1812. Hours: daily 9 A.M. to 5 P.M., summer until 6 P.M. Adults, $2; 6 to 16, $.50 (boarding the ship is free) ● *John Hancock Observatory,* John Hancock Building, Copley Square at Trinity Place and St. James Avenue, 247-1977. Hours: May to October, Monday to Saturday 9 A.M. to 11 P.M., Sunday 10 A.M. to 11 P.M., rest of year from 12 noon. Adults, $2.75; children, $2 ● *John F. Kennedy Library,* off Morrissey Boulevard, I-93 south, exit 17, Dorchester, 929-4523. Hours: daily 9 A.M. to 5 P.M. Adults, $2.50; under 16, free ● *Museum of Fine Arts,* 465 Huntington Avenue, 267-9300. Hours: Tuesday to Sunday, 10 A.M. to 5 P.M., Wednesday to 10 P.M.; West Wing only, Thursday and Friday to 10 P.M. Adults, $4 (West Wing only, $3); under 16, free; free to all Saturday 10 A.M. to 12 noon ● *Museum of Science,* Science Park, 742-6088. Hours: Tuesday to Sunday, 9 A.M. to 5 P.M., Friday to 10 P.M. Adults, $5; under 17, $3; half-price Friday 5 P.M. to 10 P.M. ● *New England Aquarium,* Central Wharf, 742-8870. Hours: Monday to Thursday, 9 A.M. to 5 P.M., Friday to 8 P.M., Saturday, Sunday, holidays and summer Wednesdays to 6 P.M. Adults, $6; 4 to 15, $3.50; $1 discount on Friday 4 P.M. to 8 P.M. ● *Paul Revere House,* North End, 523-1676. Hours: daily 9:30 A.M. to 5:15 P.M., to 4:15 P.M. in winter. Adults, $1.50; children 17 and under, $.50 ● *Skywalk Observation Deck,* Prudential Tower, Prudential Center, 236-3318. Hours: Monday to Saturday, 10 A.M. to 10 P.M., Sunday from 12 noon. Adults, $2; children 5 to 15, $1 ● *"Whites of Their Eyes,"* Bunker Hill Pavilion, Charlestown. Hours: daily 9:30 A.M. to 5 P.M. Adults, $1.50; children, $.75; family rate, $4 ● *Boston Harbor Cruises,* Long Wharf, 227-4320; phone for varying schedules and rates.

INFORMATION Boston Common Visitor Information Booth, Tremont Street, and Prudential Center Visitors' Center, 9 A.M. to 5 P.M. daily. National Park Service Visitors' Center, 15 State Street, same hours. For written information, Greater Boston Convention and Tourist Bureau, Prudential Plaza, PO Box 490, Boston, MA 02199, 536-4100; send $2 for guidebook, map, and Freedom Trail guide.

WINTER

Overleaf: Old Sturbridge Village, Massachusetts

Merry Days at Mystic

Seaman John Blood was puzzled. Here it was Christmas Eve 1885. His boat had overcome rough seas to dock in the evening, and just as he was hurrying home he was asked to take time out to show a group of strangers through the town. An unlikely lot they were at that, wearing odd clothes like none he had ever seen before.

But it was, after all, the holiday season, so Blood decided not to leave the strangers stranded. He took up his lantern and led the way, lighting the paths of the town for his charges as they wended their way to see how Christmas was celebrated a hundred years ago in seaside towns like Mystic, Connecticut.

Lantern-light tours at Mystic Seaport have become a treasured tradition in southeastern Connecticut, the way that many families choose to mark the official start of the holiday season.

The seaport staff and local volunteers love the custom too, and they thoroughly enjoy getting into the spirit of Christmas past, taking the part of characters who might have lived in Mystic a century ago. The hour-long tours, which are usually held nightly for about two weeks before Christmas, cover a variety of homes as well as the local tavern, store, and chapel, where the occupants are in the midst of celebrating the season, each in his or her own way. The dates span the century, showing how Christmas customs changed through the 1800s.

At the Buckinghams' house, for example, the time is the early nineteenth century, and a Puritan mother is complaining that she has no use for frivolity on a serious religious holiday.

There's plenty of merriment down at the tavern, however, and twentieth-century visitors are cordially invited to join in dancing to the tune of the fiddle. In the mid-1850s, families like the Burrowses decorated and baked for the holidays almost the same way we do today. But this Christmas Eve Mrs. Burrows is far from happy. Her seafaring son is overdue, and she is fearful for his life. Visitors have arrived just in time to see him slip in the back door to surprise his overjoyed mother.

At a stop on the steamboat *Sabino*, the captain reminisces about Christmases spent at sea, and in the village store the shopkeeper displays the kinds of toys children will be finding under their trees tomorrow morning. Then, as everyone pauses at the window to admire the handsome tree in the Edmondsons' house, who should appear in the living room but St. Nicholas himself, busily filling stockings with toys for the little ones who are sleeping upstairs. At the final stop, the

Thomas Greenmans' home, a prosperous Victorian family is celebrating the holiday.

Mystic tours are a little bit educational and a lot sentimental and, when followed by a glass of hot cider or a roast goose dinner at the seaport's Seaman's Inne, they lend a cheerful start to a family holiday excursion.

Though Mystic Seaport is usually thought of as a warm-weather destination, it has a special charm in the winter chill, particularly if a dusting of snow has covered the village green. Christmas trees are tied atop the masts of the tall ships to herald the season.

The Northeast's premiere maritime exhibit is more than just a collection of ships, however. It is a complete 17-acre re-creation of a nineteenth-century waterfront village, and all the exhibit buildings as well as the ships themselves remain open for winter visitors.

The village's history as a nautical center dates back to the 1800s, when the real Thomas Greenman headed a major shipbuilding company on this same site, a yard that produced some of the fastest clipper ships on the seas. In 1929 three local residents got together to form the Mystic Marine Historical Association to preserve some of this maritime heritage, and the project steadily gained support from sea-minded friends all over the country. To date, Mystic Seaport has grown to encompass 60 historic buildings, 4 major vessels, and more than 200 smaller boats, important collections of maritime artifacts and paintings, and a planetarium to teach the secrets of celestial navigation.

The planetarium's Christmas show, "The Star of Bethlehem," illustrates theories about the origins of the Christmas star. The half-hour demonstration is held both days and evenings. There are usually special Christmas programs for children only on Saturday mornings as well, when they take part in Victorian Christmas customs. Since reservations are required and the spaces fill quickly, it's well to get in touch with the Mystic Seaport office in advance to get the current schedule.

Boarding the ships remains the best part of Mystic for most people, and December or no, you're still able to walk the decks, examine the intricate riggings and enormous masts, and go below to see the cramped quarters where the captain and crew lived. In winter, you're likely to spend more time at the indoor exhibits, which sometimes get short shrift on warmer days, so you'll add a special dimension to your visit. In the village shops the warmth of coal stoves and wood fires welcomes guests, and the carver, smith, chandler, and other local craftspeople find time for an extra chat.

A visit to the Mystic Children's Museum, which is designed to resemble a cabin aboard ship, and to the Cape Horn ship *Benjamin Packard* shows how Christmas was celebrated at sea by families thousands of miles from home. For those who cannot make the lantern-light tours, there are also guided tours by day that repeat the evening itinerary, though without the good-humored dramatics.

There are several fine museums on the grounds displaying maritime art, ship models, and scrimshaw and tracing the development of the maritime and fishing industries from the seventeenth to the nineteenth centuries. One of the most delightful exhibits is the collection of ship figureheads and wood carvings in the Wendell Building.

And don't think the sights of Mystic stop when you leave the Seaport. The Mystic Marinelife Aquarium, with its dolphins and seals, is almost as popular with youngsters as the Seaport itself, and the Memory Lane Doll and Toy Museum, with 1,500 exhibits from around the world, delights young and old alike.

The town of Mystic is also appealing, with many fine old houses lining its streets and plenty of shops to explore. Olde Mystick Village, a pseudo-Colonial shopping mall, has dozens of stores and shops for just about everything, including antiques. Don't overlook the Mystic Seaport stores, which offer a tremendous selection of wares, from stick candy and fresh baked goods to Christmas ornaments, books, paintings, and tasteful gift ideas with a nautical theme.

You can shop. You can sightsee. You can relive the old-fashioned holiday traditions of yesterday. A Mystic weekend is a special way to bring back Christmas past—and to get everyone into the spirit of Christmas present.

Connecticut Area Code: 203

DRIVING DIRECTIONS Mystic Seaport is located on Route 27, one mile south of I-95 at exit 90. Mystic is about 95 miles from Boston, 127 miles from New York, and 55 miles from Hartford.

PUBLIC TRANSPORTATION Mystic is served by Greyhound buses and by Amtrak.

ACCOMMODATIONS *Mystic Hilton,* Coogan Boulevard, 572-0731, $$–$$$$ ● *Mystic Motor Inn,* Route 1 at Route 27, 536-9604, a motel as well as a very attractive and luxurious inn, $$$–$$$$$ ● *Ramada Inn,* Route 27, just off I-95, 536-9604, $$–$$$ ● *Day's Inn,* also off I-95 at Route 27, 572-0574, $$ ● *Howard Johnson,* I-95 at Route 27, 536-2654, $$ ● *Red Brook Inn,* 10 Welles Road, Old Mystic, 572-0349, Colonial bed and breakfast, $$$–$$$$ CP ● *Norwich Inn,* Route 32, Norwich, a 20-minute drive from Mystic, elegant, very festive for the holidays, $$$–$$$$$ ● *Palmer Inn,* 25 Church Street, Noank, 572-9000, restored mansion, $$$–$$$$ CP.

BED AND BREAKFAST   *Seacoast Landings Bed and Breakfast Registry,* 133 Neptune Drive, Groton, CT 06340, 442-1940.

DINING   *Seamen's Inne,* Greenmanville Avenue, 536-9649, Colonial decor, seafood specialties, special Christmas dinners, $$–$$$ ● *Steamboat Café,* 73 Steamboat Wharf, 536-1975, seafood, $–$$$ ● *J. P. Daniels,* Route 184, 572-9564, $$–$$$ ● *Captain Daniel Packer Inne,* 32 Water Street, 536-3555, tavern atmosphere, $–$$ ● *The Mooring,* Mystic Hilton (see above), innovative American cuisine, $$–$$$ ● *The Fisherman,* Groton Long Point Road, Noank, 536-1717, $$–$$$.

SIGHTSEEING   *Mystic Seaport Museum,* Route 27, Mystic, 536-2631. Hours: daily except Christmas, winter 9 A.M. to 4 P.M., summer until 5 P.M. Adults, $10; children, $5; under 5, free. Lantern-light tours, daily 5 P.M. to 9 P.M. in December. Adults, $7.50; children, $3.75 ● *Mystic Marinelife Aquarium,* Route 27, Mystic, 536-3323. Hours: daily 9 A.M. to 5 P.M.; hourly dolphin, sea lion, and whale demonstrations from 10 A.M. Adults, $6.25; children, $3.25 ● *Memory Lane Doll and Toy Museum,* Route 27, 536-3450. Hours: Monday to Saturday, 10 A.M. to 6 P.M., Sunday from 12 noon. Adults, $.75; children, $.25.

INFORMATION   Mystic Tourist Information Center, Building 1D, Olde Mistick Village, CT 06355, 536-1641.

Christmas Card Country in Hanover

No doubt about it. This is Christmas card country.

Cradled in the beautiful upper Connecticut River Valley between the White Mountains of New Hampshire and the Green Mountains across the state line in Vermont, Hanover and its heart, the picture-perfect Dartmouth College campus, make an idyllic scene any time of year. Sprinkle a cover of snow on the combination campus green and town center, add a twinkling Christmas tree, and you'll have to look far to find a more magical holiday setting.

With that kind of inspiration, it's no wonder the season is celebrated in a big way here. With a shopper's weekend straight out of the pages of Dickens, the annual Chrsitmas Revels entertainment that literally has folks dancing in the aisles, and Christmas festivities at the Hanover

Inn that rival home for their warmth and tradition, Hanover is just the place to spend a memorable December weekend.

It's impossible to talk about Hanover without talking about Dartmouth because, even more than most college towns, this little community of 6,800 was shaped from the start by the school. The town was founded in 1761 by a venturesome band of Connecticut families ready to carve a new frontier in what was then wilderness. Just nine years later Dartmouth was established beside the new settlement, a dream that many thought would be impossible to achieve.

Eleazar Wheelock, a Connecticut missionary with a vision of civilizing the wilderness, chose this unlikely site for his "grand design" precisely because it was on the frontier of the northern colonies and near the Indians, in whose education he had a special interest. Against all odds, Dartmouth survived to become one of the nation's great names in higher education, with an unbroken succession of graduating classes since the first enrolled in 1771.

A walking tour of the campus with its original Colonial buildings and many handsome later additions is a first order of business on a Hanover visit. Be sure to go into the Baker Memorial Library, the imposing spired building on the green, to see the 3,000-square-foot fresco by the great Mexican muralist Jose Clemente Orozco.

An excellent way to make sure you don't miss anything is to rent the tape available from the Hanover Inn for $2.50. It tells you all the campus lore, points out where Daniel Webster lived as an undergraduate, and gives such missing information as the name of the row of white buildings on the east side of the campus.

When you see this lovely school, you may better understand Webster's sentiments 150 years ago when he defended the independence of his young alma mater in a famed case before the U.S. Supreme Court: "It is, as I have said, sir, a small college, but there are those who love it."

The history of the Hanover Inn, also just across the green from the college, is inextricably tied to that of the school. Eleven years after Dartmouth's founding, General Ebenezer Brewster arrived in Hanover to accept a position as college steward and redesigned his home on the present inn site to serve as a tavern, no doubt to supplement his academic earnings. One historian noted that the new enterprise was "not altogether, it would seem, to the gratification of the college authorities," but still the business flourished—so much so that Brewster's son had the tavern moved to another site and put up a much larger building in its place, naming it the Dartmouth Hotel.

When that structure burned in 1887, a new hotel, the Wheelock, was built, and in 1901 the college undertook extensive remodeling and renamed the building the Hanover Inn. With many additions and modernizations, that building still stands, and it is as gracious a Colonial hostelry as you could wish for. The furnishings are on the formal side—wing chairs, Queen Anne tables, canopied beds—as is the handsome dining room with its fireplaces and chandeliers. But the perennial presence of young Dartmouth men and women keeps things from becoming stuffy, even at afternoon tea, a favorite local tradition.

At Christmas time the inn puts up two giant trees covered with luscious, brightly decorated cookies, one in the dining room and the other right in the front window. Since the decorations are all but irresistible, the trees bear a sign pleading, "Please don't eat the cookies."

Hanover Inn is the only place to stay right in Hanover, but there is a very attractive bed-and-breakfast inn, Trumbull House, on the edge of town, with cross-country trails right outside the door. And if you prefer a more traditional cozy country inn, you need drive only nine miles to the Lyme Inn on the green in Lyme, another traditional tiny New England village. There are a couple of excellent restaurants in nearby smaller towns as well, the most touted of them being Home Hill in Plainfield. And both Quechee and Woodstock are near enough to be home bases or dinner choices should you want a change of scene.

Still, for location, you can't beat the Hanover Inn. It is connected by a covered walkway to the Hood Museum and the Hopkins Center, both sources of culture and entertainment for the whole community as well as for the campus. The Hood Museum's rotating art exhibits are always well recommended. The most treasured local holiday tradition, the Christmas Revels, takes place at the Hopkins Center, usually on the second weekend of December each year.

The Revels are a combination hometown musicale and salute to the season. Though the look and the direction are professional, the actors are locals and the costumes are made by volunteers. Each year the cast salutes the customs of another culture. The production is unusual, lively, and full of color and music, with a minimum of the expected caroling. Just about everybody in town turns out for one of the three performances, which are perennial sellouts. So faithfully do they come that the audiences seem to know in unison exactly when the moment has arrived to join the cast in song and dance. If you're not prepared, you may be shocked when your neighbor all but leaps over you to get to the merriment in the aisles.

The Christmas Revels are unique—guaranteed to lift your spirits— but if you can't make that weekend, there are other wonderful happenings throughout December in Hanover.

For the pleasantest Christmas shopping you can imagine, come on the first weekend in December, when local merchants pay their annual homage to the season with a Victorian Christmas celebration. A recent weekend was dubbed "A Dickens of a Christmas."

Get there early on Friday night in time to see Santa arrive on the green. That's when the tree is officially lit, to the accompaniment of fireworks. On Saturday, Main Street turns into a Victorian promenade with all kinds of period decorations. No cars are allowed to spoil things, and a steady stream of street entertainers—dulcimer players, Old English folk dancers, jugglers, mimes, and carolers—keeps everyone in the Christmas spirit. There's even a free movie with caretakers for the kids so moms and dads can shop in peace.

Hanover shops are on the traditional side, but you may be able to pick up some one-of-a-kind treasures from the League of New Hampshire Craftsmen shop at 13 Lebanon Street. The league has showcased the best crafts of the state's artisans for more than 50 years. Works by local artists are also on display at the AVA Gallery on Allen Street.

There's more shopping to be found about 20 minutes away in the many shops of Woodstock, Vermont. Make a detour off Route 4 into Quechee to see glassblower Simon Pearce's studio in a restored mill. Besides the exquisite glassware, pottery and Irish sweaters and woolens are for sale.

If you'd rather enjoy the out of doors than browse the shops, there's every opportunity around Hanover. You can set off cross-country skiing within a few blocks of Main Street and continue in all directions. There's downhill skiing at the Dartmouth Skiway 13 miles away or at the smaller Oak Hill area on the edge of town, and ice skating is excellent at Occum Pond, adjacent to the Dartmouth Outing Club. The pond is cleared and lighted for night skating. There's also indoor skating at Thompson Arena and at Davis Rink, in case you don't want to brave the winter weather.

The final special holiday observance each year takes place on Christmas Eve and Christmas Day at the Hanover Inn, a celebration so special it may change your mind about spending the holiday at home. The festivities include a wassailing party, caroling, storytelling around the Hanover Inn tree, and learning to make "stained glass" cookies, and clove oranges from the inn's chef right in his own kitchen.

Celebrate Christmas Eve sleigh riding, skating, and tobogganing at the Dartmouth Outing Club, with blazing fires in the clubhouse to warm frosty noses and fingers and lots of tea and hot chocolate available for all.

The inn's Christmas Eve candlelight dinner is served family style so that friends old and new can share the evening. You wake on Christmas morning to find that Santa has left a little something outside your door, and following the afternoon dinner of turkey plus trimmings, there's a "second time around" buffet starting at six when the turkeys and other goodies reappear so you can make sandwiches and nibble on the stuffing—just like home.

Whether you come to celebrate Christmas or to get into the spirit of things in advance, you may agree that there's no place like Hanover as a second home for the holidays.

New Hampshire Area Code: 603

DRIVING DIRECTIONS   Hanover can be reached off I-89 at exit 18, Lebanon, or I-91 at exit 13, Norwich. It is 135 miles from Boston, 270 miles from New York, and 150 miles from Hartford.

PUBLIC TRANSPORTATION   Vermont Transit bus service and Amtrak to White River Junction, VT; American Eagle and Eastern Express air service to Lebanon, ten miles away.

ACCOMMODATIONS   _Hanover Inn,_ at Dartmouth College green, Hanover, 643-4300, $$$–$$$$; write for special Christmas brochure and prices ● _Lyme Inn,_ on the green, Lyme, 795-2222, $$ ● _Trumbull House,_ Etna Road, Hanover, 643-1400, $$$ CP.

DINING   Both of the above inns offer good dining. Also recommended ● _Home Hill,_ River Road, Plainfield, 675-6165, highly regarded French chef-owner, prix fixe, $$$$ ● _D'Artagnan,_ 13 Dartmouth College Highway, Route 10, Lyme, 795-2137, French Nouvelle, prix fixe $$$ ● _Café La Fraise,_ 8 West Wheelock, Hanover, 643-8588, French food in a Colonial setting, $$$ ● _Molly's Balloon,_ 45 South Main Street, 643-2570, casual, cheerful, wide menu, $–$$ ● _Bentley's,_ South Main Street, 643-4075, campus favorite, good Sunday brunch, $–$$ ● _Peter Christian's Tavern,_ 39 Main Street, Hanover, 643-2345, informal, good for families, $–$$. Also see Quechee, page 69, and Woodstock, page 6.

SIGHTSEEING   _Christmas Revels,_ contact Hopkins Center, Hanover, NH 03755, 646-2422 for current dates and prices.

INFORMATION   Hanover Chamber of Commerce, PO Box A-105, Hanover, NH 03755, 643-3115.

Holiday Cheer in Hartford

 Some might say it was gilding an already flamboyant lily to add Christmas trimmings to the elaborate home of Mark Twain in Hartford, Connecticut. But Twain, a consummate showman who loved decorating and entertaining for the holidays, would no doubt be pleased to know that each year his home is set up just as it was when he and his family were getting ready to receive guests.

For that matter, Twain would likely approve of several of the special

Christmas scenes in his onetime hometown, for Hartford is a city that makes the most of the holidays.

At the Wadsworth Atheneum, the city's fine art museum, dozens of trees lavishly decorated by local garden clubs and other organizations go on display and are for sale to benefit the museum. At the Old State House, the yearly gathering of work by Connecticut craftsmen is a perfect place to find unusual Christmas gifts. At Constitution Plaza in the city's center, the Festival of Lights transforms the plaza into a glittery scene of sculptured reindeer, trumpeting angels, and thousands of tiny twinkling lights. Add the annual performances of the *Nutcracker* by the Hartford Ballet and you have a capital December weekend.

You will probably want to spend Saturday seeing the many sights in the center of Hartford. A traditional old-fashioned Christmas scene in town is the Butler-McCook Homestead, a 1782 house that has managed to survive in the middle of modern downtown Hartford. The tree is adorned with antique ornaments, gingerbread animals, and garlands of popcorn and cranberries. In the kitchen, paper cornucopias are filled with fruits, nuts, and candies, just as they were when Reverend McCook and his family used to distribute these gifts to neighborhood children.

Since the family was a large one, there are lots of leftover Victorian toys to see, including sleds, cannons, a steamboat, toy soldiers, and china dolls. The house, which until 1971 was occupied by one family for four generations, is particularly interesting for the continuity of life within its walls.

The other historic building that has remained in the heart of Hartford is the 1796 Old State House, a masterpiece of Federal-style architecture designed by Charles Bullfinch. The object of a recent major restoration that brought its courtroom, senate, and office chambers back to their original splendor, the building now serves as an exhibition and concert hall for the community. The gift shop here is always an excellent place to look for folk art and handicrafts, and the Christmas show and sale in the upstairs galleries, featuring works by 100 top Connecticut craftsmen, is an ideal place to find original jewelry, pewter pieces, quilts, and all kinds of collectibles. A traditional Christmas setup of toy trains has perennial appeal to youngsters—and nostalgic oldsters as well.

The Wadsworth Atheneum, America's first free public art museum, is still outstanding, even more so with recent additions and renovations. The museum has benefited over the years from wealthy patrons such as J. P. Morgan, who once lived in Hartford and donated a wing to the Atheneum. The total complex consists of four buildings and a sculpture garden, and contains works from every period, including modern paintings by Picasso, Monet, Andrew Wyeth, and Hartford-born Frederick Church. The gift shop is another treasure trove of ideas, and the tree collection is guaranteed to inspire you if not tempt you to take one home somehow.

A strongpoint here is American arts, including the Wallace Nutting Collection, the largest and best-known collection of early Colonial furniture, with over 1,000 examples from the "Pilgrim century," 1630 to 1730. The noted Philip H. Hammerslough Collection of more than 600 items made by the finest Early American silversmiths is also displayed, along with the priceless personal collection of Samuel Colt, the noted gunsmith, who was yet another prominent Hartford resident.

Colt's gun collection, one of the outstanding exhibits of its kind, is at the Museum of Connecticut History. If you want to see it, plan to do so early, however, since the museum closes on Saturday at 1 P.M.

If you still have time and energy and the weather is cooperative, when you've seen the indoor sights, pick up a walking tour at the Old State House and take in the unusual mix of old and new that marks downtown Hartford. You'll see, for example, the white steeple of Center Church, circa 1788, reflected in the gold-mirrored walls of the Bushnell Tower, designed by I. M. Pei in 1969. Stroll over to Bushnell Park to see the ornate state capitol with its gold dome, then walk to Constitution Plaza to view what is considered one of the earliest successful urban renewal efforts. You'll want to come back at night for the light show, which includes a cascading fountain of lights.

On Sunday, sleep late and have a hearty Sunday brunch to fortify yourself for the short drive to see Mark Twain's masterpiece, the home that he described as part steamboat, part medieval stronghold, and part cuckoo clock. Nook Farm, the literary colony that housed the homes of both Twain and his neighbor Harriet Beecher Stowe, is a prime Christmas attraction. The house that Twain built cost $130,000, a whopping sum back in 1874, and includes decorations by such artisans as Louis Comfort Tiffany. It is filled with lavish touches—patterned ceilings, carved doors, massive fireplaces, stenciling, elaborate wallpaper that looks like tooled leather—and with the last word in high Victorian furnishings.

For the holidays the staircases and mantels are festooned with greenery, and a glittering Victorian Christmas tree stands tall in the library. Gifts in all stages of wrapping are set about in the Mahogany Room, where the Twains used to hide presents from curious young eyes. Upstairs in the schoolroom, Christmas stockings hang as though waiting to be discovered by the three young daughters of the household.

The scene is simpler in the cottage of Harriet Beecher Stowe, where the author of *Uncle Tom's Cabin* lived from 1873 until her death in 1896, but the Christmas spirit is just as strong. A replica of the Stowe family Christmas tree stands in the rear parlor, along with a number of Victorian pieces owned by the author. The dining room table is set for a Yuletide feast, with ribbons descending from the chandelier to each place setting, where a tiny gift is set for each guest. Period Christmas trees also adorn the mantel and tables in the living room.

After your tour, stop in the gift shop, where you can buy copies of *Tom Sawyer* or *Uncle Tom* as well as charming Victorian lace pillows, delicate Christmas tree ornaments, and reproductions of exquisite period jewelry. There are even Mark Twain and Harriet Beecher Stowe T-shirts for sale, if you want to surprise a literary friend.

If you continue west from Nook Farm, you'll come to West Hartford and, on its Main Street, the historic home of another important early Hartford citizen, Noah Webster. It's a simple homestead, but interesting to tour nevertheless—to see Mr. Webster's first volumes and realize how he changed our language by insisting that Americans needed their own dictionary.

Once again, a festive old-fashioned Christmas tree heralds the season. It's the last stop on a holiday tour of Hartford—a capital city to visit anytime and a gilded lily at Christmas.

Connecticut Area Code: 203

DRIVING DIRECTIONS   Hartford can be reached via I-91 and I-84. It is 100 miles from Boston and 110 miles from New York.

PUBLIC TRANSPORTATION   The city is served by major bus lines, Amtrak, and several major airlines. The central part of the city can be navigated easily without a car.

ACCOMMODATIONS   There are lots of center city hotels and motels to choose from; ask about their special weekend packages ● *Hotel Summit,* Constitution Plaza, 278-2000, the best place to view the Festival of Lights, $$$–$$$$$ ● *Ramada Inn,* 440 Asylum Street, 246-6591, $$ ● *Holiday Inn of Hartford,* 50 Morgan Street, 549-2400, $$$ ● *Sheraton-Hartford,* Trumbull Street at Civic Center Plaza, 728-5151, $$$$–$$$$$ ● *Susse Chalet,* 185 Brainard Road, 525-9306, budget motel, $.

BED AND BREAKFAST   *Nutmeg Bed and Breakfast,* 222 Girard Avenue, Hartford, CT 06105, 235-6698.

DINING   *L'Americain,* 2 Hartford Square West, 522-6500, superelegant continental, one of the city's best, $$$ ● *The Brownstone,* 124 Asylum Street, 525-1171, antiques and stained glass, $$–$$$ ● *Carbone's Restaurant,* 588 Franklin, 249-9646, Italian restaurant popular with political types, $$–$$$ ● *Congress Rotisserie,* 7 Maple Avenue,

560-1965, grill specialties, $$ ● *36 Lewis Street,* at that address, 247-2300, popular spot on a historic street, good for Sunday brunch, $$–$$$ ● *Panache,* 357 Main Street, 724-0810, tiny with interesting menu, $$–$$$ ● *Spencer's,* 10 Capitol Avenue, 247-0400, tavern fare upstairs, $–$$; elegant continental dining downstairs, prix fixe $$$$ ● *Apricots,* 1593 Farmington Avenue, Farmington, 673-5405, worth the drive to the suburbs, $$$ (prix fixe $$$$) ● *Simsbury House,* 731 Hopmeadow Street, Simsbury, 658-7658, another elegant suburban winner, $$$.

SIGHTSEEING *Nook Farm,* Farmington Avenue at Forest Street (I-84, exit 46), 525-9317. Hours: Tuesday to Saturday, 9:30 A.M. to 4 P.M., Sunday 1 P.M. to 4 P.M. Combined admission to Twain and Stowe houses: adults, $6; children under 16, $3.75; Stowe home only: adults, $3; children, $1.25; Twain home only: adults, $3.75; children, $1.50 ● *Wadsworth Atheneum,* 600 Main Street, 278-2670. Hours: Tuesday to Sunday, 11 A.M. to 5 P.M. Adults, $3; 13 to 18, $1.50; under 13, free; free to all Thursday and Saturday from 11 A.M. to 1 P.M. ● *Butler-McCook Homestead,* 396 Main Street, 522-1806. Winter hours vary; best to call and check. Adults, $2; children, $.50 ● *Old State House,* 800 Main Street, 522-6766. Hours: Monday to Saturday, 10 A.M. to 5 P.M., Sunday from 12 noon. Free ● *Noah Webster Foundation and Historical Society,* 227 South Main Street, West Hartford, 521-5362. Hours: October to mid-June, weekdays except Wednesday, 10 A.M. to 4 P.M., Saturday and Sunday from 1 P.M. Adults, $2; children, $1.50 ● *Museum of Connecticut History,* Connecticut State Library, 231 Capitol Avenue, 566-3056. Hours: Monday to Friday, 9 A.M. to 5 P.M., Saturday to 1 P.M. Free.

INFORMATION Greater Hartford Convention and Visitors Bureau, 1 Civic Center Plaza, Hartford, CT 06103, 728-6789.

Shopping by the Sea in Portsmouth

"Have yourself a merry little Christmas," caroled the speaker in one of the shops in Portsmouth, New Hampshire. We were doing just that.

Portsmouth is a lovely old seafaring town, with handsome sea captain's homes and a long, proud history. In summer it is filled with tourists—and therefore it is a town filled with shops. Come December, the crowds are gone but the many shops remain, offering choice selections of unusual wares for shoppers in the most pleasant of surroundings. There's a bonus too, since New Hampshire has no sales tax.

Things are made even more inviting with gala decorations and music. Little Prescott Park sets the waterfront aglow with tiny twinkling lights on every tree. Portsmouth also offers an event absolutely guaranteed to imbue even Ebenezer Scrooge with Christmas spirit—the annual Candlelight Stroll at Strawbery Banke.

When the first settlers arrived in Portsmouth, they found the area covered with luscious wild strawberries, inspiring them to name their new home "Strawbery Banke." It became the third settlement in the New World, preceded only by Plymouth and Jamestown. Though the town name changed in 1653, Strawbery Banke lives on today in the form of 30 original buildings in various stages of restoration, a historic village representing 350 years of the town's history. On the first and second weekends of December, the streets are lit by candleglow and music fills the village with a melodious salute to the season.

Each home in the Candlelight Stroll is bedecked with period holiday decorations, and when you enter, each one holds its own delightful musical surprise—professional musicians playing early Christmas airs. A harpsichord and early winds consort may greet you in one, a flutist in another, perhaps a chorus in yet a third.

The village is unique in using its historic houses as places for local artisans to live and work, displaying their skills and selling their wares. The weaver, potter, cooper, resident artist, and others are present for the evening festivities, offering you a chance to pick up handmade one-of-a-kind gifts for special names on your Christmas list as you stroll.

More gifts are to be found at the Dunaway Store, the old-fashioned country store on the grounds, where bell ringers are in residence for the night, and at the other gift shops run by the Guild of Strawbery Banke—all good bets for tasteful and unusual presents, many with a strawberry motif. You'll spy yet another Guild gift shop in town at Kingsbury House on State Street.

Outdoors, children arrive with decorations to help complete the big blue spruce tree on the museum green, and carolers around the tree lead everyone in the traditional songs of the season.

It's an unbeatable evening in a town that makes the chore of gift shopping a true pleasure. On State and Market, the two main streets, and Bow and Ceres and others running off them toward the water, you'll find just about anything you could ask for—wooden ware, art deco glass, candles, mugs, clothing, you name it. Handmade crafts are plentiful, from leather goods to hand-forged iron pieces to jewelry. You might find a handsome trunk at the Trunk Shop on Ceres, hand-blown art glass at Salamandra on Market Street, or one-of-a-kind handcrafted gifts at one of the many excellent craft galleries such as

Gallery 33 on Bow Street, Tulips on Market, and N. W. Barrett on Commercial Alley. The Marcy Street Doll Company on Pleasant Street is filled with lovable teddy bears in all shapes and sizes.

Portsmouth also has a number of art galleries on these same streets to provide a change of pace, many offering special holiday shows and gift ideas, and there are plenty of antiques shops if you want to splurge for someone special—including yourself.

For bargains, check the Discount House on Lafayette Road for electronics and ask directions to Mirona Road near the McDonald's on Route 1 for the Artisans Outlet, where brand-name clothing and shoes for men and women are sold at discount prices. Albert Nipon, Ralph Lauren, Calvin Klein, Pierre Cardin, and Stanley Blacker are just a few of the many lines carried.

Remember, too, that prices at the state-run liquor stores in New Hampshire are excellent. The nearest one, at the Portsmouth traffic circle on I-95, is the biggest in the state.

Just across the bridge in Kittery, Maine, you'll find more discount shopping, including outlet stores for Dansk, Mikasa, Lenox, Hathaway, Bass, and Timberland and labels such as Van Heusen, Royal Doulton, Towle, Mighty Mac, and Le Sportsac at the Kittery Outlet Center.

Portsmouth restaurants are plentiful—the Blue Strawberry in a restored 1797 granary on Ceres is generally considered the best among many good ones. They book up fast for their six-course price-fixed nouvelle cuisine dinners, so reserve early for one of the two sittings.

Though it is technically off-season, there are still plenty of places to go at night for jazz or other live music. Look for the little local paper called *re: Ports,* an arts and entertainment journal, to find out what is happening where.

Though the Candlelight Stroll enables December visitors to get inside Strawbery Banke's homes, you'll have to return in summer to go into the historic showplaces on the "Portsmouth Trail." But you can have a look at some of them, and at many other fine homes as well, by making your own compact driving tour. Be sure to see the Wentworth-Gardner House at 141 Mechanic Street, the Moffatt-Ladd House at 154 Market, the Rundlet-May House at 364 Middle Street, the Warner House at the corner of Daniel and Chapel, and finally, the most historic of all, the John Paul Jones House at Middle and State. This is the place where the admiral oversaw fittings for his new command, the *Ranger,* which sailed out of Portsmouth Harbor on November 1, 1777, bearing the first American flag flown at sea. The Portsmouth Tourist Information Office is not usually open on a winter weekend, but you can write in advance for a street map to guide you on your tour.

Portsmouth has much to offer in the summer when the houses are open, the gardens are in bloom in Prescott Park, and the sightseeing cruise boats are out in the harbor or heading for the Shoals Islands. But there's nothing to match the town on a frosty December night, when Strawbery Banke is aglow with candlelight and music. And when it comes to Christmas shopping, you won't find a snugger port anywhere.

New Hampshire Area Code: 603

DRIVING DIRECTIONS   Portsmouth is on I-95, 60 miles north of Boston, 268 miles from New York, and 158 miles from Hartford.

PUBLIC TRANSPORTATION   Greyhound buses serve Portsmouth. If you stay at an inn in town, you can walk to everything.

ACCOMMODATIONS   The choices are small bed-and-breakfast inns, motels, or the accommodations in York, Maine, ten minutes north (see page 90) ● *Inn at Strawbery Banke,* 314 Court Street, 436-7242, historic house conveniently near the restoration village, $$ CP ● *Inn at Christian Shore,* 335 Maplewood, 431-6770, Federal house with period furnishings and huge breakfasts, $$ CP ● *Martin Hill Inn,* 404 Islington, 436-2287, more period furniture and hearty breakfast fare, $–$$ CP ● *Howard Johnson,* at US 1 just off I-95, 436-7600, $$–$$$.

BED AND BREAKFAST   *New Hampshire Bed and Breakfast,* RFD 3, Box 53, Laconia, NH 03246, 279-8348.

DINING   *The Blue Strawberry,* 29 Ceres Street, 431-6420, prix fixe $$$$ ● *The Oar House,* 55 Ceres Street, 436-4205, varied menu, good also for Sunday brunch, $$ ● *Pier 11,* State Street on the harbor, 436-0669, seafood, $–$$ ● *BG's Boathouse Restaurant,* 191 Wentworth, 431-1074, seafood, informal, $–$$ ● *The Metro,* 20 High Street, 436-0521, varied menu, good chowder, $$ ● *The Library at the Rockingham House,* 401 State Street, 431-5202, book-lined walls and a varied menu, $$ ● *The Codfish,* the Hill, 431-8503, converted carriage house, fun atmosphere, moderate prices, $ ● *The Dolphin Striker,* 15 Bow Street, 431-5222, restored warehouse, seafood specialties, $$–$$$ ● *Strawberry Court,* 20 Atkinson Street adjacent to Strawbery Banke, gracious 1815 Federal home, French cuisine, prix fixe $$$ ● *The Tavern,* 38 Marcy Steet at Strawbery Banke, 431-2816, New England menu with continental flair, $$–$$$. Also see York, Maine, pages 90–91.

SIGHTSEEING   *Strawbery Banke,* Hancock and Marcy streets,

436-1100, candlelight stroll, usually first and second weekends in December. Hours: Friday and Saturday evenings, 4:30 P.M. to 8:30 P.M. Adults, $7; children, $3. Regular hours May 1 to October 31, daily 9:30 A.M. to 5 P.M. Adults, $6; 6 to 16, $3.50.

INFORMATION Seacoast Council on Tourism, 500 Market Street, PO Box 239, Portsmouth, NH 03801, 436-7678.

Winter Carnival at Stowe

"Stowe is King," proclaimed the ice sculptures at a recent Winter Carnival in Stowe, Vermont.

Three generations of skiers would agree, but you don't have to be a skier to love the hometown of Mt. Mansfield, Vermont's highest mountain peak.

Stowe blends the charm of an old-fashioned New England village nestled in a stunning mountain setting with sophisticated food and lodgings that few ski resorts can match. Come Winter Carnival week, when fanciful ice carvings, dog sled races, parades, ski racing, and other gala events are added to the agenda, it is a stellar winter destination for all.

Stowe differs from many ski destinations in that it is a long-established town as well as a ski resort. Its diverse landscape includes not only the state's tallest mountain but Vermont's largest town in terms of land area—some 50,000 acres of rich agricultural bottomland and hillside for grazing.

The Stowe scenery has been attracting visitors since the 1840s, when the first inn was built under the mountain and another, Mansfield House, arose in Stowe village to house 600 guests. The Dartmouth College team was skiing the Toll Road as early as 1914; but it was in 1933, just as agriculture was declining as a source of revenue, that the Civilian Conservation Corps cut a four-mile trail down the mountain and serious skiing began. The next year Mt. Mansfield Ski Club was formed, setting up lodging in a former logging camp at the bottom of the trail, and by 1937 the first rope tow was in place. Those who are used to paying upward of $30 a day to ski might like to know that first lift cost $.50 daily, $5 for the season.

Winter recreation saved the town of Stowe from the hard times that the demise of small farming brought to many other Vermont communities. Mt. Mansfield emerged as the eastern skier's supreme test, with steep trails such as Star and Goat and National becoming legendary for their challenge. And though it has been rivaled by emerging giants like Killington, now Vermont's biggest mountain, Stowe's cachet remains unmatched. The proliferation of fine facilities that grew up around skiing now makes it a prime year-round resort destination.

The first Winter Carnival, held in 1921, consisted of ski jumping and tobogganing on a hill in the village. The tradition was abandoned for a time but was reborn in 1974 as an antidote to the mid-January doldrums common to ski areas. Today Stowe hosts the "king of carnivals," offering something for everyone—sports enthusiast and spectator alike.

The kickoff carnival event, known as Village Night, is a small-town affair with lights and balloons festooning Main Street and a parade of locals in storybook costumes. Each year's theme is spelled out in an ice sculpture contest, with fanciful carvings appearing in front of almost every inn and restaurant—a special delight for photographers, who can enter a photo competition with their prize snaps. Popeye, King Kong, and the *Star Wars* crew are just a few of the elaborate sculptures seen in recent years.

Carnival sporting competitions are both serious and silly, with top contenders on hand for ski races and speed skating and everyone invited to the "Fun X-C Race," as well as to the Mogul Challenge and the Trivia tournament, a less strenuous indoor contest for all ages.

Almost everyone turns out also to watch the excitement of sled dogs streaking down the track with their drivers standing on sleds at the rear and urging the racers onward.

Evening carnival festivities include Tyrolean Night, with Alpine entertainment, Las Vegas Night, with a chance to try your luck at gaming tables, and hearty homemade church suppers. Whatever is slated over your weekend visit, you can count on a spirited schedule.

When it comes to choosing a place to stay at Stowe, the possibilities are enormous, with something for every pocketbook and taste. At the top of the scale, Top Notch is just that. You can skate here, go sledding or sleigh riding, use the on-premises Cross-Country Center, take advantage of the indoor tennis facilities, the lavish new spa, and the pool, or just sit in front of the giant fireplace and look out the 12-foot windows at snow-covered Mt. Mansfield in a living room that is a fortuitous and tasteful blend of rustic fieldstone and country antiques.

Stowehof is another luxury establishment that appeals to some for its picture-window views and unusual ambience, which includes a sculptured tree in the center of a multilevel living room filled with antiques and oddities. It is not my top choice for the price, however.

Skiers may well prefer the former Toll House, now the Inn at the Mountain, which offers a condominium lodge and town houses with comfortable, simple decor and the advantage of closest proximity to the slopes via shuttle as well as direct access to the mountain trails from the inn's own double chairlift. In-room steam baths here are a special luxury, and the restaurant is highly rated.

Ten Acres Lodge is the definite choice for those who enjoy a more traditional antique-filled Colonial-style New England inn, and the new Trapp Family Lodge, recently rebuilt after a fire, is big but gracious, with an Alpine atmosphere. The lodge is also well known for its Ski Touring Center and extensive trails.

On a somewhat more modest scale, the Gables is a congenial country inn that welcomes you home each afternoon with hot soup and hors d'oeuvres on the house, and Edson Hill Manor has a rustic feel and a ski touring and riding center on its 500 acres. For the budget-minded, there's the warm and cozy Golden Kitz, a happily cluttered establishment that offers not only hot soup but wine and cheese as antidotes to wintry afternoons. And Timberholm Inn is tucked away on a delightful, quiet wooded hillside just one block away from the mountain road.

There are dozens of other lodgings—over 60 at last count. Contact the Stowe Area Association for further information and for free reservation service.

When it comes to food, Stowe offers some of the best dining in ski country, with 35 restaurants to choose from. Recommendations include Hungarian delights at the Charda, Italian fare at Foxfire, fine French at Isle de France and continental specialties at Stowehof, where dinner is preceded by a sleigh ride and hot rum drinks.

Popular for après-ski are B. K. Clark's, the Matterhorn, and the Rusty Nail for those who want a lively scene, and Mr. Pickwick's Pub in Ye Olde England Inne for a quieter world of British folk songs and a pint of ale. Among the prize breakfast places in town are the Gables, where you can choose from the extensive menu until noon, and the Ten Acres Lodge.

Even without Winter Carnival, you can stay busy at Stowe with a dozen different activities, beginning but not ending with the 350 miles of Alpine skiing terrain and over 100 miles of cross-country trails. Besides the tough stuff for the experts, there are many new trails for novices on Spruce Peak, thanks to the recently opened 6,400-foot Toll House Chairlift. The original Toll Road is now a 4½-mile run down one of the most scenic novice trails to be found.

If you don't ski, you can choose from ice skating at the indoor Jackson Arena in the village or outdoor and indoor activities open to the public at some of the area resorts: a sleigh ride for two at Stowehof Inn, a sleigh wagon for 20 at the Trapp Family Lodge, tennis lessons from the pros at Top Notch, or exercise at the Top Notch spa or Golden Eagle Resort Spa, with whirlpool, sauna, and massage to take away the aches and pains. Snowmobiles are for rent at Nichols on Route 100, and you can soak your sore muscles at Stowe Hot Tubs on Route 100 South.

If your favorite sport is shopping, you've still come to the right place. There are plenty of possibilities in town and all along Mountain Road (Route 108). Some of the places to watch for on the road are Samara, for fine crafts by Vermont artisans (there's an outpost in the Green Mountain Inn in the village as well); Stowe Pottery, a converted old red mill with a studio and showroom for stoneware made by resident potter Jean-Paul Patnode; Stowe Trading Post and Leather, with clothing, leather goods, and sheepskin accessories; the Yellow Turtle, for everything you can think of in the way of children's winter wear; and the Christmas Place, a haven for collectors of unusual tree ornaments. In town there is the Wool and Feathers Shop for handmade sweaters and fine woolen yarns, Green Mountain, Stowe Antique Center, and the Four Antiques for collectibles, and Shaw's General Store for almost anything.

If you want a souvenir emblazoned with that ever present Vermont cow, try Everything Cows on Main Street—and if you want a tour of the Ben and Jerry's Ice Cream Factory, the people who made the cow almost a national symbol, you'll find them on Route 100 in Waterbury, just ten miles away.

South of town on Route 100, you can pick up cob-smoked ham and bacon and aged Vermont cheddar cheese at Harrington's. And there are bargains to be found at Wheelwright's Name Brand Store on Main Street.

In fact, there's just not much of anything you can't find around Stowe, a town that richly deserves its title as king—Winter Carnival or not.

Vermont Area Code: 802

DRIVING DIRECTIONS   Stowe is in northern Vermont on Route 100, ten minutes north of exit 10, Route I-89. It is about 185 miles from Boston, 325 miles from New York, and 200 miles from Hartford.

PUBLIC TRANSPORTATION   Air service to Burlington, 45 minutes away; shuttle service to Stowe from the airport, as well as many car rentals offering special ski packages. Vermont Transit and Greyhound provide bus service and Amtrak rail service runs to Waterbury, 10 miles away, with taxis available for the rest of the route. Regular shuttle bus service from the village to the slopes makes it easy to get around without a car during the day, and many restaurants are within walking distance of lodgings.

ACCOMMODATIONS   Free reservation service: Stowe Area Association, Box 1230, Stowe, VT 05672, (800) 24-STOWE • *Top Notch at Stowe,* Mountain Road, 253-8585, $$$$ • *Stowehof Inn,* Edson Hill Road, 253-9722, $$$$$ MAP ● *The Inn at the Mountain,* Mountain Road, 253-7311, $$$$$ (MAP for the inn, EP for Condominium Lodge and Town Houses) ● *Ten Acres Lodge,* Luce Hill, 253-7638, $$$–$$$$ CP; $$$$–$$$$$ MAP ● *Trapp Family Lodge,* Luce Hill Road, 253-8511, $$$$–$$$$$ MAP ● *Timberholm Inn,* Cottage Club Road, 253-7603, $–$$ CP ● *Edson Hill Manor,* Edson Hill Road, 253-7371, $$$$–$$$$$ MAP ● *Green Mountain Inn,* Main Street, 253-7301, $$–$$$$ ● *The Gables Inn and Motel,* Mountain Road, 253-7730, $$$ MAP (weekend packages available) ● *Golden Kitz,* Mountain Road, 253-4217, $–$$ CP. Ask about weekend or ski packages at all.

DINING   *The Charda Inn,* Route 100 North, 253-4598, $$ ● *Foxfire,* Route 100 North, 253-4887, $$ ● *Ten Acres* (see above), $$–$$$ ● *Stowehof* (see above), continental menu, $$$ ● *Top Notch* (see above), excellent, $$$ ● *Trapp Family Lodge* (see above), Austrian-German, $$–$$$ ● *Isle de France,* Mountain Road, 253-7751, classic French, $$$ ● *Partridge Inn,* Mountain Road, 253-8000, seafood specialties, moderate prices, $$ ● Breakfast: *The Gables* (see above). Light fare: *The Shed, Hapleton's West Branch Café*, and the *Swisspot,* a tiny charmer noted for fondue and quiche.

SIGHTSEEING   *Stowe Winter Carnival,* one week in middle to late January; dates and schedule of events available from Stowe Winter Carnival, PO Box 1230, Stowe, VT 05676, 253-7321 ● *Stowe Skiing information,* including ski vacation packages, Mt. Mansfield Company, Inc., Stowe, VT 05672, 253-7311; snow reports, 253-8521 ● *Ben & Jerry's Ice Cream Factory,* Route 100, Waterbury. Hours: tours year round Monday to Saturday, 9 A.M. to 4 P.M. $1 admission donation goes to charity; under 12 free.

INFORMATION   Stowe Area Association, PO Box 1230, Stowe, VT 05672, (800) 24-STOWE, for all general Stowe information and free instant lodging reservations year round.

 # Stirring Things Up at Sturbridge

The soup kettle was simmering and the spit was being turned, searing the joint of beef to a crispy brown and sending heavenly smells through the kitchen. Several guests were busy preparing potatoes, carrots, and onions to be browned in the drippings, the men as involved with the chores as the women.

Another group was filling a pottery dish with whole-wheat pie crust, ready to receive chicken and gravy and vegetables, then be baked into savory pies in the cast-iron Dutch oven that was heating in the hot coals.

Meanwhile, others were busy forming wafers fresh from the wafer iron into cone shapes that would hold sweet fillings for dessert.

It's one thing to visit the Colonial kitchen of a restored New England home. It's a lot more fun to roll up your sleeves and pitch in preparing dinner on the open hearth, just the way it was done 150 years ago. That's just what you can do if you sign up for "Dinner in a Country Village," a cooking and dining program held each Saturday night during the winter months at Old Sturbridge Village in Massachusetts.

New England's largest historical restoration, Old Sturbridge Village is a lively re-creation of a rural New England village of the early nineteenth century, with "villagers" in authentic dress demonstrating what work and daily life were like in early America. The 200-acre property includes more than 40 New England houses as well as mills, churches, crafts shops, and a fully operating period farm.

But for the lucky 14 who snag a place at Saturday dinner, the real fun begins when the gates close and everyone else heads home. That's when the kitchen of the red saltbox Parsonage on the village common swings into action.

Dinner guests are escorted into the 1748 home, restored to reflect the fashions and furnishings of a clergyman's family in the 1830s, and are greeted by three members of the village staff who are well versed in the art of fireplace cooking. Everyone helps in the preparation of an authentic full-course Colonial meal using historical kitchen utensils reproduced from the Sturbridge Village collections.

With the group limited in number, everyone really gets a chance to participate, and while dinner cooks there is time to socialize and learn to play some early nineteenth-century parlor games.

It's a delicious way to relive a bit of the past, something you can also do by day at Old Sturbridge Village. A coat of winter white only makes the village more beautiful—and gives you a chance to ride in a horse-drawn sleigh. A cold weather visit also allows you to see the special activities of the peaceful winter season. Outdoors you can find farmers hauling logs with a team of oxen to make repairs in the split-rail fences or to provide material for the sawmill. Indoors you can join country artisans in front of a cheery fireplace or cast-iron stove, a mighty welcome invention in the 1830s. Weaving, printing, and tinning are among the traditional crafts to be seen.

This is also a time to linger over some of the indoor exhibits that tend to be forgotten in the summer. The Cheney Wells Clock Gallery

houses an outstanding collection of New England clocks from the eighteenth and early nineteenth centuries, and also provides a rare opportunity to see a tower clock mechanism in operation. The adjoining Folk
Art Gallery showcases examples of New England folk painting, por-
traiture, and decorative arts and crafts.

There are special activities at Old Sturbridge to mark the weekend of
George Washington's birthday, beginning with a Saturday display of
1830s dress and hairstyles and the preparation of fancy foods. Meet-
inghouse services are held on Sunday afternoon, and later in the day
there is an early nineteenth-century toasting ceremony at the Tavern,
all intended to show how New Englanders of 150 years ago might have
commemorated the birthday of the young nation's first president.

Seeing Old Sturbridge Village and visiting a few of the shops in the
town of Sturbridge will fill Saturday to the brim. Among the interesting stops on Route 20 are Basketville for its hundreds of wicker items,
the Sturbridge Yankee Workshop for reproductions of Early American
furniture, and Quilter's Quarters for a selection of handsome quilts. To
the east, Sturbridge Marketplace houses all sorts of shops and factory
outlets, and Sturbridge Antique Shops offers 75 dealers in one
complex.

If you have doll fanciers along, you will want to find time also for
the Fairbanks Doll Museum, a collection of 2,700 dolls and accessories. The museum claims to have every American doll made from the
year 1830 to present times.

When it comes to choosing lodging for the night, the most attractive
Sturbridge inn by far is the 1771 Publick House, a longtime New England standby that is full of Colonial charm, and its equally attractive,
cozier, and quieter adjunct, the Colonel Ebenezer Crafts Inn. The Publick House runs a series of very pleasant ''Yankee Winter Weekends,''
featuring lots of hearty fare and visits to Old Sturbridge. However, the
package includes dinner, something of a waste if you plan to take part
in the cooking at the village. Old Sturbridge Village has a motor lodge
adjoining the grounds, as well as the Oliver Wight House, a handsome, restored Early American home that is a very fitting lodging for
the weekend. The Wildwood Inn in Ware, about 20 miles away, is
another charmer, a Victorian home with very reasonable prices.

On Sunday, you have a choice of destinations, depending on
whether you want indoor or outdoor activity. For starters, you might
follow Route 20 a few miles east to Auburn for the year-round antiques
fair and flea market held on Route 12.

Clock fanciers should take the Mass Pike east a few miles to Grafton
for the Willard House and Clock Museum, the birthplace of the famous
Willard clockmakers. Featured are many fine early clocks, including
some prize tall clocks, as well as eighteenth-century furnishings.

Worcester, Massachusetts's second-largest city, is just 20 miles from Sturbridge via Routes 90 and 290. This city is a sleeper, still thought of by many as primarily a factory town, but actually much more. In addition to having a Colonial heritage dating back to 1673, an attractively hilly terrain, and lovely residential areas, Worcester is the home of twelve college campuses and two fine small museums.

The New England Science Center is unique and worth a visit. The self-sufficient energy system running the center also serves as an exhibit to educate the public. There are some clever demonstrations of scientific principles—a push-pull device to show how a fulcrum works, a hot air compressor to show what makes balloons go up—as well as more traditional natural science exhibits, a solar/lunar observatory, an African hall, and an indoor-outdoor zoo. In winter, the stars of the outdoor show are the polar bears, Ursa Minor and her daughter, Kenda. A special window lets you watch them swimming underwater.

The Worcester Art Museum, a handsome traditional stone building, may surprise you as well, with a collection of paintings that tell the story of art through 50 centuries of development. Rembrandts, Goyas, Matisses, and Picassos are among the treasures here, and one particularly fine exhibit is a thirteeth-century French chapel rebuilt here stone by stone.

The museums are easy to find, as road signs are posted no matter which way you enter the city. And when you're done with gallery hopping, you'll find that some of those dull factories in the city have been converted into very lively places for food and drink. The Northworks on Grove Street and Maxwell Silverman's Tool House on Union are two prime examples.

Another conversion in town is Exchange Place, at Exchange and Walden just across from Worcester's Centrum Civic Center. This is not a factory but a transformed police station/firehouse complex, which now holds restaurants, stores, and an art gallery. You can have a drink served from a 1922 Mack fire engine here at the Firehouse Café, eat Mexican food in a former jail cell at Margaritaville, or visit a branch of Boston's well-known Legal Sea Foods.

If you prefer ski slopes to city venues, follow Route 20 east to Route 31 north and turn off on Route 62 in Princeton for Wachusett Mountain, a small, friendly ski area with good snowmaking facilities and a most attractive lodge.

Another good reason to drive to Princeton is to eat at the very fine Inn at Princeton, a beautifully restored Victorian mansion with a marvelous continental menu. There are lodgings here as well, though it's a bit far from Sturbridge unless you plan to be here on Sunday anyway.

But if you spend the afternoon in Worcester, Princeton is within easy driving range for dinner—as is the Salem Cross Inn in West Brookfield, northwest of Sturbridge, a fine restaurant in a beamed and beautiful Colonial home that is listed in the National Register of Historic Places. Meats are roasted here in a giant 42-foot fireplace, and now that you're an amateur expert, you can test their cook's mettle.

Sturbridge Area Code: 508

DRIVING DIRECTIONS   Sturbridge is located on Route 20 in south-central Massachusetts, exit 9 on I-90, the Massachusetts Turnpike. It is 55 miles from Boston, 160 miles from New York, and 40 miles from Hartford.

PUBLIC TRANSPORTATION   Sturbridge can be reached by Amtrak to Worcester, Springfield, or Boston; Peter Pan bus lines from all three towns. Transport service is also available from Boston, Worcester, and Hartford-Springfield's Bradley International Airport.

ACCOMMODATIONS   *The Publick House,* Main Street (Route 131), Sturbridge, 347-3313, $$$ ● Under same management: *Publick House Motor Lodge,* $$; *Colonel Ebenezer Crafts Inn,* Fiske Hill (off Route 20), Colonial bed and breakfast, $$$–$$$$ CP ● *Old Sturbridge Village Motor Lodge,* Route 20, 347-3327, $$–$$$; under same management, *Oliver Wight House,* $$$ ● *Sheraton Sturbridge Inn,* Route 20, Sturbridge, 347-7393, resort-motel with indoor pool, cross-country trails, $$$–$$$$ ● *Wildwood Inn,* 121 Church Street, Ware, 967-7798, $–$$ CP ● *The Inn at Princeton,* Route 31, Princeton, 464-2030, $$$$$ CP ● There are many motels in Sturbridge; write for complete list.

BED AND BREAKFAST   *Folkstone Bed and Breakfast*, PO Box 131, Station 1, Boylston, MA 01505, 869-2687.

DINING   *The Publick House* (see above), $$$–$$$$ ● *Inn at Princeton* (see above), $$$–$$$$ ● *Salem Cross Inn,* Route 9, West Brookfield, 867-2345, $–$$$ ● *The Northworks,* 106 Grove Street, Worcester, 755-9657, $ ● *Maxwell Silverman's Tool House,* 25 Union Street, Worcester, 755-9657, $$–$$$ ● *El Morocco,* 100 Wall Street, Worcester, 756-7117, Middle Eastern, $$ ● And in Exchange Place, Exchange and Walden streets: *Legal Sea Foods,* 792-1600, $–$$$; *Margaritaville,* 792-6733, $; *Firehouse Café,* 753-7899, drinks and sandwiches, $.

SIGHTSEEING   *Old Sturbridge Village,* Route 20, Sturbridge, MA 01566, 347-3362, "Dinner in a Country Village," Saturday nights at 5 P.M., December through March, limited to 14 people, minimum age 14, reservations required, approximately $40 per person. General admission to the restoration: November to March, daily except Monday, 10 A.M. to 4 P.M.; rest of year, 9 A.M. to 5 P.M. Adults, $9.50; children, $4 • *Fairbanks Doll Museum,* Hall Road, Sturbridge, 347-9690. Hours: Tuesday through Sunday, 1 P.M. to 5 P.M. and 7 P.M. to 9 P.M. Adults, $1; children, $.50 • *Willard House and Clock Museum, Inc.,* 11 Willard Street, Grafton, 839-3500. Hours: Tuesday to Saturday, 10 A.M. to 4 P.M., Sunday 1 P.M. to 5 P.M. Adults, $2; children, $.75. • *Worcester Art Museum,* 55 Salisbury Street, 799-4406. Hours: Tuesday to Friday, 10 A.M. to 4 P.M., Saturday from 5 P.M., Sunday 1 P.M. to 5 P.M. Free • *New England Science Center,* 222 Harrington Way, Worcester, 791-9211. Hours: Wednesday to Saturday, 10 A.M. to 5 P.M.; Sunday from 12 noon. Adults, $3.50; age 3 to 16, $2.75 *Wachusett Mountain State Reservation,* Princeton, 464-2712, ski area with triple and two double chairlifts, beginner's area, and teaching facilities.

INFORMATION Sturbridge Area Tourist Association, PO Box 66, Route 20, Sturbridge, MA 01566, 347-7594. Central Massachusetts Tourist Council, Inc., 850 Mechanics Tower, Worcester, MA 01608, 753-2920.

Happy Landings in Salisbury

They fly through the air with the greatest of ease, those graceful ski jumpers in Salisbury, Connecticut.

Ever since 1926 the best of these daring young men, including many top Olympic contenders, have shown off their style each year in early February at the U.S. Eastern Ski Jump Championships held at Salisbury's Satre Hill. Even the most sedentary spectator will appreciate the extraordinary coordination and skill required to make a 55-meter jump with a happy landing, and sports enthusiasts and firesiders alike will also appreciate the many cozy inns and other attractions of this particulary charming corner of the state.

Northwestern Connecticut is Currier and Ives country, set in the rolling foothills of the Berkshire Mountains and blessed with a string of picture-pretty Colonial towns. It has long attracted writers and artists, and though the area has now been well discovered by wealthy New Yorkers looking for vacation homes, it has escaped any obvious kind of commercialization. Except for inflated real estate prices and the appearance of gourmet pasta and cheese in local grocery stores, villages like Salisbury, Sharon, and Lakeville retain the unspoiled air that attracted the newcomers in the first place.

This is also ideal country for anyone who wants to learn to ski, either downhill or cross-country, with low-key Mohawk Mountain a few miles south in Cornwall offering excellent facilities without the hassles found at the bigger areas farther north. This area is so civilized that the ski lodge hangs up potted plants and provides a library of books for nonskiers. There are extensive snowmaking facilities to help ensure the necessary white stuff on the slopes as well as miles of cross-country trails in the adjacent state forest.

The ski jump championship, a one-of-kind event in the East, is held both Saturday and Sunday from 11 A.M. Saturday's jump is the annual Salisbury invitational, Sunday's, the official competition. With a renovation of the jump ramp in 1984, the leaps are more exciting than ever, and the old 217-foot record may have already been bettered by this time.

In their slick skin-tight jump suits, with special light boots, bindings, and skis, the jumpers are a thrilling sight leaping off into space. All it takes is some watching to begin to understand the standards that go into making a champion. In addition to length of jump, the bend of the body, the position of the skis, the spring of the takeoff, and the grace of the landing are all calculated by the judges before each competitor is given a score.

Even with all the excitement, plus the coffee or hot chocolate served at a convenient stand, a couple of hours in the cold is enough for most viewers, so there is plenty of time to explore Salisbury and some of the surrounding towns. Don't expect rows of shops, however. The lack of such touristy sights is one of this area's chief delights. There is just enough to keep you occupied for a pleasant hour in town and to give you an excuse to tour some of the nearby territory.

Right in the village you'll find the Salisbury Antiques Center on Library Street, just off Route 44, with an interesting and eclectic selection. Serious antiquers should proceed north on Route 7 across the Massachusetts state line to Sheffield, where every other house on the main street seems to have blossomed into an antiques shop.

Other attractions in Salisbury are For the Birds, featuring many locally made crafts, and Garlande Limited, where an elegant selection of heirloom Christmas tree decorations is the specialty of a store "where every day is Christmas." Lauray on Undermountain Road is a top source for cacti and succulent plants, in person or by mail.

Go back on Route 41 and take Route 44 west to Lakeville, home of the prestigious Hotchkiss School and a few upscale shops.

Or you can follow Route 44 east into East Canaan for the Connecticut Woodcarvers' Gallery, a shop featuring hand-carved birds, animals, clocks, frames, and other objects done by some 14 professional wood carvers. If you don't see what you want, they'll carve it to order for you.

Drive farther east on Route 44 into Norfolk to discover one of the prettiest towns around, complete with village green, church steeples, shuttered Colonial houses, and a mansion in the middle of town that serves as summer quarters for the Yale School of Music. Check out the current art exhibit in the handsome 1889 library here, and then mark Norfolk down as a place to return for summer concerts.

Continue east to Winsted if you want to visit Folkcraft Instruments, which features handcrafted harps, dulcimers, and psalteries. The owners claim they'll teach you to play the dulcimer in 10 minutes—15 for slow students. There are interesting records and books here too in this folk music center.

Then take Route 20 north, and you'll arrive in Riverton, once known as Hitchcockville for the factory that opened here in 1826 when Lambert Hitchcock produced the famous painted and stenciled chairs that bear his name. A collection of the originals can be seen in the Hitchcock Museum in an old church in the center of town. Chairs are still made in the factory, using many of the original handmade procedures, and new models of the old patterns are for sale at the showroom and shop next door. Plan your stop for Saturday, however, as both museum and factory close on Sundays.

Riverton offers some other interesting shopping as well. Sarah Hubbard Putnam Antiques and Herbs, located in an 1865 Victorian house, offers old and new baskets, spices and wreaths, and kitchen collectibles. Graphics and works in pewter, blown glass, pottery, fiber, and wood are to be found at the Contemporary Crafts Gallery. You'll also find a Seth Thomas factory outlet here for good buys on mantel, wall, and grandfather clocks from America's oldest clockmaker.

Riverton is home to one of Connecticut's oldest inns, a good bet for a meal or an overnight stay. Other traditional inn lodgings are to be found back in Salisbury and in Norfolk, and Lakeville's Interlaken Inn is a mini-resort. If your idea of a winter weekend means cuddling by the fire, most of the inns can oblige with the proper setting.

If you have more touring time after the ski jump competitions on Sunday, drive south about 25 miles from Salisbury on Route 7 and then take Route 63 to Litchfield, a town invariably high on the list of most beautiful main streets in New England. You'll likely recognize the Congregational church on the green, since it shows up in countless magazine photos of New England scenes. Next door is the 1787 Parsonage, where Harriet Beecher Stowe was born.

The extraordinarily fine homes here are still occupied, some by descendents of the original occupants. Take a walk or a slow drive along North and South streets to see the handsome early architecture, and make special note of the little house on South where Tapping Reeve opened the nation's first law school in 1773, with his brother-in-law, Aaron Burr, as his first pupil.

Follow Route 202 west out of Litchfield to Bantam Lake to end your winter outing by watching yet another speedy sport, for this is the home course for the Connecticut Ice Yachting Club. Up to 30 boats gather here every weekend for this unusual activity, which requires just the kind of winter conditions most of us try to avoid—high winds and frigid temperatures. The hardy competitors seem to find the thrills and high speeds ample compensation, however, and when conditions are right, it's not unusual to see a DN-60 or Skeeter-class boat skimming up to 100 miles an hour. It's great fun to watch—just be sure to dress for the weather.

Connecticut Area Code: 203

DRIVING DIRECTIONS Salisbury is on Route 44, reached via Route 7 from the east and Route 22 from the west. It is about 150 miles from Boston, 103 miles from New York, and 65 miles from Hartford.

PUBLIC TRANSPORTATION Bonanza buses serve Canaan, Connecticut, just a few miles from Salisbury.

ACCOMMODATIONS *Undermountain Inn,* Undermountain Road (Route 41), Salisbury, 435-0242, attractive 1700s home, warm hosts, $$$$$ MAP ● *Old Riverton Inn,* Route 20, Riverton, 379-8678, atmospheric 1796 Colonial, $$ ● *Mountain View Inn,* Route 272, Norfolk, 542-5595, homey Victorian, $$–$$$ CP ● *Manor House,* PO Box 701, Maple Avenue, Norfolk, 542-5690, showplace Victorian, $$–$$$$ CP ● *Greenwoods Gate,* Greenwoods Road East, Norfolk, 542-5439, beautifully furnished Colonial, $$$$ CP ● *Interlaken Inn,* Route 112, Lakeville, 435-2515, modern inn with Victorian home lodgings also on grounds, indoor sauna and Jacuzzi, ice skating nearby, $$$–$$$$.

BED AND BREAKFAST *Covered Bridge Bed and Breakfast,* PO Box 447, Norfolk, CT 06058, 542-5944.

DINING *Old Riverton Inn* (see above), $$ ● *Undermountain Inn* (see above), British specialties, cozy ambience, $$ ● *White Hart Inn,* Routes 41 and 44, Salisbury, 435-2372, landmark on the green, $$ ● *Holley Place,* Pocketknife Square, Lakeville, 435-2727, attractive restored factory, $$–$$$ ● *Interlaken Inn* (see above), $$–$$$ ● *The Woodland,* Route 41, Lakeville, 435-0578, casual, popular locally, a good bet for Sunday brunch, $–$$.

SIGHTSEEING *U.S. Eastern Ski Jumping Championships,* two days, usually first weekend in February; single tickets or combination for both days. Write Salisbury Winter Sports Association, Salisbury, CT 06068, for current dates and ticket prices, or contact the Salisbury Chamber of Commerce ● *Mohawk Mountain Ski Area,* Route 4, Cornwall, 672-6464 ● *Horse and Carriage Livery,* PO Box 264, Loon Meadow Drive, Norfolk, 542-6085, carriage and sleigh rides.

INFORMATION Salisbury Chamber of Commerce, PO Box 1732, Lakeville, CT 06039, 435-2666. Litchfield Hills Travel Council, PO Box 1776, Marbledale, CT 06777, 868-2214.

Wintering in the White Mountains

Winter is the magic season in the White Mountains of New Hampshire.

Well-paved roads lead through mountain passes beneath imposing peaks that are all the more beautiful under their winter coats of white. The snow adds its crowning softness to the tall pines and maples in the pristine national forests that surround the mountains and to the rooftops and greens in tiny roadside villages where skaters on the ponds make living Grandma Moses scenes.

The stupendous scenery, unmatched in the East, and the great variety of activities and facilities available in the White Mountains make New England's highest peaks the peak choice for couples or families who have differing abilities on or enthusiasm for the ski slopes.

Whatever your winter pleasure, you'll find it here. Skiers can take their turns at more than half a dozen nearby slopes for all abilities, and ski tourers have miles and miles of exquisite cross-country trails to choose from. There's also ample opportunity for such pastimes as sledding, tobogganing, snowshoeing, and ice skating. And for indoor challenge, the North Conway bargains await—a total of almost 30 discount outlets in the general area.

The unsurpassed setting makes many content to spend a weekend just driving the scenic highways, riding the mountain cable cars for the views, or simply settling in before the fireplace at a cozy inn and enjoying the picture from a picture window.

For those who do come to ski, White Mountain loyalists claim that the sport here still has an old-fashioned, no-frills flavor that is missing in the slicker, newer areas to the west. Tradition is strong, after all, and Northeastern skiing was born in these mountains. Norwegian immigrants were skiing here as early as the 1870s, and the first American

Alpine ski school, started in the 1920s by Austrian champion Sigi Buchmayr, made Franconia the Northeast's first great winter resort.

The boom continued when the first aerial tramway was built at Cannon Mountain in 1938, and prospered even further when Austrian Hannes Schneider came to North Conway in 1939 and built the first ski tram, the same skimobile that is still moving people up Mt. Cranmore despite the addition of more modern chairlifts and pomas. It adds a certain quirky charm to the scene, and is a treasured sight for families who are into the third generation of skiing here.

Cranmore is homey and popular with families, has extensive snow-making operations, and is within walking distance of North Conway. There are six other ski areas in the White Mountains, with something for just about everyone. In the North Conway–Jackson area, Wildcat, located near Mt. Washington and legendary for its howling winds, is a challenging mountain known for its long trails and views. Bretton Woods is new and small, gentler than Wildcat, and also prides itself on spectacular views. Black Mountain, another family area, has its own bit of history—the first overhead cable tow in America, built in 1935. Newer Attitash offers 20 trails with one of the most extensive snow-making operations in the East, and limits ticket sales, promising no more than a 15-minute lift wait.

Across the mountains in Franconia, Cannon Mountain, owned by the state, is the largest ski resort in the area with 35 trails, 8 of them for experts but plenty left for everyone else, and 50 miles of ski-touring trails past scenery that may tempt you to trade your ski poles for a paintbrush.

The New England Ski Museum opened at Cannon in 1983 with audiovisual exhibits showing some early skiers in action, and displays of the wooden skis belonging to Sigi Buchmayr and other adventurers such as Lowell Thomas.

To the south are two newer complexes that don't quite fit the old-fashioned mold. Loon Mountain has a high-speed gondola, good intermediate slopes, and a resort ski complex with its own lodge. Waterville Valley, with two mountains and trails for all abilities, is a chic resort that is a village in itself, with hundreds of condominiums and four choice inns. The Snowy Owl, the most attractive of the inns, once won *Ski* magazine's prize as the best-designed mountain inn in the United States.

Waterville is a convenient choice for families, since a bus makes the rounds from village accommodations to the slopes regularly, allowing parents to sleep while the kids get to the trails first.

For cross-country skiing, Cannon and Bretton Woods take the prize for mountain scenery, but Jackson, one of the prettiest of the White Mountain villages, offers the largest ski-touring complex in the East, run by the Jackson Ski Touring Foundation and offering lessons and 80 miles of trails for all abilities. Several trails link village inns to allow for pleasant stops along the way. Experts can try their mettle on the Wildcat Valley Trail, which begins at the top of Wildcat Mountain and then swoops down 3,400 feet to meet the rest of the trail system.

The accommodations are as extensive as the skiing choices, ranging from lodges on the slopes to secluded country inns.

When you're settled in and the skiers are happily challenging the slopes, nonskiers will probably want to take the "scenic tour." From North Conway, the recommended route is the drive along Route 16 north to Pinkham Notch, then down to Conway and west on the magnificent 32-mile Kancamagus Highway, through the White Mountain National Forest from Cannon to Lincoln. At Lincoln, take Route 3 north to the fabulous attractions of Franconia Notch State Park.

Franconia Notch is a natural mountain pass between the towering peaks of the Kinsman and Franconia ranges, with some of the most spectacular scenery in the White Mountains. Here's where you'll meet the symbol of New Hampshire, the Old Man of the Mountain, that famous face carved in granite by some celestial sculptor on the mountainside.

The views and picture-book villages continue north on Route 18 to Sugar Hill, then back down and west on Route 3 to connect with 302 at Twin Mountain for the drive back to North Conway, past Bretton Woods and Crawford Notch.

Shopping is the thing in North Conway. If you need ski equipment or outdoor clothing, you won't do better than the Carroll Reed, Eastern Mountain Sports, and International Mountain Equipment stores here, and there are several local sports stores in town as well as a shop at each ski area.

Check the Scottish Lion for a fine selection of wares and choice sweaters from Scotland, Ireland, England, and Wales. You'll find casual clothing, country collectibles, and a few art galleries to explore as well as On the Wall, a print and poster shop, and a dozen antiques shops on Main Street.

If you are interested in new Early American furniture, stop by Yield House for pine and oak.

For bargains, there are outlet stores galore in North Conway, including Anne Klein, Barbizon, Converse, Corning, Frye, London Fog, Oshkosh, Gorham, Manhattan, Polo/Ralph Lauren, and Timberland. And just a few miles farther in Conway: Hathaway, Bass, Cannon Mills, White Stag, and other outlet stores await.

And the League of New Hampshire Craftsmen Shops in Franconia and North Conway are always worth a look for their fine selection of work by state artisans.

Between skiing, scenery, and shopping, the days fly by and come dinner hour, there are more fine choices than can ever fit into a weekend. For après-ski, try the Wildcat Tavern in Jackson, the Red Parka Pub in Glen, or in North Conway, the Up Country Saloon, Barnaby's, or the Oxen Yoke, an old barn turned nightclub that has been bringing in crowds for three generations.

Day or night, about the only thing you may find lacking in the White Mountains is time to do justice to the cornucopia of winter pleasures.

New Hampshire Area Code: 603

DRIVING DIRECTIONS   North Conway and Jackson in the Mt. Washington Valley are reached via Routes 16 or 302, connecting from I-95; Franconia is on Route I-93/3; Waterville Valley is reached via I-93 to exit 28, then 11 miles on Route 49 to the Valley. North Conway is 145 miles from Boston, 335 miles from New York, 225 miles from Hartford; Franconia and Waterville are roughly 15 miles closer.

PUBLIC TRANSPORTATION   Vermont Transit bus service to North Conway; American Eagle or Eastern Express air service to Lebanon, New Hampshire.

ACCOMMODATIONS   In addition to inns listed for Mt. Washington Valley on page 85 and Franconia on page 168, the following accommodations are convenient for ski areas; ask about weekend ski packages • *The Lodge at Bretton Woods,* 278-1000, contemporary lodge built in 1981, pool, sauna, Jacuzzi, $$$ • *Attitash Mountain Village,* Bartlett, 374-6501, slopeside motel and condos, $$–$$$ • *Whitney's Village Inn at Black Mountain,* Jackson, 383-6886, ice skating, convenient to mountain, $$$$$ MAP • *Mill House Inn* at the Mill, Loon Mountain, Lincoln, 745-6261, attractive, part of restored shopping complex, rooms and condos, $$$–$$$$$ • *The Mountain Club on Loon,* Lincoln, 745-8111, $$$–$$$$$ • *Waterville Valley Lodging Bureau,* (800) 258-8988, village with condos and attractive modern inns with indoor pools, saunas, Jacuzzis • Condos: *Snowy Owl Inn, Black Bear Lodge,* and *Valley Inn,* all $$$$ • *Cranmore Mt. Lodge,* Kearsage Road, North Conway, 447-2181, $$ CP, and *Nestlenook Inn,* PO Box Q, Jackson Village, 383-9443, $$–$$$ CP, have their own ski touring trails and Nestlenook offers sleigh rides as well.

BED AND BREAKFAST   *New Hampshire Bed and Breakfast,* RFD 3, Box 52, Laconia, NH 03246, 279-8348.

DINING   See Mt. Washington Valley, page 86, and Franconia, page 168.

SKI AREAS   Write for trail maps and current rates ● *Attitash*, Route 302, Bartlett, lodging, 374-2386; information, 374-2369; ski conditions, (800) 258-0316 out of state ● *Black Mountain*, Jackson, 383-4490 ● *Bretton Woods*, Route 302, Bretton Woods, 278-5000; conditions, 278-5051 ● *Mt. Cranmore*, off Route 302/16, North Conway, 356-5544; conditions, 356-5545 ● *Wildcat*, Route 16, Pinkham Notch, 466-3326; conditions (800) 272-2550 out of state ● *Loon Mountain*, Lincoln, 745-8111 ● *Cannon Mountain*, Route 3, Franconia, 823-5561 ● *Waterville Valley*, (800) 552-4767 or (800) 258-8983 out of state; conditions, (800) 552-0388 or (800) 258-8983 out of state ● *Jackson Ski Touring Foundation*, Jackson, 383-9355; conditions, 383-9356.

INFORMATION   Mt. Washington Valley Chamber of Commerce, Route 16, North Conway, PO Box 385, Washington Valley, NH 03860, 356-3171; Franconia–Sugar Hill Chamber of Commerce, Franconia, NH 03580, 823-5661.

Back to Nature in Bethel

When a noted Cleveland surgeon, Dr. John Gehring, suffered a nervous breakdown in 1887, he came to the peaceful New England village of Bethel, Maine, to recover.

The cure worked so well that Gehring opened a pioneer clinic in Bethel that became famous. Many prominent people regained their good health and spirits here through a program that mixed outdoor physical activity, including planting crops and cutting wood, with contemplating the physical beauty of the rivers, forests, and mountains around Bethel.

Visitors to Bethel these days are more likely to get their exercise sightseeing or skiing, but for a restorative weekend close to nature, it's still hard to beat this quiet and beautiful corner of southwestern Maine. For skiers who have suffered through long lift lines elsewhere, relaxed and uncrowded Maine skiing may prove to be a rejuvenating experience in itself.

The history of this handsome Colonial town of 2,500 goes back much farther than Dr. Gehring's day, and much of it can be revisited with a walk through town. Bethel was founded in 1774 as Sudbury, Canada, after the original grantees from Sudbury, Massachusetts, all of whom had fought in the campaign to conquer Canada. The early sawmills and farms along the Androscoggin River prospered after the Revolutionary War, and in 1796 the town was incorporated as Bethel, a biblical name meaning House of God.

With the arrival of the railway, wood products became (and remain) an important factor in the town's economy. The trains also brought the first summer visitors to enjoy the town's extraordinary setting in the White Mountain foothills.

The 1836 founding of Gould Academy, one of Maine's oldest prep schools, brought notice to the town. Later, the residency of William Rogers Chapman, an outstanding musician who attracted many of the nation's music greats to visit, and the 1947 founding of the National Training Laboratories with their experimental human relations and leadership programs further helped give Bethel a prominence beyond its size.

Much of the center of Bethel is now a National Historic District marking the early landmarks. Stroll down to the end of the aptly named Broad Street and you can see Dr. Gehring's original clinic, an 1896 Queen Anne home that is presently the headquarters of the National Training Laboratories.

It was Dr. Gehring and one of his patients, William Bingham II, who in 1913 built the Bethel Inn on the choice spot facing the long town common. The inn presently consists of the old main building and a series of surrounding 1800s residences bought up over the years for additional lodging space. It isn't as formal or as elegant as it once was, but it is still attractive, with big, warming fireplaces and picture windows in the dining room and main lounges that look out on an evergreen-rimmed golf course and the White Mountains beyond.

In winter, the golf course is a perfect place for cross-country skiers. The inn offers 22 miles of trails connecting to some of the many other touring trails in the area, plus a sauna to ease aching muscles when tired skiers come home. It also hosts a touring center with rental and instruction open to all. The excellent dining room has well-prepared American dishes, with such basics as prime rib, steak, and lamb chops as the specialties.

Across from the Bethel Inn are some classic clapboard mansions, including the 1848 Greek revival Major Gideon Hastings House, built by the founder of one of western Maine's timberland and lumbering dynasties, and the Moses Mason House, the circa 1813 Federal-style home of one of the town's leading early residents. The Mason House is now a museum of eight period rooms restored by the Bethel Historical Society, and is open to visitors by appointment. Some of the other attractive homes around the common are now bed-and-breakfast lodgings.

The handsome Gould Academy campus at the other end of town includes the James B. Owen Art Gallery, which is open from 9 A.M. to 3 P.M. on weekdays and on weekend afternoons. The white-spired West Parish Congregational Church near the school housed the congregation led by Reverend Daniel Gould, a teacher and pastor, for whom the academy was named.

Having seen the sights of Bethel, skiers will want to make haste north on Route 26 to Sunday River, a small ski mountain that still manages to have trails for everyone except the most expert. Though Sunday River is growing as condominiums are multiplying near the slopes, it still offers good intermediate skiing on trails through the tall Maine timber, easy slopes for beginners, and lift lines that are quick and efficient for all.

South of Bethel are Mount Abram, five miles from town on Route 26, and Pleasant Mountain, a bit farther on in Bridgton, both pleasant, low-key family areas.

For those who don't ski, Bridgton is the place to go to while away some time in pleasant shops. There are more than a dozen antiques and crafts shops in town right on Main Street or on Route 302.

A tour of some of the other little towns in the area will bring you to more shops as well as some lovely winter scenery. If your travels take you to Lynchville, south of Bethel on Route 35, you can photograph the famous road sign leading to such faraway places as Norway, Paris, Denmark, Naples, Poland, Peru, and China, all of them nearby villages in Maine.

While you are driving, be sure to include the perfect little Colonial hamlet of Waterford in your travels, another good prospect for lodging with three exceptional small inns to choose from.

For interesting stops, Bonnema Pottery in Bethel and Freiden Dorf Pottery in Bryant Pond are both places where you can watch the potters at their craft. More shops dot many of the villages in the area—Sleepy Hollow Collectibles in Denmark and Oxford Common in Oxford to name just a few. Western buffs may want to visit the library in Fryeburg for the Hopalong Cassidy Room, full of memorabilia belonging to Hoppy's creator, Clarence Mulford, including his gun collection.

Generally, all is peaceful in these little towns, but there's a bit of excitement in February when Bridgton stages its annual Winter Carnival, a strictly hometown event that is fun to see. The festivities include ice sculptures, dog sled races, and Klondike Night at the local Lion's Club, featuring casino games where you can try your luck.

Win or lose, you've picked a good bet with Bethel and its environs. Whether you prefer traversing uncrowded ski slopes, traveling the scenic back roads, or simply contemplating the fire in a cozy inn, this serene section of western Maine is just what the doctor ordered.

Maine Area Code: 207

DRIVING DIRECTIONS Bethel is about 70 miles northwest of Portland and its airport. It can be reached via Route 26 from the Gray exit of the Maine Turnpike or from the west via Route 2, which connects to I-91 at St. Johnsbury, Vermont. It is 175 miles from Boston, 385 miles from New York, and 275 miles from Hartford.

PUBLIC TRANSPORTATION   Closest air service is Portland; nearest bus service is Vermont Transit to North Conway, New Hampshire.

ACCOMMODATIONS   *Bethel Inn and Country Club,* Bethel, 824-2175, $$–$$$$ MAP; weekend ski packages ● *L'Auberge,* PO Box 21, Bethel, 824-2774, simple secluded village inn, dorm rooms for skiers, $$ CP ● *Sudbury Inn,* PO Box 521, Bethel, 824-2174, another unpretentious and reasonable village inn with a good dining room, $$ CP ● *The Norseman Inn,* Bethel, 824-2002, homey, popular ski lodge on the way to Sunday Mountain, $$$ MAP ● *Chapman Inn,* on the common, Bethel, 824-2657, gracious 1865 home, $–$$ CP ● *Hammons House,* Broad Street, PO Box 16, Bethel, 824-3170, historic 1859 home, $$ ● *Four Seasons Inn,* Upper Main Street, Bethel, 824-2755, elegant 1895 Victorian with afternoon tea, $$ CP ● *Condominiums at Sunday Mountain,* 824-2187, attractive modern units, $$$–$$$$ ● *Pleasant Mountain Inn,* Bridgton, 647-2431, condo accommodations near the slopes, $$$$ ● *Philbrook Farm Inn,* off Route 2, Shelburne, NH, 466-3831, cozy farmhouse on 100 acres with its own cross-country trails, $$$ MAP ● Waterford accommodations, see page 155.

BED AND BREAKFAST   *Bed and Breakfast of Maine,* 32 Colonial Village, Falmouth, ME 04105, 781-4528.

DINING   *Bethel Inn and Country Club* (see above), $$ ● *Sudbury Inn* (see above), $$ ● *Olde Rawley Inn,* Route 35, North Waterford, 583-4143, historic Colonial inn, best in the region, $$ ● *Center Lovell Inn,* Route 5, Center Lovell, 925-1575, northern Italian specialties, $–$$ ● *Maurice,* Main Street (Route 26), South Paris, 743-2532, continental menu, $–$$ ● For informal fare and lively atmosphere, *Mother's* in Bethel or *D.W. McKeen's* on the access road to Sunday River ● Also see Waterford, pages 155–56.

SKIING AREAS   All have both downhill and cross-country ● *Sunday River Ski Resort,* Route 26, 6 miles north of Bethel, 824-2187 ● *Mount Abram Ski Slopes,* Route 26, Locke Mills (5 miles south of Bethel), 875-2601 ● *Pleasant Valley Ski Area,* Mountain Road off Route 302, Bridgton, 647-8444.

INFORMATION   Greater Bethel Chamber of Commerce, PO Box

121, Bethel, ME 04217, 824-2346. Bridgton Chamber of Commerce, Box 236, Bridgton, ME 04009, 647-3472.

Beyond the Mansions in Newport

Newport, Rhode Island, is a town that might have an identity problem if all its various personalities were not so exceptional.

There's the opulent Newport, private summer bastion of the super-wealthy, evidenced by some of the grandest mansions in the country.

There's the nautical Newport, also easy to discern in summer by the dozens of yachts in the harbor and enough visitors clad in topsiders to sink a ship. The old wharfs have bloomed anew with restaurants and shops to accommodate all the sailors plus the army of landlubbers who join them on crowded warm-weather weekends, giving rise to the touristy Newport.

Then there's the scenic Newport, which tends to get lost in all the tourist activity—a town of rare beauty to be seen best on the spectacular ten-mile Ocean Drive along a cliff overlooking the sea and further savored on the Cliff Walk along the bluffs. Not to mention the Colonial Newport, a town of enormous charm whose narrow old streets have undergone one of the most impressive restorations in the country.

In the quiet off season when the harbor is still, it is these last and sometimes neglected aspects of Newport that shine through. And with the mansions and many other attractions still open for sightseeing and the shops and restaurants still very much in business, there's plenty of activity when you want it. Add the drama of wintry winds that send waves dashing against the cliffs, and you have a winning winter getaway.

If Newport today seems to have more than its share of personalities, it may be because of the town's unusual past. It was founded in 1639 by settlers seeking religious freedom but soon prospered as a major seaport of the infamous Triangle Trade—actually an extension of the slave trade using African slaves to obtain West Indian sugar and molasses to be made into Newport rum.

Newport's era of prominence as a port ended when the British burned the harbor, first during the Revolutionary War and then during the War of 1812. Later it became a haunt of artists and writers who were taken with its natural beauty, followed in the late 1800s by the wealthy, who put up the opulent summer palaces they called "cottages'' for a feverish six-week season that became the nation's most elaborate social scene.

Though many wealthy summer people remain today, Newport's gilded age died out with changing times. But the mansions survive as prime tourist attractions. The seven homes operated by the Newport Preservation Society currently draw a million visitors a year.

The building of a bridge connecting Newport to Jamestown in 1969 made it far more accessible for travelers, and the Newport Jazz Festival, born in the same period, brought even more crowds. Newport was going public, and in 1973 when the Navy relocated the base that had helped support the town economy, the city fathers began to encourage the trend. The waterfront was turned into shops and restaurants, attracting a seasonal flood of tourists.

During all this activity, part-time resident Doris Duke began to take interest in the many fine early eighteenth-century buildings that had been allowed to decay. She set up a foundation that renovated some six dozen houses, renting them at reasonable rates to residents who would appreciate and protect their heritage. Others followed suit, spreading the restoration area.

If you want to start your Newport tour chronologically, a stroll along the cobbled streets leading uphill from the town center and along the waterfront on Washington Street—the area known as the Point—will show you early Newport in a series of some 400 pastel-hued town houses that are one of the nation's most extensive collection of authentic Colonial dwellings. Washington Street has some particularly fine homes.

Hunter House, the grandest of the Colonial dwellings, is owned by the Newport Historical Society and can be seen in winter by appointment. You can rent a taped driving or walking tour at the Chamber of Commerce if you want to know more about the history of this fascinating area as well as about the rest of the town.

Next, a tour on the well-marked Ocean Drive past the mansions and out on the bluffs will show you the views that attracted all those millionaires to Newport. If the weather is kind, stop off along Bellevue Avenue, bundle up, and follow some of the Cliff Walk, a 3½-mile path along the top that gives you a rare perspective of lawns and mansions on one side, an eagle's-eye ocean view on the other.

By now you'll probably be dying to see the inside of the houses. If you think America had no royalty, you may well change your mind when you see the massive scale, the marble floors and chandeliers, and the priceless brocades of the summer palaces of America's upper crust. Three of the finest of the houses remain open weekends for touring all year: Marble House, designed by Richard Morris Hunt for William K. Vanderbilt and named for the many colors of marble used in its construction and decorations; The Elms, a summer residence of Philadelphia coal magnate Edward Berwind, modeled after the Château d'Asnieres near Paris; and Château-sur-Mer, one of the most lavish examples of Victorian architecture and the home of Newport's first ballroom.

Back in town, everything centers on the harbor, where the first American navy was established in 1775 to protect against the British fleet. Along the restored wooden wharves, in old warehouses and new structures with Colonial-modern lines, is the touristy Newport, with the usual assortment of shops to be found where visitors congregate. At Bowen's and Bannister's wharves, right on the waterfront, you'll find clothing from the Greek isles or Ireland, original gold and silver jewelry designs, handcrafted leather, children's clothing and toys, and a candy store noted for homemade fudge. Across the street in the Brick Marketplace, a cobbled maze of condominiums and 30 shops, there is even more variety.

If antiquing is your goal, you'll find shops on lower Thames and on parallel Spring Street, as well as the side streets in between. Newport shop hours are irregular in the winter, so check the times for the stores that interest you or call for an appointment.

When it comes to lodgings, once again you can pick your Newport: Colonial-style rooms at the Inntowne, brass beds and a warming fire in the parlor at the Admiral Benbow, an unparalleled harbor view at the rambling shingled Inn at Castle Hill, and modern condominium accommodations around the wharves. The Sheraton Islander Inn is a mini-resort off to itself on Goat Island, a few minutes away across a causeway. There are many bed-and-breakfast choices as well. Two of the most appealing are on Clarke Street in the heart of the historic district. Melville House is a snug and welcoming Colonial, circa 1750, where in the late afternoon everyone gathers in the living room for sherry, and the Admiral Farragut next door is a 1702 charmer decorated with flair, whimsy, and handsome handmade furniture.

Excellent restaurants are plentiful, many a bit on the formal side, so men should be prepared with jacket and tie in the better places.

If Saturday was filled with mansions and scenery, Sunday brings another set of Newport sights, mostly clustered around Touro Street and Bellevue Avenue. From the grand days, there is the Tennis Hall of Fame, located on Bellevue in the old Newport Casino building, designed by Stanford White. Pass through the arch to see the fashionable resort that once was the epitome of recreation for the "cottage set" with lawn games, tennis and racquetball courts, and bowling alleys.

You can try your hand at tennis here at the Casino Indoor Racquet Club or in summer on those gorgeous grass courts.

Touro Synagogue, a National Historic Site, is the oldest Jewish house of worship in the country, a sign of the religious freedom of the early Rhode Island colony. Dedicated in 1763, it is a beautiful edifice done by Peter Harrison, the nation's first architect, in Colonial style that has been carefully preserved. It is worth a visit for anyone interested in Early American architecture.

In Queen Anne Square on Spring Street you can see Trinity Church, the first Anglican parish in the state, with Tiffany windows, an organ tested by Handel, and the silver service and bell dating from its dedication in 1726. The Second Congregational Church on Clarke Street is another early building, commissioned in 1735 and attended by many prominent Colonial citizens. St. Mary's Church on Spring Street is of interest as the place where John Kennedy married Jacqueline Bouvier, who summered in Newport at her mother's home, Hammersmith Farm, which is now open to the public in summer.

More? The Newport Historical Society on Touro Street has Colonial art, prize Newport silver and china, and Early American glass and furniture. Changing exhibits are featured at the Newport Art Museum on Bellevue Avenue, and the Museum of Yachting on Ocean Drive is open to fans in winter by appointment. Even the Redwood Library on Bellevue is historic, the oldest library building in the country in continuous use. Among those who used it were Gilbert Stuart, William and Henry James, and Edith Wharton.

Mansion or not, almost every building in Newport seems to have a history worth noting, and this is a town where you could spend hours tracing the past. That is, unless you'd rather forget it all to head back to the Cliff Walk and gaze a little longer at the mesmerizing winter seascape. It's the side of Newport that many people like best of all.

Rhode Island Area Code: 401

DRIVING DIRECTIONS From the south, take I-95 to Route 138 and the Newport Bridge; from the north, follow I-195 to Route 114 south; from Boston take Route 128 south to Route 24 south via Sakonnet River Bridge to Route 114 south into town. Newport is about 75 miles from Boston, 185 miles from New York, and 75 miles from Hartford.

PUBLIC TRANSPORTATION Amtrak trains from New York and Boston to Providence; bus connection from station to Newport. Bonanza bus service from Providence or Boston. Major airlines service Providence, limo connections from the airport.

ACCOMMODATIONS *Inn at Castle Hill,* Ocean Drive, 849-3800, $$–$$$$$ ● *Inntowne,* 6 Mary Street, 846-9200, afternoon tea, $$$–$$$$ CP ● *Admiral Benbow Inn,* 93 Pelham Street, 846-4256, $$–$$$ ● *Melville House,* 39 Clarke Street, 847-0640, $$–

$$$ CP • *Admiral Farragut Inn*, 31 Clarke Street, 849-0006, $$–$$$ CP • *Sheraton Islander Inn*, Goat Island, 849-2600, $$$$$ • *Tread-way Inn*, America's Cup Avenue on the wharf, 847-9000, $$$–$$$$$. • Other pleasant, modest small inns: *Brinley Victorian*, 23 Brinley Street, 849-7645, $$–$$$ CP; *Pilgrim House*, 123 Spring Street, 846-0040, $$$ CP • For a brochure listing member inns, write to *Guest House Association of Newport*, PO Box 981, Newport, RI 02840, 846-5444. Write to Chamber of Commerce for list of numerous motels.

BED AND BREAKFAST *Bed and Breakfast of Rhode Island*, PO Box 3291, Newport, RI 02840, 849-1298. *Castle Keep*, 44 Everett Street, Newport, RI 02840, 846-0362.

DINING *Le Petite Auberge*, 19 Charles Street, 849-6669, elegant and authentic French, $$$ • *Clark Cooke House*, Bannister's Wharf, 846-2900, continental, historic wharf location, $$$ • *Black Pearl*, Bannister's Wharf, 846-3000, nouvelle, popular, $$–$$$; Both Clarke Cooke and Black Pearl have excellent, less expensive cafés adjoining the restaurants • *Le Bistro*, Bowen's Wharf, 849-7778, innovative menu, $$–$$$ • *Canfield House*, 5 Memorial Boulevard, 847-0416, continental menu in old Victorian gambling casino, $$–$$$ • *White Horse Tavern*, Marlborough and Farewell streets, 849-3600, nation's oldest continuously operating tavern, $$–$$$ • *The Ark*, 348 Thames Street, 849-3808, American, reasonable, especially in downstairs pub, $–$$ • For informal fare: *Rhumb Line*, 92 Bridge Street, 849-6950; *Brick Alley Pub*, 140 Thames, 849-6334; and *Cobblestone*, 206 Thames Street, 846-4285. All $–$$ • For brunch with a view, the *Inn at Castle Hill* is hard to beat.

SIGHTSEEING *Newport Mansions*, the Preservation Society of Newport County, 118 Mill Street, Newport, 847-1000, winter tours of Marble House, The Elms, Château-sur-Mer. Hours: Saturdays and Sundays, 10 A.M. to 4 P.M.; from April all homes open weekends, from May to November, open daily. Three mansions: adults, $10; children, $4. Individual houses: Marble House, adults, $4.50; children $2; other houses: adults, $4; children, $2. • *International Tennis Hall of Fame and Tennis Museum*, Newport Casino, 194 Bellevue Avenue, 849-3990. Hours: November to April, daily 11 A.M. to 4 P.M., rest of year 10 A.M. to 5 P.M. Adults, $4; children, $2; • *Touro Synagogue National Historic Site*, 72 Touro Street, 847-4794. Hours: Sunday 2 P.M. to 4 P.M. or by appointment. Free • *Redwood Library*, 50 Bellevue Avenue, 847-0292. Hours: daily except Sunday, 9:30 A.M. to 5:30 P.M. Free • *Newport Historical Society Museum*, 82 Touro Street, 846-0813. Hours: Tuesday to Friday, 9:30 A.M. to 4:30 P.M., June 15

June 15 to Labor Day also open Saturday to 12 noon. Donation • *Old Colony House,* Washington Street, 846-2980. Hours: July to Labor Day, Monday to Friday 9:30 A.M. to 12 noon, and 1 P.M. to 4 P.M., Saturday to noon; rest of year by appointment. Free • *Newport Art Museum,* Bellevue Avenue at Touro Park, 847-0179. Hours: Tuesday to Saturday, 10 A.M. to 5 P.M., Sunday from 1 P.M. Adults, $2; under 18, free; free to all on Fridays. • *Museum of Yachting*, Fort Adams Park, Ocean Drive, 847-1018. Hours: Mid-May to mid-October, 10 A.M. to 5 P.M.; rest of the year by appointment. $2.50.

INFORMATION Newport County Chamber of Commerce, 10 America's Cup Avenue, 847-1600. Hours: winter weekdays 9 A.M. to 5 P.M., Saturday 9 A.M. to 2 P.M., Sunday 10 A.M. to 2 P.M.

Boning Up on Cambridge

Without its colleges, Cambridge, Massachusetts, might be any other town on the perimeter of Boston. But its two very prominent residents, Harvard, the nation's oldest and proudest university, and MIT, considered by many to be the birthplace of modern technology, make Cambridge as rightful an attraction for American visitors as Oxford or the original Cambridge University are for travelers to Britain.

Since a visit to Boston seldom leaves enough time to do justice to the town across the Charles River, a weekend in Cambridge can give you a chance to tour the famous universities, explore the many bookstores and shops, join the crowds in the coffee houses, enjoy the fine films and theater in the area, and generally bone up on a fascinating community.

To begin with, Cambridge is not a typical college town. A city of 95,000 that is in many ways a microcosm of a metropolis, it is more than its universities and more than a Boston suburb. A large part of the population is working class and represents a wide mix of nationalities. Another part is intellectual and creative, people ranging from economist John Kenneth Galbraith to author John Irving to chef Julia Child, who live in the handsome and historic residential neighborhoods that mark a city that is now more than 350 years old.

It is almost impossible to separate the history of Cambridge from that of Harvard, the institution that shaped it. The town was founded in 1630 as Newtowne; the college came along just six years later. It was named for local minister John Harvard, who died in 1638, leaving his fortune and library to the campus.

As Harvard grew to greatness, Cambridge flowered as well. Great universities tend to collect impressive architecture, famous people, and fine museums, and Cambridge has them all. Students and visitors usually attract good restaurants, shops, and attractive lodgings, and Cambridge offers all these in abundance as well.

There is so much, in fact, that at first glance academic Cambridge is a jumble of impressions. Busy Harvard Square, the hub of activity, seems to be in perpetual motion, filled with people and traffic. The big out-of-town newspaper stand, the sprawling Harvard Coop, and the string of stores and sandwich shops and banks say little about the past, yet the square opens directly into the gate to Harvard Yard, a tranquil ivied repository of history. A new information booth in the square makes it easier to get your bearings.

Since the university is the major lure for most visitors, you'll likely want to spend Saturday getting to know that campus and its rich variety of sights, beginning with the Yard. Harvard has its own information center on the plaza of Holyoke Center, 1350 Massachusetts Avenue, where you can pick up a free map that identifies every Harvard-owned building and all the streets in the immediate area. Student-guided tours of the campus also leave from this point.

If you prefer to tour on your own, cross the street and enter Harvard Yard through the Quincy Gate to see the oldest part of the campus. Massachusetts Hall, where the president of Harvard has his office, has stood on this spot since 1720. Holden Chapel, dating from 1744, is a gem of Georgian architecture. Untold numbers of students and visitors to the campus have had their picture taken with the seated statue of John Harvard that stands in front of University Hall, the gray stone building designed in 1815 by Charles Bullfinch.

The quadrangle in back of University Hall is dominated by the bulk of Widener Library, the largest university library in the world. Behind Widener's Corinthian portico are ten stories holding the equivalent of 50 miles of books, some 3 million volumes. Walk inside to see panoramic models of Harvard and Cambridge, old and new.

Across the quadrangle are the steepled 1932 Memorial Chapel and Sever Hall, an 1880 classroom building designed by H. H. Richardson, the late nineteenth-century master architect, two of many architectural treasures spanning almost three centuries.

Straight on to Robinson Hall, then left past Emerson Hall and onto Quincy Street will bring you to the Fogg Art Museum, whose collections include almost every significant period of Western art and Oriental art as well. It is one of eight museums on campus, and is a training ground for curators the world over. Next door is the Carpenter Center for the Visual Arts, a sweep of glass and concrete that is the only Le Corbusier building in North America.

Exit the museum on Quincy, turn right, and continue to Broadway and the Arthur M. Sackler Museum, the newest of the campus art repositories. The ancient Islamic and Oriental art here includes the world's richest collection of Chinese jades. Continuing on Quincy, on the left is Memorial Hall, a massive brick building with a tiled roof where many of the area's music and dance groups perform. Continuing down Quincy past Cambridge and onto Kirkland Street, you'll find the Busch-Reisinger Museum, one of the few museums in the country specializing in the art of northern and central Europe. The collection of German Expressionist paintings here is among the best in the world.

Back on Kirkland, turn right on Oxford and you'll come to the Harvard University Museum building, four museums under one roof that include everything from dinosaurs to rare jewels. The garden of Blaschka glass flowers in the Botanical Museum is world renowned—bigger than life and absolutely true to nature.

In addition to the interesting museum displays of North, Central, and South American cultures, the gift shop in the Peabody Museum of Archaeology and Ethnology is worth a visit. It is filled with the finest in Indian baskets, Eskimo carvings, beadwork, and fine Navajo jewelry, among many other unique handicrafts.

The printed guide will show you more of Harvard/Radcliffe and Cambridge sights. In addition to the museums, you can see the fine residence houses of the campus between Harvard Square and the Charles River. Dunster, Lowell, and Eliot houses are the three domes you see standing out. A campus map will show you where the specific schools are located.

Outside the campus Cambridge history merges with that of the college. At the edge of Harvard Yard is the Wadsworth House, a 1726 frame house that was for 100 years the residence of Harvard presidents and was also the site of George Washington's militia offices in 1775. It now houses the Harvard alumni office.

Across the square from the Yard is the 1631 Ancient Burying Ground where Harvard presidents and important Revolutionary leaders are buried. Beside it is the nineteenth-century wooden gothic building of the First Parish Unitarian Church. Next to the burying ground on Garden Street opposite the common is the Christ Church, the town's oldest, worth a look inside for its handsome Georgian interior. The church became a barracks during the American Revolution, but was restored to its intended use by George Washington, who worshipped here in 1775–76.

Historic Cambridge Common, the starting place for many events that led to our nation's freedom, is where the Massachusetts Bay Colony held its elections in the seventeenth century, where French militia trained for the French and Indian Wars, and where Washington took command of the First Continental Army. Today it is crowded by twentieth-century buildings, including the Harvard Law School.

When you've finished the sights, go back to Harvard Square to explore the mix of bookstores, cafés, and shops that are a hub not only for Harvard but for all the thousands of students at Boston's many colleges. You certainly needn't be a student to enjoy Harvard Square, however. The Harvard Coop is all but overwhelming—a sort of intellectual department store now occupying several buildings, selling clothing and almost everything else you can think of, including a stock of books and art prints that is nothing short of extraordinary.

All of Cambridge, in fact, is an extraordinary place for book lovers. Words Worth on Brattle Street is a discount bookstore, Pangloss on Mt. Auburn Street has an impressive collection of rare and out-of-print volumes, Shoenhof's has foreign books, and the Grolier and Harvard bookstores add to the incredible variety of books available in this small area.

What else is around the square? Jeans and fine tailoring, stationery and wares from Greece, Russian wooden dolls and exotic earrings, pricey women's clothing and inexpensive cottons from India, posters and housewares, and traditional Ivy League dress at J. Press and the Crimson Shop. You'll see the shops as you walk Mt. Auburn, Dunster, and the other narrow streets off Harvard Square and in small complexes such as the Garage on Dunster and the Mall at 99 Mt. Auburn.

A good street for browsing is Brattle, where the Brattle Street Theater offers old film fare to delight buffs. Radcliffe Yard, another lovely academic complex, is on Brattle across from the Loeb Drama Center, the home of the excellent productions of the American Repertory Theater.

Brattle was once known as Tory Row and you'll see why if you continue walking past the impressive houses on the street. Number 105, the Longfellow House, is a National Historic Site, the place where the poet lived and wrote many of his poems while he taught at Harvard. The Blacksmith House nearby is the present home of the Cambridge Center for Adult Education, which offers many interesting evening programs. It was at one time the home of the "village smithy" made famous by Longfellow's poem.

Cambridge is still home to creative minds producing a prodigious number of books, poems, theories, music, art, and ideas. The feeling of creativity is almost tangible, particularly in the coffee houses and cafés. The Café Pamplona is a favored hangout of the Cambridge literati, who often seem to arrive with works in progress, and Algiers Coffee House and Au Bon Pain, a French bakery, are also popular spots. The outdoor café in front of the latter is a gathering spot for chatters and chess players on all but the most frigid days.

The restaurants in Cambridge reflect the community's cosmopolitan makeup. You'll find everything from haute cuisine to Greek, Indian, Korean, Thai, and Ethiopian, something to suit every taste and budget as well. Top rated for fine dining are Rarities, Autre Chose, and Panache. Among many other favorites are the long-established Harvest, the romantic Upstairs at the Pudding (above the famous Hasty Puddy Club), and Michela's, an Italian restaurant where you'll have to fight for a reservation.

There is a range of hotels as well, with the stylish Charles at the top of the list. There's a first-class spa and indoor pool here, and The Regatta Bar is a favorite gathering place to hear jazz.

The Hyatt Regency affords the best view of the Charles and the Boston skyline from its revolving rooftop restaurant, and the Sonesta offers excellent weekend packages. There are also motels with lower rates, including one almost right on Harvard Square. This is a particularly good town for bed-and-breakfast accommodations, since you may find yourself in one of the very private neighborhoods of lovely old homes.

Having given Saturday to Harvard and Harvard Square, fortify yourself with Sunday brunch and move on to the impressive campus of MIT, where the formal atmosphere is as different from Harvard as is the architecture. Instead of red brick ivied halls, you'll find stately stone neoclassical buildings and stunning modern architecture. Many of the newer buildings are significant contributions by modern architectural greats like Eero Saarinen.

As you might expect, the major MIT museum (open weekdays only) is devoted to tracing the development of science and technology. The Hart Nautical Galleries, in a separate building, can be visited on weekends for an interesting survey of ship and marine engineering from the days of rigged merchant ships to the present, with many half-models and engine models on display. All is not science, however. Contemporary art may be seen at the Hayden Gallery, and the entire MIT campus is a museum of outdoor sculpture by Calder, Moore, Picasso, and other masters.

MIT is also built along the Charles, and from the campus you can drive directly over the Massachusetts Avenue Bridge and be in Boston in two minutes' time. An eight-minute ride on "the T" from Harvard Square will also put you in the heart of the city. Assuming this is a winter weekend, it may be just the chance to catch up on some of the indoor attractions you may have missed in warmer weather—the treasure-filled Museum of Fine Arts, perhaps, or the Museum of Science, the new Computer Museum, or the John F. Kennedy Library.

Though easy access to Boston has always been a plus, it's in Cambridge, whether sightseeing at Harvard and MIT, shopping in the Harvard Coop, or sipping espresso in a café, that you know you are in the company of people and ideas that not only shaped America's past but are molders of its future.

Cambridge Area Code: 617

DRIVING DIRECTIONS Cambridge is on the northwest banks of the Charles River, four miles west of Boston and connected to the city by many bridges over the Charles as well as via "the T," the local subway system. See Boston access roads, page 59.

ACCOMMODATIONS *Charles Hotel*, 1 Bennett Street at Eliot Street, 864-1200, $$$$$ • *Hyatt Regency Hotel*, 575 Memorial Drive, 492-1234, $$$$$ • *Royal Sonesta Hotel*, 5 Cambridge Parkway, 491-3600, $$$$$ • *Sheraton Commander*, 16 Garden Street, opposite the common, 547-4800, $$$$–$$$$$ • *Howard Johnson*, 777 Memorial Drive, 492-7777, $$$–$$$$ • *Quality Inn*, 1651 Massachusetts Avenue, 491-1000, $$$ • *Harvard Motor House*, 110 Mt. Auburn Street, 854-5200, nothing special but particularly convenient, $$$ CP. Ask about weekend packages at all.

BED AND BREAKFAST See Boston, page 60.

DINING *Rarities*, Charles Hotel (see above), top of the line in quality and price, $$$$ • *Michela's*, 245 First Street, 494-5419, expensive Italian, $$$ • *Harvest Restaurant*, 44 Brattle Street, 492-1115, perennial favorite, $$–$$$ • *Upstairs at the Pudding*, 10 Holyoke Street, 864-1933, elegant northern Italian, prix fixe $$$$$ • *Legal Sea Foods*, 5 Cambridge Center, Kendall Square, 864-3400, a local institution, $–$$$ • *Autre Chose*, 1105 Massachusetts Avenue, 661-0852, fine French, $$$ • *Panache*, 708 Main Street, 492-9500, excellent nouvelle, $$$ • *Averof*, 1924 Massachusetts Avenue, 354-4500, Middle Eastern, complete with belly dancers, $–$$ • *Shilla*, 95 Winthrop Street, 547-7971, interesting Japanese/Korean menu, sushi, $–$$ • *Peacock*, 5 Craigie Circle, 661-4073, continental, $$ • *Henry IV*, 96 Winthrop Street, 876-5200, modern American cuisine, $$–$$$ • *Acropolis*, 1680 Massachusetts Avenue, 354-8335, moderately priced Greek, $–$$ • *Iruna*, 56 John Kennedy Street, 868-5633, Spanish, $ • *The Daily Catch*, 1 Kendall Square, 225-2300, Sicilian seafood, $$–$$$ • For cocktails, other than hotels, try *Pistachios*, 50 Church Street; *Casablanca*, 40 Brattle, downstairs from the Brattle Theater; or *Grendel's*, 91 Winthrop, where you'll find lots of complimentary hors d'oeuvres.

SIGHTSEEING AT HARVARD *Information Center*, 1350 Massachusetts Avenue, 495-1573. Hours: Monday through Saturday, 9 A.M. to 4:45 P.M. • *Fogg Art Museum*, 32 Quincy Street, 495-2387. Hours: Monday to Saturday, 10 A.M. to 5 P.M., Sunday from 1 P.M.

Adults, $3; under 18, free ● *University Museum*, 24 Oxford Street, 495-1910. Hours: Monday to Saturday, 9 A.M. to 4:30 P.M., Sunday from 1 P.M. Adults, $2; under 15, $.50 ● *Busch-Reisinger Museum*, 29 Kirkland Street, 495-2338. Hours: Monday to Saturday, 9 A.M. to 5 P.M., Sunday from 1 P.M. Adults, $3; children, $1.50 ● *Arthur M. Sackler Museum*, 485 Broadway, 495-2387. Hours: Monday to Saturday, 10 A.M. to 5 P.M., Sunday from 1 P.M. Adults, $3; children, $1.50. All Harvard museums are free to all on Saturdays, 9 A.M. to 11 A.M.

SIGHTSEEING AT MIT *Massachusetts Institute of Technology Information Center*, 77 Massachusetts Avenue, 253-1000. Hours: weekdays only, 9 A.M. to 5 P.M. ● *MIT Museum*, 265 Massachusetts Avenue, 253-4444. Hours: Monday to Friday, 9 A.M. to 5 P.M. Free ● *Hart Nautical Galleries*, 77 Massachusetts Avenue, 253-4444. Hours: daily 9 A.M. to 5 P.M. Free ● *Hayden Gallery*, 160 Memorial Drive, 253-4680. Hours: Monday to Friday, 10 A.M. to 4 P.M., Saturday and Sunday 1 P.M. to 5 P.M., closed July and August. Free.

INFORMATION Cambridge Chamber of Commerce, 859 Massachusetts Avenue, Cambridge MA, 02139, 876-4100.

Sugaring Off in Grafton, Vermont

Maples and Vermont are all but synonymous, and maple sugaring—a major state industry and a livelihood for hundreds of Vermont farmers—is a cause for local celebration, the first welcome sign of spring, despite the layers of snow still on the ground.

Seeing how the sugaring is done and getting in on a traditional "sugar on snow" party with fresh syrup hardened into candy in the snow is good reason for a late winter visit. Dozens of Vermont sugarmakers welcome visitors, though most appreciate a call for an appointment first. A list of sugarmaking farms is available from the state travel service.

It takes cold nights and warm days to make the sap rise, so the timing of the sugaring season is entirely in the hands of Mother Nature. Usually early to mid-March is the peak in the southern part of the state; it takes a little longer up north.

Old-fashioned small-town maple festivals are held in late April way up north in St. Albans and in St. Johnsbury, but since the most interesting sight for most visitors is a visit to a farm, you needn't journey quite so far or wait so long. Farms all over the state carry on the traditional tapping of the trees and gathering of the buckets, a task that still is often accomplished best by horse and sled despite all the modern improvements in methods.

One southern location to view this century-old operation is around Grafton, a town with a wonderful inn and a special ambience that will add much to your stay. Remember, however, that weather can speed the season, so be sure to phone and check before you set off on a trip. In one recent warm year, for example, Thomas Eldridge and his sons fired up the first kettles in their Baltimore, Vermont, sugar house by February 23.

The Eldridges have a large operation, with some 2,000 taps to tend. The syrup they produce and sell has been ordered and shipped to customers as far away as New Guinea. They use tractors to pick up buckets from the trees nearest to the road, but in late afternoon you can usually see a team of horses setting out into the woods to gather the buckets from more remote areas, just the way it has been done for a hundred years or more.

They don't use horses these days at the Putney farm of Donald and Madeline Harlow, but they do set up a treat booth during sugaring season where you can buy homemade goodies such as maple-coated apples, corn fritters with fresh syrup, and the traditional "sugar on snow" treat. The Harlows have also assembled a small exhibit of old-time sugaring methods, with photos of the oxen-drawn sleds that were used to gather the buckets and displays of old kettles and other utensils. A film about the Vermont maple-sugaring industry is shown regularly in their little gift shop, where you can also buy syrup and maple candy.

If you've never seen how maple syrup is made, you may be surprised to learn that the sweet sap running into the buckets is as thin and clear as water. When the buckets are full, they are taken to the sugar house, where the sap is emptied into an evaporator to simmer slowly over the fire until it thickens into a golden, gooey, and delicious syrup. On hillsides all over Vermont, you can see the clouds of smoke day and night, marking a sugar house in action.

A good tree will produce 40 quarts of syrup, drip by drip, which must be hauled down day by day to the evaporator. You may understand better why the syrup is so costly when you learn it takes 40 *gallons* of sap to produce 1 gallon of syrup. To provide enough heat to boil down that much sap requires a log as big as a man, split, sawed, and dried.

The sap continues in a rolling, steaming boil until an ample aroma tells the maker that "she's ready to draw off." The draw-off valve is opened and out pours the sweet syrup. The first day of boiling is a great occasion for the whole crew, enough to make them forget the trials of the frozen buckets or tangled lines that slowed the process.

The finished syrup comes in grades: fancy for the lightest and sweetest; medium-amber grade A for use on pancakes and French toast; dark grade B, a robust caramel flavor used in cooking; and grade C, an even stronger flavor also used for cooking. Pick your syrup according to your personal taste and how you plan to use it.

The picture-perfect village of Grafton is located about midway between the Eldridge and Harlow farms, and is within reach of farms in Marlboro, Putney, Jamaica, and several other locations as well. Grafton still looks much the way it did in its 1800s prime, and that is no accident. It is a town that had the good fortune to be "adopted" by the Windham Foundation, which was founded by millionaire Dean Mathey, former chairman of the Bank of New York.

Mathey had no children, so most of his fortune went to the foundation after his death in 1962. The trustees of the estate looked for a project they felt he would have approved, and decided there was no more appropriate idea than the salvation of the tiny town of Grafton, a place that Mathey loved. He had his own summer home right on Main Street, and many of his family members were long-time residents as well.

Once a prosperous mill and agricultural center, Grafton, like many such towns, had declined by the early twentieth century. The population dwindled to less than 500, and many of the old buildings were left to deteriorate, though their original charm could still be seen.

In the 1960s, the Windham Foundation, named for Grafton's home county, set out to bring the town back to its former self. The first project was a practical one. The old grocery store was in sad shape, and the townspeople found themselves having to travel elsewhere for food and other daily necessities. So the derelict building was shored up, sagging floors were leveled, warped walls were straightened, and pretty soon the Village Store was looking much the way it had when it was finished back in 1841, at least on the outside. Inside it became a complete modern market.

One by one the village houses were also purchased and refurbished. At the same time, the Windham Foundation took on the renewal of the Old Tavern, once a noted stopping place when Grafton was a trading center. The old guest books list such notables as Rudyard Kipling, Ulysses S. Grant, Daniel Webster, Oliver Wendell Holmes, Theodore Roosevelt, and Ralph Waldo Emerson.

With the restoration the tavern became one of New England's most elegant little inns, described by the *New York Times* as "perhaps the choicest inn of all." People now come to Grafton from around the country and around the world. Early reservations are a must.

What to do in Grafton? Very little, which is very much part of this town's charm. If there is snow, you can ski at Windham, Stratton, or Magic Mountain nearby. If the spring thaw has set in, or if you don't ski, you can simply stroll through Grafton's picturesque streets or take a bike ride or a hike on the walking trails that abound around town. The inn will give you a folder of nine walks that will show you the Grafton of old. (If you hike the more wooded trails, be forewarned that spring is known as "mud season" in Vermont, so wear proper footgear.)

Cheese is still made at the restored cheese factory in Grafton, and visitors are welcome to come by to see how it is done. There's a little gift shop operated by the foundation and an excellent antiques store to explore. And the Country Store, just a few miles south in Newfane, is one of the best sources in New England for quilts, as well as a place to shop for handicrafts, homemade baked goods, and old-fashioned penny candy. There are more shops just behind the store selling crafts and sweaters and other collectibles.

Newfane is another particularly lovely Vermont town, and you'll want to bring the camera to capture its perfect village green. Plan to stay for dinner too, for both local inns, the Four Columns and the Old Newfane Inn, have renowned dining rooms. Either is also a happy alternative should Grafton's Old Tavern be filled.

This is a weekend that will take you back to the tranquillity of another time—a visit to the farm, a stroll through peaceful country towns and village shops. At day's end there's lots of time to savor a drink in front of a roaring fire and dine in a cozy beamed dining room. To make it even better, there's that delicious maple syrup to bring home as a sweet reminder of the trip.

Vermont Area Code: 802

DRIVING DIRECTIONS From I-91, exit 5 (North Westminster and Bellows Falls), take Route 121 west to Grafton. Alternate route: From I-91, exit 2, Brattleboro, follow Route 30 west to Newfane, then Route 35 north to Grafton. Call each farm for specific driving directions. Grafton is 152 miles from Boston, 221 miles from New York, and 111 miles from Hartford.

PUBLIC TRANSPORTATION Vermont Transit bus service to Brattleboro.

ACCOMMODATIONS AND DINING *The Old Tavern at Grafton*, Grafton, 843-2231, $$–$$$ ● *The Four Columns Inn*, 230 West Street, Route 30, Newfane, 365-7713, $$–$$$ CP ● *Old Newfane Inn*, Route 30, Newfane, 365-4427, $$$.

BED AND BREAKFAST   *Vermont Bed and Breakfast Reservation Service,* PO Box 1, East Fairfield, VT 05448, 827-3827.

SIGHTSEEING   Farm visits to watch maple sugaring are free, but you must call ahead to make sure the weather is right and syrup is being made. Ask for driving directions as well. The Vermont Department of Agriculture prints a complete listing of farms in the state that invite visitors. Write to the department at 116 State Street, Montpelier, VT 05602, 828-2418. Farms mentioned here are *Eldridge C. Thomas and Sons,* Baltimore Road, Route 4, Box 336, Chester (though the post office is Chester, the location is actually in Baltimore), 263-5680 (evenings are the best time to reach Mr. Eldridge); *Donald and Madline Harlow,* Route 4, RD 1, Box 100, Putney, 387-5852.

INFORMATION   Vermont Travel Division, Agency of Development and Community Affairs, Montpelier, VT 05602, 828-3236.

MAPS

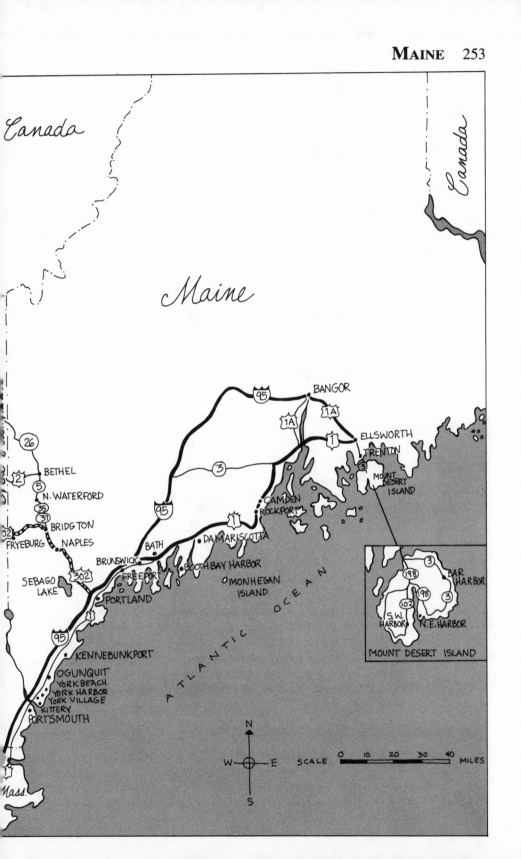

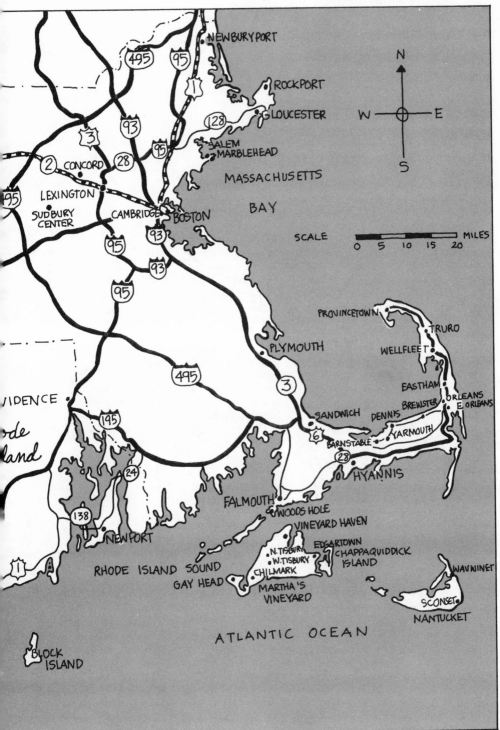

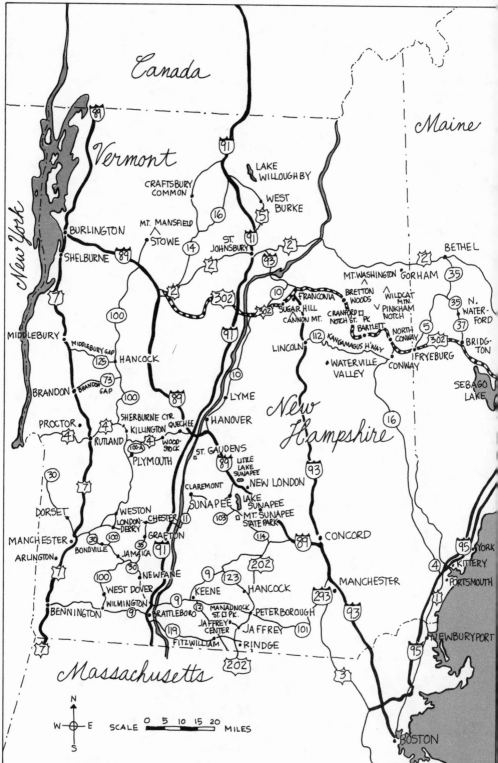

General Index

Category Index

Museums and Galleries